HOLES

HOLES

LOUIS SACHAR

ISBN 979-11-91343-98-4 14740

Longtail Books

TO SHERRE, JESSICA, LORI, KATHLEEN, AND EMILY

AND TO JUDY ALLEN,
A FIFTH-GRADE TEACHER FROM
WHOM WE ALL CAN LEARN

PART ONE

YOU ARE ENTERING CAMP GREEN LAKE

1

There is no lake at Camp Green Lake. There once was a very large lake here, the largest lake in Texas. That was over a hundred years ago. Now it is just a dry, flat **wasteland**.

There used to be a town of Green Lake as well. The town **shrivel**ed and dried up along with the lake, and the people who lived there.

During the summer the **daytime** temperature **hover**s around ninety-five **degree**s★ in the **shade**—if you can find any shade. There's not much shade in a big dry lake.

The only trees are two old **oak**s on the eastern edge of the "lake." A hammock✳ is stretched between the two trees, and a **log cabin** stands behind that.

The campers are **forbid**den to lie in the hammock. It

★ **ninety-five degrees** 여기서 95도는 화씨 온도 95℉를 말한다. 화씨온도 95℉는 섭씨온도로 약 35℃이다.
✳ **hammock** 해먹. 나무나 기둥에 달아매는 그물·천으로 된 침대.

belongs to the Warden.* The Warden owns the shade.

Out on the lake, **rattlesnake**s and **scorpion**s find shade under rocks and in the holes **dug** by the campers.

Here's a good rule to remember about rattlesnakes and scorpions: If you don't **bother** them, they won't bother you.

Usually.

Being bitten by a scorpion or even a rattlesnake is not the worst thing that can happen to you. You won't die.

Usually.

Sometimes a camper will try to be bitten by a scorpion, or even a small rattlesnake. Then he will get to spend a day or two recovering in his tent, instead of having to dig a hole out on the lake.

But you don't want to be bitten by a yellow-**spotted lizard**. That's the worst thing that can happen to you. You will die a slow and painful death.

Always.

If you get bitten by a yellow-spotted lizard, you **might as well** go into the shade of the oak trees and lie in the hammock.

There is nothing anyone can do to you anymore.

---

* **Warden** 기숙사나 보호 시설 등의 관리인·교도소장. 여기서는 소년원과 유사한 캠프의 관리인을 지칭하는 말이다.

2

The reader is probably asking: Why would anyone go to Camp Green Lake?

Most campers weren't given a choice. Camp Green Lake is a camp for bad boys.

If you take a bad boy and make him **dig** a hole every day in the hot sun, it will turn him into a good boy.

That was what some people thought.

Stanley Yelnats was given a choice. The judge said, "You may go to **jail**, or you may go to Camp Green Lake."

Stanley was from a poor family. He had never been to camp before.

3

Stanley Yelnats was the only **passenger** on the bus, not **count**ing the driver or the guard. The guard sat next to the driver with his seat turned around **facing** Stanley. A **rifle** lay across his **lap**.

Stanley was sitting about ten rows back, **handcuff**ed to his **armrest**. His backpack lay on the seat next to him. It contained his **toothbrush, toothpaste,** and a box of **stationery** his mother had given him. He'd promised to write to her at least once a week.

He looked out the window, although there wasn't much to see—mostly fields of **hay** and **cotton**. He was on a long bus ride to nowhere. The bus wasn't **air-conditioned,** and the hot, heavy air was almost as **stifling** as the handcuffs.

Stanley and his parents had tried to pretend that he was just going away to camp for a while, just like rich kids do. When Stanley was younger he used to play with **stuff**ed animals,* and pretend the animals were at camp. Camp Fun and Games he called it. Sometimes he'd have them play soccer with a **marble**. Other times they'd run an **obstacle** course,* or go bungee jumping* off a table, tied to broken **rubber** bands. Now Stanley tried to pretend he was going to Camp Fun and Games Maybe he'd make some friends, he thought. At least he'd get to swim in the lake.

He didn't have any friends at home. He was **overweight** and the kids at his middle school often **tease**d him about his size. Even his teachers sometimes made **cruel** comments without realizing it. On his last day of school, his math teacher, Mrs. Bell, taught **ratio**s. As an example, she chose the heaviest kid in the class and the lightest kid in the class, and had them weigh themselves. Stanley weighed three times as much as the other boy. Mrs. Bell wrote the ratio on the board, 3:1, **unaware** of how much **embarrass**ment she had caused both of them.

Stanley was **arrest**ed later that day.

He looked at the guard who sat **slump**ed in his seat and wondered if he had fallen asleep. The guard was wearing sunglasses, so Stanley couldn't see his eyes.

Stanley was not a bad kid. He was **innocent** of the crime for which he was **convict**ed. He'd just been in the wrong place at the wrong time.

It was all because of his no-good-dirty-rotten-pig-stealing-great-great-grandfather!

★ stuffed animal 솜 등으로 속을 채운(stuffed) 동물 모양 봉제인형.
✻ obstacle course 장애물 경주 코스.
✻ bungee jumping 번지점프. 긴 고무줄에 몸을 묶고 높은 곳에서 뛰어내리는 스포츠.

He smiled. It was a family joke. Whenever anything went wrong, they always blamed Stanley's no-good-dirty-rotten-pig-stealing-great-great-grandfather.

Supposedly, he had a great-great-grandfather who had stolen a pig from a **one-legged** Gypsy,* and she put a **curse** on him and all his **descendant**s. Stanley and his parents didn't believe in curses, of course, but whenever anything went wrong, it felt good to be able to blame someone.

Things went wrong a lot. They always seemed to be in the wrong place at the wrong time.

He looked out the window at the **vast** emptiness. He watched the rise and fall of a telephone **wire**. In his mind he could hear his father's **gruff** voice softly singing to him.

*"If only, if only," the **woodpecker** sighs,*
*"The **bark** on the tree was just a little bit softer."*
While the wolf waits below, hungry and lonely,
He cries to the moo—oo—oon,
"If only, if only."

It was a song his father used to sing to him. The melody was sweet and sad, but Stanley's favorite part was when his father would **howl** the word "moon."

The bus hit a small **bump** and the guard sat up, instantly **alert**.

Stanley's father was an **inventor**. To be a successful

★**Gypsy** 집시. 정처 없이 떠돌아다니며 방랑 생활을 하는 사람을 말한다.

inventor you need three things: **intelligence, perseverance**, and just a little bit of luck.

Stanley's father was smart and had a lot of perseverance. Once he started a project he would work on it for years, often going days without sleep. He just never had any luck.

Every time an **experiment** failed, Stanley could hear him cursing his dirty-rotten-pig-stealing-great-grandfather.

Stanley's father was also named Stanley Yelnats. Stanley's father's full name was Stanley Yelnats III. Our Stanley is Stanley Yelnats IV.

Everyone in his family had always liked the fact that "Stanley Yelnats" was spelled the same **frontward** and backward. So they kept naming their sons Stanley. Stanley was an only child, as was every other Stanley Yelnats before him.

All of them had something else in common. Despite their **awful** luck, they always remained hopeful. As Stanley's father liked to say, "I learn from failure."

But perhaps that was part of the curse as well. If Stanley and his father weren't always hopeful, then it wouldn't hurt so much every time their hopes were crushed.

"Not every Stanley Yelnats has been a failure," Stanley's mother often **point**ed **out**, whenever Stanley or his father became so **discourage**d that they actually started to believe in the curse. The first Stanley Yelnats, Stanley's great-grandfather, had made a **fortune** in the **stock** market. "He couldn't have been too unlucky."

At such times she **neglect**ed to mention the bad luck

that **befell** the first Stanley Yelnats. He lost his entire fortune when he was moving from New York to California. His **stagecoach** was **rob**bed by the **outlaw** Kissin' Kate Barlow.

If it weren't for that, Stanley's family would now be living in a **mansion** on a beach in California. Instead, they were **cram**med in a tiny apartment that smelled of burning rubber and foot **odor**.

If only, if only . . .

The apartment smelled the way it did because Stanley's father was trying to invent a way to **recycle** old **sneakers**. "The first person who finds a use for old sneakers," he said, "will be a very rich man."

It was this latest project that led to Stanley's arrest.

The bus ride became **increasingly bumpy** because the road was no longer **paved**.

Actually, Stanley had been impressed when he first found out that his great-grandfather was robbed by Kissin' Kate Barlow. True, he would have preferred living on the beach in California, but it was still kind of cool to have someone in your family robbed by a famous outlaw.

Kate Barlow didn't actually kiss Stanley's great-grandfather. That would have been really cool, but she only kissed the men she killed. Instead, she robbed him and left him **strand**ed in the middle of the **desert**.

"He was lucky to have survived," Stanley's mother was quick to point out.

The bus was slowing down. The guard **grunt**ed as he

stretched his arms.

"Welcome to Camp Green Lake," said the driver.

Stanley looked out the dirty window. He couldn't see a lake.

And hardly anything was green.

4

Stanley felt somewhat **dazed** as the guard unlocked his **handcuffs** and led him off the bus. He'd been on the bus for over eight hours.

"Be careful," the bus driver said as Stanley walked down the steps.

Stanley wasn't sure if the bus driver meant for him to be careful going down the steps, or if he was telling him to be careful at Camp Green Lake. "Thanks for the ride," he said. His mouth was dry and his throat hurt. He stepped onto the hard, dry dirt. There was a band of **sweat** around his **wrist** where the handcuff had been.

The land was **barren** and **desolate**. He could see a few **rundown** buildings and some tents. Farther away there was a **cabin** beneath two tall trees. Those two trees were the only plant life he could see. There weren't even **weed**s.

The guard led Stanley to a small building. A sign on front said, YOU ARE ENTERING CAMP GREEN LAKE JUVENILE

CORRECTIONAL FACILITY. Next to it was another sign which declared that it was a **violation** of the Texas **Penal** Code* to bring guns, **explosive**s, weapons, **drug**s, or **alcohol** onto the **premise**s.

As Stanley read the sign he couldn't help but think, *Well, duh!**

The guard led Stanley into the building, where he felt the welcome relief of **air-conditioning**.

A man was sitting with his feet up on a desk. He turned his head when Stanley and the guard entered, but otherwise didn't move. Even though he was inside, he wore sunglasses and a cowboy hat. He also held a can of soda, and the **sight** of it made Stanley even more aware of his own thirst.

He waited while the bus guard gave the man some papers to sign.

"That's a lot of sunflower seeds," the bus guard said.

Stanley noticed a burlap* **sack** filled with sunflower seeds* on the floor next to the desk.

"I quit smoking last month," said the man in the cowboy hat. He had a **tattoo** of a **rattlesnake** on his arm, and as he signed his name, the snake's **rattle** seemed to **wiggle**. "I used to smoke a pack a day. Now I eat a sack of these every week."

The guard laughed.

There must have been a small **refrigerator** behind his desk, because the man in the cowboy hat **produced** two more cans of soda. For a second Stanley hoped that one might be for him, but the man gave one to the guard and said the other was for the driver.

"Nine hours here, and now nine hours back," the guard **grumbled**. "What a day."

Stanley thought about the long, **miserable** bus ride and felt a little sorry for the guard and the bus driver.

The man in the cowboy hat **spit** sunflower seed shells into a **wastepaper basket**. Then he walked around the desk to Stanley. "My name is Mr. Sir," he said "Whenever you speak to me you must call me by my name, is that clear?"

Stanley hesitated. "Uh, yes, Mr. Sir," he said, though he couldn't imagine that was really the man's name.

"You're not in the Girl Scouts anymore," Mr. Sir said.

Stanley had to remove his clothes in front of Mr. Sir, who made sure he wasn't hiding anything. He was then given two sets of clothes and a towel. Each set consisted of a long-sleeve orange jumpsuit,* an orange T-shirt, and yellow socks. Stanley wasn't sure if the socks had been yellow originally.

He was also given white **sneaker**s, an orange cap, and a **canteen** made of heavy plastic, which unfortunately was empty. The cap had a piece of cloth **sewn** on the back of it,

---

*jumpsuit 바지와 상의가 하나로 붙어 있는 옷.

20

for neck **protection.**

Stanley got dressed. The clothes smelled like soap.

Mr. Sir told him he should wear one set to work in and one set for **relaxation. Laundry** was done every three days. On that day his work clothes would be washed. Then the other set would become his work clothes, and he would get clean clothes to wear while resting.

"You are to **dig** one hole each day, including Saturdays and Sundays. Each hole must be five feet* deep, and five feet across in every direction. Your **shovel** is your measuring stick.* Breakfast is served at 4:30."

Stanley must have looked surprised, because Mr. Sir went on to explain that they started early to avoid the hottest part of the day. "No one is going to **baby-sit** you," he added. "The longer it takes you to dig, the longer you will be out in the sun. If you dig up anything interesting, you are to report it to me or any other **counselor.** When you finish, the rest of the day is yours."

Stanley **nod**ded to show he understood.

"This isn't a Girl Scout camp," said Mr. Sir.

He checked Stanley's backpack and allowed him to keep it. Then he led Stanley outside into the **blazing** heat.

"Take a good look around you," Mr. Sir said. "What do you see?"

Stanley looked out across the **vast wasteland.** The air

★ **feet/foot** 길이의 단위 피트. 1피트는 약 30.48센티미터이다. (복수형은 feet이지만 뒤에 tall이 올 때는 feet 대신에 foot을 사용하는 경우가 많다.)
✳ **measuring stick** 길이를 측정하는 도구.

seemed thick with heat and dirt. "Not much," he said, then hastily added, "Mr. Sir."

Mr. Sir laughed. "You see any guard towers?*"

"No."

"How about an electric fence?"

"No, Mr. Sir."

"There's no fence at all, is there?"

"No, Mr. Sir."

"You want to run away?" Mr. Sir asked him.

Stanley looked back at him, **unsure** what he meant.

"If you want to run away, go ahead, start running. I'm not going to stop you."

Stanley didn't know what kind of game Mr. Sir was playing.

"I see you're looking at my gun. Don't worry. I'm not going to shoot you." He **tap**ped his **holster**. "This is for yellow-**spotted lizard**s. I wouldn't waste a **bullet** on you."

"I'm not going to run away," Stanley said.

"Good thinking," said Mr. Sir. "Nobody runs away from here. We don't need a fence. Know why? Because we've got the only water for a hundred miles.* You want to run away? You'll be buzzard* food in three days."

Stanley could see some kids dressed in orange and carrying shovels **dragging** themselves toward the tents.

"You thirsty?" asked Mr. Sir.

★ guard tower 감시탑.
✳ mile 거리의 단위 마일. 1마일은 1,609미터이다.
❉ buzzard 대머리수리. 독수리 같이 큰 맹금류.

"Yes, Mr. Sir," Stanley said **gratefu**lly.

"Well, you better get used to it. You're going to be thirsty for the next eighteen months."

5

There were six large gray tents, and each one had a black letter on it: A, B, C, D, E, or F. The first five tents were for the campers. The **counselor**s slept in F.

Stanley was **assign**ed to D tent. Mr. Pendanski was his counselor.

"My name is easy to remember," said Mr. Pendanski as he shook hands with Stanley just outside the tent. "Three easy words: pen, dance, key."

Mr. Sir returned to the office.

Mr. Pendanski was younger than Mr. Sir, and not nearly as scary looking. The top of his head was shaved so close it was almost **bald**, but his face was covered in a thick **curly** black **beard**. His nose was badly **sunburn**ed.

"Mr. Sir isn't really so bad," said Mr. Pendanski. "He's just been in a bad mood ever since he quit smoking. The person you've got to worry about is the Warden. There's really only one rule at Camp Green Lake: Don't upset the

Warden."

Stanley **nod**ded, as if he understood.

"I want you to know, Stanley, that I respect you," Mr. Pendanski said. "I understand you've made some bad mistakes in your life. Otherwise you wouldn't be here. But everyone makes mistakes. You may have done some bad things, but that doesn't mean you're a bad kid."

Stanley nodded. It seemed **pointless** to try and tell his counselor that he was **innocent**. He figured that everyone probably said that. He didn't want Mr. Pen-dance-key to think he had a bad **attitude**.

"I'm going to help you turn your life around," said his counselor. "But you're going to have to help, too. Can I **count on** your help?"

"Yes, sir," Stanley said.

Mr. Pendanski said, "Good," and **pat**ted Stanley on the back.

Two boys, each carrying a **shovel**, were coming across the **compound**. Mr. Pendanski called to them. "Rex! Alan! I want you to come say hello to Stanley. He's the newest member of our team."

The boys **glance**d **wearily** at Stanley.

They were **drip**ping with **sweat**, and their faces were so dirty that it took Stanley a moment to notice that one kid was white and the other black.

"What happened to Barf Bag?*" asked the black kid.

★ **Barf Bag** 비행기 등에 비치된 구토 봉지. 본문에서는 사람의 별명으로 쓰였다.

"Lewis is still in the hospital," said Mr. Pendanski. "He won't be returning." He told the boys to come shake Stanley's hand and introduce themselves, "like gentlemen."

"Hi," the white kid **grunt**ed.

"That's Alan," said Mr. Pendanski.

"My name's not Alan," the boy said. "It's Squid.* And that's X-Ray."

"Hey," said X-Ray. He smiled and shook Stanley's hand. He wore glasses, but they were so dirty that Stanley wondered how he could see out of them.

Mr. Pendanski told Alan to go to the Rec Hall* and bring the other boys to meet Stanley. Then he led him inside the tent.

There were seven **cot**s, each one less than two feet from the one next to it.

"Which was Lewis's cot?" Mr. Pendanski asked.

"Barf Bag slept here," said X-Ray, kicking at one of the beds.

"All right, Stanley, that'll be yours," said Mr. Pendanski.

Stanley looked at the cot and nodded. He wasn't particularly **thrill**ed about sleeping in the same cot that had been used by somebody named Barf Bag.

Seven **crate**s were **stack**ed in two piles at one side of the tent. The open end of the crates faced outward. Stanley put his backpack, change of clothes, and towel in what used to

---

★**Squid** 원래는 '오징어'라는 뜻이지만, 역시 별명으로 쓰였다.
＊**Rec Hall** 레크리에이션(recreation)을 하는 강당(hall).

be Barf Bag's crate. It was at the bottom of the stack that had three in it.

Squid returned with four other boys. The first three were introduced by Mr. Pendanski as Jose, Theodore, and Ricky. They called themselves Magnet,* Armpit,* and Zigzag.

"They all have **nickname**s," explained Mr. Pendanski. "However, I prefer to use the names their parents gave them—the names that *society will recognize them* by when they return to become useful and hardworking members of society."

"It ain't just a nickname," X-Ray told Mr. Pendanski. He **tap**ped the **rim** of his glasses. "I can see inside you, Mom. You've got a big fat heart."

The last boy either didn't have a real name or else he didn't have a nickname. Both Mr. Pendanski and X-Ray called him Zero.

"You know why his name's Zero?" asked Mr. Pendanski. "Because there's nothing inside his head." He smiled and **playful**ly shook Zero's shoulder.

Zero said nothing.

"And that's Mom!" a boy said.

Mr. Pendanski smiled at him. "If it makes you feel better to call me Mom, Theodore, go ahead and call me Mom." He turned to Stanley. "If you have questions, Theodore will help you. You got that, Theodore. I'm depending on you."

★ **Magnet** 원래는 '자석'이라는 뜻이다.
✳ **Armpit** 원래는 '겨드랑이'라는 뜻이다.

Theodore **spit** a thin line of **saliva** between his teeth, causing some of the other boys to complain about the need to keep their "home" **sanitary**.

"You were all new here once," said Mr. Pendanski, "and you all know what it feels like. I'm counting on every one of you to help Stanley."

Stanley looked at the ground.

Mr. Pendanski left the tent, and soon the other boys began to **file out** as well, taking their towels and change of clothes with them. Stanley was relieved to be left alone, but he was so thirsty he felt as if he would die if he didn't get something to drink soon.

"Hey, uh, Theodore," he said, going after him. "Do you know where I can fill my **canteen**?"

Theodore **whirl**ed and grabbed Stanley by his **collar**. "My name's not Thee-o-dore," he said. "It's Armpit." He threw Stanley to the ground.

Stanley stared up at him, **terrified**.

"There's a water **spigot** on the wall of the shower **stall**."

"Thanks . . . Armpit," said Stanley.

As he watched the boy turn and walk away, he **couldn't for the life of** him **figure out** why anyone would want to be called Armpit.

In a way, it made him feel a little better about having to sleep in a cot that had been used by somebody named Barf Bag. Maybe it was a term of respect.

6

Stanley took a shower—if you could call it that, ate dinner—if you could call it that, and went to bed—if you could call his smelly and **scratchy cot** a bed.

Because of the **scarcity** of water, each camper was only allowed a four-minute shower. It took Stanley nearly that long to get used to the cold water. There was no **knob** for hot water. He kept stepping into, then jumping back from, the spray, until the water shut off automatically. He never managed to use his bar of soap, which was just as well, because he wouldn't have had time to **rinse** off the **suds**.

Dinner was some kind of **stew**ed meat and vegetables. The meat was brown and the vegetables had once been green. Everything tasted pretty much the same. He ate it all, and used his slice of white bread to **mop up** the juice. Stanley had never been one to leave food on his plate, no matter how it tasted.

"What'd you do?" one of the campers asked him.

At first Stanley didn't know what he meant.

"They sent you here for a reason."

"Oh," he realized. "I stole a pair of sneakers."

The other boys thought that was funny. Stanley wasn't sure why. Maybe because their crimes were a lot worse than stealing shoes.

"From a store, or were they on someone's feet?" asked Squid.

"Uh, neither," Stanley answered. "They belonged to Clyde Livingston."

Nobody believed him.

"Sweet Feet?" said X-Ray. "Yeah, *right!*"

"No way," said Squid.

Now, as Stanley lay on his cot, he thought it was kind of funny in a way. Nobody had believed him when he said he was innocent. Now, when he said he stole them, nobody believed him either.

Clyde "Sweet Feet" Livingston was a famous baseball player. He'd led the American League* in stolen bases* over the last three years. He was also the only player in history to ever hit four triples* in one game.

Stanley had a poster of him hanging on the wall of his bedroom. He used to have the poster anyway. He didn't

---

★ **American League** National League와 함께 미국 프로 야구 메이저 리그를 구성하는 양대 리그 중 하나이다. 매년 양 리그의 우승팀은 월드 시리즈에서 메이저 리그 전체의 챔피언을 결정한다.

✷ **steal a base** 야구에서 도루하다.

✳ **triple** 야구에서 삼루타.

know where it was now. It had been taken by the police and was used as **evidence** of his **guilt** in the **courtroom**.

Clyde Livingston also came to court. In spite of everything, when Stanley found out that Sweet Feet was going to be there, he was actually excited about the **prospect** of meeting his hero.

Clyde Livingston **testified** that they were his sneakers and that he had **donate**d them to help raise money for the **homeless shelter**. He said he couldn't imagine what kind of **horrible** person would steal from homeless children.

That was the worst part for Stanley. His hero thought he was a no-good-dirty-rotten **thief**.

As Stanley tried to turn over on his cot, he was afraid it was going to **collapse** under all his weight. He barely fit in it. When he finally managed to **roll over** on his stomach, the smell was so bad that he had to turn over again and try sleeping on his back. The cot smelled like sour milk.

Though it was night, the air was still very warm. Armpit was **snoring** two cots away.

Back at school, a **bully** named Derrick Dunne used to **torment** Stanley. The teachers never took Stanley's **complaint**s seriously, because Derrick was so much smaller than Stanley. Some teachers even seemed to find it **amusing** that a little kid like Derrick could **pick on** someone as big as Stanley.

On the day Stanley was **arrest**ed, Derrick had taken

Stanley's notebook and, after a long game of come-and-get-it, finally dropped it in the toilet in the boys' restroom. By the time Stanley **retrieve**d it, he had missed his bus and had to walk home.

It was while he was walking home, carrying his wet notebook, with the prospect of having to copy the ruined pages, that the sneakers fell from the sky.

"I was walking home and the sneakers fell from the sky," he had told the judge. "One hit me on the head."

It had hurt, too.

They hadn't exactly fallen from the sky. He had just walked out from under a **freeway overpass** when the shoe hit him on the head.

Stanley took it as some kind of sign. His father had been trying to **figure out** a way to **recycle** old sneakers, and suddenly a pair of sneakers fell on top of him, **seemingly** out of nowhere, like a gift from God.

Naturally, he had no way of knowing they belonged to Clyde Livingston. In fact, the shoes were anything but sweet. Whoever had worn them had had a bad case of foot **odor**.

Stanley couldn't help but think that there was something special about the shoes, that they would somehow provide the key to his father's invention. It was too much of a **coincidence** to be a **mere** accident. Stanley had felt like he was holding destiny's shoes.

He ran. Thinking back now, he wasn't sure why he ran. Maybe he was in a hurry to bring the shoes to his father, or maybe he was trying to run away from his **miserable** and

humiliating day at school.

A **patrol** car pulled alongside him. A policeman asked him why he was running. Then he took the shoes and made a call on his radio. Shortly thereafter, Stanley was arrested.

It turned out the sneakers had been stolen from a display at the homeless shelter. That evening rich people were going to come to the shelter and pay a hundred dollars to eat the food that the poor people ate every day for free. Clyde Livingston, who had once lived at the shelter when he was younger, was going to speak and sign **autograph**s. His shoes would be **auction**ed, and it was expected that they would sell for over five thousand dollars. All the money would go to help the homeless.

Because of the baseball schedule, Stanley's **trial** was **delay**ed several months. His parents couldn't **afford** a lawyer. "You don't need a lawyer," his mother had said. "Just tell the truth."

Stanley told the truth, but perhaps it would have been better if he had lied a little. He could have said he found the shoes in the street. No one believed they fell from the sky.

It wasn't destiny, he realized. It was his no-good-dirty-rotten-pig-stealing-great-great-grandfather!

The judge called Stanley's crime **despicable**. "The shoes were valued at over five thousand dollars. It was money that would provide food and shelter for the homeless. And you stole that from them, just so you could have a **souvenir**."

The judge said that there was an opening at Camp Green

Lake, and he suggested that the **discipline** of the camp might **improve** Stanley's **character**. It was either that or **jail**. Stanley's parents asked if they could have some time to find out more about Camp Green Lake, but the judge advised them to make a quick decision. "**Vacancies** don't last long at Camp Green Lake."

7

The shovel felt heavy in Stanley's soft, **fleshy** hands. He tried to **jam** it into the earth, but the **blade bang**ed against the ground and **bounce**d off without making a **dent**. The **vibration**s ran up the **shaft** of the shovel and into Stanley's **wrist**s, making his bones **rattle**.

It was still dark. The only light came from the moon and the stars, more stars than Stanley had ever seen before. It seemed he had only just gotten to sleep when Mr. Pendanski came in and woke everyone up.

Using all his **might**, he brought the shovel back down onto the dry lake bed.* The force **stung** his hands but made no **impression** on the earth. He wondered if he had a **defective** shovel. He **glance**d at Zero, about fifteen feet away, who **scoop**ed out a **shovelful** of dirt and **dump**ed it on a pile that was already almost a foot tall.

★ **lake bed** 호수의 바닥. 특히 호숫물이 마른 경우를 말한다.

For breakfast they'd been served some kind of **lukewarm cereal**. The best part was the orange juice. They each got a pint* **carton**. The cereal actually didn't taste too bad, but it had smelled just like his cot.

Then they filled their canteens, got their shovels, and were marched out across the lake. Each group was **assign**ed a different area.

The shovels were kept in a **shed** near the showers. They all looked the same to Stanley, although X-Ray had his own special shovel, which no one else was allowed to use. X-Ray claimed it was shorter than the others, but if it was, it was only by a **fraction** of an inch.

The shovels were five feet long, from the **tip** of the steel blade to the end of the wooden shaft. Stanley's hole would have to be as deep as his shovel, and he'd have to be able to lay the shovel flat across the bottom in any direction. That was why X-Ray wanted the shortest shovel.

The lake was so full of holes and **mound**s that it reminded Stanley of pictures he'd seen of the moon. "If you find anything interesting or unusual," Mr. Pendanski had told him, "you should report it either to me or Mr. Sir when we come around with the water truck. If the Warden likes what you found, you'll get the rest of the **day off**."

"What are we supposed to be looking for?" Stanley asked him.

"You're not looking for anything. You're **digg**ing to build

---

* pint 액량의 단위 파인트. 1파인트는 0.473리터이다.

character. It's just if you find anything, the Warden would like to know about it."

He glanced **helpless**ly at his shovel. It wasn't defective. He was defective.

He noticed a thin **crack** in the ground. He placed the point of his shovel on top of it, then jumped on the back of the blade with both feet.

The shovel sank a few inches into the **packed** earth.

He smiled. For once in his life it paid to be **overweight**.

He leaned on the shaft and **pried** up his first shovelful of dirt, then dumped it off to the side.

Only ten million more to go, he thought, then placed the shovel back in the crack and jumped on it again.

He **unearth**ed several shovelfuls of dirt in this **manner**, before it occurred to him that he was dumping his dirt within the **perimeter** of his hole. He laid his shovel flat on the ground and marked where the edges of his hole would be. Five feet was **awful**ly wide.

He moved the dirt he'd already dug up out past his mark. He took a drink from his canteen. Five feet would be awfully deep, too.

The digging got easier after a while. The ground was hardest at the surface, where the sun had **baked** a **crust** about eight inches deep. Beneath that, the earth was looser. But by the time Stanley broke past the crust, a **blister** had formed in the middle of his right thumb, and it hurt to hold the shovel.

Stanley's great-great-grandfather was named Elya Yelnats. He was born in Latvia* When he was fifteen years old he fell in love with Myra Menke.

(He didn't know he was Stanley's great-great-grandfather.)

Myra Menke was fourteen. She would turn fifteen in two months, at which time her father had decided she should be married.

Elya went to her father to **ask for her hand**, but so did Igor Barkov, the pig farmer. Igor was fifty-seven years old. He had a red nose and fat **puffy** cheeks.

"I will trade you my fattest pig for your daughter," Igor offered.

"And what have you got?" Myra's father asked Elya.

"A heart full of love," said Elya.

"I'd rather have a fat pig," said Myra's father.

Desperate, Elya went to see Madame Zeroni, an old Egyptian* woman who lived on the edge of town. He had become friends with her, though she was quite a bit older than him. She was even older than Igor Barkov.

The other boys of his village liked to mud wrestle. Elya preferred visiting Madame Zeroni and listening to her many stories.

Madame Zeroni had dark skin and a very wide mouth. When she looked at you, her eyes seemed to expand, and

---

★ Latvia 라트비아. 발트 해 연안의 공화국.
✳ Egyptian 이집트사람.

38

you felt like she was looking right through you.

"Elya, what's wrong?" she asked, before he even told her he was upset. She was sitting in a homemade wheelchair. She had no left foot. Her leg stopped at her **ankle**.

"I'm in love with Myra Menke," Elya confessed. "But Igor Barkov has offered to trade his fattest pig for her. I can't **compete** with that."

"Good," said Madame Zeroni. "You're too young to get married. You've got your whole life ahead of you."

"But I love Myra."

"Myra's head is as empty as a **flowerpot**."

"But she's beautiful."

"So is a flowerpot. Can she push a **plow**? Can she milk a goat? No, she is too **delicate**. Can she have an intelligent conversation? No, she is silly and foolish. Will she take care of you when you are sick? No, she is **spoil**ed and will only want you to take care of her. So, she is beautiful. So what? Ptuui!"

Madame Zeroni spat on the dirt.

She told Elya that he should go to America. "Like my son. That's where your future lies. Not with Myra Menke."

But Elya would hear none of that. He was fifteen, and all he could see was Myra's **shallow** beauty.

Madame Zeroni hated to see Elya so **forlorn**. Against her better judgment, she agreed to help him.

"It just so happens, my **sow** gave birth to a **litter** of **piglet**s yesterday," she said. "There is one little **runt** whom she won't **suckle**. You may have him. He would die anyway."

Madame Zeroni led Elya around the back of her house where she kept her pigs.

Elya took the tiny piglet, but he didn't see what good it would do him. It wasn't much bigger than a rat.

"He'll grow," Madame Zeroni assured him. "Do you see that mountain on the edge of the forest?"

"Yes," said Elya.

"On the top of the mountain there is a stream where the water runs **uphill**. You must carry the piglet every day to the top of the mountain and let it drink from the stream. As it drinks, you are to sing to him."

She taught Elya a special song to sing to the pig.

"On the day of Myra's fifteenth birthday, you should carry the pig up the mountain for the last time. Then take it directly to Myra's father. It will be fatter than any of Igor's pigs."

"If it is that big and fat," asked Elya, "how will I be able to carry it up the mountain?"

"The piglet is not too heavy for you now, is it?" asked Madame Zeroni.

"Of course not," said Elya.

"Do you think it will be too heavy for you tomorrow?"

"No."

"Every day you will carry the pig up the mountain. It will get a little bigger, but you will get a little stronger. After you give the pig to Myra's father, I want you to do one more thing for me."

"Anything," said Elya.

40

"I want you to carry me up the mountain. I want to drink from the stream, and I want you to sing the song to me."

Elya promised he would.

Madame Zeroni warned that if he failed to do this, he and his **descendants** would be **doom**ed for all of **eternity**.

At the time, Elya thought nothing of the **curse**. He was just a fifteen-year-old kid, and "eternity" didn't seem much longer than a week from Tuesday. Besides, he liked Madame Zeroni and would be glad to carry her up the mountain. He would have done it right then and there, but he wasn't yet strong enough.

Stanley was still digging. His hole was about three feet deep, but only in the center. It **slope**d upward to the edges. The sun had only just come up over the **horizon**, but he already could feel its hot **rays** against his face.

As he reached down to pick up his canteen, he felt a sudden rush of **dizziness** and put his hands on his knees to **steady** himself. For a moment he was afraid he would **throw up**, but the moment passed. He drank the last drop of water from his canteen. He had blisters on every one of his fingers, and one in the center of each palm.

Everyone else's hole was a lot deeper than his. He couldn't actually see their holes but could tell by the size of their dirt piles.

He saw a cloud of dust moving across the **wasteland** and noticed that the other boys had stopped digging and were watching it, too. The dirt cloud moved closer, and he could see that it **trail**ed behind a red pickup truck.*

The truck stopped near where they were digging, and the boys lined up behind it, X-Ray in front, Zero at the **rear**. Stanley got in line behind Zero.

Mr. Sir filled each of their canteens from a tank of water in the bed of the pickup. As he took Stanley's canteen from him, he said, "This isn't the Girl Scouts, is it?"

Stanley raised and lowered one shoulder.

Mr. Sir followed Stanley back to his hole to see how he was doing. "You better get with it," he said. "Or else you're going to be digging in the hottest part of the day." He **pop**ped some sunflower seeds into his mouth, **deft**ly removed the shells with his teeth, and spat them into Stanley's hole.

Every day Elya carried the little piglet up the mountain and sang to it as it drank from the stream. As the pig grew fatter, Elya grew stronger.

On the day of Myra's fifteenth birthday, Elya's pig weighed over fifty stones.* Madame Zeroni had told him to carry the pig up the mountain on that day as well, but Elya didn't want to present himself to Myra smelling like a pig.

Instead, he took a bath. It was his second bath in less than a week.

Then he led the pig to Myra's.

★ **pickup truck** 뚜껑 없이 뒷부분이 열려있어서 짐을 실을 수 있는 소형 트럭.
⁂ **stone** 무게의 단위 스톤. 1스톤은 6.35킬로그램이다.

Igor Barkov was there with his pig as well.

"These are two of the finest pigs I've ever seen," Myra's father declared.

He was also impressed with Elya, who seemed to have grown bigger and stronger in the last two months. "I used to think you were a good-for-nothing book reader," he said. "But I see now you could be an excellent mud wrestler."

"May I marry your daughter?" Elya **bold**ly asked.

"First, I must weigh the pigs."

Alas,[*] poor Elya should have carried his pig up the mountain one last time. The two pigs weighed exactly the same.

Stanley's blisters had **rip**ped open, and new blisters formed. He kept changing his **grip** on the shovel to try to avoid the pain. Finally, he removed his cap and held it between the shaft of his shovel and his raw hands. This helped, but digging was harder because the cap would slip and slide. The sun beat down on his unprotected head and neck.

Though he tried to **convince** himself otherwise, he'd been aware for a while that his piles of dirt were too close to his hole. The piles were outside his five-foot circle, but he could see he was going to run out of room. Still, he pretended otherwise and kept adding more dirt to the piles, piles that he would **eventually** have to move.

The problem was that when the dirt was in the ground,

★ **alas** [감탄사] 아아. 슬픔·유감을 나타내는 소리.

it was **compact**ed. It expanded when it was **excavat**ed. The piles were a lot bigger than his hole was deep.

It was either now or later. **Reluctant**ly, he climbed up out of his hole, and once again dug his shovel into his previously dug dirt.

Myra's father got down on his hands and knees and closely examined each pig, tail to **snout**.

"Those are two of the finest pigs I have ever seen," he said at last. "How am I to decide? I have only one daughter."

"Why not let Myra decide?" suggested Elya.

"That's **preposterous**!" exclaimed Igor, **expell**ing **saliva** as he spoke.

"Myra is just an empty-headed girl," said her father. "How can she possibly decide, when I, her father, can't?"

"She knows how she feels in her heart," said Elya.

Myra's father **rub**bed his **chin**. Then he laughed and said, "Why not?" He **slap**ped Elya on the back. "It doesn't matter to me. A pig is a pig."

He **summon**ed his daughter.

Elya **blush**ed when Myra entered the room. "Good afternoon, Myra," he said.

She looked at him. "You're Elya, right?" she asked.

"Myra," said her father. "Elya and Igor have each offered a pig for your hand in marriage. It doesn't matter to me. A pig is a pig. So I will let you make the choice. Whom do you wish to marry?"

Myra looked confused. "You want me to decide?"

"That's right, my **blossom**," said her father.

"Gee, I don't know," said Myra. "Which pig weighs more?"

"They both weigh the same," said her father.

"Golly,* " said Myra, "I guess I choose Elya— No, Igor. No, Elya. No, Igor. Oh, I know! I'll think of a number between one and ten. I'll marry whoever guesses the closest number. Okay, I'm ready."

"Ten," guessed Igor.

Elya said nothing.

"Elya?" said Myra. "What number do you guess?"

Elya didn't pick a number. "Marry Igor," he **mutter**ed. "You can keep my pig as a wedding present."

The next time the water truck came it was driven by Mr. Pendanski, who also brought **sack** lunches.* Stanley sat with his back against a pile of dirt and ate. He had a baloney* sandwich, potato chips, and a large chocolate-chip cookie.

"How you doin'?" asked Magnet.

"Not real good," said Stanley.

"Well, the first hole's the hardest," Magnet said.

Stanley took a long, deep breath. He couldn't **afford** to **dawdle**. He was way behind the others, and the sun just kept getting hotter. It wasn't even noon yet. But he didn't

---

★ **golly** [감탄사] 어머나, 아이고, 저런.

✳ **sack lunch** 손잡이가 없는 황색 종이 봉투(sack)에 싸온 점심(lunch).

✳ **baloney** 이탈리아 도시 Bologna에서 유래한 양념된 소시지. 주로 얇게 썰어 샌드위치로 먹는다.

know if he had the strength to stand up.

He thought about quitting. He wondered what they would do to him. What could they do to him?

His clothes were **soak**ed with sweat. In school he had learned that sweating was good for you. It was nature's way of keeping you cool. So why was he so hot?

Using his shovel for support, he managed to get to his feet.

"Where are we supposed to go to the bathroom?" he asked Magnet.

Magnet **gesture**d with his arms to the great **expanse** around them. "Pick a hole, any hole," he said.

Stanley **stagger**ed across the lake, almost falling over a dirt pile.

Behind him he heard Magnet say, "But first make sure nothing's living in it."

After leaving Myra's house, Elya **wander**ed **aimless**ly through the town, until he found himself down by the **wharf**. He sat on the edge of a **pier** and stared down into the cold, black water. He could not understand how Myra had trouble deciding between him and Igor. He thought she loved him. Even if she didn't love him, couldn't she see what a **foul** person Igor was?

It was like Madame Zeroni had said. Her head was as empty as a flowerpot.

Some men were gathering on another **dock**, and he went to see what was going on. A sign read:

46

DECK HANDS WANTED

FREE **PASSAGE** TO AMERICA

He had no sailing experience, but the ship's captain
signed him **aboard**. The captain could see that Elya was
a man of great strength. Not everybody could carry a full-
grown pig up the side of a mountain.

It wasn't until the ship had cleared the **harbor** and
was heading out across the Atlantic* that he suddenly
remembered his promise to carry Madame Zeroni up the
mountain. He felt terrible.

He wasn't afraid of the curse. He thought that was a lot
of nonsense. He felt bad because he knew Madame Zeroni
had wanted to drink from the stream before she died.

Zero was the smallest kid in Group D, but he was the first
one to finish digging.

"You're finished?" Stanley asked **enviously**.

Zero said nothing.

Stanley walked to Zero's hole and watched him measure
it with his shovel. The top of his hole was a perfect circle,
and the sides were smooth and **steep**. Not one dirt **clod**
more than necessary had been removed from the earth.

Zero pulled himself up to the surface. He didn't even
smile. He looked down at his perfectly dug hole, spat in it,

★ **Atlantic** 대서양.

then turned and headed back to the camp **compound**.

"Zero's one **weird dude**," said Zigzag.

Stanley would have laughed, but he didn't have the strength. Zigzag had to be the "weirdest dude" Stanley had ever seen. He had a long skinny neck, and a big round head with wild **frizzy** blond hair that **stuck out** in all directions. His head seemed to **bob** up and down on his neck, like it was on a spring.

Armpit was the second one to finish digging. He also spat into his hole before heading back to the camp compound. One by one, Stanley watched each of the boys spit into his hole and return to the camp compound.

Stanley kept digging. His hole was almost up to his shoulders, although it was hard to tell exactly where ground level was because his dirt piles completely surrounded the hole. The deeper he got, the harder it was to raise the dirt up and out of the hole. Once again, he realized, he was going to have to move the piles.

His cap was **stain**ed with blood from his hands. He felt like he was digging his own **grave**.

In America, Elya learned to speak English. He fell in love with a woman named Sarah Miller. She could push a plow, milk a goat, and, most important, think for herself. She and Elya often stayed up half the night talking and laughing together.

Their life was not easy. Elya worked hard, but bad luck seemed to follow him everywhere. He always seemed to be in the wrong place at the wrong time.

He remembered Madame Zeroni telling him that she had a son in America. Elya was forever looking for him. He'd walk up to complete strangers and ask if they knew someone named Zeroni, or had ever heard of anyone named Zeroni.

No one did. Elya wasn't sure what he'd do if he ever found Madame Zeroni's son anyway. Carry him up a mountain and sing the pig **lullaby** to him?

After his **barn** was **struck** by lightning for the third time, he told Sarah about his broken promise to Madame Zeroni. "I'm worse than a pig **thief**," he said. "You should leave me and find someone who isn't cursed."

"I'm not leaving you," said Sarah. "But I want you to do one thing for me."

"Anything," said Elya.

Sarah smiled. "Sing me the pig lullaby."

He sang it for her.

Her eyes **sparkle**d. "That's so pretty. What does it mean?"

Elya tried his best to **translate** it from Latvian into English, but it wasn't the same. "It **rhyme**s in Latvian," he told her.

"I could tell," said Sarah.

A year later their child was born. Sarah named him Stanley because she noticed that "Stanley" was "Yelnats" spelled backward.

Sarah changed the words of the pig lullaby so that they

rhymed, and every night she sang it to little Stanley.

*"If only, if only," the **woodpecker** sighs,*
*"The **bark** on the tree was as soft as the skies."*
While the wolf waits below, hungry and lonely,
Crying to the moo—oo—oon,
"If only, if only."

Stanley's hole was as deep as his shovel, but not quite wide enough on the bottom. He **grimace**d as he sliced off a **chunk** of dirt, then raised it up and **flung** it onto a pile.

He laid his shovel back down on the bottom of his hole and, to his surprise, it fit. He **rotate**d it and only had to **chip off** a few chunks of dirt, here and there, before it could lie flat across his hole in every direction.

He heard the water truck approaching, and felt a strange sense of pride at being able to show Mr. Sir, or Mr. Pendanski, that he had dug his first hole.

He put his hands on the **rim** and tried to pull himself up.

He couldn't do it. His arms were too weak to lift his heavy body.

He used his legs to help, but he just didn't have any strength. He was trapped in his hole. It was almost funny, but he wasn't in the mood to laugh.

"Stanley!" he heard Mr. Pendanski call.

Using his shovel, he dug two **foothold**s in the hole wall. He climbed out to see Mr. Pendanski walking over to him.

50

"I was afraid you'd **faint**ed," Mr. Pendanski said. "You wouldn't have been the first."

"I'm finished," Stanley said, putting his blood-spotted cap back on his head.

"All right!" said Mr. Pendanski, raising his hand for a high five, but Stanley ignored it. He didn't have the strength.

Mr. Pendanski lowered his hand and looked down at Stanley's hole. "Well done," he said. "You want a ride back?"

Stanley shook his head. "I'll walk."

Mr. Pendanski climbed back into the truck without filling Stanley's canteen. Stanley waited for him to drive away, then took another look at his hole. He knew it was nothing to be proud of, but he felt proud nonetheless.

He **suck**ed up his last bit of saliva and spat.

8

A lot of people don't believe in **curse**s.

A lot of people don't believe in yellow-**spotted lizard**s either, but if one bites you, it doesn't make a difference whether you believe in it or not.

Actually, it is kind of **odd** that scientists named the lizard after its yellow spots. Each lizard has exactly eleven yellow spots, but the spots are hard to see on its yellow-green body.

The lizard is from six to ten inches long and has big red eyes. In truth, its eyes are yellow, and it is the skin around the eyes which is red, but everyone always speaks of its red eyes. It also has black teeth and a **milky** white tongue.

Looking at one, you would have thought that it should have been named a "red-eyed" lizard, or a "black-toothed" lizard, or perhaps a "white-tongued" lizard.

If you've ever been close enough to see the yellow spots, you are probably dead.

The yellow-spotted lizards like to live in holes, which offer **shade** from the sun and **protection** from **predatory** birds. Up to twenty lizards may live in one hole. They have strong, powerful legs, and can **leap** out of very deep holes to **attack** their **prey**. They eat small animals, **insects**, certain **cactus thorn**s, and the shells of sunflower seeds.

9

Stanley stood in the shower and let the cold water pour over his hot and **sore** body. It was four minutes of heaven. For the second day in a row he didn't use soap. He was too tired.

There was no roof over the shower building, and the walls were raised up six inches off the ground except in the corners. There was no **drain** in the floor. The water ran out under the walls and **evaporate**d quickly in the sun.

He put on his clean set of orange clothes. He returned to his tent, put his duty clothes in his **crate**, got out his pen and box of **stationery**, and headed to the rec room.

A sign on the door said WRECK ROOM.[*]

Nearly everything in the room was broken; the TV, the pinball machine,[*] the furniture. Even the people looked

---

★ **wreck** 레크리에이션 강당(Rec Room)의 rec과 발음이 같은 'wreck'을 사용하여 재미있게 표현했다.
✻ **pinball** 바늘이 군데군데 박혀있는 사이로 구슬로 움직이며 점수를 따는 게임.

broken, with their **worn-out** bodies **sprawl**ed over the various chairs and sofas.

X-Ray and Armpit were playing pool.* The surface of the table reminded Stanley of the surface of the lake. It was full of **bump**s and holes because so many people had **carve**d their initials into the felt.*

There was a hole in the far wall, and an electric fan had been placed in front of it. Cheap **air-conditioning**. At least the fan worked.

As Stanley made his way across the room, he **trip**ped over an **outstretch**ed leg.

"Hey, watch it!" said an orange **lump** on a chair.

"You watch it," **mutter**ed Stanley, too tired to care.

"What'd you say?" the Lump demanded.

"Nothin'," said Stanley.

The Lump rose. He was almost as big as Stanley and a lot tougher. "You said something." He **poke**d his fat finger in Stanley's neck. "What'd you say?"

A crowd quickly formed around them.

"Be cool," said X-Ray. He put his hand on Stanley's shoulder. "You don't want to **mess with** the Caveman," he warned.

"The Caveman's cool," said Armpit.

"I'm not looking for trouble," Stanley said. "I'm just tired, that's all."

★ **pool** 포켓볼. 여러 색깔의 공 16개로 하는 당구의 일종.
✳ **felt** 펠트. 모직이나 털을 압축해서 만든 부드럽고 두꺼운 천.

The Lump **grunt**ed.

X-Ray and Armpit led Stanley over to a **couch**. Squid slid over to make room as Stanley sat down.

"Did you see the Caveman back there?" X-Ray asked.

"The Caveman's one tough **dude**," said Squid, and he lightly punched Stanley's arm.

Stanley leaned back against the torn **vinyl upholstery**. Despite his shower, his body still **radiate**d heat. "I wasn't trying to start anything," he said.

The last thing he wanted to do after killing himself all day on the lake was to get in a fight with a boy called the Caveman. He was glad X-Ray and Armpit had come to his rescue.

"Well, how'd you like your first hole?" asked Squid.

Stanley **groan**ed, and the other boys laughed.

"Well, the first hole's the hardest," said Stanley.

"No way," said X-Ray. "The second hole's a lot harder. You're hurting before you even get started. If you think you're sore now, just wait and see how you feel tomorrow morning, right?"

"That's right," said Squid.

"Plus, the fun's gone," said X-Ray.

"The fun?" asked Stanley.

"Don't lie to me," said X-Ray. "I bet you always wanted to dig a big hole, right? Am I right?"

Stanley had never really thought about it before, but he knew better than to tell X-Ray he wasn't right.

"Every kid in the world wants to dig a great big hole,"

said X-Ray. "To China, right?"

"Right," said Stanley.

"See what I mean," said X-Ray. "That's what I'm saying. But now the fun's gone. And you still got to do it again, and again, and again."

"Camp Fun and Games," said Stanley.

"What's in the box?" asked Squid.

Stanley had forgotten he had brought it. "Uh, paper. I was going to write a letter to my mother."

"Your mother?" laughed Squid.

"She'll worry if I don't."

Squid **scowl**ed.

Stanley looked around the room. This was the one place in camp where the boys could enjoy themselves, and what'd they do? They wrecked it. The glass on the TV was **smash**ed, as if someone had put his foot through it. Every table and chair seemed to be missing at least one leg. Everything leaned.

He waited to write the letter until after Squid had gotten up and joined the game of pool.

Dear Mom,

Today was my first day at camp, and I've already made some friends. We've *been* out on the lake all day, so I'm pretty tired. Once I pass the swimming test, *I'll* get to learn how to water-ski.* I

He stopped writing as he became aware that somebody was reading over his shoulder. He turned to see Zero, standing behind the couch.

"I don't want her to worry about me," he explained.

Zero said nothing. He just stared at the letter with a serious, almost angry look on his face.

Stanley slipped it back into the stationery box.

"Did the shoes have red X's on the back?" Zero asked him.

It took Stanley a moment, but then he realized Zero was asking about Clyde Livingston's shoes.

"Yes, they did," he said. He wondered how Zero knew that. Brand X was a popular brand of **sneaker**s. Maybe Clyde Livingston made a **commercial** for them.

Zero stared at him for a moment, with the same **intensity** with which he had been staring at the letter.

Stanley poked his finger through a hole in the vinyl couch and pulled out some of the **stuff**ing. He wasn't aware of what he was doing.

"C'mon, Caveman, dinner," said Armpit.

"You coming, Caveman?" said Squid.

Stanley looked around to see that Armpit and Squid were talking to him. "Uh, sure," he said. He put the piece of stationery back in the box, then got up and followed the boys out to the tables.

The Lump wasn't the Caveman. He was.

He **shrug**ged his left shoulder. It was better than Barf Bag.

★ **water-ski** 수상 스키. 양발에 스키를 신고 보트에 매달려 물 위를 활주하는 스포츠.

10

Stanley had no trouble falling asleep, but morning came much too quickly. Every **muscle** and **joint** in his body **ache**d as he tried to get out of bed. He didn't think it was possible but his body hurt more than it had the day before. It wasn't just his arms and back, but his legs, **ankle**s, and waist also hurt. The only thing that got him out of bed was knowing that every second he wasted meant he was one second closer to the rising of the sun. He hated the sun.

He could hardly lift his spoon during breakfast, and then he was out on the lake, his spoon replaced by a **shovel**. He found a **crack** in the ground, and began his second hole.

He stepped on the shovel **blade**, and pushed on the very back of the **shaft** with the base of his thumb. This hurt less than trying to hold the shaft with his **blister**ed fingers.

As he dug, he was careful to **dump** the dirt far away from the hole. He needed to save the area around the hole for when his hole was much deeper.

He didn't know if he'd ever get that far. X-Ray was right. The second hole was the hardest. It would take a miracle.

As long as the sun wasn't out yet, he removed his cap and used it to help protect his hands. Once the sun rose, he would have to put it back on his head. His neck and **forehead** had been badly burned the day before.

He took it one **shovelful** at a time, and tried not to think of the **awesome** task that lay ahead of him. After an hour or so, his **sore** muscles seemed to loosen up a little bit.

He **grunt**ed as he tried to stick his shovel into the dirt. His cap slipped out from under his fingers, and the shovel fell free.

He let it lie there.

He took a drink from his **canteen**. He guessed that the water truck should be coming soon, but he didn't finish all the water, just in case he was wrong. He'd learned to wait until he saw the truck, before drinking the last drop.

The sun wasn't yet up, but its **rays arc**ed over the **horizon** and brought light to the sky.

He reached down to pick up his cap, and there next to it he saw a wide flat rock. As he put his cap on his head, he continued to look down at the rock.

He picked it up. He thought he could see the shape of a fish, **fossiliz**ed in it.

He **rub**bed off some dirt, and the **outline** of the fish became clearer. The sun **peek**ed over the horizon, and he could actually see tiny lines where every one of the fish's bones had been.

He looked at the **barren** land all around him. True, everyone referred to this area as "the lake," but it was still hard to believe that this dry **wasteland** was once full of water.

Then he remembered what Mr. Sir and Mr. Pendanski had both said. If he dug up anything interesting, he should report it to one of them. If the Warden liked it, he would get the rest of the **day off**.

He looked back down at his fish. He'd found his miracle.

He continued to dig, though very slowly, as he waited for the water truck. He didn't want to bring attention to his find, afraid that one of the other boys might try to take it from him. He tossed the rock, face down, beside his dirt pile, as if it had no special value. A short while later he saw the cloud of dirt heading across the lake.

The truck stopped and the boys lined up. They always lined up in the same order, Stanley realized, no matter who got there first. X-Ray was always at the front of the line. Then came Armpit, Squid, Zigzag, Magnet, and Zero.

Stanley got in line behind Zero. He was glad to be at the back, so no one would notice the **fossil**. His pants had very large pockets, but the rock still made a **bulge**.

Mr. Pendanski filled each boy's canteen, until Stanley was the only one left.

"I found something," Stanley said, taking it out of his pocket.

Mr. Pendanski reached for Stanley's canteen, but Stanley

handed him the rock instead.

"What's this?"

"It's a fossil," said Stanley. "See the fish?"

Mr. Pendanski looked at it again.

"See, you can even see all of its little bones," said Stanley.

"Interesting," said Mr. Pendanski. "Let me have your canteen."

Stanley handed it to him. Mr. Pendanski filled it, then returned it.

"So do I get the rest of the day off?"

"What for?"

"You know, you said if I found something interesting, the Warden would give me the day off."

Mr. Pendanski laughed as he gave the fossil back to Stanley. "Sorry, Stanley. The Warden isn't interested in fossils."

"Let me see that," said Magnet, taking the rock from Stanley.

Stanley continued to stare at Mr. Pendanski.

"Hey, Zig, dig this rock."

"Cool," said Zigzag.

Stanley saw his fossil being passed around.

"I don't see nothing," said X-Ray. He took off his glasses, **wipe**d them on his dirty clothes, and put them back on.

"See, look at the little fishy," said Armpit.

11

Stanley returned to his hole. It wasn't fair. Mr. Pendanski had even said his **fossil** was interesting. He **slam**med his shovel into the ground and **pried** up another piece of earth.

After a while, he noticed X-Ray had come by and was watching him dig.

"Hey, Caveman, let me talk to you a second," X-Ray said.

Stanley put down his shovel and stepped up out of his hole.

"Say, listen," said X-Ray. "If you find something else, give it to me, okay?"

Stanley wasn't sure what to say. X-Ray was clearly the leader of the group, and Stanley didn't want to get on his bad side.

"You're new here, right?" said X-Ray. "I've been here for almost a year. I've never found anything. You know, my **eyesight**'s not so good. No one knows this, but you know why my name's X-Ray?"

Stanley **shrugged** one shoulder.

"It's pig latin* for Rex. That's all. I'm too blind to find anything."

Stanley tried to remember how pig latin worked.

"I mean," X-Ray went on, "why should you get a day off when you've only been here a couple of days? If anybody gets a day off, it should be me. That's only fair, right?"

"I guess," Stanley agreed.

X-Ray smiled. "You're a good guy, Caveman."

Stanley picked up his shovel.

The more he thought about it, the more he was glad that he agreed to let X-Ray have anything he might find. If he was going to survive at Camp Green Lake, it was far more important that X-Ray think he was a good guy than it was for him to get one day off. Besides, he didn't expect to find anything anyway. There probably wasn't anything "of interest" out there, and even if there was, he'd never been what you could call lucky.

He slammed his blade into the ground, then dumped out another shovelful of dirt. It was a little surprising, he thought, that X-Ray was the leader of the group, since he obviously wasn't the biggest or the toughest. In fact, except for Zero, X-Ray was the smallest. Armpit was the biggest.

★ **pig latin** 피그 라틴. 은어를 만드는 방법 중 하나로, 단어의 맨 앞에 있는 자음을 맨 뒤로 보내고 거기에 ay를 덧붙이는 말장난이다. 본문에서 X-Ray라는 이름도 Rex에서 R을 ex(X) 뒤로 보낸 후 ay를 붙여서 나오게 된 이름이다.

Zigzag may have been taller than Armpit, but that was only because of his neck. Yet Armpit, and all the others, seemed to be willing to do whatever X-Ray asked of them.

As Stanley **dug** up another shovelful of dirt, it occurred to him that Armpit wasn't the biggest. He, the Caveman, was bigger.

He was glad they called him Caveman. It meant they accepted him as a member of the group. He would have been glad even if they'd called him Barf Bag.

It was really quite **remarkable** to him. At school, **bullies** like Derrick Dunne used to **pick on** him. Yet Derrick Dunne would be scared **senseless** by any of the boys here.

As he dug his hole, Stanley thought about what it would be like if Derrick Dunne had to fight Armpit or Squid. Derrick wouldn't stand a chance.

He imagined what it would be like if he became good friends with all of them, and then for some reason they all went with him to his school, and then Derrick Dunne tried to steal his notebook . . .

"Just what do you think you're doing?" asks Squid, as he slams his hands into *Derrick Dunne's* **smug** *face.*

"Caveman's our friend," says Armpit, *grabbing him by the shirt* **collar.**

Stanley played the scene over and over again in his mind, each time watching another boy from Group D **beat up** Derrick Dunne. It helped him dig his hole and **ease** his own suffering. Whatever pain he felt was being felt ten times worse by Derrick.

12

Again, Stanley was the last one to finish digging. It was late afternoon when he **dragged** himself back to the **compound**. This time he would have accepted a ride on the truck if it was offered.

When he got to the tent, he found Mr. Pendanski and the other boys sitting in a circle on the ground.

"Welcome, Stanley," said Mr. Pendanski.

"Hey, Caveman. You get your hole dug?" asked Magnet.

He managed to **nod**.

"You **spit** in it?" asked Squid.

He nodded again. "You're right," he said to X-Ray. "The second hole's the hardest."

X-Ray shook his head. "The third hole's the hardest," he said.

"Come join our circle," said Mr. Pendanski.

Stanley **plop**ped down between Squid and Magnet. He needed to rest up before taking a shower.

"We've been discussing what we want to do with our lives," said Mr. Pendanski. "We're not going to be at Camp Green Lake forever. We need to prepare for the day we leave here and join the rest of society."

"Hey, that's great, Mom!" said Magnet. "They're going to finally let you out of here?"

The other boys laughed.

"Okay, José," said Mr. Pendanski. "What do you want to do with your life?"

"I don't know," said Magnet.

"You need to think about that," said Mr. Pendanski. "It's important to have goals. Otherwise you're going to end up right back in **jail**. What do you like to do?"

"I don't know," said Magnet.

"You must like something," said Mr. Pendanski.

"I like animals," said Magnet.

"Good," said Mr. Pendanski. "Does anyone know of any jobs that involve animals?"

"**Veterinarian**," said Armpit.

"That's right," said Mr. Pendanski.

"He could work in a zoo," said Zigzag.

"He belongs in the zoo," said Squid, then he and X-Ray laughed.

"How about you, Stanley? Any ideas for José?"

Stanley sighed. "Animal trainer," he said. "Like for the circus, or movies, or something like that."

"Any of those jobs sound good to you, José?" asked Mr. Pendanski.

"Yeah, I like what Caveman said. About training animals for movies. I think it would be fun to train monkeys."

X-Ray laughed.

"Don't laugh, Rex," said Mr. Pendanski. "We don't laugh at people's dreams. Someone is going to have to train monkeys for the movies."

"Who are you kidding, Mom?" asked X-Ray. "Magnet's never going to be a monkey trainer."

"You don't know that," said Mr. Pendanski. "I'm not saying it's going to be easy. Nothing in life is easy. But that's no reason to give up. You'll be surprised what you can **accomplish** if you set your mind to it. After all, you only have one life, so you should try to make the most of it."

Stanley tried to **figure out** what he'd say if Mr. Pendanski asked him what he wanted to do with his life. He used to think he wanted to work for the F.B.I.,★ but this didn't seem the **appropriate** place to mention that.

"So far you've all done a pretty good job at **mess**ing **up** your lives," said Mr. Pendanski. "I know you think you're cool." He looked at Stanley. "So you're Caveman, now, huh? You like digging holes, Caveman?"

Stanley didn't know what to say.

"Well, let me tell you something, Caveman. You are here **on account of** one person. If it wasn't for that person, you wouldn't be here digging holes in the hot sun. You know who that person is?"

★ **F.B.I.** 미국 연방 수사국(Federal Bureau of Investigation). 미국 법무부 산하의 수사 기관으로 범죄 수사와 정보 수집 업무를 담당하고 있다.

"My no-good-dirty-rotten-pig-stealing-great-great-grand-father."

The other boys **howl**ed with laughter.

Even Zero smiled.

It was the first time Stanley had ever seen Zero smile. He usually had such an angry expression on his face. Now he had such a huge smile it almost seemed too big for his face, like the smile on a jack-o'-lantern.★

"No," said Mr. Pendanski. "That person is you, Stanley. You're the reason you are here. You're responsible for yourself. You messed up your life, and it's up to you to fix it. No one else is going to do it for you—for any of you."

Mr. Pendanski looked from one boy to another. "You're all special in your own way," he said. "You've all got something to offer. You have to think about what you want to do, then do it. Even you, Zero. You're not completely **worthless**."

The smile was now gone from Zero's face.

"What do you want to do with your life?" Mr. Pendanski asked him.

Zero's mouth was shut tight. As he **glare**d at Mr. Pendanski, his dark eyes seemed to expand.

"What about it, Zero?" asked Mr. Pendanski. "What do you like to do?"

"I like to dig holes."

★ **jack-o'-lantern** 호박에 얼굴 모양으로 구멍을 뚫고 안에 촛불을 꽂은 등. 할로윈 때 장식용으로 사용한다.

13

All too soon Stanley was back out on the lake, sticking his shovel into the dirt. X-Ray was right: the third hole was the hardest. So was the fourth hole. And the fifth hole. And the sixth, and the . . .

He dug his shovel into the dirt.

After a while he'd **lost track of** the day of the week, and how many holes he'd dug. It all seemed like one big hole, and it would take a year and a half to dig it. He guessed he'd lost at least five pounds.* He figured that in a year and a half he'd be either in great physical condition, or else dead.

He dug his shovel into the dirt.

It couldn't always be this hot, he thought. Surely it got cooler in December. Maybe then they **froze**.

He dug his shovel into the dirt.

His skin had gotten tougher. It didn't hurt so much to

---

*★ **pound** 중량을 나타내는 단위인 파운드. 1파운드는 0.4536킬로그램이다.

hold the shovel.

As he drank from his canteen he looked up at the sky. A cloud had appeared earlier in the day. It was the first cloud he could remember seeing since coming to Camp Green Lake.

He and the other boys had been watching it all day, hoping it would move in front of the sun. **Occasionally** it got close, but it was just **teasing** them.

His hole was waist deep. He dug his shovel into the dirt. As he dumped it out, he thought he saw something **glisten** as it fell onto the dirt pile. Whatever it was, it was quickly buried.

Stanley stared at the pile a moment, **unsure** if he'd even seen it. Even if it was something, what good would it do him? He'd promised to give anything he found to X-Ray. It didn't seem worth the effort to climb out of his hole to check it out.

He **glance**d up at the cloud, which was close enough to the sun that he had to **squint** to look at it.

He dug his shovel back into the earth, **scoop**ed out some dirt, and lifted it over his dirt pile. But instead of dumping it there, he tossed it off to the side. His **curiosity** had **gotten the better of** him.

He climbed up out of his hole and **sift**ed his fingers through the pile. He felt something hard and **metallic**.

He pulled it out. It was a gold tube, about as long and as wide as the second finger on his right hand. The tube was open at one end and closed at the other.

He used a few drops of his **precious** water to clean it.

There seemed to be some kind of design on the flat, closed end. He poured a few more drops of water on it and **rub**bed it on the inside of his pants pocket.

He looked again at the design **engrave**d into the flat bottom of the tube. He could see an **outline** of a heart, with the letters K B **etch**ed inside it.

He tried to figure out some way that he wouldn't have to give it to X-Ray. He could just keep it, but that wouldn't do him any good. He wanted a day off.

He looked at the large piles of dirt near where X-Ray was digging. X-Ray was probably almost finished for the day. Getting the rest of the day off would hardly do him much good. X-Ray would first have to show the tube to Mr. Sir or Mr. Pendanski, who would then have to show it to the Warden. By then X-Ray might be done anyway.

Stanley wondered about trying to secretly take the tube directly to the Warden. He could explain the situation to the Warden, and the Warden might make up an excuse for giving him the day off, so X-Ray wouldn't **suspect**.

He looked across the lake toward the **cabin** under the two **oak** trees. The place scared him. He'd been at Camp Green Lake almost two weeks, and he still hadn't seen the

Warden. That was just as well. If he could go his entire year and a half without seeing the Warden, that would be fine with him.

Besides, he didn't know if the Warden would find the tube "interesting." He looked at it again. It looked familiar. He thought he'd seen something like it, somewhere before, but couldn't quite **place** it.

"What you got there, Caveman?" asked Zigzag.

Stanley's large hand closed around the tube. "Nothin', just, uh . . ." It was useless. "I think I might have found something."

"Another **fossil**?"

"No, I'm not sure what it is."

"Let me see," said Zigzag.

Instead of showing it to Zigzag, Stanley brought it to X-Ray. Zigzag followed.

X-Ray looked at the tube, then rubbed his dirty glasses on his dirty shirt and looked at the tube again. One by one, the other boys dropped their shovels and came to look.

"It looks like an old **shotgun** shell,*" said Squid.

"Yeah, that's probably what it is," said Stanley. He decided not to mention the engraved design. Maybe nobody would notice it. He doubted X-Ray could see it.

"No, it's too long and thin to be a shotgun shell," said Magnet.

★ **shell** 보통 열매·씨 등의 '껍질, 조가비'라는 뜻으로 쓰이는 단어이지만, 여기서는 '탄약통'으로 쓰였다.

"It's prob'ly just a piece of **junk**," said Stanley.

"Well, I'll show it to Mom," said X-Ray. "See what he thinks. Who knows? Maybe I'll get the day off."

"Your hole's almost finished," said Stanley.

"Yeah, so?"

Stanley raised and lowered his shoulder. "So, why don't you wait until tomorrow to show it to Mom?" he suggested. "You can pretend you found it first thing in the morning. Then you can get the whole day off, instead of just an hour or so this afternoon."

X-Ray smiled. "Good thinking, Caveman." He dropped the tube into his large pocket on the right leg of his dirty orange pants.

Stanley returned to his hole.

When the water truck came, Stanley started to take his place at the end of the line, but X-Ray told him to get behind Magnet, in front of Zero.

Stanley moved up one place in line.

74

14

That night, as Stanley lay on his **scratchy** and smelly **cot**, he tried to figure out what he could have done differently, but there was nothing he could do. For once in his unlucky life, he was in the right place at the right time, and it still didn't help him.

"You got it?" he asked X-Ray the next morning at breakfast.

X-Ray looked at him with half-opened eyes behind his dirty glasses. "I don't know what you're talking about," he **grumble**d.

"You know . . ." said Stanley.

"No, I don't know!" X-Ray **snap**ped. "So just leave me alone, okay? I don't want to talk to you."

Stanley didn't say another word.

Mr. Sir marched the boys out to the lake, chewing sunflower seeds along the way and spitting out the shells. He **scrape**d the ground with his boot heel, to mark where each boy was supposed to dig.

Stanley **stamp**ed down on the back of the **blade** of the **shovel**, **piercing** the hard, dry earth. He couldn't figure out why X-Ray snapped at him. If he wasn't going to **produce** the tube, why did he make Stanley give it to him? Was he just going to keep it? The tube was gold in color, but Stanley didn't think it was real gold.

The water truck came a little after sunrise. Stanley finished his last drop of water and stepped up out of his hole. At this time of day, Stanley sometimes could see some **distant** hills or mountains on the other side of the lake. They were only visible for a short while and would soon disappear behind the **haze** of heat and dirt.

The truck stopped, and the dust cloud **drift**ed past it. X-Ray took his place at the front of the line. Mr. Pendanski filled his **canteen**. "Thanks, Mom," X-Ray said. He didn't mention the tube.

Mr. Pendanski filled all the canteens, then climbed back into the **cab** of the pickup. He still had to bring water to Group E. Stanley could see them digging about two hundred yards* away.

"Mr. Pendanski!" X-Ray shouted from his hole. "Wait! Mr. Pendanski! I think I might have found something!"

The boys all followed Mr. Pendanski as he walked over to X-Ray's hole. Stanley could see the gold tube **stick**ing **out** of some dirt on the end of X-Ray's shovel.

★ **yard** 길이의 단위 야드. 1야드는 0.9144미터이다.

Mr. Pendanski examined it and took a long look at its flat bottom. "I think the Warden is going to like this."

"Does X-Ray get the **day off**?" asked Squid.

"Just keep digging until someone says otherwise," Mr. Pendanski said. Then he smiled. "But if I were you, Rex, I wouldn't dig too hard."

Stanley watched the cloud of dust move across the lake to the cabin beneath the trees.

The boys in Group E were just going to have to wait.

It didn't take long for the pickup to return. Mr. Pendanski stepped out of the cab. A tall woman with red hair stepped out of the **passenger** side. She looked even taller than she was, since Stanley was down in his hole. She wore a black cowboy hat and black cowboy boots which were **stud**ded with turquoise stones.* The sleeves on her shirt were rolled up, and her arms were covered with **freckle**s, as was her face. She walked right up to X-Ray.

"This where you found it?"

"Yes, ma'am."

"Your good work will be **reward**ed." She turned to Mr. Pendanski. "Drive X-Ray back to camp. Let him take a double shower, and give him some clean clothes. But first I want you to fill everyone's canteen."

"I just filled them a little while ago," said Mr. Pendanski.

The Warden stared hard at him. "Excuse me," she said. Her voice was soft.

★ turquoise (stone) 터키석. 청록색·녹색을 띠는 보석으로, 12월의 탄생석이기도 하다.

"I had just filled them when Rex—"

"Excuse me," the Warden said again. "Did I ask you when you last filled them?"

"No, but it's just—"

"Excuse me."

Mr. Pendanski stopped talking. The Warden **wiggle**d her finger for him to come to her. "It's hot and it's only going to get hotter," she said. "Now, these fine boys have been working hard. Don't you think it might be possible that they might have taken a drink since you last filled their canteens?"

Mr. Pendanski said nothing.

The Warden turned to Stanley. "Caveman, will you come here, please?"

Stanley was surprised she knew his name. He had never seen her. Until she stepped out of the truck, he didn't even know the Warden was a woman.

He nervously went toward her.

"Mr. Pendanski and I have been having a discussion. Have you taken a drink since Mr. Pendanski last filled your canteen?"

Stanley didn't want to cause any trouble for Mr. Pendanski. "I still got plenty left," he said.

"Excuse me."

He stopped. "Yeah, I drank some."

"Thank you. May I see your canteen please."

Stanley handed it to her. Her fingernails were painted dark red.

She gently shook the canteen, letting the water **swish** inside the plastic container. "Do you hear the empty spaces?" she asked.

"Yes," said Mr. Pendanski.

"Then fill it," she said. "And the next time I tell you to do something, I expect you to do it without questioning my **authority**. If it's too much trouble for you to fill a canteen, I'll give you a shovel. You can dig the hole, and the Caveman can fill your canteen." She turned back to Stanley. "I don't think that would be too much trouble for you, would it?"

"No," said Stanley.

"So what will it be?" she asked Mr. Pendanski. "Do you want to fill the canteens or do you want to dig?"

"I'll fill the canteens," said Mr. Pendanski.

"Thank you."

15

Mr. Pendanski filled the canteens.

The Warden got a pitchfork* out of the back of the pickup. She **poke**d it through X-Ray's dirt pile, to see if anything else might have been buried in there as well.

"After you drop off X-Ray, I want you to bring back three wheelbarrows,*" she said.

X-Ray got in the pickup. As the truck pulled away, he leaned out the wide window and waved.

"Zero," said the Warden. "I want you to **take over** X-Ray's hole." She seemed to know that Zero was the fastest digger.

"Armpit and Squid, you will keep **dig**ging where you have been," she said. "But you're each going to have a helper. Zigzag, you help Armpit. Magnet will help Squid. And Caveman, you'll work with Zero. We're going to dig

---

★ **pitchfork** 쇠스랑. 땅을 일구는 데 쓰는 농기구.
＊ **wheelbarrow** 외바퀴손수레.

the dirt twice. Zero will dig it out of the hole, and Caveman will carefully shovel it into a wheelbarrow. Zigzag will do the same for Armpit, and the same with Magnet and Squid. We don't want to miss anything. If either of you find something, you'll both get the rest of the day off, and a double shower.

"When the wheelbarrows are full, you are to **dump** them away from this area. We don't want any dirt piles to **get in the way.**"

The Warden remained at the site for the **remainder** of the day, along with Mr. Pendanski and Mr. Sir, who showed up after a while. **Occasional**ly Mr. Sir would leave to take water to the other groups of campers, but otherwise he and the water truck stayed parked there. The Warden saw to it that nobody in Group D was ever thirsty.

Stanley did as he was told. He carefully looked through all the dirt dug up by Zero, as he shoveled it into a wheelbarrow, though he knew he wouldn't find anything.

It was easier than digging his own hole. When the wheelbarrow was full, he took it a good distance away before dumping it.

The Warden couldn't keep **still**. She kept walking around, looking over the boys' shoulders, and sticking her pitchfork through the dirt piles. "You're doing fine, just fine," she told Stanley.

After a while, she told the boys to switch places, so that Stanley, Zigzag, and Magnet dug in the holes, and Zero, Armpit, and Squid shoveled the **excavate**d dirt into the wheelbarrows.

After lunch, Zero took over the digging again, and Stanley returned to the wheelbarrow. "There's no hurry," the Warden said several times. "The main thing is not to miss anything."

The boys dug until each hole was well over six feet deep and wide. Still, it was easier for two boys to dig a six-foot hole than it was for one boy to dig a five-foot hole.

"All right, that's enough for today," the Warden said. "I've waited this long, I can wait another day."

Mr. Sir drove her back to her cabin.

"I wonder how she knew all our names," Stanley said as he walked back to the compound.

"She watches us all the time," said Zigzag. "She's got hidden **microphone**s and cameras all over the place. In the tents, the Wreck Room, the shower."

"The shower?" asked Stanley. He wondered if Zigzag was just being **paranoid**.

"The cameras are tiny," said Armpit. "No bigger than the **toenail** on your little toe."

Stanley had his doubts about that. He didn't think they could make cameras that small. Microphones, maybe.

He realized that was why X-Ray didn't want to talk to him about the gold tube at breakfast. X-Ray was afraid the Warden might have been listening.

One thing was certain: They weren't just digging to "build **character**." They were **definitely** looking for something.

And whatever they were looking for, they were looking

in the wrong place.

Stanley **gaze**d out across the lake, toward the spot where he had been digging yesterday when he found the gold tube. He dug the hole into his memory.

16

As Stanley entered the Wreck Room, he could hear X-Ray's voice from all the way across the room.

"See what I'm saying," X-Ray said. "Am I right, or am I right?"

The other bodies in the room were little more than bags of **flesh** and bones, dumped across broken chairs and **couch**es. X-Ray was full of life, laughing and waving his arms around as he talked. "Yo, Caveman, my man!" he called out.

Stanley made his way across the room.

"Hey, slide on over, Squid," said X-Ray. "Make room for the Caveman."

Stanley **crash**ed on the couch.

He had looked for a hidden camera in the shower. He hadn't seen anything, and he hoped the Warden hadn't either.

"What's the matter?" asked X-Ray. "You guys tired or something?" He laughed.

"Hey, keep it down, will you," **groan**ed Zigzag. "I'm trying to watch TV."

Stanley glanced **uncertain**ly at Zigzag, who was staring very **intent**ly at the **bust**ed television screen.

The Warden greeted the boys at breakfast the next morning and went with them to the holes. Four **dug** in the holes, and three **tend**ed to the wheelbarrows. "Glad you're here, X-Ray," she said to him. "We need your sharp eyes."

Stanley spent more time pushing the wheelbarrow than digging, because he was such a slow digger. He **cart**ed away the **excess** dirt and dumped it into previously dug holes. He was careful not to dump any of it in the hole where the gold tube was actually found.

He could still see the tube in his mind. It seemed so familiar, but he just couldn't **place** it. He thought that it might have been the **lid** to a **fancy** gold pen. *K B* could have been the initials of a famous author. The only famous authors he could think of were Charles Dickens,* William Shakespeare,* and Mark Twain.* Besides, it didn't really look like the top of a pen.

By lunchtime the Warden was beginning to lose her patience. She made them eat quickly, so they could get back to work. "If you can't get them to work any faster," she told

---

★ **Charles Dickens** 영국의 소설가 찰스 디킨스. 『크리스마스 캐럴』, 『올리버 트위스트』등을 썼다.
✳ **William Shakespeare** 영국이 낳은 세계 최고 시인 겸 극작가 셰익스피어.
✴ **Mark Twain** 미국 소설가 마크 트웨인. 『톰소여의 모험』으로 유명하다.

Mr. Sir, "then you're going to have to climb down there and dig with them."

After that, everyone worked faster, especially when Mr. Sir was watching them. Stanley practically ran when he pushed his wheelbarrow. Mr. Sir reminded them that they weren't Girl Scouts.

They didn't quit digging until after every other group had finished.

Later, as Stanley sat **sprawl**ed across an **understuffed** chair, he tried to think of a way to tell the Warden where the tube was really found, without getting himself or X-Ray into trouble. It didn't seem possible. He even thought about **sneak**ing out at night and digging in that hole by himself. But the last thing he wanted to do after digging all day was to dig at night, too. Besides, the shovels were locked up at night, **presumably** so they couldn't be used as weapons.

Mr. Pendanski entered the Wreck Room. "Stanley," he called as he made his way to him.

"His name's Caveman," said X-Ray.

"Stanley," said Mr. Pendanski.

"My name's Caveman," said Stanley.

"Well, I have a letter here for someone named Stanley Yelnats," said Mr. Pendanski. He turned over an envelope in his hands. "It doesn't say Caveman anywhere."

"Uh, thanks," Stanley said, taking it.

It was from his mother.

"Who's it from?" Squid asked. "Your *mother?*"

Stanley put it in the big pocket of his pants.

"Aren't you going to read it to us?" asked Armpit.

"Give him some space," said X-Ray. "If Caveman doesn't want to read it to us, he doesn't have to. It's probably from his girlfriend."

Stanley smiled.

He read it later, after the other boys had gone to dinner.

> *Dear Stanley,*
>
> *It was wonderful to hear from you. Your letter made me feel like one of the other moms who can **afford** to send their kids to summer camp. I know it's not the same, but I am very proud of you for trying to make the best of a bad situation. Who knows? Maybe something good will come of this.*
>
> *Your father thinks he is real close to a **breakthrough** on his **sneaker** project. I hope so. The **landlord** is **threaten**ing to **evict** us because of the **odor**.*
>
> *I feel sorry for the little old lady who lived in a shoe.* It must have smelled **awful**!*
>
> *Love from both of us,*

"What's so funny?" Zero asked.

It **startle**d him. He thought Zero had gone to dinner with the others.

★ **little old lady who lived in a shoe** 유명한 자장가 중 하나. 신발 속에 사는 늙은 엄마의 이야기.

"Nothing. Just something my mom wrote."

"What'd she say?" Zero asked.

"Nothing."

"Oh, sorry," said Zero.

"Well, see my dad is trying to invent a way to **recycle** old sneakers. So the apartment kind of smells bad, because he's always cooking these old sneakers. So anyway, in the letter my mom said she felt sorry for that little old lady who lived in a shoe, you know, because it must have smelled bad in there."

Zero stared **blank**ly at him.

"You know, the nursery **rhyme**?"

Zero said nothing.

"You've heard the nursery rhyme about the little old lady who lived in a shoe?"

"No."

Stanley was amazed.

"How does it go?" asked Zero.

"Didn't you ever watch *Sesame Street?**" Stanley asked.

Zero stared blankly.

Stanley headed on to dinner. He would have felt pretty silly **reciting** nursery rhymes at Camp Green Lake.

★ **Sesame Street** 미국 CTW가 제작한 장수 어린이 프로그램. 취학 이전의 아동들에게 자연스럽게 영어 알파벳을 알려주는 교육 프로그램이다.

17

For the next week and a half, the boys continued to dig in and around the area where X-Ray had supposedly found the gold tube. They widened X-Ray's hole, as well as the holes Armpit and Squid had been digging, until the fourth day, when all three holes met and formed one big hole.

As the days **wore on**, the Warden became less and less patient. She arrived later in the morning and left earlier in the afternoon. Meanwhile, the boys continued to dig later and later.

"This is no bigger than it was when I left you yesterday," she said after arriving late one morning, well after sunrise. "What have you been doing down there?"

"Nothing," said Squid.

It was the wrong thing to say.

At just that moment, Armpit was returning from a bathroom break.

"How nice of you to join us," she said. "And what have

you been doing?"

"I had to . . . you know . . . go."

The Warden **jab**bed at Armpit with her pitchfork, **knock**ing him backward into the big hole. The pitchfork left three holes in the front of his shirt, and three tiny spots of blood.

"You're giving these boys too much water," the Warden told Mr. Pendanski.

They continued to dig until late afternoon, long after all the other groups had finished for the day. Stanley was down in the big hole, along with the other six boys. They had stopped using the wheelbarrows.

He dug his shovel into the side of the hole. He **scoop**ed up some dirt, and was raising it up to the surface when Zigzag's shovel caught him in the side of the head.

He **collapse**d.

He wasn't sure if he **pass**ed **out** or not. He looked up to see Zigzag's wild head staring down at him. "I ain't digging that dirt up," Zigzag said. "That's your dirt."

"Hey, Mom!" Magnet called. "Caveman's been hurt."

Stanley brought his fingers up the side of his neck. He felt his wet blood and a pretty big **gash** just below his ear.

Magnet helped Stanley to his feet, then up and out of the hole. Mr. Sir made a **bandage** out of a piece of his **sack** of sunflower seeds and taped it over Stanley's **wound**. Then he told him to get back to work. "It isn't **nap** time."

When Stanley returned to the hole, Zigzag was waiting

90

for him.

"That's your dirt," Zigzag said. "You have to dig it up. It's covering up my dirt."

Stanley felt a little **dizzy**. He could see a small pile of dirt. It took him a moment to realize that it was the dirt which had been on his shovel when he was hit.

He scooped it up, then Zigzag dug his shovel into the ground underneath where "Stanley's dirt" had been.

18

The next morning Mr. Sir marched the boys to another section of the lake, and each boy dug his own hole, five feet deep and five feet wide. Stanley was glad to be away from the big hole. At least now he knew just how much he had to dig for the day. And it was a relief not to have other shovels swinging past his face, or the Warden hanging around.

He dug his shovel into the dirt, then slowly turned to dump it into a pile. He had to make his turns smooth and slow. If he jerked too quickly, he felt a throbbing pain just above his neck where Zigzag's shovel had hit him.

That part of his head, between his neck and ear, was considerably swollen. There were no mirrors in camp, but he imagined he looked like he had a hard-boiled egg sticking out of him.

The remainder of his body hardly hurt at all. His muscles had strengthened, and his hands were tough and callused. He was still the slowest digger, but not all that much slower than Magnet. Less than thirty minutes after Magnet returned to camp, Stanley **spat** into his hole.

After his shower, he put his dirty clothes in his **crate** and got out his box of **stationery**. He stayed in the tent to write the letter so Squid and the other boys wouldn't make fun of him for writing to his mother.

Dear Mom and Dad,

*Camp is hard, but **challenging**. We've been running **obstacle** courses, and have to swim long distances on the lake. Tomorrow we learn*

He stopped writing as Zero walked into the tent, then returned to his letter. He didn't care what Zero thought. Zero was nobody.

to rock climb. I know that sounds scary, but don't worry,

Zero was standing beside him now, watching him write.

Stanley turned, and felt his neck throb. "I don't like it when you read over my shoulder, okay?"

Zero said nothing.

I'll be careful. It's not all fun and games here, but I think I'm getting a lot out of it. It builds character. The other boys

"I don't know how," said Zero.

"What?"

"Can you teach me?"

Stanley didn't know what he was talking about. "Teach you what, to rock climb?"

Zero stared at him with **penetrating** eyes.

"What?" said Stanley. He was hot, tired, and **sore**.

"I want to learn to read and write," said Zero.

Stanley let out a short laugh. He wasn't laughing at Zero. He was just surprised. All this time he had thought Zero was reading over his shoulder. "Sorry," he said. "I don't know how to teach."

After digging all day, he didn't have the strength to try to teach Zero to read and write. He needed to save his energy for the people who **count**ed.

"You don't have to teach me to write," said Zero. "Just to read. I don't have anybody to write to."

"Sorry," Stanley said again.

His muscles and hands weren't the only parts of his body that had toughened over the past several weeks. His heart had hardened as well.

He finished his letter. He barely had enough **moisture** in his mouth to **seal** and **stamp** the envelope. It seemed that no matter how much water he drank, he was always thirsty.

19

He was **awaken**ed one night by a strange noise. At first he thought it might have been some kind of animal, and it **frighten**ed him. But as the sleep cleared from his head, he realized that the noise was coming from the **cot** next to him.

Squid was crying.

"You okay?" Stanley whispered.

Squid's head **jerk**ed around. He **sniff**ed and caught his breath. "Yeah, I just . . . I'm fine," he whispered, and sniffed again.

In the morning Stanley asked Squid if he was feeling better.

"What are you, my mother?" asked Squid.

Stanley raised and lowered one shoulder.

"I got **allergies**, okay?" Squid said.

"Okay," said Stanley.

"You open your mouth again, and I'll break your **jaw**."

Stanley kept his mouth shut most of the time. He didn't talk too much to any of the boys, afraid that he might say the wrong thing. They called him Caveman and all that, but he couldn't forget that they were dangerous, too. They were all here for a reason. As Mr. Sir would say, this wasn't a Girl Scout camp.

Stanley was thankful that there were no **racial** problems. X-Ray, Armpit, and Zero were black. He, Squid, and Zigzag were white. Magnet was Hispanic.* On the lake they were all the same reddish brown color*—the color of dirt.

He looked up from his hole to see the water truck and its **trail**ing dust cloud. His **canteen** was still almost a quarter full. He quickly drank it down, then took his place in line, behind Magnet and in front of Zero. The air was thick with heat, dust, and **exhaust fume**s.

Mr. Sir filled their canteens.

The truck pulled away. Stanley was back in his hole, shovel in hand, when he heard Magnet call out. "Anybody want some sunflower seeds?"

Magnet was standing at ground level, holding a sack of seeds. He **pop**ped a **handful** into his mouth, chewed, and **swallow**ed, shells and all.

"Over here," called X-Ray.

The sack looked to be about half full. Magnet rolled up the top, then tossed it to X-Ray.

★ **Hispanic** 주로 미국이나 캐나다에 사는 라틴 아메리카계 사람을 말한다.
✳ **reddish brown color** 적갈색. 갈색과 빨간색의 중간.

"How'd you get them without Mr. Sir seeing you?" asked Armpit.

"I can't help it," Magnet said. He held both hands up, **wiggle**d his fingers, and laughed. "My fingers are like little magnets."

The sack went from X-Ray to Armpit to Squid.

"It's sure good to eat something that doesn't come from a can," said Armpit.

Squid tossed the sack to Zigzag.

Stanley knew it would come to him next. He didn't even want it. From the moment Magnet shouted, "Anybody want some sunflower seeds," he knew there would be trouble. Mr. Sir was sure to come back. And anyway, the **salt**ed shells would only make him thirsty.

"Coming your way, Caveman," said Zigzag. "Airmail★ and special delivery . . ."

It's unclear whether the seeds spilled before they got to Stanley or after he dropped the bag. It seemed to him that Zigzag hadn't rolled up the top before throwing it, and that was the reason he didn't catch it.

But it all happened very fast. One moment the sack was flying through the air, and the next thing Stanley knew the sack was in his hole and the seeds were spilled across the dirt.

"Oh, man!" said Magnet.

"Sorry," Stanley said as he tried to **sweep** the seeds back

---

★ **airmail** 항공 우편.

into the sack.

"I don't want to eat dirt," said X-Ray.

Stanley didn't know what to do.

"The truck's coming!" shouted Zigzag.

Stanley looked up at the approaching dust cloud, then back down at the spilled seeds. He was in the wrong place at the wrong time.

What else is new?

He **dug** his shovel into his hole, and tried to turn over the dirt and bury the seeds.

What he should have done, he realized later, was **knock** one of his dirt piles back into his hole. But the idea of putting dirt into his hole was **unthinkable**.

"Hello, Mr. Sir," said X-Ray. "Back so soon?"

"It seems like you were just here," said Armpit.

"Time flies when you're having fun," said Magnet.

Stanley continued to turn the dirt over in his hole.

"You Girl Scouts having a good time?" asked Mr. Sir. He moved from one hole to another. He kicked a dirt pile by Magnet's hole, then he moved toward Stanley.

Stanley could see two seeds at the bottom of his hole. As he tried to cover them up, he **unearth**ed a corner of the sack.

"Well, what do you know, Caveman?" said Mr. Sir, standing over him. "It looks like you found something."

Stanley didn't know what to do.

"Dig it out," Mr. Sir said. "We'll take it to the Warden. Maybe she'll give you the rest of the **day off**."

"It's not anything," Stanley **mutter**ed.

"Let me be the judge of that," said Mr. Sir.

Stanley reached down and pulled up the empty burlap sack. He tried to hand it to Mr. Sir, but he wouldn't take it.

"So, tell me, Caveman," said Mr. Sir. "How did my sack of sunflower seeds get in your hole?"

"I stole it from your truck."

"You did?"

"Yes, Mr. Sir."

"What happened to all the sunflower seeds?"

"I ate them."

"By yourself."

"Yes, Mr. Sir."

"Hey, Caveman!" shouted Armpit. "How come you didn't share any with us?"

"That's cold, man," said X-Ray.

"I thought you were our friend," said Magnet.

Mr. Sir looked around from one boy to another, then back to Stanley. "We'll see what the Warden has to say about this. Let's go."

Stanley climbed up out of his hole and followed Mr. Sir to the truck. He still held the empty sack.

It felt good to sit inside the truck, out of the direct **ray**s of the sun. Stanley was surprised he could feel good about anything at the moment, but he did. It felt good to sit down on a comfortable seat for a change. And as the truck **bounce**d along the dirt, he was able to **appreciate** the air blowing through the open window onto his hot and **sweaty** face.

20

It felt good to walk in the **shade** of the two **oak** trees. Stanley wondered if this was how a **condemn**ed man felt on his way to the electric chair*—appreciating all of the good things in life for the last time.

They had to step around holes to get to the **cabin** door. Stanley was surprised to see so many around the cabin. He would have expected the Warden to not want the campers digging so close to her home. But several holes were right up against the cabin wall. The holes were closer together here as well, and were of different shapes and sizes.

Mr. Sir **knock**ed on the door. Stanley still held the empty sack.

"Yes?" the Warden said, opening the door.

"There's been a little trouble out on the lake," Mr. Sir said. "Caveman will tell you all about it."

★ **electric chair** 사형 집행용 전기의자.

The Warden stared at Mr. Sir a moment, then her **gaze** turned toward Stanley. He felt nothing but **dread** now.

"Come in, I suppose," said the Warden. "You're letting the cold out."

It was **air-conditioned** inside her cabin. The television was going. She picked up the **remote** and turned it off.

She sat down on a canvas chair.★ She was **barefoot** and wearing shorts. Her legs were as **freckle**d as her face and arms.

"So what is it you have to tell me?"

Stanley took a breath to **steady** himself. "While Mr. Sir was filling the canteens, I **snuck** into the truck and stole his sack of sunflower seeds."

"I see." She turned to Mr. Sir. "That's why you brought him here?"

"Yes, but I think he's lying. I think someone else stole the sack, and Caveman is **cover**ing **up** for X-Ray or somebody. It was a twenty-pound sack, and he claims to have eaten them all by himself." He took the sack from Stanley and handed it to the Warden.

"I see," the Warden said again.

"The sack wasn't full," said Stanley. "And I spilled a lot. You can check my hole."

"In that room, Caveman, there's a small **flowered** case. Will you get it for me, please?" She pointed to a door.

Stanley looked at the door, then at the Warden, then

★ **canvas chair** 나무틀에 캔버스 천을 친 의자.

back at the door. He slowly walked toward it.

It was a kind of dressing room, with a sink and a mirror. Next to the sink he saw the case, white with pink roses.

He brought it back out to the Warden, and she set it on the glass coffee table in front of her. She **unclasp**ed the **latch** and opened the case.

It was a makeup case. Stanley's mother had one similar to it. He saw several bottles of nail polish,* polish remover,* a couple of lipstick tubes, and other **jar**s and powders.

The Warden held up a small jar of dark-red nail polish. "You see this, Caveman?"

He **nod**ded.

"This is my special nail polish. Do you see the dark rich color? You can't buy that in a store. I have to make it myself."

Stanley had no idea why she was showing it to him. He wondered why the Warden would ever have the need to wear nail polish or makeup.

"Do you want to know my secret **ingredient**?"

He raised and lowered one shoulder.

The Warden opened the bottle. "**Rattlesnake venom.**" With a small paintbrush she began applying it to the nails on her left hand. "It's perfectly **harmless** . . . when it's dry."

She finished her left hand. She waved it in the air for a few seconds, then began painting the nails on her right

---

★ **nail polish** 손톱에 바르는 매니큐어.
✳ **polish remover** 매니큐어를 지우는 화장품.

hand. "It's only **toxic** while it's wet."

She finished painting her nails, then stood up. She reached over and touched Stanley's face with her fingers. She ran her sharp wet nails very gently down his cheek. He felt his skin **tingle**.

The nail on her **pinkie** just barely touched the **wound** behind his ear. A sharp **sting** of pain caused him to jump back.

The Warden turned to **face** Mr. Sir, who was sitting on the **fireplace hearth**.

"So you think he stole your sunflower seeds?"

"No, he says he stole them, but I think it was—"

She stepped toward him and **struck** him across the face.

Mr. Sir stared at her. He had three long red marks **slant**ing across the left side of his face. Stanley didn't know if the redness was caused by her nail polish or his blood.

It took a moment for the venom to sink in. Suddenly, Mr. Sir screamed and **clutch**ed his face with both hands. He let himself fall over, rolling off the hearth and onto the **rug**.

The Warden spoke softly. "I don't especially care about your sunflower seeds."

Mr. Sir **moan**ed.

"If you must know," said the Warden, "I liked it better when you smoked."

For a second, Mr. Sir's pain seemed to **recede**. He took several long, deep breaths. Then his head jerked **violent**ly, and he let out a **shrill** scream, worse than the one before.

The Warden turned to Stanley. "I suggest you go back

to your hole now."

Stanley started to go, but Mr. Sir lay in the way. Stanley could see the muscles on his face jump and **twitch**. His body **writhe**d in **agony**.

Stanley stepped carefully over him. "Is he—?"

"Excuse me?" said the Warden.

Stanley was too **frighten**ed to speak.

"He's not going to die," the Warden said. "Unfortunately for you."

21

It was a long walk back to his hole. Stanley looked out through the **haze** of heat and dirt at the other boys, lowering and raising their shovels. Group D was the farthest* away.

He realized that once again he would be digging long after everyone else had quit. He hoped he'd finish before Mr. Sir recovered. He didn't want to be out there alone with Mr. Sir.

He won't die, the Warden had said. *Unfortunately for you.*

Walking across the **desolate wasteland**, Stanley thought about his great-grandfather—not the pig stealer but the pig stealer's son, the one who was **rob**bed by Kissin' Kate Barlow.

He tried to imagine how he must have felt after Kissin' Kate had left him **strand**ed in the **desert**. It probably wasn't a whole lot different from the way he himself felt now. Kate

---

★ **farthest** far의 최상급. 가장 먼, 가장 멀리. (far-farther-farthest)

Barlow had left his great-grandfather to **face** the hot **barren** desert. The Warden had left Stanley to face Mr. Sir.

Somehow his great-grandfather had survived for seventeen days, before he was rescued by a couple of rattlesnake hunters. He was **insane** when they found him.

When he was asked how he had lived so long, he said he "found **refuge** on God's thumb."

He spent nearly a month in a hospital. He ended up marrying one of the nurses. Nobody ever knew what he meant by God's thumb, including himself.

Stanley heard a **twitch**ing sound. He stopped in mid-step, with one foot still in the air.

A rattlesnake lay **coil**ed beneath his foot. Its tail was pointed upward, **rattling**.

Stanley backed his leg away, then turned and ran.

The rattlesnake didn't chase after him. It had rattled its tail to warn him to stay away.

"Thanks for the warning," Stanley whispered as his heart **pound**ed.

The rattlesnake would be a lot more dangerous if it didn't have a rattle.

"Hey, Caveman!" called Armpit. "You're still alive."

"What'd the Warden say?" asked X-Ray.

"What'd you tell her?" asked Magnet.

"I told her I stole the seeds," said Stanley.

"Good going," said Magnet.

"What'd she do?" asked Zigzag.

Stanley **shrug**ged one shoulder. "Nothing. She got mad at Mr. Sir for **bother**ing her."

He didn't feel like going into details. If he didn't talk about it, then maybe it didn't happen.

He went over to his hole, and to his surprise it was nearly finished. He stared at it, amazed. It didn't make sense.

Or perhaps it did. He smiled. Since he had taken the blame for the sunflower seeds, he realized, the other boys had dug his hole for him.

"Hey, thanks," he said.

"Don't look at me," said X-Ray.

Confused, Stanley looked around—from Magnet, to Armpit, to Zigzag, to Squid. None of them took **credit** for it.

Then he turned to Zero, who had been quietly digging in his hole since Stanley's return. Zero's hole was smaller than all the others.

22

Stanley was the first one finished. He **spat** in his hole, then showered and changed into his cleaner set of clothes. It had been three days since the **laundry** was done, so even his clean set was dirty and smelly. Tomorrow, these would become his work clothes, and his other set would be washed.

He could think of no reason why Zero would dig his hole for him. Zero didn't even get any sunflower seeds.

"I guess he likes to dig holes," Armpit had said.

"He's a **mole**," Zigzag had said. "I think he eats dirt."

"Moles don't eat dirt," X-Ray had **point**ed **out**. "**Worm**s eat dirt."

"Hey, Zero?" Squid had asked. "Are you a mole or a worm?"

Zero had said nothing.

Stanley never even thanked him. But now he sat on his cot and waited for Zero to return from the shower room.

"Thanks," he said as Zero entered through the tent **flap**.

Zero **glance**d at him, then went over to the **crate**s, where he **deposit**ed his dirty clothes and towel.

"Why'd you help me?" Stanley asked.

Zero turned around. "You didn't steal the sunflower seeds," he said.

"So, neither did you," said Stanley.

Zero stared at him. His eyes seemed to expand, and it was almost as if Zero were looking right through him. "You didn't steal the **sneaker**s," he said.

Stanley said nothing.

He watched Zero walk out of the tent. If anybody had X-ray vision, it was Zero.

"Wait!" he called, then hurried out after him.

Zero had stopped just outside the tent, and Stanley almost ran into him.

"I'll try to teach you to read if you want," Stanley offered. "I don't know if I know how to teach, but I'm not that **worn-out** today, since you dug a lot of my hole."

A big smile spread across Zero's face.

They returned to the tent, where they were less likely to be bothered. Stanley got his box of **stationery** and a pen out of his crate. They sat on the ground.

"Do you know the alphabet?" Stanley asked.

For a second, he thought he saw a flash of **defiance** in Zero's eyes, but then it passed.

"I think I know some of it," Zero said. "A, B, C, D."

"Keep going," said Stanley.

Zero's eyes looked upward. "E . . ."

"F," said Stanley.

"G," said Zero. He blew some air out of the side of his mouth. "H . . . I . . . K, P."

"H, I, J, K, L," Stanley said.

"That's right," said Zero. "I've heard it before. I just don't have it **memorize**d exactly."

"That's all right," said Stanley. "Here, I'll say the whole thing, just to kind of **refresh** your memory, then you can try it."

He **recite**d the alphabet for Zero, then Zero repeated it without a single mistake.

Not bad for a kid who had never seen Sesame Street!

"Well, I've heard it before, somewhere," Zero said, trying to act like it was nothing, but his big smile **gave** him **away**.

The next step was harder. Stanley had to **figure out** how to teach him to recognize each letter. He gave Zero a piece of paper, and took a piece for himself. "I guess we'll start with A."

He **print**ed a capital A, and then Zero copied it on his sheet of paper. The paper wasn't lined, which made it more difficult, but Zero's A wasn't bad, just a little big. Stanley told him he needed to write smaller, or else they'd run out of paper real quick. Zero printed it smaller.

"Actually, there are two ways to write each letter," Stanley said, as he realized this was going to be even harder than he thought. "That's a capital A. But usually you'll see a small a. You only have capitals at the beginning of a word, and only if it's the start of a sentence, or if it's a **proper** noun, like a name."

Zero nodded as if he understood, but Stanley knew he had made very little sense.

He printed a **lowercase** a, and Zero copied it.

"So there are fifty-two," said Zero.

Stanley didn't know what he was talking about.

"Instead of twenty-six letters. There are really fifty-two."

Stanley looked at him, surprised. "I guess that's right. How'd you figure that out?" he asked.

Zero said nothing.

"Did you add?"

Zero said nothing.

"Did you **multiply**?"

"That's just how many there are," said Zero.

Stanley raised and lowered one shoulder. He didn't even know how Zero knew there were twenty-six in the first place. Did he **count** them as he recited them?

He had Zero write a few more **upper**-and lowercase A's, and then he moved on to a capital B. This was going to take a long time, he realized.

"You can teach me ten letters a day," suggested Zero. "Five capitals and five smalls. After five days I'll know them all. Except on the last day I'll have to do twelve. Six capitals and six smalls."

Again Stanley stared at him, amazed that he was able to figure all that out.

Zero must have thought he was staring for a different reason, because he said, "I'll dig part of your hole every day.

I can dig for about an hour, then you can teach me for an hour. And since I'm a faster digger anyway, our holes will get done about the same time. I won't have to wait for you."

"Okay," Stanley agreed.

As Zero was printing his B's, Stanley asked him how he figured out it would take five days. "Did you multiply? Did you **divide**?"

"That's just what it is," Zero said.

"It's good math," said Stanley.

"I'm not stupid," Zero said. "I know everybody thinks I am. I just don't like answering their questions."

Later that night, as he lay on his cot, Stanley **reconsider**ed the deal he had made with Zero. Getting a break every day would be a relief, but he knew X-Ray wouldn't like it. He wondered if there might be some way Zero would agree to dig part of X-Ray's hole as well. But then again, why should he? I'm the one teaching Zero. *I need the break so I'll have the energy to teach him. I'm the one who took the blame for the sunflower seeds. I'm the one who Mr. Sir is mad at.*

He closed his eyes, and images from the Warden's cabin **float**ed inside his head: her red fingernails, Mr. Sir **writhing** on the floor, her **flowered** makeup kit.

He opened his eyes.

He suddenly realized where he'd seen the gold tube before.

He'd seen it in his mother's bathroom, and he'd seen it again in the Warden's cabin. It was half of a lipstick container.

KB?

KB?

He felt a **jolt** of **astonishment**.

His mouth silently formed the name Kate Barlow, as he wondered if it really could have belonged to the kissin' **outlaw**.

23

One hundred and ten years ago, Green Lake was the largest lake in Texas. It was full of clear cool water, and it **sparkle**d like a giant emerald in the sun. It was especially beautiful in the spring, when the peach trees, which lined the **shore**, **bloom**ed with pink and rose-colored **blossom**s.

There was always a town picnic on the Fourth of July.★ They'd play games, dance, sing, and swim in the lake to keep cool. Prizes were awarded for the best peach pie and peach jam.

A special prize was given every year to Miss Katherine Barlow for her **fabulous spice**d peaches. No one else even tried to make spiced peaches, because they knew none could be as delicious as hers.

Every summer Miss Katherine would pick bushels✳ of

★ **the Fourth of July** 7월 4일은 미국의 독립기념일이다.
✳ **bushel** 용량의 단위 부셸. 1부셸은 약 35리터이다.

peaches and preserve them in **jar**s with cinnamon, cloves,* nutmeg,* and other spices which she kept secret. The jarred peaches would last all winter. They probably would have lasted a lot longer than that, but they were always eaten by the end of winter.

It was said that Green Lake was "heaven on earth" and that Miss Katherine's spiced peaches were "food for the angels."

Katherine Barlow was the town's only schoolteacher. She taught in an old one-room schoolhouse. It was old even then. The roof **leak**ed. The windows wouldn't open. The door hung **crooked** on its bent **hinge**s.

She was a wonderful teacher, full of knowledge and full of life. The children loved her.

She taught classes in the evening for adults, and many of the adults loved her as well. She was very pretty. Her classes were often full of young men, who were a lot more interested in the teacher than they were in getting an education.

But all they ever got was an education.

One such young man was Trout* Walker. His real name was Charles Walker, but everyone called him Trout because his two feet smelled like a couple of dead fish.

This wasn't entirely Trout's fault. He had an **incurable** foot fungus.* In fact, it was the same foot fungus that

---

★ **clove** [식물] 정향(丁香). 향신료로 사용한다.
✻ **nutmeg** [식물] 육두구. 향신료로 사용한다.
✴ **trout** 송어.
✳ **foot fungus** 무좀.

a hundred and ten years later would **afflict** the famous **ballplayer** Clyde Livingston. But at least Clyde Livingston showered every day.

"I take a bath every Sunday morning," Trout would **brag**, "whether I need to or not."

Most everyone in the town of Green Lake expected Miss Katherine to marry Trout Walker. He was the son of the richest man in the **county**. His family owned most of the peach trees and all the land on the east side of the lake.

Trout often showed up at night school but never paid attention. He talked in class and was **disrespectful** of the students around him. He was loud and stupid.

A lot of men in town were not educated. That didn't bother Miss Katherine. She knew they'd spent most of their lives working on farms and **ranch**es and hadn't had much **schooling**. That was why she was there—to teach them.

But Trout didn't want to learn. He seemed to be proud of his **stupidity**.

"How'd you like to take a ride on my new boat this Saturday?" he asked her one evening after class.

"No, thank you," said Miss Katherine.

"We've got a **brand-new** boat," he said. "You don't even have to **row** it."

"Yes, I know," said Miss Katherine.

Everyone in town had seen—and heard—the Walkers' new boat. It made a **horrible** loud noise and **spew**ed ugly black smoke over the beautiful lake.

Trout had always gotten everything he ever wanted. He

found it hard to believe that Miss Katherine had **turn**ed him **down**. He pointed his finger at her and said, "No one ever says 'No' to Charles Walker!"

"I believe I just did," said Katherine Barlow.

24

Stanley was half asleep as he got in line for breakfast, but the **sight** of Mr. Sir **awaken**ed him. The left side of Mr. Sir's face had **swollen** to the size of half a cantaloupe.★ There were three dark-purple **jagged** lines running down his cheek where the Warden had scratched him.

The other boys in Stanley's tent had obviously seen Mr. Sir as well, but they had the **good sense** not to say anything. Stanley put a **carton** of juice and a plastic spoon on his tray. He kept his eyes down and hardly breathed as Mr. Sir **ladle**d some oatmeal-like **stuff** into his bowl.

He brought his tray to the table. Behind him, a boy from one of the other tents said, "Hey, what happened to your face?"

There was a **crash**.

Stanley turned to see Mr. Sir holding the boy's head

★ **cantaloupe** 껍질은 녹색에 과육은 오렌지색인 멜론.

against the oatmeal pot. "Is something wrong with my face?"

The boy tried to speak but couldn't. Mr. Sir had him by the throat.

"Does anyone see anything wrong with my face?" asked Mr. Sir, as he continued to **choke** the boy.

Nobody said anything.

Mr. Sir let the boy go. His head **bang**ed against the table as he fell to the ground.

Mr. Sir stood over him and asked, "How does my face look to you now?"

A **gurgling** sound came out of the boy's mouth, then he managed to **gasp** the word, "Fine."

"I'm kind of handsome, don't you think?"

"Yes, Mr. Sir."

Out on the lake, the other boys asked Stanley what he knew about Mr. Sir's face, but he just shrugged and **dug** his hole. If he didn't talk about it, maybe it would go away.

He worked as hard and as fast as he could, not trying to **pace** himself. He just wanted to get off the lake and away from Mr. Sir as soon as possible. Besides, he knew he'd get a break.

"Whenever you're ready, just let me know," Zero had said.

The first time the water truck came, it was driven by Mr. Pendanski. The second time, Mr. Sir was driving.

No one said anything except "Thank you, Mr. Sir" as he filled each **canteen**. No one even **dare**d to look at his

grotesque face.

As Stanley waited, he ran his tongue over the roof of his mouth and inside his cheeks. His mouth was as dry and as **parched** as the lake. The bright sun reflected off the side mirror of the truck, and Stanley had to shield his eyes with his hand.

"Thank you, Mr. Sir," said Magnet, as he took his canteen from him.

"You thirsty, Caveman?" Mr. Sir asked.

"Yes, Mr. Sir," Stanley said, handing his canteen to him.

Mr. Sir opened the **nozzle**, and the water flowed out of the tank, but it did not go into Stanley's canteen. Instead, he held the canteen right next to the stream of water.

Stanley watched the water **splatter** on the dirt, where it was quickly **absorb**ed by the thirsty ground.

Mr. Sir let the water run for about thirty seconds, then stopped. "You want more?" he asked.

Stanley didn't say anything.

Mr. Sir turned the water back on, and again Stanley watched it pour onto the dirt.

"There, that should be plenty." He handed Stanley his empty canteen.

Stanley stared at the dark spot on the ground, which quickly **shrank** before his eyes.

"Thank you, Mr. Sir," he said.

25

There was a doctor in the town of Green Lake, one hundred and ten years ago. His name was Dr. Hawthorn. And whenever people got sick, they would go see Doc* Hawthorn. But they would also see Sam, the onion man.

"Onions! Sweet, fresh onions!" Sam would call, as he and his **donkey**, Mary Lou, walked up and down the **dirt road**s of Green Lake. Mary Lou pulled a cart full of onions.

Sam's onion field was somewhere on the other side of the lake. Once or twice a week he would **row** across the lake and pick a new **batch** to fill the cart. Sam had big strong arms, but it would still take all day for him to row across the lake and another day for him to return. Most of the time he would leave Mary Lou in a **shed**, which the Walkers let him use at no **charge**, but sometimes he would take Mary Lou on his boat with him.

★ **doc** doctor의 줄임말.

Sam claimed that Mary Lou was almost fifty years old, which was, and still is, **extraordinarily** old for a donkey.

"She eats nothing but raw onions," Sam would say, holding up a white onion between his dark fingers. "It's nature's magic vegetable. If a person ate nothing but raw onions, he could live to be two hundred years old."

Sam was not much older than twenty, so nobody was quite sure that Mary Lou was really as old as he said she was. How would he know?

Still, nobody ever argued with Sam. And whenever they were sick, they would go not only to Doc Hawthorn but also to Sam.

Sam always gave the same advice: "Eat plenty of onions."

He said that onions were good for the **digestion**, the **liver**, the stomach, the **lung**s, the heart, and the brain. "If you don't believe me, just look at old Mary Lou here. She's never been sick a day in her life."

He also had many different **ointment**s, lotions, syrups, and **paste**s all made out of onion juice and different parts of the onion plant. This one **cure**d asthma.* That one was for warts* and **pimple**s. Another was a **remedy** for arthritis.*

He even had a special ointment which he claimed would cure **bald**ness. "Just **rub** it on your husband's head every night when he's sleeping, Mrs. Collingwood, and soon his

---

★ asthma 천식. 주기적으로 일어나는 호흡곤란.
✳ wart 피부에 나는 사마귀.
✲ arthritis 관절염.

hair will be as thick and as long as Mary Lou's tail."

Doc Hawthorn did not **resent** Sam. The **folk**s of Green Lake were afraid to take chances. They would get regular medicine from Doc Hawthorn and onion **concoction**s from Sam. After they got over their illness, no one could be sure, not even Doc Hawthorn, which of the two **treatment**s had done the **trick**.

Doc Hawthorn was almost completely **bald**, and in the morning his head often smelled like onions.

Whenever Katherine Barlow bought onions, she always bought an extra one or two and would let Mary Lou eat them out of her hand.

"Is something wrong?" Sam asked her one day as she was feeding Mary Lou. "You seem **distract**ed."

"Oh, just the weather," said Miss Katherine. "It looks like rain clouds moving in."

"Me and Mary Lou, we like the rain," said Sam.

"Oh, I like it fine," said Miss Katherine, as she rubbed the donkey's rough hair on top of its head. "It's just that the roof **leak**s in the schoolhouse."

"I can fix that," said Sam.

"What are you going to do?" Katherine joked. "Fill the holes with onion paste?"

Sam laughed. "I'm good with my hands," he told her. "I built my own boat. If it leaked, I'd be in big trouble."

Katherine couldn't help but notice his strong, firm hands.

They made a deal. He agreed to fix the **leaky** roof in exchange for six **jar**s of **spice**d peaches.

It took Sam a week to fix the roof, because he could only work in the afternoons, after school let out and before night classes began. Sam wasn't allowed to attend classes because he was a Negro,★ but they let him fix the building.

Miss Katherine usually stayed in the schoolhouse, grading papers and such, while Sam worked on the roof. She enjoyed what little conversation they were able to have, shouting up and down to each other. She was surprised by his interest in **poetry**. When he took a break, she would sometimes read a **poem** to him. On more than one occasion, she would start to read a poem by Poe※ or Longfellow,※ only to hear him finish it for her, from memory.

She was sad when the roof was finished.

"Is something wrong?" he asked.

"No, you did a wonderful job," she said. "It's just that . . . the windows won't open. The children and I would enjoy a **breeze** now and then."

"I can fix that," said Sam.

She gave him two more jars of peaches and Sam fixed the windows.

It was easier to talk to him when he was working on

★ **Negro** 흑인을 부르는 모욕적인 표현.

※ **Edgar Allan Poe** 미국의 시인·소설가·평론가 애드가 앨런 포. 대표작으로 『검은 고양이』가 있다.

※ **Henry Wadsworth Longfellow** 미국의 시인 헨리 롱펠로. 역사·전승 이야기가 담긴 시를 많이 썼다.

the windows. He told her about his secret onion field on the other side of the lake, "where the onions grow all year round, and the water runs **uphill**."

When the windows were fixed, she complained that her desk **wobble**d.

"I can fix that," said Sam.

The next time she saw him, she mentioned that "the door doesn't hang straight," and she got to spend another afternoon with him while he fixed the door.

By the end of the first semester, Onion Sam had turned the old **run-down** schoolhouse into a well-**craft**ed, freshly painted jewel of a building that the whole town was proud of. People passing by would stop and **admire** it. "That's our schoolhouse. It shows how much we value education here in Green Lake."

The only person who wasn't happy with it was Miss Katherine. She'd run out of things needing to be fixed.

She sat at her desk one afternoon, listening to the pitter-patter* of the rain on the roof. No water leaked into the classroom, except for the few drops that came from her eyes.

"Onions! Hot sweet onions!" Sam called, out on the street.

She ran to him. She wanted to throw her arms around him but couldn't bring herself to do it. Instead she hugged Mary Lou's neck.

"Is something wrong?" he asked her.

★ **pitter-patter** 후드득하는 빗소리.

"Oh, Sam," she said. "My heart is breaking."

"I can fix that," said Sam.

She turned to him.

He took hold of both of her hands, and kissed her.

Because of the rain, there was nobody else out on the street. Even if there was, Katherine and Sam wouldn't have noticed. They were lost in their own world.

At that moment, however, Hattie Parker stepped out of the **general store**. They didn't see her, but she saw them. She pointed her **quiver**ing finger in their direction and whispered, "God will **punish** you!"

26

There were no telephones, but word spread quickly through the small town. By the end of the day, everyone in Green Lake had heard that the schoolteacher had kissed the onion picker.

Not one child showed up for school the next morning.

Miss Katherine sat alone in the classroom and wondered if she had **lost track of** the day of the week. Perhaps it was Saturday. It wouldn't have surprised her. Her brain and heart had been spinning ever since Sam kissed her.

She heard a noise outside the door, then suddenly a **mob** of men and women came **storm**ing into the school building. They were led by Trout Walker.

"There she is!" Trout shouted. "The Devil Woman!"

The mob was turning over desks and **rip**ping down **bulletin board**s.

"She's been **poison**ing your children's brains with books," Trout declared.

They began piling all the books in the center of the room.

"Think about what you are doing!" cried Miss Katherine.

Someone made a grab for her, tearing her dress, but she managed to get out of the building. She ran to the **sheriff**'s office.

The sheriff had his feet up on his desk and was drinking from a bottle of whiskey. "Mornin', Miss Katherine," he said.

"They're destroying the schoolhouse," she said, **gasp**ing for breath. "They'll burn it to the ground if someone doesn't stop them!"

"Just calm your pretty self down a second," the sheriff said in a slow **drawl**. "And tell me what you're talking about." He got up from his desk and walked over to her.

"Trout Walker has—"

"Now don't go saying nothing bad about Charles Walker," said the sheriff.

"We don't have much time!" **urge**d Katherine. "You've got to stop them."

"You're sure pretty," said the sheriff.

Miss Katherine stared at him in horror.

"Kiss me," said the sheriff.

She **slap**ped him across the face.

He laughed. "You kissed the onion picker. Why won't you kiss me?"

She tried to slap him again, but he caught her by the hand.

She tried to **wriggle** free. "You're drunk!" she yelled.

"I always get drunk before a **hang**ing."

"A hanging? Who—"

"It's against the law for a Negro to kiss a white woman."

"Well, then you'll have to hang me, too," said Katherine. "Because I kissed him back."

"It ain't against the law for you to kiss him," the sheriff explained. "Just for him to kiss you."

"We're all equal under the eyes of God," she declared.

The sheriff laughed. "Then if Sam and I are equal, why won't you kiss me?" He laughed again. "I'll make you a deal. One sweet kiss, and I won't hang your boyfriend. I'll just run him out of town."

Miss Katherine **jerk**ed her hand free. As she hurried to the door, she heard the sheriff say, "The law will **punish** Sam. And God will punish you."

She stepped back into the street and saw smoke rising from the schoolhouse. She ran down to the **lakefront**, where Sam was **hitch**ing Mary Lou to the onion cart.

"Thank God, I found you," she sighed, hugging him. "We've got to get out of here. Now!"

"What—"

"Someone must have seen us kissing yesterday," she said. "They set fire to the schoolhouse. The sheriff said he's going to hang you!"

Sam hesitated for a moment, as if he couldn't quite believe it. He didn't want to believe it. "C'mon, Mary Lou."

"We have to leave Mary Lou behind," said Katherine.

Sam stared at her a moment. There were tears in his eyes.

"Okay."

Sam's boat was in the water, tied to a tree by a long rope. He untied it, and they **wade**d through the water and climbed **aboard**. His powerful arms rowed them away from the **shore**.

But his powerful arms were no match for Trout Walker's **motorized** boat. They were little more than halfway across the lake when Miss Katherine heard the loud **roar** of the engine. Then she saw the ugly black smoke . . .

These are the facts:

The Walker boat **smash**ed into Sam's boat. Sam was shot and killed in the water. Katherine Barlow was rescued against her wishes. When they returned to the shore, she saw Mary Lou's body lying on the ground. The **donkey** had been shot in the head.

That all happened one hundred and ten years ago. Since then, not one drop of rain has fallen on Green Lake.

You make the decision: Whom did God punish?

Three days after Sam's death, Miss Katherine shot the sheriff while he was sitting in his chair drinking a cup of coffee. Then she carefully applied a fresh **coat** of red lipstick and gave him the kiss he had asked for.

For the next twenty years Kissin' Kate Barlow was one of the most feared **outlaw**s in all the West.

27

Stanley dug his **shovel** into the ground. His hole was about three and a half feet deep in the center. He **grunt**ed as he **pried** up some dirt, then **flung** it off to the side. The sun was almost directly overhead.

He **glance**d at his canteen lying beside his hole. He knew it was half full, but he didn't take a drink just yet. He had to drink **sparing**ly, because he didn't know who would be driving the water truck the next time it came.

Three days had passed since the Warden had scratched Mr. Sir. Every time Mr. Sir delivered water, he poured Stanley's straight onto the ground.

Fortunately, Mr. Pendanski delivered the water more often than Mr. Sir. Mr. Pendanski was obviously aware of what Mr. Sir was doing, because he always gave Stanley a little extra. He'd fill Stanley's canteen, then let Stanley take a long drink, then top it off for him.

It helped, too, that Zero was digging some of Stanley's

hole for him. Although, as Stanley had expected, the other boys didn't like to see Stanley sitting around while they were working. They'd say things like "Who died and made you king?" or "It must be nice to have your own personal **slave**."

When he tried **point**ing **out** that he was the one who took the blame for the sunflower seeds, the other boys said it was his fault because he was the one who spilled them. "I **risk**ed my life for those seeds," Magnet had said, "and all I got was one **lousy handful**."

Stanley had also tried to explain that he needed to save his energy so he could teach Zero how to read, but the other boys just **mock**ed him.

"Same old story, ain't it, Armpit?" X-Ray had said. "The white boy sits around while the black boy does all the work. Ain't that right, Caveman?"

"No, that's not right," Stanley replied.

"No, it ain't," X-Ray agreed. "It ain't right at all."

Stanley dug out another **shovelful** of dirt. He knew X-Ray wouldn't have been talking like that if he was the one teaching Zero to read. Then X-Ray would be talking about how important it was that he got his rest, *right?* So he could be a better teacher, *right?*

And that was true. He did need to save his strength so he could be a better teacher, although Zero was a quick learner. Sometimes, in fact, Stanley hoped the Warden was watching them, with her secret cameras and **microphone**s, so she'd know that Zero wasn't as stupid as everyone thought.

From across the lake he could see the approaching dust

cloud. He took a drink from his canteen, then waited to see who was driving the truck.

The **swelling** on Mr. Sir's face had gone down, but it was still a little **puffy**. There had been three scratch marks down his cheek. Two of the marks had faded, but the middle scratch must have been the deepest, because it still remained. It was a **jagged** purple line running from below his eye to below his mouth, like a **tattoo** of a scar.

Stanley waited in line, then handed him his canteen.

Mr. Sir held it up to his ear and shook it. He smiled at the **swish**ing sound.

Stanley hoped he wouldn't **dump** it out.

To his surprise, Mr. Sir held the canteen under the stream of water and filled it.

"Wait here," he said.

Still holding Stanley's canteen, Mr. Sir walked past him, then went around the side of the truck and into the **cab**, where he couldn't be seen.

"What's he doing in there?" asked Zero.

"I wish I knew," said Stanley.

A short while later, Mr. Sir came out of the truck and handed Stanley his canteen. It was still full.

"Thank you, Mr. Sir."

Mr. Sir smiled at him. "What are you waiting for?" he asked. "Drink up." He **pop**ped some sunflower seeds into his mouth, chewed, and **spit** out the shells.

Stanley was afraid to drink it. He hated to think what

kind of **vile substance** Mr. Sir might have put in it.

He brought the canteen back to his hole. For a long time, he left it beside his hole as he continued to dig. Then, when he was so thirsty that he could hardly stand it anymore, he **unscrew**ed the cap, turned the canteen over, and poured it all out onto the dirt. He was afraid that if he'd waited another second, he might have taken a drink.

After Stanley taught Zero the final six letters of the alphabet, he taught him to write his name.

"Capital Z-e-r-o."

Zero wrote the letters as Stanley said them. "Zero," he said, looking at his piece of paper. His smile was too big for his face.

Stanley watched him write it over and over again.

Zero Zero Zero Zero Zero Zero Zero . . .

In a way, it made him sad. He couldn't help but think that a hundred times zero was still nothing.

"You know, that's not my real name," Zero said as they headed to the Wreck Room for dinner.

"Well, yeah," Stanley said, "I guess I knew that." He had never really been sure.

"Everyone's always called me Zero, even before I came here."

"Oh. Okay."

"My real name is Hector."

"Hector," Stanley repeated.

"Hector Zeroni."

28

After twenty years, Kate Barlow returned to Green Lake. It was a place where nobody would ever find her—a ghost town on a ghost lake.

The peach trees had all died, but there were a couple of small **oak** trees still growing by an old **abandon**ed **cabin**. The cabin used to be on the eastern shore of the lake. Now the edge of the lake was over five miles away, and it was little more than a small **pond** full of dirty water.

She lived in the cabin. Sometimes she could hear Sam's voice **echo**ing across the emptiness. "Onions! Sweet fresh onions."

She knew she was crazy. She knew she'd been crazy for the last twenty years.

"Oh, Sam," she would say, speaking into the **vast** emptiness. "I know it is hot, but I feel so very cold. My hands are cold. My feet are cold. My face is cold. My heart is cold."

And sometimes she would hear him say, "I can fix that," and she'd feel his warm arm across her shoulders.

She'd been living in the cabin about three months when she was **awaken**ed one morning by someone kicking open the cabin door. She opened her eyes to see the **blurry** end of a **rifle**, two inches from her nose.

She could smell Trout Walker's dirty feet.

"You've got exactly ten seconds to tell me where you've hidden your **loot**," said Trout. "Or else I'll blow your head off."

She **yawn**ed.

A **redheaded** woman was there with Trout. Kate could see her **rummaging** through the cabin, dumping **drawer**s and **knock**ing things from the shelves of cabinets.

The woman came to her. "Where is it?" she demanded.

"Linda Miller?" asked Kate. "Is that you?"

Linda Miller had been in the fourth grade when Kate Barlow was still a teacher. She had been a cute **freckle**-faced girl with beautiful red hair. Now her face was **blotchy**, and her hair was dirty and **scraggly**.

"It's Linda Walker now," said Trout.

"Oh, Linda, I'm so sorry," said Kate.

Trout **jab**bed her throat with the rifle. "Where's the loot?"

"There is no loot," said Kate.

"Don't give me that!" shouted Trout. "You've **rob**bed every bank from here to Houston."

"You better tell him," said Linda. "We're desperate."

"You married him for his money, didn't you?" asked Kate.

Linda **nod**ded. "But it's all gone. It dried up with the lake. The peach trees. The **livestock**. I kept thinking: It has to rain soon. The **drought** can't last forever. But it just kept getting hotter and hotter and hotter . . ." Her eyes fixed on the shovel, which was leaning up against the **fireplace**. "She's buried it!" she declared.

"I don't know what you're talking about," said Kate.

There was a loud **blast** as Trout **fire**d his rifle just above her head. The window behind her **shatter**ed. "Where's it buried?" he demanded.

"Go ahead and kill me, Trout," said Kate. "But I sure hope you like to **dig**. 'Cause you're going to be digging for a long time. It's a big vast **wasteland** out there. You, and your children, and their children, can dig for the next hundred years and you'll never find it."

Linda grabbed Kate's hair and jerked her head back. "Oh, we're not going to kill you," she said. "But by the time we're finished with you, you're going to wish you were dead."

"I've been wishing I was dead for the last twenty years," said Kate.

They **drag**ged her out of bed and pushed her outside. She wore blue silk **pajama**s. Her turquoise-**stud**ded black boots remained beside her bed.

They loosely tied her legs together so she could walk, but she couldn't run. They made her walk **barefoot** on the hot ground.

They wouldn't let her stop walking.

"Not until you take us to the loot," said Trout.

Linda hit Kate on the back of her legs with the shovel. "You're going to take us to it sooner or later. So you **might as well** make it sooner."

She walked one way, then the other, until her feet were black and **blister**ed. Whenever she stopped, Linda **whack**ed her with the shovel.

"I'm losing my patience," warned Trout.

She felt the shovel jab into her back, and she fell onto hard dirt.

"Get up!" ordered Linda.

Kate **struggled to her feet**.

"We're being easy on you today," said Trout. "It's just going to keep getting worse and worse for you until you take us to it."

"Look out!" shouted Linda.

A **lizard leap**ed toward them. Kate could see its big red eyes.

Linda tried to hit it with the shovel, and Trout shot at it, but they both missed.

The lizard landed on Kate's bare **ankle**. Its sharp black teeth bit into her leg. Its white tongue **lap**ped up the **droplet**s of blood that **leak**ed out of the **wound**.

Kate smiled. There was nothing they could do to her anymore. "Start digging," she said.

"Where is it?" Linda **screech**ed.

"Where'd you bury it?" Trout demanded.

Kate Barlow died laughing.

PART TWO

THE LAST HOLE

29

There was a change in the weather.

For the worse.

The air became **unbearably humid**. Stanley was **drench**ed in **sweat**. **Bead**s of **moisture** ran down the handle of his shovel. It was almost as if the temperature had gotten so hot that the air itself was sweating.

A loud **boom** of thunder **echo**ed across the empty lake.

A **storm** was way off to the west, beyond the mountains. Stanley could **count** more than thirty seconds between the flash of lightning and the **clap** of thunder. That was how far away the storm was. Sound travels a great distance across a **barren** wasteland.

Usually, Stanley couldn't see the mountains at this time of day. The only time they were visible was just at **sunup**, before the air became **hazy**. Now, however, the sky was very dark off to the west, and every time the lightning flashed, the dark shape of the mountains would **briefly** appear.

"C'mon, rain!" shouted Armpit. "Blow this way!"

"Maybe it'll rain so hard it will fill up the whole lake," said Squid. "We can go swimming."

"Forty days and forty nights," said X-Ray. "Guess we better start building us an ark.★ Get two of each animal, right?"

"Right," said Zigzag. "Two **rattlesnake**s. Two **scorpion**s. Two yellow-**spotted** lizards."

The **humidity**, or maybe the electricity in the air, had made Zigzag's head even more wild-looking. His **frizzy** blond hair stuck almost straight out.

The **horizon** lit up with a huge web of lightning. In that **split second** Stanley thought he saw an unusual rock **formation** on top of one of the mountain **peak**s. The peak looked to him exactly like a giant **fist**, with the thumb sticking straight up.

Then it was gone.

And Stanley wasn't sure whether he'd seen it or not.

*"I found **refuge** on God's thumb."*

That was what his great-grandfather had supposedly said after Kate Barlow had robbed him and left him **strand**ed in the **desert**.

No one ever knew what he meant by that. He was **delirious** when he said it.

"But how could he live for three weeks without food or water?" Stanley had asked his father.

★ **ark** 성경에 나오는 노아의 방주. 대홍수를 대비하여 노아가 만든 배를 말한다.

"I don't know. I wasn't there," replied his father. "I wasn't born yet. My father wasn't born yet. My grandmother, your great-grandmother, was a nurse in the hospital where they **treat**ed him. He'd always talked about how she'd **dab** his **forehead** with a cool wet cloth. He said that's why he fell in love with her. He thought she was an angel."

"A real angel?"

His father didn't know.

"What about after he got better? Did he ever say what he meant by God's thumb, or how he survived?"

"No. He just blamed his no-good-pig-stealing-father."

The storm moved off farther west, along with any hope of rain. But the image of the fist and thumb remained in Stanley's head. Although, instead of lightning flashing behind the thumb, in Stanley's mind, the lightning was coming out of the thumb, as if it were the thumb of God.

30

The next day was Zigzag's birthday. Or so he said. Zigzag lay in his **cot** as everyone headed outside. "I get to sleep in, because it's my birthday."

Then a little while later he **cut in**to the breakfast **line**, just in front of Squid. Squid told him to go to the end of the line. "Hey, it's my birthday," Zigzag said, staying where he was.

"It's not your birthday," said Magnet, who was standing behind Squid.

"Is too," said Zigzag. "July 8."

Stanley was behind Magnet. He didn't know what day of the week it was, let alone the date. It could have been July 8, but how would Zigzag know?

He tried to **figure out** how long he'd been at Camp Green Lake, if indeed it was July 8. "I came here on May 24," he said aloud. "So that means I've been here . . ."

"Forty-six days," said Zero.

Stanley was still trying to remember how many days there were in May and June. He looked at Zero. He'd learned not to doubt him when it came to math.

Forty-six days. It felt more like a thousand. He didn't dig a hole that first day, and he hadn't dug one yet today. That meant he'd dug forty-four holes—if it really was July 8.

"Can I have an extra **carton** of juice?" Zigzag asked Mr. Sir. "It's my birthday."

To everyone's surprise, Mr. Sir gave it to him.

Stanley dug his shovel into the dirt. Hole number 45. "The forty-fifth hole is the hardest," he said to himself.

But that really wasn't true, and he knew it. He was a lot stronger than when he first arrived. His body had **adjust**ed somewhat to the heat and **harsh** conditions.

Mr. Sir was no longer **depriving** him of water. After having to get by on less water for a week or so, Stanley now felt like he had all the water he could want.

Of course it helped that Zero dug some of his hole for him each day, but that wasn't as great as everyone thought it was. He always felt **awkward** while Zero was digging his hole, **unsure** of what to do with himself. Usually he stood around awhile, before sitting off by himself on the hard ground, with the sun beating down on him.

It was better than digging.

But not a lot better.

When the sun came up a couple of hours later, Stanley looked for "the thumb of God." The mountains were little more than dark shadows on the **horizon**.

He thought he could make out a spot where the top of one mountain seemed to **jut** upward, but it didn't seem very **impressive**. A short time later the mountains were no longer visible, hidden behind the **glare** of the sun, reflecting off the dirty air.

It was possible, he realized, that he was somewhere near where Kate Barlow had **rob**bed his great-grandfather. If that was really her lipstick tube he'd found, then she must have lived somewhere around here.

Zero took his turn before the lunch break. Stanley climbed out of his hole, and Zero climbed down into it.

"Hey, Caveman," said Zigzag. "You should get a **whip**. Then if your **slave** doesn't dig fast enough, you can **crack** it across his back."

"He's not my slave," said Stanley. "We have a deal, that's all."

"A good deal for you," said Zigzag.

"It was Zero's idea, not mine."

"Don't you know, Zig?" said X-Ray, coming over. "Caveman's doing Zero a big favor. Zero likes to dig holes."

"He sure is a nice guy to let Zero dig his hole for him," said Squid.

"Well, what about me?" asked Armpit. "I like to dig holes, too. Can I dig for you, Caveman, after Zero's finished?"

The other boys laughed.

"No, I want to," said Zigzag. "It's my birthday."

Stanley tried his best to ignore them.

Zigzag kept at it. "Come on, Caveman. Be a **pal**. Let me dig your hole."

Stanley smiled, as if it were all a big joke.

When Mr. Pendanski arrived with water and lunch, Zigzag offered Stanley his place in line. "Since you're so much better than me."

Stanley remained where he was. "I didn't say I was bet—"

"You're **insult**ing him, Zig," said X-Ray. "Why should Caveman take your place, when he deserves to be at the very front? He's better than all of us. Aren't you, Caveman?"

"No," said Stanley.

"Sure you are," said X-Ray. "Now come to the front of the line where you belong."

"That's okay," said Stanley.

"No, it's not okay," said X-Ray. "Get up here."

Stanley hesitated, then moved to the front of the line.

"Well, this is a first," Mr. Pendanski said, coming around the side of the truck. He filled Stanley's **canteen** and handed him a **sack** lunch.

Stanley was glad to get away. He sat down between his hole and Zero's. He was glad that he'd be digging his own hole for the rest of the day. Maybe the other boys would leave him alone. Maybe he shouldn't let Zero dig his hole for him anymore. But he needed to save his energy to be a good teacher.

He bit into his sandwich, which contained some kind of meat-and-cheese mixture that came in a can. Just about everything at Green Lake came in a can. The supply truck came once a month.

He glanced up to see Zigzag and Squid walking toward him.

"I'll give you my cookie if you let me dig your hole," said Zigzag.

Squid laughed.

"Here, take my cookie," said Zigzag, holding it out for him.

"No, thanks," said Stanley.

"C'mon, take my cookie," said Zigzag, sticking it in his face.

"Leave me alone," said Stanley.

"Please eat my cookie," said Zigzag, holding it under Stanley's nose.

Squid laughed.

Stanley pushed it away.

Zigzag pushed him back. "Don't push me!"

"I didn't . . ." Stanley got to his feet. He looked around. Mr. Pendanski was filling Zero's canteen.

Zigzag pushed him again. "I said, 'Don't push me.'"

Stanley took a step backward, carefully avoiding Zero's hole.

Zigzag kept after him. He **shove**d Stanley and said, "Quit pushing!"

"**Lay off**," said Armpit, as he, Magnet, and X-Ray joined

them.

"Why should he?" snapped X-Ray. "Caveman's bigger. He can take care of himself."

"I don't want any trouble," Stanley said.

Zigzag pushed him hard. "Eat my cookie," he said.

Stanley was glad to see Mr. Pendanski coming toward them, along with Zero.

"Hi, Mom," said Armpit. "We were just fooling around."

"I saw what was going on," Mr. Pendanski said. He turned to Stanley. "Go ahead, Stanley," he said. "Hit him back. You're bigger."

Stanley stared at Mr. Pendanski in astonishment.

"Teach the bully a lesson," said Mr. Pendanski.

Zigzag hit Stanley on the shoulder with his open hand. "Teach me a lesson," he challenged.

Stanley made a feeble attempt to punch Zigzag, then he felt a flurry of fists against his head and neck. Zigzag had hold of his collar with one hand and was hitting him with the other.

The collar ripped and Stanley fell backward onto the dirt.

"That's enough!" Mr. Pendanski yelled.

It wasn't enough for Zigzag. He jumped on top of Stanley. "Stop!" shouted Mr. Pendanski.

The side of Stanley's face was pressed flat against the dirt. He tried to protect himself, but Zigzag's fists slammed off his arms and pounded his face into the ground.

All he could do was wait for it to be over.

Then, suddenly, Zigzag was off of him. Stanley managed to look up, and he saw that Zero had his arm around Zigzag's long neck.

Zigzag made a **gag**ging sound, as he desperately tried to pry Zero's arm off of him.

"You're going to kill him!" shouted Mr. Pendanski.

Zero kept **squeezing**.

Armpit **charge**d into them, freeing Zigzag from Zero's **choke** hold. The three boys fell to the ground in different directions.

Mr. Pendanski **fire**d his **pistol** into the air.

The other **counselor**s came running from the office, the tents, or out on the lake. They had their guns drawn, but **holster**ed them when they saw the trouble was over.

The Warden walked over from her cabin.

"There was a **riot**," Mr. Pendanski told her. "Zero almost **strangle**d Ricky."

The Warden looked at Zigzag, who was still stretching and massaging his neck. Then she turned her attention to Stanley, who was obviously in the worst condition. "What happened to you?"

"Nothing. It wasn't a riot."

"Ziggy was **beat**ing **up** the Caveman," said Armpit. "Then Zero started choking Zigzag, and I had to pull Zero off of Zigzag. It was all over before Mom fired his gun."

"They just got a little hot, that's all," said X-Ray. "You know how it is. In the sun all day. People get hot, right? But everything's cool now."

"I see," the Warden said. She turned to Zigzag. "What's the matter? Didn't you get a puppy for your birthday?"

"Zig's just a little hot," said X-Ray. "Out in the sun all day. You know how it is. The blood starts to **boil**."

"Is that what happened, Zigzag?" asked the Warden.

"Yeah," said Zigzag. "Like X-Ray said. Working so hard in the hot sun, while Caveman just sits around doing nothing. My blood boiled."

"Excuse me?" said the Warden. "Caveman digs his holes, just like everyone else."

Zigzag **shrug**ged. "Sometimes."

"Excuse me?"

"Zero's been digging part of Caveman's hole every day," said Squid.

The Warden looked from Squid to Stanley to Zero.

"I'm teaching him to read and write," said Stanley. "It's sort of a trade. The hole still gets dug, so what does it matter who digs it?"

"Excuse me?" said the Warden.

"Isn't it more important for him to learn to read?" Stanley asked. "Doesn't that build **character** more than digging holes?"

"That's his character," said the Warden. "What about your character?"

Stanley raised and lowered one shoulder.

The Warden turned to Zero. "Well, Zero, what have you learned so far?"

Zero said nothing.

"Have you just been digging Caveman's hole for nothing?" the Warden asked him.

"He likes to dig holes," said Mr. Pendanski.

"Tell me what you learned yesterday," said the Warden. "Surely you can remember that."

Zero said nothing.

Mr. Pendanski laughed. He picked up a shovel and said, "You **might as well** try to teach this shovel to read! It's got more brains than Zero."

"The 'at' sound," said Zero.

"The 'at' sound," repeated the Warden. "Well then, tell me, what does c-a-t spell?"

Zero glanced around uneasily.

Stanley knew he knew the answer. Zero just didn't like answering questions.

"Cat," Zero said.

Mr. Pendanski **clap**ped his hands. "Bravo! Bravo! The boy's a **genius**!"

"F-a-t?" asked the Warden.

Zero thought a moment.

Stanley hadn't taught him the "f" sound yet.

"Eff," Zero whispered. "Eff-at. Fat."

"How about h-a-t?" asked the Warden.

Stanley hadn't taught him the "h" sound either.

Zero **concentrate**d hard, then said, "Chat."

All the counselors laughed.

"He's a genius, all right!" said Mr. Pendanski. "He's so

stupid, he doesn't even know he's stupid."

Stanley didn't know why Mr. Pendanski seemed to **have it in for** Zero. If Mr. Pendanski only thought about it, he'd realize it was very **logical** for Zero to think that the letter "h" made the "ch" sound.

"Okay, from now on, I don't want anyone digging anyone else's hole," said the Warden. "And no more reading lessons."

"I'm not digging another hole," said Zero.

"Good," said the Warden. She turned to Stanley. "You know why you're digging holes? Because it's good for you. It teaches you a lesson. If Zero digs your hole for you, then you're not learning your lesson, are you?"

"I guess not," Stanley **mumble**d, although he knew they weren't digging just to learn a lesson. She was looking for something, something that belonged to Kissin' Kate Barlow.

"Why can't I dig my own hole, but still teach Zero to read?" he asked. "What's wrong with that?"

"I'll tell you what's wrong with that," the Warden said. "It leads to trouble. Zero almost killed Zigzag."

"It causes him stress," said Mr. Pendanski. "I know you mean well, Stanley, but **face** it. Zero's too stupid to learn to read. That's what makes his blood boil. Not the hot sun."

"I'm not digging another hole," said Zero.

Mr. Pendanski handed him the shovel. "Here, take it, Zero. It's all you'll ever be good for."

Zero took the shovel.

Then he **swung** it like a baseball **bat**.

The metal **blade smash**ed across Mr. Pendanski's face. His knees **crumple**d beneath him. He was **unconscious** before he hit the ground.

The counselors all drew their guns.

Zero held the shovel out in front of him, as if he were going to try to bat away the **bullet**s. "I hate digging holes," he said. Then he slowly backed away.

"Don't shoot him," said the Warden. "He can't go anywhere. The last thing we need is an **investigation**."

Zero kept backing up, out past the **cluster** of holes the boys had been digging, then farther and farther out onto the lake.

"He's going to have to come back for water," the Warden said.

Stanley noticed Zero's canteen lying on the ground near his hole.

A couple of the counselors helped Mr. Pendanski to his feet and into the truck.

Stanley looked out toward Zero, but he had disappeared into the **haze**.

The Warden ordered the counselors to take turns guarding the shower room and Wreck Room, all day and all night. They were not to let Zero drink any water. When he returned, he was to be brought directly to her.

She examined her fingernails and said, "It's almost time for me to paint my nails again."

Before she left, she told the six remaining members of Group D that she still expected seven holes.

31

Stanley angrily dug his **shovel** into the dirt. He was angry at everyone—Mr. Pendanski, the Warden, Zigzag, X-Ray, and his no-good-dirty-rotten-pig-stealing-great-great-grandfather. But mostly he was angry at himself.

He knew he never should have let Zero dig part of his hole for him. He still could have taught him to read. If Zero could dig all day and still have the strength to learn, then he should have been able to dig all day and still have the strength to teach.

What he should do, he thought, was go out after Zero.

But he didn't.

None of the others helped him dig Zero's hole, and he didn't expect them to. Zero had been helping him dig his hole. Now he had to dig Zero's.

He remained out on the lake, digging during the hottest part of the day, long after everyone else had gone in. He kept an eye out for Zero, but Zero didn't come back.

It would have been easy to go out after Zero. There was nobody to stop him. He kept thinking that's what he should do.

Maybe they could climb to the top of Big Thumb.

If it wasn't too far away. And if it was really the same place where his great-grandfather found refuge. And if, after a hundred years or so, water was still there.

It didn't seem likely. Not when an entire lake had gone dry.

And even if they did find refuge on Big Thumb, he thought, they'd still have to come back here, **eventually**. Then they'd both have to **face** the Warden, and her rattlesnake fingers.

Instead, he came up with a better idea, although he didn't have it quite all **figure**d **out** yet. He thought that maybe he could make a deal with the Warden. He'd tell her where he really found the gold tube if she wouldn't scratch Zero.

He wasn't sure how he'd make this deal without getting himself in deeper trouble. She might just say, Tell me where you found it or I'll scratch you, too. Plus, it would mean X-Ray would get in trouble, too. She'd probably scratch him up as well.

X-Ray would be out to get him for the next sixteen months.

He dug his shovel into the dirt.

By the next morning, Zero still hadn't returned. Stanley

saw one of the counselors sitting guard by the water **spigot** outside the shower wall.

Mr. Pendanski had two black eyes and a **bandage** over his nose. "I always knew he was stupid," Stanley heard him say.

Stanley was required to dig only one hole the next day. As he dug, he kept a **constant watchout** for Zero, but never saw him. Once again he considered going out on the lake to look for him, but he began to realize that it was already too late.

His only hope was that Zero had found God's thumb on his own. It wasn't impossible. His great-grandfather had found it. For some reason his great-grandfather had felt the **urge** to climb to the top of that mountain. Maybe Zero would feel the same urge.

If it was the same mountain. If water was still there.

He tried to **convince** himself it wasn't impossible. There had been a **storm** just a few days ago. Maybe Big Thumb was actually some kind of natural **water tower** that caught and stored the rain.

It wasn't impossible.

He returned to his tent to find the Warden, Mr. Sir, and Mr. Pendanski all waiting for him.

"Have you seen Zero?" the Warden asked him.

"No."

"No sign of him at all?"

"No."

"Do you have any idea where he went?"

"No."

"You know you're not doing him any favors if you're lying," said Mr. Sir. "He can't survive out there for more than a day or two."

"I don't know where he is."

All three stared at Stanley as if they were trying to figure out if he was telling the truth. Mr. Pendanski's face was so **swollen,** he could barely open his eyes. They were just **slit**s.

"You sure he has no family?" the Warden asked Mr. Pendanski.

"He's a **ward** of the state,*" Mr. Pendanski told her. "He was living on the streets when he was **arrest**ed."

"Is there anyone who might ask questions? Some social worker who took an interest in him?"

"He had nobody," said Mr. Pendanski. "He was nobody."

The Warden thought a moment. "Okay, I want you to destroy all of his records."

Mr. Pendanski nodded.

"He was never here," said the Warden.

Mr. Sir nodded.

"Can you get into the state files from our computer?" she asked Mr. Pendanski. "I don't want anyone in the A.G.'s office* to know he was here."

★ **ward of the state** 주(state)의 법률적 보호를 받는 피보호자.

✳ **A.G.** Attorney General의 약자로, 각 주에서 가장 높은 법률 집행자.

"I don't think I can erase him completely from all the state files," said Mr. Pendanski. "Too many cross-references.* But I can make it so it would be very difficult for anyone to ever find a record of him. Like I said, though, no one will ever look. No one cares about Hector Zeroni."

"Good," said the Warden.

★ cross-reference 상호 참조.

32

Two days later a new kid was **assign**ed to Group D. His name was Brian, but X-Ray called him **Twitch** because he was always **fidget**ing. Twitch was assigned Zero's bed, and Zero's **crate**.

Vacancies don't last long at Camp Green Lake.

Twitch had been arrested for stealing a car. He claimed he could break into a car, disconnect the alarm, and hot-wire* the engine, all in less than a minute.

"I never plan to, you know, steal one," he told them. "But sometimes, you know, I'll be walking past a real nice car, parked in a **desert**ed area, and, you know, I'll just start twitching. If you think I twitch now, you should see me when I'm around a car. The next thing I know, I'm behind the **wheel**."

Stanley lay on his **scratchy** sheets. It occurred to him

★ hot-wire 열쇠 대신에 철사를 이용하여 차에 시동을 걸다.

that his **cot** no longer smelled bad. He wondered if the smell had gone away, or if he had just gotten used to it.

"Hey, Caveman," said Twitch. "Do we really have to get up at 4:30?"

"You get used to it," Stanley told him. "It's the coolest part of the day."

He tried not to think about Zero. It was too late. Either he'd made it to Big Thumb, or . . .

What worried him the most, however, wasn't that it was too late. What worried him the most, what really **ate at** his insides, was the fear that it wasn't too late.

What if Zero was still alive, desperately **crawl**ing across the dirt searching for water?

He tried to force the image out of his mind.

The next morning, out on the lake, Stanley listened as Mr. Sir told Twitch the requirements for his hole: ". . . as wide and as deep as your shovel."

Twitch fidgeted. His fingers **drum**med against the wooden **shaft** of his shovel, and his neck moved from side to side.

"You won't be twitching so much after **dig**ging all day," Mr. Sir told him. "You won't have the strength to **wiggle** your **pinkie**." He **pop**ped some sunflower seeds in his mouth, **deft**ly chewed them, and **spat** out the shells. "This isn't a Girl Scout camp."

The water truck came shortly after sunrise. Stanley got in line behind Magnet, ahead of Twitch.

What if it's not too late?

He watched Mr. Sir fill X-Ray's canteen. The image of Zero crawling across the hot dry dirt remained in his head.

But what could he do about it? Even if Zero was somehow alive after more than four days, how would Stanley ever find him? It would take days. He'd need a car.

Or a pickup truck. A pickup truck with a tank of water in the back.

Stanley wondered if Mr. Sir had left the keys in the **ignition**.

He slowly backed away from the line, then circled over to the side of the truck. He looked through the window. The keys were there, **dangling** in the ignition.

Stanley felt his fingers start to twitch.

He took a deep breath to **steady** himself and tried to think clearly. He had never driven before.

But how hard could it be?

This is really crazy, he told himself. Whatever he did, he knew he'd have to do it quickly, before Mr. Sir noticed.

It's too late, he told himself. Zero couldn't have survived.

But what if it wasn't too late?

He took another deep breath. Think about this, he told himself, but there wasn't time to think. He **flung** open the door to the truck and climbed quickly inside.

"Hey!" shouted Mr. Sir.

He turned the key and stepped on the gas **pedal**. The engine **rev**ved.

The truck didn't move.

He pressed the pedal to the floor. The engine **roar**ed, but the truck was **motionless**.

Mr. Sir came running around the side of the truck. The door was still open.

"Put it in **gear**!" shouted Twitch.

The gear shift was on the floor next to the seat. Stanley pulled the lever back until the arrow pointed to the letter D, for Drive.

The truck **lurch**ed forward. Stanley **jerk**ed back against the seat and tightly **grip**ped the wheel as the truck **accelerate**d. His foot was pressed to the floor.

The truck went faster and faster across the dry lake bed. It **bounce**d over a pile of dirt. Suddenly Stanley was slammed forward, then instantly backward as an airbag **explode**d in his face. He fell out of the open door and onto the ground.

He had driven straight into a hole.

He lay on the dirt staring at the truck, which stuck **lopsided** into the ground. He sighed. He couldn't blame his no-good-dirty-rotten-pig-stealing-great-great-grandfather this time. This time it was his own fault, one hundred percent. He had probably just done the stupidest thing he had ever done in his short and **miserable** life.

He managed to get to his feet. He was **sore** but didn't think he had broken any bones. He **glance**d back at Mr. Sir, who remained where he was, staring at Stanley.

He ran. His canteen was **strap**ped around his neck. It **bang**ed against his chest as he ran, and every time it hit against him, it reminded him that it was empty, empty, empty.

33

He slowed to a walk. As far as he could tell, nobody was chasing him. He could hear voices coming from back by the truck but couldn't make out the words. **Occasional**ly he'd hear the **rev**ving of the engine, but the truck wasn't going anywhere anytime soon.

He headed in what he thought was the direction of Big Thumb. He couldn't see it through the haze.

Walking helped calm him down and allowed him to think clearly. He doubted he could make it to Big Thumb, and with no water in his canteen, he didn't want to **risk** his life on the hope that he'd find **refuge** there. He'd have to return to camp. He knew that. But he was in no hurry. It would be better to return later, after everyone had a chance to calm down. And as long as he'd come this far, he **might as well** look for Zero.

He decided he would walk as long as he could, until he was too weak to go any farther, then he'd turn around and go back.

He smiled as he realized that wouldn't quite work. He would only go *halfway*—halfway as far as he thought he could go, so that he'd still have the strength to return. Then he'd have to make a deal with the Warden, tell her where he found Kate Barlow's lipstick tube, and **beg** for **mercy**.

He was surprised by how far out the holes extended. He couldn't even see the camp **compound** anymore, but he still kept passing holes. Just when he thought he'd passed the last hole, he'd come across another **cluster** of them, a little farther away.

Back at the compound, they had dug in a **systematic** order, row upon row, allowing space for the water truck. But out here there was no system. It was as if every once in a while, in a **fit** of **frustration**, the Warden would just pick a spot at random, and say, "What the hell, dig here." It was like trying to guess the winning numbers★ in a **lottery**.

Stanley found himself looking down into each hole he passed. He didn't admit to himself what he was looking for.

After more than an hour had gone by, he thought he had surely seen the last hole, but then off to the left he saw another cluster of them. He didn't actually see the holes. He saw the **mound**s of dirt that surrounded them.

He stepped over the mounds and looked into the first hole. His heart stopped.

Down at the bottom was a family of yellow-**spotted**

★ **winning numbers** (복권 등의) 당첨번호.

lizards. Their large red eyes looked up at him.

He **leap**t back over the mound and ran.

He didn't know if they were chasing after him. He thought he might have seen one leap out of the hole.

He ran until he couldn't run any farther, then **collapse**d. They hadn't come after him.

He sat there awhile and caught his breath. As he got back to his feet, he thought he noticed something on the ground, maybe fifty yards away. It didn't look like much, maybe just a big rock, but in a land of nothingness, any little thing seemed unusual.

He walked slowly toward it. The **encounter** with the lizards had made him very **cautious**.

It turned out to be an empty sack of sunflower seeds. He wondered if it was the same one Magnet had stolen from Mr. Sir, although that didn't seem likely.

He turned it inside out and found one seed stuck to the burlap.

Lunch.

34

The sun was almost directly overhead. He figured he could walk for no more than another hour, maybe two, before he had to turn back.

It seemed **pointless**. He could see there was nothing ahead of him. Nothing but emptiness. He was hot, tired, hungry, and, most of all, thirsty. Maybe he should just turn around now. Maybe he'd already gone halfway and didn't know it.

Then, looking around, he saw a **pool** of water less than a hundred yards away from where he was standing. He closed his eyes and opened them to make sure he wasn't imagining it. The pool was still there.

He hurried toward it. The pool hurried away from him, moving as he moved, stopping when he stopped.

There wasn't any water. It was a **mirage** caused by the **shimmer**ing waves of heat rising off the dry ground.

He kept walking. He still carried the empty **sack** of

sunflower seeds. He didn't know if he might find something to put in it.

After a while he thought he could make out the shape of the mountains through the **haze**. At first he wasn't sure if this was another kind of mirage, but the farther he walked, the clearer they came into a view. Almost straight ahead of him, he could see what looked like a **fist**, with its thumb sticking up.

He didn't know how far away it was. Five miles? Fifty miles? One thing was certain. It was more than halfway.

He kept walking toward it, although he didn't know why. He knew he'd have to turn around before he got there. But every time he looked at it, it seemed to **encourage** him, giving him the **thumbs-up** sign.

As he continued walking, he became aware of a large object on the lake. He couldn't tell what it was, or even if it was natural or **man-made**. It looked a little like a fallen tree, although it didn't seem likely that a tree would grow here. More likely, it was a **ridge** of dirt or rocks.

The object, whatever it was, was not on the way to Big Thumb but off to the right. He tried to decide whether to go to it or continue toward Big Thumb. Or maybe just turn around.

There was no point in heading toward Big Thumb, he decided. He would never make it. For all he knew it was like chasing the moon. But he could make it to the mysterious object.

He changed directions. He doubted it was anything, but the fact that there was something in the middle of all this nothing made it hard for him to pass up. He decided to make the object his halfway point, and he hoped he hadn't already gone too far.

He laughed to himself when he saw what it was. It was a boat—or part of a boat anyway. It **struck** him as funny to see a boat in the middle of this dry and **barren wasteland**. But after all, he realized, this was once a lake.

The boat lay **upside down**, half buried in the dirt.

Someone may have **drown**ed here, he thought **grim**ly—at the same spot where he could very well die of thirst.

The name of the boat had been painted on the back. The upside-down red letters were **peel**ed and faded, but Stanley could still read the name: *Mary Lou.*

On one side of the boat there was a pile of dirt and then a tunnel leading down below the boat. The tunnel looked big enough for a good-sized animal to **crawl** through.

He heard a noise. Something **stir**red under the boat.

It was coming out.

"Hey!" Stanley shouted, hoping to scare it back inside. His mouth was very dry, and it was hard to shout very loudly.

"Hey," the thing answered weakly.

Then a dark hand and an orange sleeve reached up out of the tunnel.

35

Zero's face looked like a jack-o'-lantern that had been left out too many days past Halloween—half **rotten**, with **sunken** eyes and a **droop**ing smile. "Is that water?" he asked. His voice was weak and **raspy**. His lips were so pale they were almost white, and his tongue seemed to **flop** around uselessly in his mouth as he spoke, as if it kept **getting in the way**.

"It's empty," said Stanley. He stared at Zero, not quite believing that he was real. "I tried to bring you the whole water truck, but," he smiled **sheepish**ly, "I drove it into a hole. I can't believe you're . . ."

"Me neither," said Zero.

"C'mon, we got to get back to camp."

Zero shook his head. "I'm not going back."

"You have to. We both have to."

"You want some sploosh?" Zero asked.

"What?"

Zero **shade**d his eyes with his **forearm**. "It's cooler under the boat," he said.

Stanley watched Zero crawl back through his hole. It was a miracle he was still alive, but Stanley knew he would have to get him back to camp soon, even if he had to carry him.

He crawled after him, and was just able to **squeeze** his body through the hole. He never would have fit when he first came to Camp Green Lake. He'd lost a lot of weight.

As he pulled himself through, his leg struck something sharp and hard. It was a **shovel**. For a second Stanley wondered how it got there, but then remembered that Zero had taken it with him after striking Mr. Pendanski.

It was cooler under the boat, which was half buried in the dirt. There were enough **crack**s and holes in the bottom of the boat, now the roof, to provide light and **ventilation**. He could see empty **jar**s **scatter**ed about.

Zero held a jar in his hand and **grunt**ed as he tried to **unscrew** the **lid**.

"What is it?"

"Sploosh!" His voice was strained as he worked on the jar. "That's what I call it. They were buried under the boat."

He still couldn't get the lid off. "I found sixteen jars. Here, hand me the shovel."

Stanley didn't have a lot of room to move. He reached behind him, grabbed the wooden end of the shovel, and held it out to Zero, **blade** first.

"Sometimes you just have to . . ." Zero said, then he hit

the jar against the blade of the shovel, breaking the top of the jar clean off. He quickly brought the jar to his mouth and licked the sploosh off the **jagged** edges before it spilled.

"Careful," Stanley warned.

Zero picked up the cracked lid and **lick**ed the sploosh off that as well. Then he handed the broken jar to Stanley. "Drink some."

Stanley held it in his hand and stared at it a moment. He was afraid of the broken glass. He was also afraid of the sploosh. It looked like mud. Whatever it was, he realized, it must have been in the boat when the boat sank. That meant it was probably over a hundred years old. Who knew what kind of bacteria might be living in it?

"It's good," said Zero, **encouraging** him.

He wondered if Zero had heard of bacteria. He raised the jar to his mouth and carefully took a **sip**.

It was a warm, **bubbly**, **mushy nectar**, sweet and **tangy**. It felt like heaven as it flowed over his dry mouth and down his **parched** throat. He thought it might have been some kind of fruit at some time, perhaps peaches.

Zero smiled at him. "I told you it was good."

Stanley didn't want to drink too much, but it was too good to **resist**. They passed the jar back and forth until it was empty. "How many are left?" he asked.

"None," said Zero.

Stanley's mouth dropped. "Now I have to take you back," he said.

"I'm not digging any more holes," said Zero.

"They won't make you dig," Stanley promised. "They'll probably send you to a hospital, like Barf Bag."

"Barf Bag stepped on a **rattlesnake**," said Zero.

Stanley remembered how he'd almost done the same. "I guess he didn't hear the **rattle**."

"He did it on purpose," said Zero.

"You think?"

"He took off his shoe and sock first."

Stanley **shiver**ed as he tried to imagine it.

"What's Mar-ya Luh-oh-oo?" asked Zero.

"What?"

Zero **concentrate**d hard. "Mar ya, Luh oh oo."

"I have no idea."

"I'll show you," said Zero. He crawled back out from under the boat.

Stanley followed. Back outside, he had to shield his eyes from the brightness.

Zero walked around to the back of the boat and pointed to the **upside-down** letters. "Mm-ar-yuh. Luh-oh-oo."

Stanley smiled. "Mary Lou. It's the name of the boat."

"Mary Lou," Zero repeated, studying the letters. "I thought 'y' made the 'yuh' sound."

"It does," said Stanley. "But not when it's at the end of a word. Sometimes 'y' is a vowel⋆ and sometimes it's a consonant.⋆"

Zero suddenly **groan**ed. He grabbed his stomach and

⋆ vowel, consonant 모음과 자음.

bent over.

"Are you all right?"

Zero dropped to the ground. He lay on his side, with his knees pulled up to his chest. He continued to groan.

Stanley watched **helpless**ly. He wondered if it was the sploosh. He looked back toward Camp Green Lake. At least he thought it was the direction of Camp Green Lake. He wasn't entirely sure.

Zero stopped **moan**ing, and his body slowly **unbent**.

"I'm taking you back," said Stanley.

Zero managed to sit up. He took several deep breaths.

"Look, I got a plan so you won't get in trouble," Stanley assured him. "Remember when I found the gold tube. Remember, I gave it to X-Ray, and the Warden went crazy making us dig where she thought X-Ray found it. I think if I tell the Warden where I really found it, I think she'll let us off."

"I'm not going back," said Zero.

"You've got nowhere else to go," said Stanley.

Zero said nothing.

"You'll die out here," said Stanley.

"Then I'll die out here."

Stanley didn't know what to do. He had come to rescue Zero and instead drank the last of his sploosh. He looked off into the distance. "I want you to look at something."

"I'm not—"

"I just want you to look at that mountain up there. See the one that has something sticking up out of it?"

"Yeah, I think."

"What does it look like to you? Does it look like anything?"

Zero said nothing.

But as he studied the mountain, his right hand slowly formed into a fist. He raised his thumb. His eyes went from the mountain, to his hand, then back to the mountain.

36

They put four of the unbroken jars in the burlap sack, in case they might be able to use them. Stanley carried the sack. Zero held the shovel.

"I should warn you," Stanley said. "I'm not exactly the luckiest guy in the world."

Zero wasn't worried. "When you spend your whole life living in a hole," he said, "the only way you can go is up."

They gave each other the **thumbs-up** sign, then headed out.

It was the hottest part of the day. Stanley's empty-empty-empty **canteen** was still **strap**ped around his neck. He thought back to the water truck, and wished he'd at least stopped and filled his canteen before running off.

They hadn't gone very far before Zero had another **attack**. He **clutch**ed his stomach as he let himself fall to the ground.

Stanley could only wait for it to pass. The sploosh had saved Zero's life, but it was now destroying him from the inside. He wondered how long it would be before he, too, felt the effects.

He looked at Big Thumb. It didn't seem any closer than when they first started out.

Zero took a deep breath and managed to sit up.

"Can you walk?" Stanley asked him.

"Just give me a second," Zero said. He took another breath, then, using the shovel, pulled himself back to his feet. He gave Stanley the thumbs-up sign and they continued.

Sometimes Stanley would try to go for a long while without looking at Big Thumb. He'd make a **mental** snapshot★ of how it looked, then wait maybe ten minutes before looking at it again, to see if it seemed closer.

It never did. It was like chasing the moon.

And if they ever reached it, he realized, then they'd still have to climb it.

"I wonder who she was," said Zero.

"Who?"

"Mary Lou," said Zero.

Stanley smiled. "I guess she was once a real person on a real lake. It's hard to imagine."

"I bet she was pretty," said Zero. "Somebody must have loved her a lot, to name a boat after her."

★**mental snapshot** 마음 속의 사진이라는 말로 그만큼 뇌리에 깊이 새긴다는 표현이다.

"Yeah," said Stanley. "I bet she looked great in a bathing suit,* sitting in the boat while her boyfriend rowed."

Zero used the shovel as a third leg. Two legs weren't enough to keep him up. "I got to stop and rest," he said after a while.

Stanley looked at Big Thumb. It still didn't look any closer. He was afraid if Zero stopped, he might never get started again. "We're almost there," he said.

He wondered which was closer: Camp Green Lake or Big Thumb?

"I really have to sit down."

"Just see if you can go a little—"

Zero collapsed. The shovel stayed up a **fraction** of a second longer, perfectly balanced on the **tip** of the blade, then it fell next to him.

Zero **knelt**, bent over with his head on the ground. Stanley could hear a very low moaning sound coming from him. He looked at the shovel and couldn't help but think that he might need it to **dig** a **grave**. Zero's last hole.

And who will dig a grave for me? he thought.

But Zero did get up, once again flashing thumbs-up.

"Give me some words," he said weakly.

It took Stanley a few seconds to realize what he meant. Then he smiled and said, "R-u-n."

Zero sounded it out to himself. "Rr-un, run. Run."

"Good. F-u-n."

★ **bathing suit** 수영복.

"Fffun."

The spelling seemed to help Zero. It gave him something to concentrate on besides his pain and weakness.

It **distract**ed Stanley as well. The next time he looked up at Big Thumb, it really did seem closer.

They quit spelling words when it hurt too much to talk. Stanley's throat was dry. He was weak and **exhaust**ed, yet as bad as he felt, he knew that Zero felt ten times worse. As long as Zero could keep going, he could keep going, too.

It was possible, he thought, he hoped, that he didn't get any of the bad bacteria. Zero hadn't been able to unscrew the lid. Maybe the bad **germs** couldn't get in, either. Maybe the bacteria were only in the jars which opened easily, the ones he was now carrying in his sack.

What scared Stanley the most about dying wasn't his actual death. He figured he could handle the pain. It wouldn't be much worse than what he felt now. In fact, maybe at the moment of his death he would be too weak to feel pain. Death would be a relief. What worried him the most was the thought of his parents not knowing what happened to him, not knowing whether he was dead or alive. He hated to imagine what it would be like for his mother and father, day after day, month after month, not knowing, living on false hope. For him, at least, it would be over. For his parents, the pain would never end.

He wondered if the Warden would send out a search party★

★ **search party** 사람을 찾기 위한 수색(search)대(party). party는 파티를 한다는 뜻 외에도, '단체, 정당'이라는 뜻을 가지고 있다.

to look for him. It didn't seem likely. She didn't send anyone to look for Zero. But no one cared about Zero. They simply destroyed his files.

But Stanley had a family. She couldn't pretend he was never there. He wondered what she would tell them. And when?

"What do you think's up there?" Zero asked.

Stanley looked to the top of Big Thumb. "Oh, probably an Italian restaurant," he said.

Zero managed to laugh.

"I think I'll get a pepperoni pizza and a large root beer,*" said Stanley.

"I want an ice cream sundae,*" said Zero. "With nuts and **whip**ped cream, and bananas, and hot fudge.*"

The sun was almost directly in front of them. The thumb pointed up toward it.

They came to the end of the lake. Huge white stone **cliff**s rose up before them.

Unlike the eastern **shore**, where Camp Green Lake was **situated**, the western shore did not **slope** down **gradual**ly. It was as if they had been walking across the flat bottom of a giant **frying pan**, and now they had to somehow climb up out of it.

They could no longer see Big Thumb. The cliffs blocked

★ **root beer** 루트 비어. 생강과 여러 식물의 뿌리로 만든 탄산음료.

✳ **ice cream sundae** 아이스크림을 넣고 시럽, 견과류, 과일 조각 등을 얹은 디저트.

❋ **fudge** 초콜릿, 설탕, 버터, 우유로 만든 물렁한 사탕.

their view. The cliffs also blocked out the sun.

Zero groaned and clutched his stomach, but he remained standing. "I'm all right," he whispered.

Stanley saw a **rut**, about a foot wide and six inches deep, running down a cliff. On either side of the rut were a series of **ledge**s. "Let's try there," he said.

It looked to be about a fifty-foot climb, straight up.

Stanley still managed to hold the sack of jars in his left hand as he slowly moved up, from ledge to ledge, **crisscross**ing the rut. At times he had to use the side of the rut for support, in order to make it to the next ledge.

Zero stayed with him, somehow. His **frail** body **trembled** terribly as he climbed the stone wall.

Some of the ledges were wide enough to sit on. Others **stuck out** no more than a few inches—just enough for a quick step. Stanley stopped about two-thirds of the way up, on a **fairly** wide ledge. Zero came up alongside him.

"You okay?" Stanley asked.

Zero gave the thumbs-up sign. Stanley did the same.

He looked above him. He wasn't sure how he'd get to the next ledge. It was three or four feet above his head, and he didn't see any **foothold**s. He was afraid to look down.

"Give me a **boost**," said Zero. "Then I'll pull you up with the shovel."

"You won't be able to pull me up," said Stanley.

"Yes, I will," said Zero.

Stanley **cup**ped his hands together, and Zero stepped on his **interwoven** fingers. He was able to lift Zero high

182

enough for him to grab the **protruding slab** of rock. Stanley continued to help him from below as Zero pulled himself onto the ledge.

While Zero was getting himself situated up there, Stanley attached the sack to the shovel by **poking** a hole through the burlap. He held it up to Zero.

Zero first grabbed hold of the sack, then the shovel. He set the shovel so that half the blade was supported by the rock slab. The wooden **shaft** hung down toward Stanley. "Okay," he said.

Stanley doubted this would work. It was one thing for him to lift Zero, who was half his weight. It was quite another for Zero to try to pull him up.

Stanley grabbed hold of the shovel as he climbed up the rock wall, using the sides of the rut to help support him. His hands moved one over the other, up the shaft of the shovel.

He felt Zero's hand **clasp** his **wrist**.

He let go of the shaft with one hand and grabbed the top of the ledge.

He gathered his strength and for a **brief** second seemed to **defy gravity** as he took a quick step up the wall and, with Zero's help, pulled himself the rest of the way over the ledge.

He caught his breath. There was no way he could have done that a few months ago.

He noticed a large spot of blood on his wrist. It took him a moment to realize that it was Zero's blood.

Zero had deep **gash**es in both hands. He had held on to

the metal blade of the shovel, keeping it in place, as Stanley climbed.

Zero brought his hands to his mouth and **suck**ed up his blood.

One of the glass jars had broken in the sack. They decided to save the pieces. They might need to make a knife or something.

They rested briefly, then continued on up. It was a fairly easy climb the rest of the way.

When they reached flat ground, Stanley looked up to see the sun, a **fiery** ball balancing on top of Big Thumb. God was **twirl**ing a basketball.

Soon they were walking in the long thin shadow of the thumb.

37

"We're almost there," said Stanley. He could see the base of the mountain.

Now that they really were *almost there*, it scared him. Big Thumb was his only hope. If there was no water, no **refuge**, then they'd have nothing, not even hope.

There was no exact place where the flat land stopped and the mountain began. The ground got **steep**er and steeper, and then there was no doubt that they were heading up the mountain.

Stanley could no longer see Big Thumb. The **slope** of the mountain was in the way.

It became too steep to go straight up. Instead they zigzagged back and forth, **increasing** their **altitude** by small **increment**s every time they changed directions.

Patches of **weed**s **dot**ted the mountainside. They walked from one patch to another, using the weeds as **foothold**s. As they got higher, the weeds got thicker. Many had **thorn**s, and they had to be careful walking through them.

Stanley would have liked to stop and rest, but he was afraid they'd never get started again. As long as Zero could keep going, he could keep going, too. Besides, he knew they didn't have much **daylight** left.

As the sky darkened, bugs began appearing above the weed patches. A **swarm** of **gnat**s **hover**ed around them, **attract**ed by their **sweat**. Neither Stanley nor Zero had the strength to try to **swat** at them.

"How are you doing?" Stanley asked.

Zero pointed thumbs up. Then he said, "If a gnat lands on me, it will **knock** me **over**."

Stanley gave him some more words. "B-u-g-s," he spelled.

Zero concentrated hard, then said, "Boogs."

Stanley laughed.

A wide smile spread across Zero's sick and **weary** face as well. "Bugs," he said.

"Good," said Stanley. "Remember, it's a short 'u' if there's no 'e' at the end. Okay, here's a hard one. How about, l-u-n-c-h?"

"Luh— Luh-un—" Suddenly, Zero made a **horrible**, **wrench**ing noise as he **doubled over** and grabbed his stomach. His **frail** body shook **violent**ly, and he **threw up**, emptying his stomach of the sploosh.

He leaned on his knees and took several deep breaths. Then he straightened up and continued going.

The swarm of gnats stayed behind, preferring the contents of Zero's stomach to the sweat on the boys' faces.

Stanley didn't give him any more words, thinking that he needed to save his strength. But about ten or fifteen minutes later, Zero said, "Lunch."

As they climbed higher, the patches of weeds grew thicker, and they had to be careful not to get their feet **tangle**d in **thorny vine**s. Stanley suddenly realized something. There hadn't been any weeds on the lake.

"Weeds and bugs," he said. "There's got to be water around somewhere. We must be getting close."

A wide **clown**-like smile spread across Zero's face. He flashed the thumbs-up sign, then fell.

He didn't get up. Stanley bent over him. "C'mon, Zero," he **urge**d. "We're getting close. C'mon, Hector. Weeds and bugs. Weeds and boogs."

Stanley shook him. "I've already ordered your hot fudge sundae," he said. "They're making it right now."

Zero said nothing.

38

Stanley took hold of Zero's **forearm**s and pulled him **upright**. Then he **stoop**ed down and let Zero fall over his right shoulder. He stood up, lifting Zero's **worn-out** body off the ground.

He left the shovel and **sack** of jars behind as he continued up the mountain. Zero's legs **dangle**d in front of him.

Stanley couldn't see his feet, which made it difficult to walk through the **tangle**d **patch**es of weeds and **vine**s. He **concentrate**d on one step at a time, carefully raising and setting down each foot. He thought only about each step, and not the impossible task that lay before him.

Higher and higher he climbed. His strength came from somewhere deep inside himself and also seemed to come from the outside as well. After focusing on Big Thumb for so long, it was as if the rock had **absorb**ed his energy and now acted like a kind of giant magnet pulling him toward it.

After a while he became aware of a **foul odor**. At first he thought it came from Zero, but it seemed to be in the air, hanging heavy all around him.

He also noticed that the ground wasn't as steep anymore. As the ground **flatten**ed, a huge stone **precipice** rose up ahead of him, just barely visible in the moonlight. It seemed to grow bigger with each step he took.

It no longer **resemble**d a thumb.

And he knew he'd never be able to climb it.

Around him, the smell became stronger. It was the **bitter** smell of **despair**.

Even if he could somehow climb Big Thumb, he knew he wouldn't find water. How could there be water at the top of a giant rock? The weeds and bugs survived only by an **occasional** rainstorm, like the one he had seen from camp.

Still, he continued toward it. If nothing else, he wanted to at least reach the Thumb.

He never made it.

His feet slipped out from under him. Zero's head **knock**ed against the back of his shoulder as he fell and **tumble**d into a small **muddy gully**.

As he lay face down in the muddy **ditch**, he didn't know if he'd ever get up again. He didn't know if he'd even try. Had he come all this way just to . . . *You need water to make mud!*

He **crawl**ed along the gully in the direction that seemed the muddiest. The ground became **gloppier**. The mud

splashed up as he **slap**ped the ground.

Using both hands, he dug a hole in the **soggy** soil. It was too dark to see, but he thought he could feel a tiny **pool** of water at the bottom of his hole. He stuck his head in the hole and **lick**ed the dirt.

He dug deeper, and as he did so, more water seemed to fill the hole. He couldn't see it, but he could feel it—first with his fingers, then with his tongue.

He dug until he had a hole that was about as deep as his arm was long. There was enough water for him to **scoop** out with his hands and drop on Zero's face.

Zero's eyes remained closed. But his tongue **poke**d out between his lips, searching out the **droplet**s.

Stanley **drag**ged Zero closer to the hole. He dug, then scooped some more water and let it pour out of his hands into Zero's mouth.

As he continued to widen his hole, his hand came across a smooth, round object. It was too smooth and too round to be a rock.

He **wipe**d the dirt off of it and realized it was an onion.

He bit into it without **peel**ing it. The hot bitter juice **burst** into his mouth. He could feel it all the way up to his eyes. And when he **swallow**ed, he felt its warmth move down his throat and into his stomach.

He only ate half. He gave the other half to Zero.

"Here, eat this."

"What is it?" Zero whispered.

"A hot fudge sundae."

39

Stanley awoke in a **meadow**, looking up at the giant rock tower. It was **layer**ed and **streak**ed with different **shade**s of red, burnt orange, brown, and **tan**. It must have been over a hundred feet tall.

Stanley lay awhile, just looking at it. He didn't have the strength to get up. It felt like the insides of his mouth and throat were **coat**ed with sand.

And no wonder. When he **roll**ed **over** he saw the water hole. It was about two and a half feet deep and over three feet wide. At the bottom lay no more than two inches of very brown water.

His hands and fingers were **sore** from digging, especially under his fingernails. He scooped some dirty water into his mouth, then **swish**ed it around, trying to filter it with his teeth.

Zero **moan**ed.

Stanley started to say something to him, but no words

came out of his mouth, and he had to try again. "How you doing?" It hurt to talk.

"Not good," Zero said quietly. With great effort, he rolled over, raised himself to his knees, and crawled to the water hole. He lowered his head into it and **lap**ped up some water.

Then he **jerk**ed back, **clutch**ed his knees to his chest, and rolled to his side. His body shook **violent**ly.

Stanley thought about going back down the mountain to look for the **shovel**, so he could make the water hole deeper. Maybe that would give them cleaner water. They could use the **jar**s as drinking glasses.

But he didn't think he had the strength to go down, let alone make it back up again. And he didn't know where to look.

He **struggle**d **to his feet**. He was in a field of greenish white flowers that seemed to extend all the way around Big Thumb.

He took a deep breath, then walked the last fifty yards to the giant **precipice** and touched it.

Tag, you're it.*

Then he walked back to Zero and the water hole. On the way he picked one of the flowers. It actually wasn't one big flower, he discovered, but instead each flower was really a **cluster** of tiny little flowers that formed a round ball. He brought it to his mouth but had to **spit** it out.

★ **tag, you're it** 잡았다(tag). 이제 네가 술래(it)다. 'tag'는 술래잡기에서 술래가 붙잡을 때 하는 말이다.

192

He could see part of the **trail** he had made the night before, when he carried Zero up the mountain. If he was going to head back down and look for the shovel, he realized, he should do it soon, while the trail was fresh. But he didn't want to leave Zero. He was afraid Zero might die while he was gone.

Zero was still lying **double**d **over** on his side. "I got to tell you something," he said with a **groan**.

"Don't talk," said Stanley. "Save your strength."

"No, listen," Zero insisted, then he closed his eyes as his face **twist**ed with pain.

"I'm listening," Stanley whispered.

"I took your shoes," Zero said.

Stanley didn't know what he was talking about. His shoes were on his feet. "That's all right," he said. "Just rest now."

"It's all my fault," said Zero.

"It's nobody's fault," said Stanley.

"I didn't know," Zero said.

"That's okay," Stanley said. "Just rest."

Zero closed his eyes. But then again he said, "I didn't know about the shoes."

"What shoes?"

"From the **shelter**."

It took a moment for Stanley to **comprehend**. "Clyde Livingston's shoes?"

"I'm sorry," said Zero.

Stanley stared at him. It was impossible. Zero was

delirious.

Zero's "**confession**" seemed to bring him some relief. The **muscle**s in his face relaxed. As he **drift**ed into sleep, Stanley softly sang him the song that had been in his family for **generation**s.

> *"If only, if only," the **woodpecker** sighs,*
> *"The **bark** on the tree was just a little bit softer."*
> *While the wolf waits below, hungry and lonely,*
> *He cries to the moo—oo—oon,*
> *"If only, if only."*

40

When Stanley found the onion the night before, he didn't question how it had come to be there. He ate it **grateful**ly. But now as he sat **gazing** at Big Thumb and the **meadow** full of flowers, he couldn't help but wonder about it.

If there was one wild onion, there could be more.

He **intertwine**d his fingers and tried to **rub** out the pain. Then he bent down and **dug** up another flower, this time pulling up the entire plant, including the root.

"Onions! Fresh, hot, sweet onions," Sam called as Mary Lou pulled the cart down Main Street. "Eight cents a dozen."

It was a beautiful spring morning. The sky was painted pale blue and pink—the same color as the lake and the peach trees along its **shore**.

Mrs. Gladys Tennyson was wearing just her nightgown[*]

---

[*] **nightgown** 주로 긴 원피스로 되어있는 잠옷.

and **robe** as she came running down the street after Sam. Mrs. Tennyson was normally a very **proper** woman who never went out in public without dressing up in fine clothes and a hat. So it was quite surprising to the people of Green Lake to see her running past them.

"Sam!" she shouted.

"Whoa, Mary Lou," said Sam, stopping his **mule** and cart. "G'morning, Mrs. Tennyson," he said. "How's little Becca doing?"

Gladys Tennyson was all smiles. "I think she's going to be all right. The **fever** broke about an hour ago. Thanks to you."

"I'm sure the good Lord and Doc Hawthorn deserve most of the **credit**."

"The Good Lord, yes," agreed Mrs. Tennyson, "but not Dr. Hawthorn. That **quack** wanted to put **leech**es on her stomach! Leeches! My word!★ He said they would **suck** out the bad blood. Now you tell me. How would a leech know good blood from bad blood?"

"I wouldn't know," said Sam.

"It was your onion **tonic**," said Mrs. Tennyson. "That's what saved her."

Other townspeople made their way to the cart. "Good morning, Gladys," said Hattie Parker. "Don't you look lovely this morning."

Several people **snicker**ed.

★ **my word** 아이고! 세상에! (놀랐을 때 하는 말)

"Good morning, Hattie," Mrs. Tennyson replied.

"Does your husband know you're **parading** about in your bed clothes?" Hattie asked.

There were more snickers.

"My husband knows exactly where I am and how I am dressed, thank you," said Mrs. Tennyson. "We have both been up all night and half the morning with Rebecca. She almost died from stomach sickness. It seems she ate some bad meat."

Hattie's face **flush**ed. Her husband, Jim Parker, was the **butcher**.

"It made my husband and me sick as well," said Mrs. Tennyson, "but it nearly killed Becca, what with her being so young. Sam saved her life."

"It wasn't me," said Sam. "It was the onions."

"I'm glad Becca's all right," Hattie said **contrite**ly.

"I keep telling Jim he needs to wash his knives," said Mr. Pike, who owned the **general store**.

Hattie Parker excused herself, then turned and quickly walked away.

"Tell Becca that when she feels up to it to come by the store for a piece of candy," said Mr. Pike.

"Thank you, I'll do that."

Before returning home, Mrs. Tennyson bought a dozen onions from Sam. She gave him a dime* and told him to keep the change.

★ **dime** 10센트짜리 동전.

"I don't take **charity**," Sam told her. "But if you want to buy a few extra onions for Mary Lou, I'm sure she'd appreciate it."

"All right then," said Mrs. Tennyson, "give me my change in onions."

Sam gave Mrs. Tennyson an additional three onions, and she fed them one at a time to Mary Lou. She laughed as the old **donkey** ate them out of her hand.

Stanley and Zero slept off and on for the next two days, ate onions, all they wanted, and **splash**ed dirty water into their mouths. In the late afternoon Big Thumb gave them shade. Stanley tried to make the hole deeper, but he really needed the shovel. His efforts just seemed to **stir** up the mud and make the water dirtier.

Zero was sleeping. He was still very sick and weak, but the sleep and the onions seemed to be doing him some good. Stanley was no longer afraid that he would die soon. Still, he didn't want to go for the shovel while Zero was asleep. He didn't want him to wake up and think he'd been **desert**ed.

He waited for Zero to open his eyes.

"I think I'll go look for the shovel," Stanley said.

"I'll wait here," Zero said **feebly**, as if he had any other choice.

Stanley headed down the mountain. The sleep and the onions had done him a lot of good as well. He felt strong.

It was **fairly** easy to follow the **trail** he had made two days earlier. There were a few places where he wasn't sure he was going the right way, but it just took a little bit of searching before he found the trail again.

He went quite a ways down the mountain but still didn't find the shovel. He looked back up toward the top of the mountain. He must have walked right past it, he thought. There was no way he could have carried Zero all the way up from here.

Still, he headed downward, just in case. He came to a bare spot between two large patches of weeds and sat down to rest. Now he had **definite**ly gone too far, he decided. He was tired out from walking down the hill. It would have been impossible to have carried Zero up the hill from here, especially after walking all day with no food or water. The shovel must be buried in some weeds.

Before starting back up, he took one last look around in all directions. He saw a large **indentation** in the weeds a little farther down the mountain. It didn't seem likely that the shovel could be there, but he'd already come this far.

There, lying in some tall weeds, he found the shovel and the sack of jars. He was amazed. He wondered if the shovel and sack might have rolled down the hill. But none of the jars were broken, except the one which had broken earlier. And if they had rolled down the hill, it is **doubtful** that he would have found the sack and shovel side by side.

On his way back up the mountain, Stanley had to sit down and rest several times. It was a long, hard climb.

41

Zero's condition continued to **improve**.

Stanley slowly peeled an onion. He liked eating them one **layer** at a time.

The water hole was now almost as large as the holes he had dug back at Camp Green Lake. It contained almost two feet of **murky** water. Stanley had dug it all himself. Zero had offered to help, but Stanley thought it better for Zero to save his strength. It was a lot harder to dig in water than it was in a dry lake.

Stanley was surprised that he himself hadn't gotten sick—either from the sploosh, the dirty water, or from **living on** onions. He used to get sick quite a lot back at home.

Both boys were **barefoot**. They had washed their socks. All their clothes were very dirty, but their socks were definitely the worst.

They didn't dip their socks into the hole, afraid to **contaminate** the water. Instead they filled the jars and poured the water over their dirty socks.

"I didn't go to the **homeless shelter** very often," Zero said. "Just if the weather was really bad. I'd have to find someone to pretend to be my mom. If I'd just gone by myself, they would have asked me a bunch of questions. If they'd found out I didn't have a mom, they would have made me a **ward** of the state."

"What's a ward of the state?"

Zero smiled. "I don't know. But I didn't like the sound of it."

Stanley remembered Mr. Pendanski telling the Warden that Zero was a ward of the state. He wondered if Zero knew he'd become one.

"I liked sleeping outside," said Zero. "I used to pretend I was a Cub Scout.★ I always wanted to be a Cub Scout. I'd see them at the park in their blue uniforms."

"I was never a Cub Scout," said Stanley. "I wasn't good at social **stuff** like that. Kids made fun of me because I was fat."

"I liked the blue uniforms," said Zero. "Maybe I wouldn't have liked being a Cub Scout."

Stanley **shrug**ged one shoulder.

"My mother was once a Girl Scout," said Zero.

"I thought you said you didn't have a mother."

"Everybody has to have a mother."

"Well, yeah, I know that."

★ **Cub Scout** 보이 스카우트에서 8세에서 10세의 어린이 단원.

"She said she once won a prize for selling the most Girl Scout cookies," said Zero. "She was real proud of that."

Stanley peeled off another layer of his onion.

"We always took what we needed," Zero said. "When I was little, I didn't even know it was *stealing*. I don't remember when I found out. But we just took what we needed, never more. So when I saw the shoes on display in the shelter, I just reached in the glass case and took them."

"Clyde Livingston's shoes?" asked Stanley.

"I didn't know they were his. I just thought they were somebody's old shoes. It was better to take someone's old shoes, I thought, than steal a pair of new ones. I didn't know they were famous. There was a sign, but of course I couldn't read it. Then, the next thing I know everybody's making this big deal about how the shoes are missing. It was kind of funny, in a way. The whole place is going crazy. There I was, wearing the shoes, and everyone's running around saying, 'What happened to the shoes?' 'The shoes are gone!' I just walked out the door. No one noticed me. When I got outside, I ran around the corner and immediately took off the shoes. I put them on top of a parked car. I remember they smelled really bad."

"Yeah, those were them," said Stanley. "Did they fit you?"

"Pretty much."

Stanley remembered being surprised at Clyde Livingston's small shoe size. Stanley's shoes were bigger. Clyde Livingston had small, quick feet. Stanley's feet were big and slow.

"I should have just kept them," said Zero. "I'd already made it out of the shelter and everything. I ended up getting **arrest**ed the next day when I tried to walk out of a shoe store with a new pair of **sneaker**s. If I had just kept those old smelly sneakers, then neither of us would be here right now."

42

Zero became strong enough to help dig the hole. When he finished, it was over six feet deep. He filled the bottom with rocks to help separate the water from the dirt.

He was still the best hole digger around.

"That's the last hole I will ever dig," he declared, throwing down the shovel.

Stanley smiled. He wished it were true, but he knew they had no choice but to **eventually** return to Camp Green Lake. They couldn't **live on** onions forever.

They had been completely around Big Thumb. It was like a giant **sundial**. They followed the shade.

They were able to see out in all directions. There was no place to go. The mountain was surrounded by desert.

Zero stared at Big Thumb. "It must have a hole in it," he said, "filled with water."

"You think?"

"Where else could the water be coming from?" Zero

asked. "Water doesn't run **uphill**."

Stanley bit into an onion. It didn't burn his eyes or nose, and, in fact, he no longer noticed a particularly strong taste.

He remembered when he had first carried Zero up the hill, how the air had smelled **bitter**. It was the smell of thousands of onions, growing and **rot**ting and **sprout**ing.

Now he didn't smell a thing.

"How many onions do you think we've eaten?" he asked.

Zero shrugged. "I don't even know how long we've been here."

"I'd say about a week," said Stanley. "And we probably each eat about twenty onions a day, so that's . . ."

"Two hundred and eighty onions," said Zero.

Stanley smiled. "I bet we really **stink**."

Two nights later, Stanley lay awake staring up at the star-filled sky. He was too happy to fall asleep.

He knew he had no reason to be happy. He had heard or read somewhere that right before a person **freeze**s to death, he suddenly feels nice and warm. He wondered if perhaps he was experiencing something like that.

It occurred to him that he couldn't remember the last time he felt happiness. It wasn't just being sent to Camp Green Lake that had made his life **miserable**. Before that he'd been unhappy at school, where he had no friends, and **bullies** like Derrick Dunne **pick**ed **on** him. No one liked him, and the truth was, he didn't especially like himself.

He liked himself now.

He wondered if he was delirious.

He looked over at Zero sleeping near him. Zero's face was lit in the starlight, and there was a flower **petal** in front of his nose that moved back and forth as he breathed. It reminded Stanley of something out of a **cartoon**. Zero breathed in, and the petal was drawn up almost touching his nose. Zero breathed out, and the petal moved toward his **chin**. It stayed on Zero's face for an **amazing**ly long time before **flutter**ing off to the side.

Stanley considered placing it back in front of Zero's nose, but it wouldn't be the same.

It seemed like Zero had lived at Camp Green Lake forever, but as Stanley thought about it now, he realized that Zero must have gotten there no more than a month or two before him. Zero was actually arrested a day later. But Stanley's **trial** kept getting **delay**ed because of baseball.

He remembered what Zero had said a few days before. If Zero had just kept those shoes, then neither of them would be here right now.

As Stanley stared at the **glitter**ing night sky, he thought there was no place he would rather be. He was glad Zero put the shoes on the parked car. He was glad they fell from the **overpass** and hit him on the head.

When the shoes first fell from the sky, he remembered thinking that destiny had **struck** him. Now, he thought so again. It was more than a **coincidence**. It had to be destiny.

Maybe they wouldn't have to return to Camp Green Lake, he thought. Maybe they could make it past the camp, then follow the **dirt road** back to **civilization**. They could fill the **sack** with onions, and the three jars with water. And he had his **canteen** as well.

They could refill their jars and canteen at the camp. Maybe **sneak** into the kitchen and get some food.

He doubted any **counselor**s were still on guard. Everyone had to think they were dead. Buzzard food.

It would mean living the rest of his life as a **fugitive**. The police would always be after him. At least he could call his parents and tell them he was still alive. But he couldn't go visit them, in case the police were watching the apartment. Although, if everyone thought he was dead, they wouldn't **bother** to watch the apartment. He would have to somehow get a new **identity**.

Now, I'm really thinking crazy, he thought. He wondered if a crazy person wonders if he's crazy.

But even as he thought this, an even crazier idea kept **pop**ping into his head. He knew it was too crazy to even consider. Still, if he was going to be a fugitive for the rest of his life, it would help to have some money, perhaps a treasure **chest** full of money.

You're crazy! he told himself. Besides, just because he found a lipstick container with K B on it, that didn't mean there was treasure buried there.

It was crazy. It was all part of his crazy feeling of happiness.

Or maybe it was destiny.

He reached over and shook Zero's arm. "Hey, Zero," he

whispered.

"Huh?" Zero **mutter**ed.

"Zero, wake up."

"What?" Zero raised up his head. "What is it?"

"You want to dig one more hole?" Stanley asked him.

43

"We weren't always **homeless**," Zero said. "I remember a yellow room."

"How old were you when you . . ." Stanley started to ask, but couldn't find the right words. ". . . **move**d **out**?"

"I don't know. I must have been real little, because I don't remember too much. I don't remember moving out. I remember standing in a **crib**, with my mother singing to me. She held my **wrist**s and made my hands **clap** together. She used to sing that song to me. That one you sang . . . It was different, though . . ."

Zero spoke slowly, as if searching his brain for memories and **clue**s. "And then later I know we lived on the street, but I don't know why we left the house. I'm pretty sure it was a house, and not an apartment. I know my room was yellow."

It was late afternoon. They were resting in the shadow of the Thumb. They had spent the morning picking onions and putting them in the **sack**. It didn't take long, but long enough so that they had to wait another day before heading down the mountain.

They wanted to leave at the first hint of **daylight**, so they'd have plenty of time to make it to Camp Green Lake before dark. Stanley wanted to be sure he could find the right hole. Then, they would hide by it until everyone went to sleep.

They would dig for as long as it seemed safe, and not a second longer. And then, treasure or no treasure, they'd head up the **dirt road**. If it was absolutely safe, they'd try to steal some food and water from the camp kitchen.

"I'm good at **sneak**ing in and out of places," Zero had said.

"Remember," Stanley had warned. "The door to the Wreck Room **squeak**s."

Now he lay on his back, trying to save his strength for the long days ahead. He wondered what happened to Zero's parents, but he didn't ask. Zero didn't like answering questions. It was better to just let him talk when he felt like it.

Stanley thought about his own parents. In her last letter, his mom was worried that they might be **evict**ed from their apartment because of the smell of burning sneakers. They could easily become homeless as well.

Again, he wondered if they'd been told that he ran away from camp. Were they told that he was dead?

An image appeared in his head of his parents hugging

each other and crying. He tried not to think about it.

Instead he tried to **recapture** the feelings he'd had the night before—the **inexplicable** feeling of happiness, the sense of destiny. But those feelings didn't return.

He just felt scared.

The next morning they headed down the mountain. They'd **dunk**ed their caps in the water hole before putting them on their heads. Zero held the **shovel**, and Stanley carried the sack, which was **cram**med with onions and the three **jar**s of water. They left the pieces of the broken jar on the mountain.

"This is where I found the shovel," Stanley said, pointing out a **patch** of **weed**s.

Zero turned and looked up toward the top of the mountain. "That's a long way."

"You were light," Stanley said. "You'd already **thrown up** everything that was inside your stomach."

He shifted the sack from one shoulder to the other. It was heavy. He stepped on a loose rock, slipped, then fell hard. The next thing he knew he was sliding down the **steep** side of the mountain. He dropped the sack, and onions spilled around him.

He slid into a patch of weeds and grabbed onto a **thorny vine**. The vine **rip**ped out of the earth, but slowed him enough so that he was able to stop himself.

"Are you all right?" Zero asked from above.

Stanley **groan**ed as he pulled a **thorn** out of the palm of his hand. "Yeah," he said. He was all right. He was worried more about the jars of water.

Zero climbed down after him, **retrieving** the sack along the way. Stanley pulled some thorns out of his pant legs.

The jars hadn't broken. The onions had protected them, like Styrofoam packing material.* "Glad you didn't do that when you were carrying me," Zero said.

They'd lost about a third of the onions, but recovered many of them as they continued down the mountain. When they reached the bottom, the sun was just rising above the lake. They walked directly toward it.

Soon they stood on the edge of a **cliff**, looking down on the dry lake bed. Stanley wasn't sure, but he thought he could see the remains of the *Mary Lou* off in the distance.

"You thirsty?" Stanley asked.

"No," said Zero. "How about you."

"No," Stanley lied. He didn't want to be the first one to take a drink. Although they didn't mention it, it had become a kind of **challenge** between him and Zero.

They climbed down into the **frying pan**. It was a different spot from where they had climbed up. They **ease**d themselves down from one **ledge** to another, and let themselves slide in other places, being especially careful with the sack.

Stanley could no longer see the *Mary Lou*, but headed in what he thought was the right direction. As the sun rose,

---

★ stryrofoam packing material 스티로폼 포장재.

so did the familiar **haze** of heat and dirt.

"You thirsty?" Zero asked.

"No," said Stanley.

"Because you have three full jars of water," said Zero. "I thought maybe it was getting too heavy for you. If you drink some, it will **lighten** your load."

"I'm not thirsty," said Stanley. "But if you want a drink, I'll give you some."

"I'm not thirsty," said Zero. "I was just worried about you."

Stanley smiled. "I'm a **camel**," he said.

They walked for what seemed like a very long time, and still never came across the *Mary Lou*. Stanley was pretty sure they were heading in the right direction. He remembered that when they left the boat, they were headed toward the **set**ting sun. Now they were headed toward the rising sun. He knew the sun didn't rise and set exactly in the east and west; more southeast and southwest, but he wasn't sure how that made a difference.

His throat felt as if it was **coat**ed with sandpaper.* "You sure you're not thirsty?" he asked.

"Not me," said Zero. His voice was dry and **raspy**.

When they did finally take a drink, they agreed to do it at the same time. Zero, who was now carrying the sack, set it down and took out two jars, giving one to Stanley. They decided to save the canteen for last, since it couldn't

---

★ **sandpaper** 사포.

accidentally break.

"You know I'm not thirsty," Stanley said, as he **unscrew**ed the **lid**. "I'm just drinking so you will."

"I'm just drinking so you will," said Zero.

They **clink**ed the jars together and, each watching the other, poured the water into their **stubborn** mouths.

Zero was the first to spot the *Mary Lou*, maybe a quarter mile away, and just a little off to the right. They headed for it.

It wasn't even noon yet when they reached the boat. They sat against the **shady** side and rested.

"I don't know what happened to my mother," Zero said. "She left and never came back."

Stanley **peel**ed an onion.

"She couldn't always take me with her," Zero said. "Sometimes she had to do things by herself."

Stanley had the feeling that Zero was explaining things to himself.

"She'd tell me to wait in a certain place for her. When I was real little, I had to wait in small areas, like on a **porch** step or a doorway. 'Now don't leave here until I get back,' she'd say.

"I never liked it when she left. I had a stuffed animal, a little giraffe, and I'd hug it the whole time she was gone. When I got bigger I was allowed to stay in bigger areas. Like, 'Stay on this block.' Or, 'Don't leave the park.' But even then, I still held Jaffy."

Stanley guessed that Jaffy was the name of Zero's giraffe.

"And then one day she didn't come back," Zero said. His voice sounded suddenly hollow. "I waited for her at Laney Park."

"Laney Park," said Stanley. "I've been there."

"You know the playscape?*" asked Zero.

"Yeah. I've played on it."

"I waited there for more than a month," said Zero. "You know that tunnel that you **crawl** through, between the slide and the **swing**ing bridge?* That's where I slept."

They ate four onions **apiece** and drank about half a jar of water. Stanley stood up and looked around. Everything looked the same in all directions.

"When I left camp, I was heading straight toward Big Thumb," he said. "I saw the boat off to the right. So that means we have to turn a little to the left."

Zero was **lost in thought**. "What? Okay," he said.

They headed out. It was Stanley's turn to carry the sack.

"Some kids had a birthday party," Zero said. "I guess it was about two weeks after my mother left. There was a picnic table next to the playscape and balloons were tied to it. The kids looked to be the same age as me. One girl said hi to me and asked me if I wanted to play. I wanted to, but I didn't. I knew I didn't belong at the party, even though it wasn't their playscape. There was this one mother who kept

---

★ **playscape** 놀이터의 놀이 기구 세트.
⁎ **swinging bridge** 구름다리.

staring at me like I was some kind of monster. Then later a boy asked me if I wanted a piece of cake, but then that same mother told me, 'Go away!' and she told all the kids to stay away from me, so I never got the piece of cake. I ran away so fast, I forgot Jaffy."

"Did you ever find him—it?"

For a moment, Zero didn't answer. Then he said, "He wasn't real."

Stanley thought again about his own parents, how **awful** it would be for them to never know if he was dead or alive. He realized that was how Zero must have felt, not knowing what happened to his own mother. He wondered why Zero never mentioned his father.

"Hold on," Zero said, stopping abruptly. "We're going the wrong way."

"No, this is right," said Stanley.

"You were heading toward Big Thumb when you saw the boat off to your right," said Zero. "That means we should have turned right when we left the boat."

"You sure?"

Zero drew a **diagram** in the dirt.

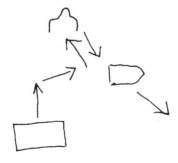

Stanley still wasn't sure.

"We need to go this way," Zero said, first drawing a line on the map and then heading that way himself.

Stanley followed. It didn't feel right to him, but Zero seemed sure.

Sometime in the middle of the afternoon, a cloud **drift**ed across the sky and blocked out the sun. It was a welcome relief. Once again, Stanley felt that destiny was on his side.

Zero stopped and held out his arm to stop Stanley, too.

"Listen," Zero whispered.

Stanley didn't hear anything.

They continued walking very quietly and Stanley began to make out the **faint** sounds of Camp Green Lake. They were still too far away to see the camp, but he could hear a **blend** of **indistinct** voices. As they got closer he **occasional**ly could hear Mr. Sir's **distinctive bark**.

They walked slowly and quietly, aware that sounds travel in both directions.

They approached a **cluster** of holes. "Let's wait here, until they go in," said Zero.

Stanley **nod**ded. He checked to make sure there was nothing living in it, then climbed down into a hole. Zero climbed into the one next to him.

Despite having gone the wrong way for a while, it hadn't taken them nearly as long as Stanley had expected. Now, they just had to wait.

The sun cut through the cloud, and Stanley felt its **ray**s

beating **down** on him. But soon more clouds filled the sky, shading Stanley and his hole.

He waited until he was certain the last of the campers had finished for the day.

Then he waited a little longer.

As quietly as possible, he and Zero climbed up out of their holes and **crept** toward camp. Stanley held the sack in front of him, cradled in his arms, instead of over his shoulder, to keep the jars from **clank**ing against each other. A wave of terror rushed over him when he saw the **compound**—the tents, the Wreck Room, the Warden's **cabin** under the two **oak** trees. The fear made him **dizzy**. He took a breath, **summon**ed his courage, and continued.

"That's the one," he whispered, pointing out the hole where he had found the gold tube. It was still about fifty yards away, but Stanley was pretty sure it was the right hole. There was no need to **risk** going any closer.

They climbed down into **adjacent** holes, and waited for the camp to fall asleep.

44

Stanley tried to sleep, not knowing when he'd get the chance again. He heard the showers and, later, the sounds of dinner. He heard the **creak**ing of the Wreck Room door. His fingers **drum**med against the side of the hole. He heard his own heart beat.

He took a drink from the **canteen**. He had given Zero the water **jar**s. They each had a good supply of onions.

He wasn't sure how long he remained in the hole, maybe five hours. He was surprised when he heard Zero whispering for him to wake up. He didn't think he'd fallen asleep. If he had, he thought it must have just been for the last five minutes. Although, when he opened his eyes, he was surprised how dark it was.

There was only one light on at camp, in the office. The sky was cloudy, so there was very little starlight. Stanley could see a sliver of a moon, which appeared and disappeared among the clouds.

He carefully led Zero to the hole, which was hard to find in the darkness. He **stumble**d over a small pile of dirt. "I think this is it," he whispered.

"You *think?*" Zero asked.

"It's it," said Stanley, sounding more certain than he really was. He climbed down. Zero handed him the **shovel**.

Stanley stuck the shovel into the dirt at the bottom of the hole and stepped on the back of the **blade**. He felt it sink beneath his weight. He **scoop**ed out some dirt and tossed it off to the side. Then he brought the shovel back down.

Zero watched for a while. "I'm going to try to refill the water jars," he said.

Stanley took a deep breath and **exhale**d. "Be careful," he said, then continued **dig**ging.

It was so dark, he couldn't even see the end of his shovel. For all he knew he could be digging up gold and diamonds instead of dirt. He brought each **shovelful** close to his face, to try to see if anything was there, before **dump**ing it out of the hole.

As he made the hole deeper, it became harder to lift the dirt up and out. It was five feet deep before he even started. He decided to use his efforts to make it wider instead.

This made more sense, he told himself. If Kate Barlow had buried a treasure **chest**, she probably wouldn't have been able to dig much deeper, so why should he?

Of course, Kate Barlow probably had a whole **gang** of **thieves** helping her.

"You want some breakfast?"

Stanley jumped at the sound of Zero's voice. He hadn't heard him approach.

Zero handed down a box of **cereal**. Stanley carefully poured some cereal into his mouth. He didn't want to put his dirty hands inside the box. He nearly **gag**ged on the ultra-sweet taste. They were sugar-**frost**ed **flake**s, and after eating nothing but onions for more than a week, he had trouble **adjust**ing to the flavor. He washed them down with a **swig** of water.

Zero **took over** the digging. Stanley **sift**ed his fingers through the fresh piles of dirt, in case he had missed anything. He wished he had a flashlight. A diamond no bigger than a **pebble** would be worth thousands of dollars. Yet there was no way he'd see it.

They finished the water that Zero had gotten from the **spigot** by the showers. Stanley said he'd go fill the jars again, but Zero insisted that he do it instead. "**No offense**, but you make too much noise when you walk. You're too big."

Stanley returned to the hole. As the hole grew wider, parts of the surface kept **caving in**. They were running out of room. To make it much wider, they would first have to move some of the surrounding dirt piles out of the way. He wondered how much time they had before the camp woke up.

"How's it going?" Zero asked when he returned with the water.

Stanley **shrug**ged one shoulder. He brought the shovel

down the side of the hole, shaving off a slice of the dirt wall. As he did so, he felt the shovel **bounce** off something hard.

"What was that?" Zero asked.

Stanley didn't know. He moved his shovel up and down the side of the hole. As the dirt **chip**ped and flaked away, the hard object became more **pronounced**.

It was **stick**ing **out** of the side of the hole, about a foot and a half from the bottom. He felt it with his hands.

"What is it?" Zero asked.

He could just feel a corner of it. Most of it was still buried. It had the cool, smooth texture of metal. "I think I might have found the treasure chest," he said. His voice was filled more with **astonishment** than with excitement.

"Really?" asked Zero.

"I think so," Stanley said.

The hole was wide enough for him to hold the shovel **lengthwise** and dig sideways into the wall. He knew he had to dig very carefully. He didn't want the side of the hole to **collapse**, along with the huge pile of dirt directly above it.

He **scrape**d at the dirt wall, until he exposed one entire side of the box-like object. He ran his fingers over it. It felt to be about eight inches tall, and almost two feet wide. He had no way of knowing how far into the earth it extended. He tried pulling it out, but it wouldn't **budge**.

He was afraid that the only way to get to it was to start back up at the surface, and dig down. They didn't have time for that.

"I'm going to try to dig a hole underneath it," he said. "Then maybe I can pull it down and slip it out."

"Go for it," said Zero.

Stanley **jam**med the shovel into the bottom edge of his hole, and carefully began to dig a tunnel underneath the metal object. He hoped it didn't cave in.

Occasionally he'd stop, **stoop** down, and try to feel the far end of the box. But even when the tunnel was as long as his arm, he still couldn't feel the other side.

Once again he tried pulling it out, but it was firmly in the ground. If he pulled too hard, he feared, he'd cause a cave-in. He knew that when he was ready to pull it out, he would have to do it quickly, before the ground above it collapsed.

As his tunnel grew deeper and wider—and more **precarious**—Stanley was able to feel **latch**es on one end of the box, and then a leather handle. It wasn't really a box. "I think it might be some kind of metal **suitcase**," he told Zero.

"Can you **pry** it loose with the shovel?" Zero suggested.

"I'm afraid the side of the hole will collapse."

"You **might as well** give it a try," said Zero.

Stanley took a **sip** of water. "Might as well," he said.

He forced the **tip** of the shovel between the dirt and the top of the metal case and tried to **wedge** it free. He wished he could see what he was doing.

He worked the end of the shovel, back and forth, up and down, until he felt the suitcase fall free. Then he felt the dirt come piling down on top of it.

But it wasn't a huge cave-in. As he **knelt** down in the hole, he could tell that only a small portion of the earth had collapsed.

He dug with his hands until he found the leather handle, and then he pulled the suitcase up and out of the dirt. "I got it!" he **exclaim**ed.

It was heavy. He handed it up to Zero.

"You did it," Zero said, taking it from him.

"*We* did it," said Stanley.

He gathered his remaining strength, and tried to pull himself up out of the hole. Suddenly, a bright light was shining in his face.

"Thank you," said the Warden. "You boys have been a big help."

45

The **beam** of the flashlight was directed away from Stanley's eyes and onto Zero, who was sitting on his knees. The **suitcase** was on his **lap**.

Mr. Pendanski was holding the flashlight. Mr. Sir stood next to him with his gun drawn and pointed in the same direction. Mr. Sir was **barefoot** and **bare-chested**, wearing only his **pajama** bottoms.

The Warden moved toward Zero. She was also in her bed clothes, wearing an extra-long T-shirt. Unlike Mr. Sir, however, she had on her boots.

Mr. Pendanski was the only one fully dressed. Perhaps he had been on guard duty.

Off in the distance, Stanley could see two more flashlights **bob**bing toward them in the darkness. He felt **helpless** in the hole.

"You boys arrived just **in the nick**—" the Warden started to say. She stopped talking and she stopped walking.

Then she slowly backed away.

A **lizard** had crawled up on top of the suitcase. Its big red eyes glowed in the beam of the flashlight. Its mouth was open, and Stanley could see its white tongue moving in and out between its black teeth.

Zero sat as still as a **statue**.

A second lizard crawled up over the side of the suitcase and stopped less than an inch away from Zero's little finger.

Stanley was afraid to look, and afraid not to. He wondered if he should try to **scramble** out of the hole before the lizards turned on him, but he didn't want to cause any **commotion**.

The second lizard crawled across Zero's fingers and halfway up his arm.

It occurred to Stanley that the lizards were probably on the suitcase when he handed it to Zero.

"There's another one!" **gasp**ed Mr. Pendanski. He shined the flashlight on the box of Frosted Flakes, which lay on its side beside Stanley's hole. A lizard was crawling out of it.

The light also **illuminate**d Stanley's hole. He **glance**d downward and had to force himself to **suppress** a scream. He was standing in a lizard nest. He felt the scream **explode** inside him.

He could see six lizards. There were three on the ground, two on his left leg, and one on his right **sneaker**.

He tried to remain very still. Something was crawling up the back of his neck.

Three other counselors approached the area. Stanley

heard one say, "What's going—" and then whisper, "Oh my God."

"What do we do?" asked Mr. Pendanski.

"We wait," said the Warden. "It won't be very long."

"At least we'll have a body to give that woman," said Mr. Pendanski.

"She's going to ask a lot of questions," said Mr. Sir. "And this time she'll have the A.G. with her."

"Let her ask her questions," said the Warden. "Just so long as I have the suitcase, I don't care what happens. Do you know how long . . ." Her voice **trail**ed **off**, then started up again. "When I was little I'd watch my parents dig holes, every weekend and holiday. When I got bigger, I had to dig, too. Even on Christmas."

Stanley felt tiny **claw**s dig into the side of his face as the lizard pulled itself off his neck and up past his **chin**.

"It won't be long now," the Warden said.

Stanley could hear his heart beat. Each beat told him he was still alive, at least for one more second.

chapter forty-five

46

Five hundred seconds later, his heart was still beating.

Mr. Pendanski screamed. The lizard which had been in the **cereal** box was **spring**ing toward him.

Mr. Sir shot it in **midair**.

Stanley felt the **blast shatter** the air around him. The lizards **scurried frantic**ally across his very still body. He did not **flinch**. A lizard ran across his closed mouth.

He glanced at Zero and Zero's eyes met his. Somehow they were both still alive, at least for one more second, one more heartbeat.

Mr. Sir lit a **cigarette**.

"I thought you quit," said one of the other **counselor**s.

"Yeah, well, sometimes sunflower seeds just won't cut it.★" He took a long **drag** on his cigarette. "I'm going to have **nightmare**s the rest of my life."

★ **not cut it** 필요한만큼 좋지 않다. 'cut'은 '자르다'라는 뜻 외에도 '해내다, 맞추다'라는 뜻을 가지고 있다.

"Maybe we should just shoot them," suggested Mr. Pendanski.

"Who?" asked a counselor. "The lizards or the kids?"

Mr. Pendanski laughed **grim**ly. "The kids are going to die anyway." He laughed again. "At least we got plenty of **grave**s to choose from."

"We've got time," said the Warden. "I've waited this long, I can wait another few . . ." Her voice **trail**ed **off**.

Stanley felt a lizard crawl in and out of his pocket.

"We're going to keep our story simple," said the Warden. "That woman's going to ask a lot of questions. The A.G. will most likely **initiate** an **investigation**. So this is what happened: Stanley tried to run away in the night, fell in a hole, and the lizards got him. That's it. We're not even going to give them Zero's body. As far as anybody knows, Zero doesn't exist. Like Mom said, we got plenty of graves to choose from."

"Why would he run away if he knew he was getting **release**d today?" asked Mr. Pendanski.

"Who knows? He's crazy. That was why we couldn't release him yesterday. He was **delirious**, and we had to keep watch over him so he wouldn't hurt himself or anybody else."

"She's not going to like it," said Mr. Pendanski.

"She's not going to like anything we tell her," said the Warden. She stared at Zero and at the suitcase. "Why aren't you dead yet?" she asked.

Stanley only half listened to the talk of the counselors. He didn't know who "that woman" was or what "A.G."

meant. He didn't even realize they were initials. It sounded like one word, "Age-ee." His mind was focused on the tiny **claw**s that moved up and down his skin and through his hair.

He tried to think about other things. He didn't want to die with the images of the Warden, Mr. Sir, and the lizards **etch**ed into his brain. Instead, he tried to see his mother's face.

His brain took him back to a time when he was very little, all **bundle**d **up** in a snowsuit.* He and his mother were walking, **hand in hand, mitten** in mitten, when they both slipped on some ice and fell and rolled down a snow-covered hillside. They ended up at the bottom of the hill. He remembered he almost cried, but instead he laughed. His mother laughed, too.

He could feel the same light-headed feeling he felt then, **dizzy** from rolling down the hill. He felt the sharp coldness of the snow against his ear. He could see **fleck**s of snow on his mother's bright and **cheery** face.

This was where he wanted to be when he died.

"Hey, Caveman, guess what?" said Mr. Sir. "You're **innocent**, after all. I thought you'd like to know that. Your lawyer came to get you yesterday. Too bad you weren't here."

The words meant nothing to Stanley, who was still in the snow. He and his mother climbed back up the hill and rolled down again, this time on purpose. Later they had hot chocolate with lots of melted marshmallows.*

★ **snowsuit** 방한복.

✱ **marshmallow** 마시멜로. 녹말·시럽·설탕·젤라틴 등으로 만들어, 씹으면 쫄깃쫄깃한 과자.

"It's getting close to 4:30," said Mr. Pendanski. "They'll be waking up."

The Warden told the counselors to return to the tents. She told them to give the campers breakfast and to make sure they didn't talk to anyone. As long as they did as they were told, they wouldn't have to dig any more holes. If they talked, they would be **severe**ly **punish**ed.

"How should we say they will be punished?" one of the counselors asked.

"Let them use their imaginations," said the Warden.

Stanley watched the counselors return to the tents, leaving only the Warden and Mr. Sir behind. He knew the Warden didn't care whether the campers dug any more holes or not. She'd found what she was looking for.

He glanced at Zero. A lizard was **perch**ed on his shoulder.

Zero remained perfectly still except for his right hand, which slowly formed into a **fist**. Then he raised his thumb, giving Stanley the **thumbs-up** sign.

Stanley thought back to what Mr. Sir had said to him earlier, and the bits of conversation he'd **overhear**d. He tried to make sense out of it. Mr. Sir had said something about a lawyer, but Stanley knew his parents couldn't **afford** a lawyer.

His legs were **sore** from remaining **rigid** for so long. Standing still was more **strenuous** than walking. He slowly allowed himself to lean against the side of the hole.

The lizards didn't seem to mind.

47

The sun was up, and Stanley's heart was still beating. There were eight lizards in the hole with him. Each one had exactly eleven yellow spots.

The Warden had dark circles under her eyes from **lack** of sleep, and lines across her **forehead** and face which seemed **exaggerate**d in the **stark** morning light. Her skin looked **blotchy**.

"Satan," said Zero.

Stanley looked at him, **unsure** if Zero had even spoken or if he'd just imagined it.

"Why don't you go see if you can take the suitcase from Zero," the Warden suggested.

"Yeah, right," said Mr. Sir.

"The lizards obviously aren't hungry," said the Warden.

"Then you go get the suitcase," said Mr. Sir.

They waited.

"Sa-tan lee," said Zero.

Sometime later Stanley saw a tarantula* **crawl** across the dirt, not too far from his hole. He had never seen a tarantula before, but there was no doubt what it was. He was **momentarily fascinate**d by it, as its big hairy body moved slowly and steadily along.

"Look, a tarantula," said Mr. Sir, also fascinated.

"I've never seen one," said the Warden. "Except in—"

Stanley suddenly felt a sharp **sting** on the side of his neck.

The lizard hadn't bitten him, however. It was **merely** pushing off.

It **leap**t off Stanley's neck and **pounce**d on the tarantula. The last Stanley saw of it was one hairy leg **stick**ing **out** of the lizard's mouth.

"Not hungry, huh?" said Mr. Sir.

Stanley tried to return to the snow, but it was harder to get there when the sun was up.

As the sun rose, the lizards moved lower in the hole, keeping mainly in the **shade**. They were no longer on his head and shoulders but had moved down to his stomach, legs, and feet.

He couldn't see any lizards on Zero, but believed there

★ tarantula 독거미의 일종.

were two, between Zero's knees, shaded from the sun by the suitcase.

"How are you doing?" Stanley asked quietly. He didn't whisper, but his voice was dry and **raspy**.

"My legs are **numb**," said Zero.

"I'm going to try to climb out of the hole," Stanley said.

As he tried to pull himself up, using just his arms, he felt a **claw** dig into his **ankle**. He gently **ease**d himself back down.

"Is your last name your first name backward?" Zero asked.

Stanley stared at him in **amazement**. Had he been working on that all night?

He heard the sound of approaching cars.

Mr. Sir and the Warden heard it as well.

"You think it's them?" asked the Warden.

"It ain't Girl Scouts selling cookies," said Mr. Sir.

He heard the cars come to a stop, and the doors open and shut. A little while later he saw Mr. Pendanski and two strangers, coming across the lake. One was a tall man in a business suit and cowboy hat. The other was a short woman holding a **briefcase**. The woman had to take three steps for every two taken by the man. "Stanley Yelnats?" she called, moving out ahead of the others.

"I suggest you don't come any closer," said Mr. Sir.

"You can't stop me," she **snap**ped, then took a second glance at him, wearing **pajama** pants and nothing else. "We'll get you out of there, Stanley," she said. "Don't you worry." She appeared to be Hispanic, with straight black hair and dark eyes. She spoke with a little bit of a Mexican accent, trilling her r's.★

"What in tarnation?" the tall man **exclaim**ed, as he came up behind her.

She turned on him. "I'm telling you right now, if any harm comes to him, we will be **filing charge**s not only against Ms. Walker and Camp Green Lake but the entire state of Texas as well. Child **abuse**. False **imprison**ment.☀ **Torture**."

The man was more than a head taller than she, and was able to look directly over her as he spoke to the Warden.

"How long have they been in there?"

"All night, as you can see by the way we're dressed. They **snuck** into my **cabin** while I was asleep, and stole my suitcase. I chased after them, and they ran out here and fell into the lizards' nest. I don't know what they were thinking."

"That's not true!" Stanley said.

"Stanley, as your **attorney**, I advise you not to say anything," said the woman, "until you and I have had a chance to talk in private."

Stanley wondered why the Warden lied about the suitcase. He wondered who it **legal**ly belonged to. That was one thing he wanted to ask his lawyer, if she really was his lawyer.

★ trill the r r을 떨리게 발음하다.
☀ false imprisonment 불법 감금.

"It's a miracle they're still alive," said the tall man.

"Yes, it is," the Warden agreed, with just a **trace** of disappointment in her voice.

"And they better come out of this alive," Stanley's lawyer warned. "This wouldn't have happened if you'd **released** him to me yesterday."

"It wouldn't have happened if he wasn't a **thief**," said the Warden. "I told him he would be set free today, and I guess he decided he'd try to take some of my valuables with him. He's been **delirious** for the last week."

"Why didn't you release him when she came to you yesterday?" the tall man asked.

"She didn't have **proper authorization**," said the Warden.

"I had a court order!*"

"It was not **authenticated**," the Warden said.

"Authenticated? It was signed by the judge who **sentenced** him."

"I needed authentication from the Attorney General," said the Warden. "How do I know it's **legitimate**? The boys in my **custody** have proven themselves dangerous to society. Am I supposed to just turn them loose any time someone hands me a piece of paper?"

"Yes," said the woman. "If it's a court order."

"Stanley has been **hospitalized** for the last few days," the Warden explained. "He's been suffering from **hallucinations** and **delirium**. **Rant**ing and **raving**. He was in no condition

---

★ court order 법원의 명령.

to leave. The fact that he was trying to steal from me on the day before his release proves . . ."

Stanley tried to climb out of his hole, using mostly his arms so as not to disturb the lizards too much. As he pulled himself upward, the lizards moved downward, keeping out of the sun's direct **ray**s. He **swung** his legs up and over, and the last of the lizards **hop**ped off.

"Thank God!" exclaimed the Warden. She started toward him, then stopped.

A lizard crawled out of his pocket and down his leg.

Stanley was **overcome** by a rush of **dizziness** and almost fell over. He **steadied** himself, then reached down, took hold of Zero's arm, and helped him slowly to his feet. Zero still held the suitcase.

The lizards, which had been hiding under it, **scurried** quickly into the hole.

Stanley and Zero **stagger**ed away.

The Warden rushed to them. She hugged Zero. "Thank God, you're alive," she said, as she tried to take the suitcase from him.

He **jerk**ed it free. "It belongs to Stanley," he said.

"Don't cause any more trouble," the Warden warned. "You stole it from my cabin, and you've been **caught red-handed**. If I **press charges**, Stanley might have to return to prison. Now I'm willing, in view of all the circumstances, to—"

"It's got his name on it," said Zero.

Stanley's lawyer pushed past the tall man to have a look.

"See," Zero showed her. "Stanley Yelnats."

Stanley looked, too. There, in big black letters, was STANLEY YELNATS.

The tall man looked over the heads of the others at the name on the suitcase. "You say he stole it from your cabin?"

The Warden stared at it in **disbelief**. "That's im . . . imposs . . . It's imposs . . ." She couldn't even say it.

48

They slowly walked back to camp. The tall man was the Texas Attorney General, the chief **law enforcement** officer for the state. Stanley's lawyer was named Ms. Morengo.

Stanley held the **suitcase**. He was so tired he couldn't think straight. He felt as if he was walking in a dream, not quite able to **comprehend** what was going on around him.

They stopped in front of the camp office. Mr. Sir went inside to get Stanley's belongings. The Attorney General told Mr. Pendanski to get the boys something to drink and eat.

The Warden seemed as **daze**d as Stanley. "You can't even read," she said to Zero.

Zero said nothing.

Ms. Morengo put a hand on Stanley's shoulder and told him to **hang in there**. He would be seeing his parents soon.

She was shorter than Stanley, but somehow gave the appearance of being tall.

Mr. Pendanski returned with two **carton**s of orange juice and two bagels.* Stanley drank the juice but didn't feel like eating anything.

"Wait!" the Warden **exclaim**ed. "I didn't say they stole the suitcase. It's his suitcase, obviously, but he put my things from my **cabin** inside it."

"That isn't what you said earlier," said Ms. Morengo.

"What's in the suitcase?" the Warden asked Stanley. "Tell us what's in it, then we'll open it and see!"

Stanley didn't know what to do.

"Stanley, as your lawyer, I advise you not to open your suitcase," said Ms. Morengo.

"He has to open it!" said the Warden. "I have the right to check the personal property of any of the **detainee**s. How do I know there aren't **drug**s or weapons in there? He stole a car, too! I've got **witness**es!" She was nearly **hysterical**.

"He is no longer under your **jurisdiction**," said Stanley's lawyer.

"He has not been officially **release**d," said the Warden. "Open the suitcase, Stanley!"

"Do not open it," said Stanley's lawyer.

Stanley did nothing.

Mr. Sir returned from the office with Stanley's backpack and clothes.

The Attorney General handed Ms. Morengo a sheet of

★ **bagel** 베이글. 밀가루·이스트·물·소금으로 만든 도넛같이 생긴 **빵**. 주로 아침 식사로 많이 먹는다.

paper. "You're free to go," he said to Stanley. "I know you're **anxious** to get out of here, so you can just keep the orange suit as a **souvenir**. Or burn it, whatever you want. Good luck, Stanley."

He reached out his hand to shake, but Ms. Morengo hurried Stanley away. "C'mon, Stanley," she said. "We have a lot to talk about."

Stanley stopped and turned to look at Zero. He couldn't just leave him here.

Zero gave him **thumbs-up**.

"I can't leave Hector," Stanley said.

"I suggest we go," said his lawyer with a sense of **urgency** in her voice.

"I'll be okay," said Zero. His eyes shifted toward Mr. Pendanski on one side of him, then to the Warden and Mr. Sir on the other.

"There's nothing I can do for your friend," said Ms. Morengo. "You are released **pursuant** to an order from the judge."

"They'll kill him," said Stanley.

"Your friend is not in danger," said the Attorney General. "There's going to be an **investigation** into everything that's happened here. For the present, I am taking **charge** of the camp."

"C'mon, Stanley," said his lawyer. "Your parents are waiting."

Stanley stayed where he was.

His lawyer sighed. "May I have a look at Hector's file?"

she asked.

"Certainly," said the Attorney General. "Ms. Walker, go get Hector's file."

She looked at him **blank**ly.

"Well?"

The Warden turned to Mr. Pendanski. "Bring me Hector Zeroni's file."

He stared at her.

"Get it!" she ordered.

Mr. Pendanski went into the office. He returned a few minutes later and announced the file was apparently **misplace**d.

The Attorney General was **outrage**d. "What kind of camp are you running here, Ms. Walker?"

The Warden said nothing. She stared at the suitcase.

The Attorney General assured Stanley's lawyer that he would get the records. "Excuse me, while I call my office." He turned back to the Warden. "I **assume** the phone works." He walked into the camp office, **slam**ming the door behind him. A little while later he reappeared and told the Warden he wanted to talk to her.

She **curse**d, then went inside.

Stanley gave Zero thumbs-up.

"Caveman? Is that you?"

He turned to see Armpit and Squid coming out of the Wreck Room. Squid shouted back into the Wreck Room, "Caveman and Zero are out here!"

Soon all the boys from Group D had gathered around

him and Zero.

"Good to see you, man," Armpit said, shaking his hand. "We thought you were buzzard food."

"Stanley is being released today," said Mr. Pendanski.

"**Way to go**," said Magnet, hitting him on the shoulder.

"And you didn't even have to step on a **rattlesnake**," said Squid.

Even Zigzag shook Stanley's hand. "Sorry about . . . you know."

"It's cool," said Stanley.

"We had to lift the truck clear out of the hole," Zigzag told him. "It took everybody in C, D, and E. We just picked it right up."

"It was really cool," said Twitch.

X-Ray was the only one who didn't come over. Stanley saw him hang back behind the others a moment, then return to the Wreck Room.

"Guess what?" said Magnet, **glancing** at Mr. Pendanski. "Mom says we don't have to **dig** any more holes."

"That's great," Stanley said.

"Will you do me a favor?" asked Squid.

"I guess," Stanley agreed, somewhat **hesitant**ly.

"I want you to—" He turned to Ms. Morengo. "Hey, lady, you have a pen and paper I can borrow?"

She gave it to him, and Squid wrote down a phone number which he gave to Stanley. "Call my mom for me, okay? Tell her . . . Tell her I said I was sorry. Tell her *Alan* said he was sorry."

Stanley promised he would.

"Now you be careful out in the real world," said Armpit. "Not everybody is as nice as us."

Stanley smiled.

The boys departed when the Warden came out of the office. The Attorney General was right behind her.

"My office is having some difficulty locating Hector Zeroni's records," the Attorney General said.

"So you have no claim of authority over him?" asked Ms. Morengo.

"I didn't say that. He's in the computer. We just can't access his records. It's like they've fallen through a hole in cyberspace."

"A hole in cyberspace," Ms. Morengo repeated. "How interesting. When is his release date?"

"I don't know."

"How long has he been here?"

"Like I said, we can't—"

"So what are you planning to do with him? Keep him confined indefinitely, without justification, while you go crawling through black holes in cyberspace?"

The Attorney General stared at her. "He was obviously incarcerated for a reason."

"Oh? And what reason was that?"

The Attorney General said nothing.

Stanley's lawyer took hold of Zero's hand. "C'mon, Hector, you're coming with us."

49

There never used to be yellow-**spotted lizard**s in the town of Green Lake. They didn't come to the area until after the lake dried up. But the **townsfolk** had heard about the "red-eyed monsters" living in the **desert** hills.

One afternoon, Sam, the onion man, and his **donkey**, Mary Lou, were returning to his boat, which was **anchor**ed just a little off **shore**. It was late in November and the peach trees had lost most of their leaves.

"Sam!" someone called.

He turned around to see three men running after him, waving their hats. He waited. "Afternoon, Walter. Bo, Jesse," he greeted them, as they walked up, catching their breath.

"Glad we caught you," said Bo. "We're going rattlesnake hunting in the morning."

"We want to get some of your lizard juice," said Walter.

"I ain't a-scared of no rattlesnake," said Jesse. "But I don't want to come across one of those red-eyed monsters. I seen one once, and that was enough. I knew about the red eyes, of course. I hadn't heard about the big black teeth."

"It's the white tongues that get me," said Bo.

Sam gave each man two bottles of pure onion juice. He told them to drink one bottle before going to bed that night, then a half bottle in the morning, and then a half bottle around lunchtime.

"You sure this **stuff** works?" asked Walter.

"I tell you what," said Sam. "If it doesn't, you can come back next week and I'll give you your money back."

Walter looked around **unsure**, as Bo and Jesse laughed. Then Sam laughed, too. Even Mary Lou let out a rare hee-haw.

"Just remember," Sam told the men before they left. "It's very important you drink a bottle tonight. You got to get it into your **bloodstream**. The lizards don't like onion blood."

Stanley and Zero sat in the backseat of Ms. Morengo's BMW. The suitcase lay between them. It was locked, and they decided they'd let Stanley's father try to open it in his **workshop**.

"You don't know what's in it, do you?" she asked.

"No," said Stanley.

"I didn't think so."

The **air-conditioning** was on, but they drove with the windows open as well, because, "**No offense**, but you boys really smell bad."

Ms. Morengo explained that she was a **patent attorney**.

"I'm helping your father with the new product he's invented. He happened to mention your situation, so I did a little **investigating**. Clyde Livingston's **sneaker**s were stolen sometime before 3:15. I found a young man, Derrick Dunne, who said that at 3:20 you were in the bathroom **fish**ing your notebook out of the toilet. Two girls remembered seeing you come out of the boys' restroom carrying a wet notebook."

Stanley felt his ears **redden**. Even after everything he'd been through, the memory still caused him to feel **shame**.

"So you couldn't have stolen them," said Ms. Morengo.

"He didn't. I did," said Zero.

"You did what?" asked Ms. Morengo.

"I stole the sneakers."

The lawyer actually turned around while driving and looked at him. "I didn't hear that," she said. "And I advise you to make sure I don't hear it again."

"What did my father invent?" Stanley asked. "Did he find a way to **recycle** sneakers?"

"No, he's still working on that," explained Ms. Morengo. "But he invented a product that **eliminate**s foot **odor**. Here, I've got a sample in my **briefcase**. I wish I had more. You two could **bathe** in it."

She opened her briefcase with one hand and passed a small bottle back to Stanley. It had a fresh and somewhat spicy smell. He handed it to Zero.

"What's it called?" Stanley asked.

"We haven't come up with a name yet," said Ms. Morengo.

"It smells familiar," said Zero.

"Peaches, right?" asked Ms. Morengo. "That's what everyone says."

A short while later both boys fell asleep. Behind them the sky had turned dark, and for the first time in over a hundred years, a drop of rain fell into the empty lake.

PART THREE

FILLING IN THE HOLES

50

Stanley's mother insists that there never was a **curse**. She even doubts whether Stanley's great-great-grandfather really stole a pig. The reader might find it interesting, however, that Stanley's father invented his **cure** for foot **odor** the day after the great-great-grandson of Elya Yelnats carried the great-great-great-grandson of Madame Zeroni up the mountain.

The Attorney General closed Camp Green Lake. Ms. Walker, who was in desperate need of money, had to sell the land which had been in her family for **generation**s. It was bought by a national organization **dedicate**d to the well-being of young girls. In a few years, Camp Green Lake will become a Girl Scout camp.

This is pretty much the end of the story. The reader probably still has some questions, but unfortunately, from here on in, the answers tend to be long and **tedious**. While Mrs. Bell, Stanley's former math teacher, might want to know the percent change in Stanley's weight, the reader probably cares more about the change in Stanley's **character** and **self-confidence**. But those changes are **subtle** and hard to measure. There is no simple answer.

Even the contents of the **suitcase** turned out to be somewhat tedious. Stanley's father **pried** it open in his **workshop**, and at first everyone **gasp**ed at the **sparkling** jewels. Stanley thought he and Hector had become **millionaire**s. But the jewels were of poor quality, worth no more than twenty thousand dollars.

Underneath the jewels was a **stack** of papers that had once belonged to the first Stanley Yelnats. These consisted of **stock certificate**s, **deed**s of **trust**, and promissory notes.* They were hard to read and even more difficult to understand. Ms. Morengo's law firm* spent more than two months going through all the papers.

They turned out to be a lot more valuable than the jewels. After **legal** fees and taxes, Stanley and Zero each received less than a million dollars.

But not a lot less.

It was enough for Stanley to buy his family a new house, with a **laboratory** in the **basement**, and for Hector to hire a

---

★ **promissory note** 약속어음. 발행인이 소지인에 대하여 일정기일에 일정금액을 지급할 것을 약속하는 어음.
✳ **law firm** 법률 사무소.

team of private investigators.*

But it would be boring to go through all the tedious details of all the changes in their lives. Instead, the reader will be presented with one last scene, which took place almost a year and a half after Stanley and Hector left Camp Green Lake.

You will have to fill in the holes yourself.

There was a small party at the Yelnats house. Except for Stanley and Hector, everyone there was an adult. All kinds of snacks and drinks were set out on the counter, including caviar,* champagne, and the fixings* to make ice cream sundaes.

The Super Bowl* was on television, but nobody was really watching.

"It should be coming on at the next break," Ms. Morengo announced.

A **time-out** was called in the football game, and a **commercial** came on the screen.

Everyone stopped talking and watched.

The commercial showed a baseball game. **Amid** a cloud of dust, Clyde Livingston slid into home plate as the **catcher** caught the ball and tried to tag him out.*

★ **private investigator** 사립 탐정.
✳ **caviar** 캐비아. 철갑상어 알을 소금에 절인 식품.
✳ **fixings** 특별한 요리·만찬에 곁들이는 음식. 여기에서는 아이스크림에 올리는 토핑이라고 보면 된다.
★ **Super Bowl** 미국 프로 미식축구의 우승팀을 결정하는 경기.
✳ **tag out** [야구] 터치아웃. 공을 잡은 손을 주자의 몸에 터치하여 아웃시키는 것.

"Safe!" shouted the **umpire** as he signaled with his arms.

The people at Stanley's house cheered, as if the run really **count**ed.

Clyde Livingston got up and dusted the dirt off his uniform. As he made his way back to the dugout,[*] he spoke to the camera. "Hi, I'm Clyde Livingston, but everyone around here calls me 'Sweet Feet.'"

"**Way to go**, Sweet Feet!" said another baseball player, **slap**ping his hand.

Besides being on the television screen, Clyde Livingston was also sitting on the **couch** next to Stanley.

"But my feet weren't always sweet," the television Clyde Livingston said as he sat down on the dugout bench. "They used to smell so bad that nobody would sit near me in the dugout."

"They really did **stink**," said the woman sitting on the couch on the other side of Clyde. She held her nose with one hand, and **fan**ned the air with the other.

Clyde **shush**ed her.

"Then a teammate told me about Sploosh," said the television Clyde. He pulled a can of Sploosh out from under the dugout bench and held it up for everyone to see. "I just spray a little on each foot every morning, and now I really do have sweet feet. Plus, I like the **tingle**."

"Sploosh," said a voice. "A **treat** for your feet. Made from all natural **ingredient**s, it **neutralize**s odor-causing **fungi** and

---

★ **dugout** 경기가 진행되는 동안 감독, 선수, 코치들이 대기하는 장소.

bacteria. Plus, you'll like the tingle."

Everyone at the party **clap**ped their hands.

"He wasn't lying," said the woman who sat next to Clyde. "I couldn't even be in the same room with his socks."

The other people at the party laughed.

The woman continued. "I'm not joking. It was so bad—"

"You've made your point," said Clyde, covering her mouth with his hand. He looked back at Stanley. "Will you do me a favor, Stanley?"

Stanley raised and lowered his left shoulder.

"I'm going to get more caviar," said Clyde. "Keep your hand over my wife's mouth." He **pat**ted Stanley on the shoulder as he rose from the couch.

Stanley looked **uncertain**ly at his hand, then at Clyde Livingston's wife.

She winked at him.

He felt himself **blush**, and turned away toward Hector, who was sitting on the floor in front of an **overstuffed** chair.

A woman sitting in the chair behind Hector was **absent-mindedly fluff**ing his hair with her fingers. She wasn't very old, but her skin had a **weathered** look to it, almost like leather. Her eyes seemed **weary**, as if she'd seen too many things in her life that she didn't want to see. And when she smiled, her mouth seemed too big for her face.

Very softly, she half sang, half **hum**med a song that her grandmother used to sing to her when she was a little girl.

If only, if only, the moon speaks no reply;

Reflecting the sun and all that's gone by.
*Be strong my weary wolf, turn around **boldly**.*
Fly high, my baby bird,
My angel, my only.

HOLES

HOLES

1판 1쇄 2012년 4월 2일
2판 4쇄 2025년 1월 20일

지은이 Louis Sachar
기획 이수영
책임편집 김보경 차소향
콘텐츠제작및감수 롱테일 교육 연구소
저작권 명채린
마케팅 두잉글 사업본부

펴낸이 이수영
펴낸곳 롱테일북스
출판등록 제2015-000191호
주소 04033 서울특별시 마포구 양화로 113, 3층(서교동, 순흥빌딩)
전자메일 help@ltinc.net

이 도서는 대한민국에서 제작되었습니다.

ISBN 979-11-91343-98-4 14740

HOLES

LOUIS SACHAR

WORKBOOK

Contents

'아동 도서계의 노벨상!' 미국 최고 권위의 아동 문학상

뉴베리 상(Newbery Award)은 미국 도서관 협회에서 해마다 미국 아동 문학 발전에 가장 크게 이바지한 작가에게 수여하는 아동 문학상입니다. 1922년에 시작된이 상은 미국에서 가장 오랜 역사를 지닌 아동 문학상이자, '아동 도서계의 노벨상'이라 불릴 만큼 높은 권위를 자랑하는 상입니다.

뉴베리 상은 그 역사와 권위만큼이나 심사 기준이 까다롭기로 유명한데, 심사단은 책의 주제 의식은 물론 정보의 깊이와 스토리의 정교함, 캐릭터와 문체의 적정성 등을 꼼꼼히 평가하여 수상작을 결정합니다.

그해 최고의 작품으로 선정된 도서에게는 '뉴베리 메달(Newbery Medal)'이라고 부르는 금색 메달을 수여하며, 최종 후보에 올랐던 주목할 만한 작품들에게는 '뉴베리 아너(Newbery Honor)'라는 이름의 은색 마크를 수여합니다.

뉴베리 상을 받은 도서는 미국의 모든 도서관에 비치되어 더 많은 독자들을 만나게 되며, 대부분 수십에서 수백만 부가 판매되는 베스트셀러가 됩니다. 뉴베리 상을 수상한 작가는 그만큼 필력과 작품성을 인정받게 되어, 수상 작가의 다른 작품들 또한 수상작 못지않게 커다란 주목과 사랑을 받습니다.

왜 뉴베리 수상작인가?
쉬운 어휘로 쓰인 '검증된' 영어원서!

뉴베리 수상작들은 '검증된 원서'로 국내 영어 학습자들에게 큰 사랑을 받고 있습니다. 뉴베리 수상작이 원서 읽기에 좋은 교재인 이유는 무엇일까요?

1. 아동 문학인 만큼 어휘가 어렵지 않습니다.
2. 어렵지 않은 어휘를 사용하면서도 '문학상'을 수상한 만큼 문장의 깊이가 상당합니다.
3. 적당한 난이도의 어휘와 깊이 있는 문장으로 구성되어 있기 때문에 초등 고학년부터 성인까지, 영어 초보자부터 실력자까지 모든 영어 학습자들이 읽기에 좋습니다.

실제로 뉴베리 수상작은 국제중·특목고에서는 입시 필독서로, 대학교에서는 영어 강독 교재로 다양하고 폭넓게 활용되고 있습니다. 이런 이유로 뉴베리 수상작은 한국어 번역서보다 오히려 원서가 훨씬 많이 판매되는 기현상을 보이고 있습니다.

'베스트 오브 베스트'만을 엄선한 「뉴베리 컬렉션」

「뉴베리 컬렉션」은 뉴베리 메달 및 아너 수상작, 그리고 뉴베리 수상 작가의 유명 작품들을 엄선하여 한국 영어 학습자들을 위한 최적의 교재로 재탄생시킨 영어 원서 시리즈입니다.

1. 어휘 수준과 문장의 난이도, 분량 등 국내 영어 학습자들에게 적합한 정도를 종합적으로 검토하여 선정하였습니다.
2. 기존 원서 독자층 사이의 인기도까지 감안하여 최적의 작품들을 선별하였습니다.
3. 판형이 좁고 글씨가 작아 읽기 힘들었던 원서 디자인을 대폭 수정하여, 판형을 시원하게 키우고 읽기에 최적화된 영문 서체를 사용하여 가독성을 극대화하였습니다.
4. 함께 제공되는 워크북은 어려운 어휘를 완벽하게 정리하고 이해력을 점검하는 퀴즈를 덧붙여 독자들이 원서를 보다 쉽고 재미있게 읽을 수 있도록 구성하였습니다.
5. 기존에 높은 가격에 판매되어 구입이 부담스러웠던 오디오북을 부록으로 제공하여 리스닝과 소리 내어 읽기에까지 원서를 두루 활용할 수 있도록 했습니다.

루이스 새커(Louis Sachar)는 현재 미국에서 가장 인기 있는 아동 문학 작가 중 한 사람입니다. 그는 1954년 미국 뉴욕에서 태어났으며 초등학교 보조 교사로 일한 경험을 바탕으로 쓴 「Wayside School」 시리즈로 잘 알려져 있습니다. 그 외에도 그는 「Marvin Redpost」 시리즈, 「There's a Boy in the Girls' Bathroom」, 「The Boy Who Lost His Face」 등 20여 권의 어린이책을 썼습니다. 그가 1998년에 발표한 「Holes」는 독자들의 큰 사랑을 받으며 전미도서상 등 많은 상을 수상하였고, 마침내 1999년에는 뉴베리 메달을 수상하였습니다. 2006년에는 「Holes」의 후속편 「Small Steps」를 출간하였습니다.

「Holes」는 고조할아버지 때부터 대대로 전해져 내려오는 '저주'에 걸린 주인공 스탠리(Stanley)의 이야기입니다. 그 저주 때문에 스탠리는 자신이 저지르지 않은 범죄로 인해 Camp Green Lake에 보내지게 됩니다. 말썽을 부린 소년들을 수용하는 Camp Green Lake. 이곳에서 소년들이 하는 일은 매일 커다란 구덩이를 파는 일입니다. 뚱뚱하고 학교에서는 따돌림을 당하던 스탠리는 비참한 상황 속에서 오히려 자신의 잠재력에 눈을 뜨고, 성장해 나갑니다. 그리고 이곳에서 친구 제로(Zero)를 만납니다.
구덩이를 파는 일, 대대손손 이어지는 가문의 저주. 언뜻 보기에 서로 상관없어 보이는 사건들이 하나의 이야기로 이어지는 순간, 독자들은 퍼즐 조각이 하나씩 맞춰지는 즐거움을 느끼며 탄성을 내뱉게 됩니다. 이렇게 탄탄한 구성력을 가진 「Holes」를 지금 영어로 읽어 보세요.

원서 본문

내용이 담긴 원서 본문입니다.
원어민이 읽는 일반 원서와 같은 텍스트지만,
암기해야 할 중요 어휘들은 볼드체로 표시되
어 있습니다. 이 어휘들은 지금 들고 계신 워
크북에 챕터별로 정리되어 있습니다.

학습 심리학 연구 결과에 따르면, 한 단어씩
따로 외우는 단어 암기는 거의 효과가 없다고
합니다. 단어를 제대로 외우기 위해서는 문맥
(context) 속에서 단어를 암기해야 하며, 한 단
어당 문맥 속에서 15번 이상 마주칠 때 완벽하
게 암기할 수 있다고 합니다.

이 책의 본문에서는 중요 어휘를 볼드체로 강조하여, 문맥 속의 단어들을 더 확
실히 인지(word cognition in context)하도록 돕고 있습니다. 또한 대부분의 중요 단
어들은 다른 챕터에서도 반복해서 등장하기 때문에 이 책을 읽는 것만으로도 자
연스럽게 어휘력을 향상시킬 수 있습니다.

또한 본문 하단에는 내용 이해를 돕기 위한
'각주'가 첨가되어 있습니다. 각주는 굳이 암기
할 필요는 없지만, 알아 두면 도움이 될 만한
정보를 설명하고 있습니다. 각주를 참고하면
스토리를 더 깊이 있게 이해할 수 있어 원서
를 읽는 재미가 배가됩니다.

워크북(Workbook)

Check Your Reading Speed
해당 챕터의 단어 수가 기록되어 있어, 리딩 속도를 측정할 수 있습니다. 특히 리딩 속도를 중시하는 독자들이 유용하게 사용할 수 있습니다.

Build Your Vocabulary
본문에 볼드 표시되어 있는 단어들이 정리되어 있습니다. 리딩 전·후에 반복해서 보면 원서를 더욱 쉽게 읽을 수 있고, 어휘력도 빠르게 향상될 것입니다.

단어는 〈스펠링 – 빈도 – 발음기호 – 품사 – 한글 뜻 – 영문 뜻〉 순서로 표기되어 있으며 빈도 표시(★)가 많을수록 필수 어휘입니다. 반복해서 등장하는 단어는 빈도 대신 '복습'으로 표기되어 있습니다. 품사는 아래와 같이 표기했습니다.

n. 명사 │ a. 형용사 │ ad. 부사 │ vi. 자동사 │ vt. 타동사 │ v. 자·타동사 모두 쓰이는 동사
conj. 접속사 │ prep. 전치사 │ int. 감탄사 │ phrasal v. 구동사 │ idiom 숙어 및 관용구

Comprehension Quiz
간단한 퀴즈를 통해 읽은 내용에 대한 이해력을 점검해 볼 수 있습니다.

「뉴베리 컬렉션」 이렇게 읽어 보세요!

아래와 같이 프리뷰(Preview) → 리딩(Reading) → 리뷰(Review) 세 단계를 거치면서 읽으면, 더욱 효과적으로 영어 실력을 향상할 수 있습니다.

1. 프리뷰(Preview) : 오늘 읽을 내용을 먼저 점검하자!

• 워크북을 통해 오늘 읽을 챕터에 나와 있는 단어들을 쭉 훑어봅니다. 어떤 단어들이 나오는지, 내가 아는 단어와 모르는 단어는 어떤 것들이 있는지 가벼운 마음으로 살펴봅니다.

• 평소처럼 하나하나 쓰면서 암기하려고 하지는 마세요! 익숙하지 않은 단어들을 주의 깊게 보되, 어차피 리딩을 하면서 점차 익숙해질 단어라는 것을 기억하며 빠르게 훑어봅니다.

• 뒤 챕터로 갈수록 '복습'이라고 표시된 단어들이 늘어나는 것을 알 수 있습니다. '복습' 단어인데도 여전히 익숙하지 않다면 더욱 신경을 써서 봐야겠죠? 매일매일 꾸준히 읽는다면, 익숙한 단어들이 점점 많아진다는 것을 몸으로 느낄 수 있습니다.

2. 리딩(Reading) : 내용에 집중하며 빠르게 읽어 나가자!

• 프리뷰를 마친 후 바로 리딩을 시작합니다. 방금 살펴봤던 어휘들을 문장 속에서 다시 만나게 되는데, 이 과정에서 단어의 쓰임새와 어감을 자연스럽게 익히게 됩니다.

• 모르는 단어나 이해되지 않는 문장이 나오더라도 멈추지 말고 전체적인 맥락을 파악하면서 속도감 있게 읽어 나가세요. 이해되지 않는 문장들은 따로 표시를 하되, 일단 넘어가고 계속 읽는 것이 좋습니다. 뒷부분을 읽다 보면 자연히 이해가 되는 경우도 있고, 정 이해가 되지 않는 부분은 리딩을 마친 이후에 따로 리뷰하는 시간을 가지면 됩니다. 문제집을 풀듯이 모든 문장을 분석하면서 원서를 읽는 것이 아니라, 리딩을 할 때는 리딩에만, 리뷰를 할 때는 리뷰에만 집중하는 것이 필요합니다.

• 볼드 처리된 단어의 의미가 궁금하더라도 워크북을 바로 펼치지 마세요. 정 궁금하다면 한 번씩 참고하는 것도 나쁘진 않지만, 워크북과 원서를 번갈아 보면서 읽는 것은 리딩의 흐름을 끊고 단어 하나하나에 집착하는 좋지 않은 리딩 습관을 심어 줄 수 있습니다.

• 같은 맥락에서 번역서를 구해 원서와 동시에 번갈아 보는 것도 좋은 방법이 아닙니다. 한글 번역을 가지고 있다고 해도 일단 영어로 읽을 때는 영어에만 집중하고 어느 정도 분량을 읽은 후에 번역서와 비교하도록 하세요. 모든 문장을 일일이 번역해서 완벽하게 이해하려는 것은 오히려 좋지 않은 리딩 습관을 심

어 주어 장기적으로는 바람직하지 않은 결과를 얻을 수 있습니다. 처음부터 완벽하게 이해하려고 하는 것보다는 빠른 속도로 2-3회 반복해서 읽는 방식이 실력 향상에 더 도움이 됩니다. 만일 반복해서 읽어도 내용이 전혀 이해되지 않아 곤란하다면 책 선정에 문제가 있다고 할 수 있습니다. 그럴 때는 좀 더 쉬운 책을 골라 실력을 다진 뒤 다시 도전하는 것이 좋습니다.

• 초보자라면 분당 150단어의 리딩 속도를 목표로 잡고 리딩을 합니다. 분당 150단어는 원어민이 말하는 속도로, 영어 학습자들이 리스닝과 스피킹으로 넘어가기 위해 가장 기초적으로 달성해야 하는 단계입니다. 분당 50-80단어 정도의 낮은 리딩 속도를 가지고 있는 경우는 대부분 영어 실력이 부족해서라기보다 '잘못된 리딩 습관'을 가지고 있어서 그렇습니다. 이해력이 조금 떨어진다고 하더라도 분당 150단어까지는 속도에 대한 긴장감을 놓치지 말고 속도감 있게 읽어 나가도록 하세요.

3. 리뷰(Review) : 이해력을 점검하고 꼼꼼하게 다시 살펴보자!

• 해당 챕터의 Comprehension Quiz를 통해 이해력을 점검해 봅니다.
• 오늘 만난 어휘들을 다시 한번 복습합니다. 이때는 읽으면서 중요하다고 생각했던 단어를 연습장에 써 보면서 꼼꼼하게 외우는 것도 좋습니다.
• 이해가 되지 않는다고 표시해 두었던 부분도 주의 깊게 분석해 봅니다. 다시 한번 문장을 꼼꼼히 읽고, 어떤 이유에서 이해가 되지 않았는지 생각해 봅니다. 따로 메모를 남기거나 노트를 작성하는 것도 좋은 방법입니다.
• 사실 꼼꼼히 리뷰하는 것은 매우 고된 과정입니다. 원서를 읽고 리뷰하는 시간을 가지는 것이 영어 실력 향상에 많은 도움이 되기는 하지만, 이 과정을 철저히 지키려다가 원서 읽기의 재미를 반감시키는 것은 바람직하지 않습니다. 그럴 때는 차라리 리뷰를 가볍게 하는 것이 좋을 수 있습니다. '내용에 빠져서 재미있게', 문제집에서는 상상도 못할 '많은 양'을 읽으면서, 매일매일 조금씩 꾸준히 실력을 키워 가는 것이 원서를 활용하는 기본적인 방법이며, 영어 공부의 왕도입니다. 문제집 풀듯이 원서 읽기를 시도하고 접근해서는 실패할 수밖에 없습니다.
• 이런 방식으로 원서를 끝까지 다 읽었다면, 다시 반복해서 읽거나 오디오북을 활용하는 등 다양한 방식으로 원서 읽기를 확장해 나갈 수 있습니다. 이에 대한 자세한 안내가 워크북 말미에 실려 있습니다.

1. What is the worst thing that could happen to you at Camp Green Lake?
   A. You could be bitten by a rattlesnake.
   B. You could be stung by a scorpion.
   C. You could fall into a deep hole.
   D. You could be bitten by a yellow-spotted lizard.

2. Camp Green Lake is for _____.
   A. bad boys
   B. children who cannot afford summer camp
   C. children who want to learn about nature
   D. girls and boys who have broken the law

3. What was true about Stanley?
   A. He had stolen a pig from a gypsy.
   B. He was an inventor.
   C. He was innocent of the crime for which he was convicted.
   D. He was very lucky.

4. What happened to Stanley's great-grandfather?
   A. He lost all his money in the stock market.
   B. He lived in a giant mansion on a beach in California.
   C. He found a use for old sneakers.
   D. He was robbed by an outlaw.

5. Which of the following is NOT true?
   A. Campers must dig a hole five feet deep and five feet across.
   B. If campers find anything interesting, they must report it to a counselor.
   C. Campers do not have to finish their hole by a specific time.
   D. Campers will be supervised by a counselor at all times.

6. Why doesn't Camp Green Lake have a fence around it?
   A. No camper could survive outside the camp without water.
   B. Mr. Sir will shoot any camper who runs away.
   C. A lake surrounds the camp.
   D. Mr. Sir wants campers to run away.

1분에 몇 단어를 읽는지 리딩 속도를 측정해보세요.

$$\frac{305 \ words}{reading \ time \ (\qquad) \ sec} \times 60 = (\qquad) \ WPM$$

Build Your Vocabulary

wasteland
[wéistlæ̀nd]

n. 황무지, 불모지
A wasteland is an area of land on which not much can grow or which has been spoiled in some way.

shrivel*
[ʃrívəl]

v. 쪼글쪼글해지다; 쪼글쪼글하게 만들다
When something shrivels or when something shrivels it, it becomes dryer and smaller, often with lines in its surface, as a result of losing the water it contains.

daytime**
[déitàim]

n. 낮 (시간), 주간
The daytime is the part of a day between the time when it gets light and the time when it gets dark.

hover**
[hʌ́vər]

v. 계속 맴돌다; 공중을 맴돌다; 서성이다
If a something such as a price, value, or score hovers around a particular level, it stays at more or less that level and does not change much.

degree***
[digríː]

n. (온도 단위인) 도; 정도, 등급
A degree is a unit of measurement that is used to measure temperatures.

shade***
[ʃeid]

n. (시원한) 그늘; 색조; **vt.** 그늘지게 하다
Shade is an area of darkness under or next to an object such as a tree, where sunlight does not reach.

oak***
[óuk]

n. 오크 나무
An oak or an oak tree is a large tree that often grows in woods and forests and has strong, hard wood.

log**
[lɔ́ːg]

n. 통나무
A log is a piece of a thick branch or of the trunk of a tree that has been cut so that it can be used for fuel or for making things.

cabin***
[kǽbin]

n. (통나무) 오두막집; 객실, 선실
A cabin is a small wooden house, especially one in an area of forests or mountains.

forbid**
[fərbíd]

v. 금하다, 허락하지 않다 (forbidden **a.** 금지된)
If you forbid someone to do something, or if you forbid an activity, you order that it must not be done.

rattlesnake*
[rǽtlsnèik]

n. [동물] 방울뱀
A rattlesnake is a poisonous American snake which can make a rattling noise with its tail.

14

scorpion* [skɔ́:rpiən]

n. [동물] 전갈
A scorpion is a small creature which looks like a large insect. Scorpions have a long curved tail, and some of them are poisonous.

dig** [díg]

v. (dug–dug) (구멍 등을) 파다; 뒤지다; n. 발굴
If people or animals dig, they make a hole in the ground or in a pile of earth, stones, or rubbish.

bother** [báðər]

v. 귀찮게 하다; 신경 쓰이게 하다, 괴롭히다; 일부러 ~하다, 애를 쓰다
If someone bothers you, they talk to you when you want to be left alone or interrupt you when you are busy.

spotted [spátid]

a. 얼룩무늬의; 물방울무늬가 있는
Something that is spotted has a pattern of spots on it.

lizard [lízərd]

n. 도마뱀
A lizard is a reptile with short legs and a long tail.

might as well

idiom ~하는 편이 낫다
If you say that you might as well do something, or that you may as well do it, you mean that you will do it although you do not have a strong desire to do it and may even feel slightly unwilling to do it.

Check Your Reading Speed

1분에 몇 단어를 읽는지 리딩 속도를 측정해보세요.

$$\frac{95 \text{ words}}{\text{reading time ( ) sec}} \times 60 = (\qquad) \text{ WPM}$$

Build Your Vocabulary

dig^{복습}
[díg]

v. (구멍 등을) 파다; 뒤지다; n. 발굴
If people or animals dig, they make a hole in the ground or in a pile of earth, stones, or rubbish.

jail**
[dʒeil]

n. 교도소, 감옥
A jail is a place where criminals are kept in order to punish them, or where people waiting to be tried are kept.

1분에 몇 단어를 읽는지 리딩 속도를 측정해보세요.

$$\frac{1,105 \text{ words}}{\text{reading time (\quad) sec}} \times 60 = (\quad) \text{ WPM}$$

Build Your Vocabulary

passenger***
[pǽsəndʒər]

n. 승객
A passenger in a vehicle such as a bus, boat, or plane is a person who is traveling in it, but who is not driving it or working on it.

count***
[káunt]

v. 포함시키다; 세다, 계산하다; 중요하다; (정식으로) 인정되다; **n.** 계산, 셈
If you count all the things in a group, you add them up in order to find how many there are.

face***
[féis]

v. ~을 마주보다, 향하다; 직면하다; 직시하다
If someone or something faces a particular thing, person, or direction, they are positioned opposite them or are looking in that direction.

rifle**
[ráifl]

① **n.** 라이플총 ② **vt.** 샅샅이 뒤지다; 강탈하다
A rifle is a gun with a long barrel.

lap**
[læp]

① **n.** 무릎; (경주에서 트랙의) 한 바퀴 ② **v.** (물이) 찰랑거리다; 할짝할짝 핥다
If you have something on your lap, it is on top of your legs and near to your body.

handcuff
[hǽndkʌf]

vt. ~에게 수갑을 채우다; **n.** 수갑, 쇠고랑
If you handcuff someone, you put handcuffs around their wrists.

armrest
[á:rmrèst]

n. (비행기나 자동차 좌석의) 팔걸이
The armrests on a chair are the two pieces on either side that support your arms when you are sitting down.

toothbrush*
[tú:θbrʌʃ]

n. 칫솔
A toothbrush is a small brush that you use for cleaning your teeth.

toothpaste
[tú:θpèist]

n. 치약
Toothpaste is a thick substance which you put on your toothbrush and use to clean your teeth.

stationery*
[stéiʃənèri]

n. 문구류, 문방구
Stationery is paper, envelopes, and other materials or equipment used for writing.

hay**
[hei]

n. 건초, 말린 풀
Hay is grass which has been cut and dried so that it can be used to feed animals.

cotton***
[kátn]

n. 목화; 면직물
Cotton is a type of cloth made from soft fibers from a particular plant.

air-conditioned
[ɛ́ər-kəndíʃənd]

a. 냉난방[공기 조절] 장치를 한
If a room or vehicle is air-conditioned, the air in it is kept cool and dry by means of a special machine.

stifling
[stáifliŋ]

a. (공기 등이) 숨 막힐 듯한, 답답한
Stifling heat is so intense that it makes you feel uncomfortable.

stuff***
[stʌ́f]

vt. 채워 넣다, 속을 채우다; n. 일[것](일반적으로 말하거나 생각하는 것);
물건, 물질 (stuffed a. 속을 채운)
If you stuff a container or space with something, you fill it with something or with a quantity of things until it is full.

marble**
[má:rbl]

n. (아이들이 가지고 노는) 구슬; 대리석
A marble is one of the small balls used in the game of marbles.

obstacle**
[ábstəkl]

n. 장애(물), 방해(물)
An obstacle is an object that makes it difficult for you to go where you want to go, because it is in your way.

rubber**
[rʌ́bər]

n. 고무; a. 고무의 (rubber band n. 고무줄)
Rubber is a strong, waterproof, elastic substance made from the juice of a tropical tree or produced chemically.

overweight*
[óuvərwèit]

a. 과체중의, 비만의; 중량 초과의
Someone who is overweight weighs more than is considered healthy or attractive.

tease**
[ti:z]

v. 놀리다, 장난하다; n. 장난, 놀림
To tease someone means to laugh at them or make jokes about them in order to embarrass, annoy, or upset them.

cruel**
[krú:əl]

a. 잔인한, 잔혹한, 무자비한
Someone who is cruel deliberately causes pain or distress to people or animals.

ratio*
[réiʃou]

n. 비율, 비
A ratio is a relationship between two things when it is expressed in numbers or amounts.

unaware*
[ʌnəwer]

a. 알지 못하는
If you are unaware of something, you do not know about it.

embarrass**
[embǽrəs]

v. 부끄럽게[무안하게] 하다; 어리둥절하게 하다; 당황하다
(embarrassment n. 당황, 당혹)
If something or someone embarrasses you, they make you feel shy or ashamed.

arrest***
[ərést]

vt. 체포하다, 저지하다; (주의 · 이목 · 흥미 등을) 끌다; n. 체포, 검거, 구속
If the police arrest you, they take charge of you and take you to a police station, because they believe you may have committed a crime.

slump*
[slʌmp]

v. 털썩 앉다; (가치 · 수량 · 가격 등이) 급감[급락]하다; n. 급감, 급락; 폭락
If you slump somewhere, you fall or sit down there heavily, for example because you are very tired or you feel ill.

18

innocent**
[ínəsnt]

a. 잘못이 없는, 결백한; 순진한
Innocent people are those who are not involved in a crime or conflict, but are injured or killed as a result of it.

convict*
[kənvíkt]

vt. 유죄를 선고하다, 유죄 판결을 내리다
If someone is convicted of a crime, they are found guilty of that crime in a law court.

one-legged
[wʌ́n-légid]

a. 다리가 하나인, 외다리의
one (형용사: 하나의) + legged (형용사: ~개의 다리가 있는)

curse**
[kəːrs]

n. 저주, 악담; vt. 저주하다, 욕설을 퍼붓다
If you say that there is a curse on someone, you mean that there seems to be a supernatural power causing unpleasant things to happen to them.

descendant**
[diséndənt]

n. 자손, 후예
Someone's descendants are the people in later generations who are related to them.

vast***
[væ(ɑ:)st]

a. 광대한, 거대한
Something that is vast is extremely large.

wire***
[wáiər]

n. 전선, (전화기 등의) 선; 철사
A wire is a cable which carries power or signals from one place to another.

gruff
[grʌf]

a. (목소리가) 걸걸한
A gruff voice sounds low and rough.

woodpecker*
[wúdpèkəːr]

n. [조류] 딱따구리
A woodpecker is a type of bird with a long sharp beak. Woodpeckers use their beaks to make holes in tree trunks.

bark***
[bɑːrk]

① n. 나무껍질 ② v. (개가) 짖다; 고함치다; n. 짖는 소리
Bark is the tough material that covers the outside of a tree.

howl**
[hául]

v. 울다, 울부짖다; n. 울부짖음
If you howl something, you say it in a very loud voice.

bump**
[bʌmp]

n. (도로의) 튀어나온 부분; 혹; v. 덜컹거리며 가다; (쾅하고) 부딪치다
A bump on a road is a raised, uneven part.

alert**
[əlɔ́ːrt]

a. 경계하는; n. 경보, 경계; v. 경고하다
If you are alert, you are paying full attention to things around you and are able to deal with anything that might happen.

inventor**
[invéntər]

n. 발명가, 발명자; 고안자
An inventor is a person who has invented something, or whose job is to invent things.

intelligence**
[intélədʒəns]

n. 지성, 지능, 정보
Intelligence is the quality of being intelligent or clever.

perseverance**
[pəːrsivírəns]

n. 인내(심)
Perseverance is the quality of continuing with something even though it is difficult.

experiment*
[ekspérimənt]

n. (과학적인) 실험; v. 실험하다
An experiment is a scientific test which is done in order to discover what happens to something in particular conditions.

frontward
[frʌ́ntwərd]

a. 정면을 향하는, 앞쪽으로의; ad. 전방으로
front (명사: 앞쪽) + ward (접미사: ~으로 향함)

awful*
[ɔ́:fəl]

a. 지독한, 대단한; 무서운
If you say that something is awful, you mean that it is extremely unpleasant, shocking, or bad.

point out

phrasal v. ~을 지적하다
If you point out a fact or mistake, you tell someone about it or draw their attention to it.

discourage*
[diskə́:ridʒ]

vt. 낙담시키다, 용기를 잃게 하다 (discouraged a. 낙담한, 낙심한)
If someone or something discourages you, they cause you to lose your enthusiasm about your actions.

fortune*
[fɔ́:rtʃən]

n. 재산, 부; 운, 행운
You can refer to a large sum of money as a fortune or a small fortune to emphasize how large it is.

stock*
[sták]

n. 주식; 재고품, 저장품
Stocks are shares in the ownership of a company, or investments on which a fixed amount of interest will be paid.

neglect*
[niglékt]

vt. 무시하다, 등한시하다; n. 태만, 소홀
If you neglect someone or something, you fail to give them the amount of attention that they deserve.

befall*
[bifɔ́:l]

v. (befell–befallen) 안 좋은 일이 닥치다
If something bad or unlucky befalls you, it happens to you.

stagecoach
[stéidʒkòutʃ]

n. 역마차, 승합 마차
Stagecoaches were large carriages pulled by horses which carried passengers and mail.

rob*
[ráb]

v. 빼앗다, 도둑질하다
If someone is robbed, they have money or property stolen from them.

outlaw
[áutlɔ̀:]

n. 범법자; vt. 불법화하다, 금지하다
An outlaw is a criminal who is hiding from the authorities.

mansion*
[mǽnʃən]

n. 대저택, 저택
A mansion is a very large house.

cram*
[kræm]

v. (좁은 공간 속으로 억지로) 밀어 넣다
If you cram things into a container or place, you put them into it, although there is hardly enough room for them.

odor*
[óudər]

n. (불쾌한) 냄새, 악취 (foot odor n. 발냄새)
An odor is a particular and distinctive smell.

recycle
[ri:sáikl]

v. 재활용하다; 재순환하다
If you recycle things that have already been used, such as bottles or sheets of paper, you process them so that they can be used again.

sneaker
[sníːkər]

n. (pl.) 고무창 운동화
Sneakers are casual shoes with rubber soles.

increasingly*
[inkríːsiŋli]

ad. 점점 더, 갈수록 더
You can use increasingly to indicate that a situation or quality is becoming greater in intensity or more common.

bumpy
[bʌ́mpi]

a. (길이) 울퉁불퉁한, 평탄치 않은
A bumpy road or path has a lot of bumps on it.

pave**
[péiv]

v. (길을) 포장하다; 덮다; n. 포장길
If a road or an area of ground has been paved, it has been covered with flat blocks of stone or concrete, so that it is suitable for walking or driving on.

strand*
[strænd]

① v. 오도 가도 못 하게 하다, 발을 묶다 ② n. (실·전선·머리카락 등의) 가닥, 끈 줄
If you are stranded, you are prevented from leaving a place, for example because of bad weather.

desert**
[dézərt]

① n. 사막, 황무지 ② v. 인적이 끊기다; 버리다, 유기하다
A desert is a large area of land, usually in a hot region, where there is almost no water, rain, trees, or plants.

grunt*
[grʌnt]

vi. (사람이) 툴툴거리다; (돼지가) 꿀꿀거리다; n. 꿀꿀[툴툴]거리는 소리
If you grunt, you make a low sound, especially because you are annoyed or not interested in something.

Check Your Reading Speed

1분에 몇 단어를 읽는지 리딩 속도를 측정해보세요.

$$\frac{1,054 \text{ words}}{\text{reading time ( ) sec}} \times 60 = (\quad) \text{ WPM}$$

Build Your Vocabulary

daze**
[déiz]

vt. 멍하게 하다; 현혹시키다; **n.** 멍한 상태; 눈이 부심 (dazed **a.** 멍한)
If someone is dazed, they are confused and unable to think clearly, often because of shock or a blow to the head.

handcuff^{복습}
[hǽndkʌf]

n. 수갑, 쇠고랑; vt. ~에게 수갑을 채우다
Handcuffs are two metal rings which are joined together and can be locked round someone's wrists, usually by the police during an arrest.

sweat**
[swét]

n. 땀; v. 땀 흘리다; 습기가 차다
Sweat is the salty colorless liquid which comes through your skin when you are hot, ill, or afraid.

wrist**
[rist]

n. 손목
Your wrist is the part of your body between your hand and your arm which bends when you move your hand.

barren**
[bǽrən]

a. 불모의, 메마른
A barren landscape is dry and bare, and has very few plants and no trees.

desolate**
[désəlit]

a. 황폐한, 황량한, 쓸쓸한
A desolate place is empty of people and lacking in comfort.

rundown
[rʌ́ndáun]

a. 허물어져 가는; (기계 등이) 멈춘, 선; 지친
A rundown building or area is in very poor condition.

cabin^{복습}
[kǽbin]

n. (통나무) 오두막집; 객실, 선실
A cabin is a small wooden house, especially one in an area of forests or mountains.

weed**
[wíːd]

n. 잡초; v. 잡초를 없애다
A weed is a wild plant that grows in gardens or fields of crops and prevents the plants that you want from growing properly.

juvenile*
[dʒúːvənàil]

a. 청소년의; 유치한, 미숙한; n. 청소년
A juvenile is a child or young person who is not yet old enough to be regarded as an adult.

correctional
[kərékʃənl]

a. (범죄자에 대한) 교정[처벌]의
Correctional means related to the punishment and rehabilitation of criminals.

22

facility‡‡
[fəsíləti]

n. 시설, 설비; 편의, 쉬움
Facilities are buildings, pieces of equipment, or services that are provided for a particular purpose.

violation‡
[vàiəléiʃən]

n. 위반, 위배; 방해, 침해
Violation is a crime less serious than a felony.

penal‡
[píːnl]

a. (법에 따라) 처벌할 수 있는, 형사상의
Penal means relating to the punishment of criminals.

explosive‡
[iksplóusiv]

n. 폭발물, 폭약; a. 폭발하는, 폭발적인
An explosive is a substance or device that can cause an explosion.

drug‡‡
[drʌg]

n. 마약; 약; v. 약을 먹이다
Drugs are substances that some people take because of their pleasant effects, but which are usually illegal.

alcohol‡‡
[ǽlkəhɔ́ːl]

n. 술, 알코올
Drinks that can make people drunk, such as beer, wine, and whisky, can be referred to as alcohol.

premise‡
[prémis]

n. (pl.) (한 사업체가 소유 · 사용하는 건물이 딸린) 부지, 구내; [논리] 전제
The premises of a business or an institution are all the buildings and land that it occupies in one place.

air-conditioning
[ɛ́ər-kəndíʃəníŋ]

n. (건물 · 자동차의) 에어컨 (장치)
Air-conditioning is a method of providing buildings and vehicles with cool dry air.

sight‡‡
[sait]

n. 보기, 봄; 시력, 시야
The sight of something is the act of seeing it or an occasion on which you see it.

sack‡‡‡
[sæk]

n. 부대, 자루; (쇼핑 물건을 담는 크고 튼튼한 종이) 봉지; vt. 자루에 넣다
Sacks are used to carry or store things such as vegetables or coal.

tattoo
[tætúː]

n. 문신
A tattoo is a design that is drawn on someone's skin using needles to make little holes and filling them with colored dye.

rattlesnake복습
[rǽtlsnèik]

n. [동물] 방울뱀
A rattlesnake is a poisonous American snake which can make a rattling noise with its tail.

rattle‡‡
[rǽtl]

n. 방울뱀의 꼬리; 덜거덕거리는 소리; v. 왈각달각 소리 나다, 덜걱덜걱 움직이다
A rattle is the series of horny structures at the end of a rattlesnake's tail.

wiggle
[wígl]

v. (몸을) 뒤흔들다, (좌우로) 움직이다; n. 뒤흔듦
If you wiggle something or if it wiggles, it moves up and down or from side to side in small quick movements.

refrigerator‡
[rifrídʒərèitəːr]

n. 냉장고
A refrigerator is a large container which is kept cool inside, usually by electricity, so that the food and drink in it stays fresh.

produce***
[prədjúːs]

v. (~에서) 꺼내 보이다, 보여 주다; 생산하다; n. 생산물
If you produce an object from somewhere, you show it or bring it out so that it can be seen.

grumble**
[grʌ́mbl]

v. 투덜거리다, 불평하다; n. 투덜댐, 불평
If someone grumbles, they complain about something in a bad-tempered way.

miserable**
[mízərəbəl]

a. 비참한, 초라한, 불쌍한
If you describe a place or situation as miserable, you mean that it makes you feel unhappy or depressed.

spit**
[spit]

v. 뱉다, 내뿜다; (폭언 등을) 내뱉다; n. 침
If you spit liquid or food somewhere, you force a small amount of it out of your mouth.

wastepaper basket

n. (= wastebasket) 휴지통
A wastepaper basket is a container for rubbish, especially paper, which is usually placed on the floor in the corner of a room or next to a desk.

sneaker^{복습}
[sníːkər]

n. (pl.) 고무창 운동화
Sneakers are casual shoes with rubber soles.

canteen
[kæntíːn]

n. (휴대용) 물통; (공장·학교 등의) 구내식당
A canteen is a small plastic bottle for carrying water and other drinks. Canteens are used by soldiers.

sew**
[sóu]

v. (sewed–sewn/sewed) 바느질하다, 꿰매다, 깁다
When you sew something such as clothes, you make them or repair them by joining pieces of cloth together by passing thread through them with a needle.

protection**
[prətékʃən]

n. 보호
To give or be protection against something unpleasant means to prevent people or things from being harmed or damaged by it.

relaxation*
[riːlækséiʃən]

n. 휴식; (규제 등의) 완화
Relaxation is a way of spending time in which you rest and feel comfortable.

laundry**
[lɔ́ːndri]

n. 세탁물; 세탁
Laundry is used to refer to clothes, sheets, and towels that are about to be washed, are being washed, or have just been washed.

dig^{복습}
[díg]

v. (구멍 등을) 파다; 뒤지다; n. 발굴
If people or animals dig, they make a hole in the ground or in a pile of earth, stones, or rubbish.

shovel**
[ʃʌ́vəl]

n. 삽; v. ~을 삽으로 뜨다[파다], 삽으로 일하다
A shovel is a tool with a long handle that is used for lifting and moving earth, coal, or snow.

baby-sit
[béibi-sit]

v. (남의 아이를) 봐주다
If you baby-sit for someone or baby-sit their children, you look after their children while they are out.

counselor[**]
[káunsələr]

n. (캠프 생활의) 지도원; 상담역, 카운슬러
A counselor is a person whose job is to give advice to people who need it, especially advice on their personal problems.

nod[***]
[nɔd]

v. 끄덕이다, 끄덕여 표시하다; n. 끄덕임(동의 · 인사 · 신호 · 명령)
If you nod, you move your head downwards and upwards to show agreement, understanding, or approval.

blaze[**]
[bleiz]

vi. 타오르다; n. 불꽃, 화염, 섬광
If something blazes with light or color, it is extremely bright.

vast[복습]
[væ(ɑ:)st]

a. 광대한, 거대한
Something that is vast is extremely large.

wasteland[복습]
[wéistlænd]

n. 황무지, 불모지
A wasteland is an area of land on which not much can grow or which has been spoiled in some way.

unsure
[ʌnʃuər]

a. 확신하지 못하는, 의심스러워하는
If you are unsure about something, you feel uncertain about it.

tap[**]
[tæp]

① v. 가볍게 두드리다; n. 가볍게 두드리기 ② n. 주둥이, (수도 등의) 꼭지
If you tap something, you hit it with a quick light blow or a series of quick light blows.

holster
[hóulstər]

n. 권총용 가죽 케이스; vt. 권총용 가죽 케이스에 넣다
A holster is a holder for a small gun, which is worn on a belt around someone's waist or on a strap around their shoulder.

spotted[복습]
[spátid]

a. 얼룩무늬의; 물방울무늬가 있는
Something that is spotted has a pattern of spots on it.

lizard[복습]
[lízərd]

n. 도마뱀
A lizard is a reptile with short legs and a long tail.

bullet[**]
[búlit]

n. (소총 · 권총의) 총탄, 탄환
A bullet is a small piece of metal with a pointed or rounded end, which is fired out of a gun.

drag[***]
[dræg]

v. 힘들게 움직이다; 끌다, 끌고 오다; n. 견인, 끌기; 빨아들이기
If you say that you drag yourself somewhere, you are emphasizing that you have to make a very great effort to go there.

grateful[**]
[gréitfəl]

a. 고맙게 여기는, 감사하는 (gratefully ad. 감사하여)
If you are grateful for something that someone has given you or done for you, you have warm, friendly feelings towards them and wish to thank them.

chapters five to seven

1. According to Mr. Pendanski, what is the one rule at Camp
   Green Lake?
   A. Don't run away.
   B. Don't upset the Warden.
   C. Don't ask for water.
   D. Be in bed by 10pm.

2. What did the campers call Mr. Pendanski?
   A. Armpit
   B. Warden
   C. Mom
   D. Squid

3. Why were Clyde Livingston's sneakers at a homeless
   shelter?
   A. Clyde worked at a homeless shelter.
   B. Clyde gave his sneakers to a homeless person.
   C. Clyde forgot them at the homeless shelter.
   D. Clyde donated them to the homeless shelter.

4. How did Stanley get Clyde's sneakers?
   A. He stole them from a homeless child.
   B. The sneakers fell on top of him.
   C. He stole them from a display case at the homeless shelter.
   D. He found them on the side of the road.

5. What would happen if a camper found something interesting?

   A. He would get a ten minute shower.

   B. He would get a special dinner.

   C. He would get the rest of the day off.

   D. He would get to leave Camp Green Lake early.

6. What did Elya want when he was 15 years old?

   A. He wanted to work for Madame Zeroni.

   B. He wanted to travel to America.

   C. He wanted to marry Myra Menke.

   D. He wanted to become a pig farmer.

7. What did Elya promise Madame Zeroni?

   A. He would take care of her pigs for one year.

   B. He would carry her up the mountain and sing to her.

   C. He would bring her water from the stream every day.

   D. He would bring her to Myra's father at the top of the mountain.

8. Why did Elya believe he was cursed?

   A. He couldn't find Madame Zeroni's son.

   B. He was struck by lightning three times.

   C. He broke his promise to Madame Zeroni.

   D. Myra refused to marry him.

1분에 몇 단어를 읽는지 리딩 속도를 측정해보세요.

$$\frac{1,009 \text{ words}}{\text{reading time (}\quad\text{) sec}} \times 60 = (\quad\quad) \text{ WPM}$$

Build Your Vocabulary

counselor^{복습}
[káunsələr]

n. (캠프 생활의) 지도원; 상담역, 카운슬러
A counselor is a person whose job is to give advice to people who need it, especially advice on their personal problems.

assign^{**}
[əsáin]

v. 배치하다; 맡기다, 배정하다
If someone is assigned to a particular place, group, or person, they are sent there, usually in order to work at that place or for that person.

bald^{**}
[bɔ́:ld]

a. (머리 등이) 벗겨진, 대머리의; **vi.** 머리가 벗겨지다
Someone who is bald has little or no hair on the top of their head.

curly[*]
[kə́:rli]

a. 곱슬곱슬한
Curly hair is full of curls.

beard^{**}
[biərd]

n. (턱)수염
A man's beard is the hair that grows on his chin and cheeks.

sunburn[*]
[sÁnbə̀:rn]

v. 햇볕에 타다; **n.** 햇볕에 탐, 햇볕으로 입은 화상 (sunburned **a.** 햇볕에 탄)
Someone who is sunburned has sore bright pink skin because they have spent too much time in hot sunshine.

nod^{복습}
[nɔd]

v. 끄덕이다, 끄덕여 표시하다; **n.** 끄덕임(동의 · 인사 · 신호 · 명령)
If you nod, you move your head downwards and upwards to show agreement, understanding, or approval.

pointless
[pɔ́intlis]

a. 무의미한, 할 가치가 없는
If you say that something is pointless, you are criticizing it because it has no sense or purpose.

innocent^{복습}
[ínəsnt]

a. 잘못이 없는, 결백한; 순진한
Innocent people are those who are not involved in a crime or conflict, but are injured or killed as a result of it.

attitude^{***}
[ǽtitjù:d]

n. 태도, 마음가짐; 자세
Your attitude to something is the way that you think and feel about it, especially when this shows in the way you behave.

count on

phrasal v. 기대하다, 의지하다
If you count on someone, you have confidence in them because you know that they will do what you want.

pat^{**}
[pǽt]

v. 톡톡 가볍게 치다, (애정을 담아) 쓰다듬다; **n.** 쓰다듬기
If you pat something or someone, you tap them lightly, usually with your hand held flat.

28

shovel^{복습}
[ʃʌvəl]

n. 삽; v. ~을 삽으로 뜨다[파다], 삽으로 일하다
A shovel is a tool with a long handle that is used for lifting and moving earth, coal, or snow.

compound
[kámpaund]

① n. (저택 · 공장의) 건물 안, 구내 ② vt. 합성하다, 조합하다, 만들어내다;
n. 합성물, 화합물
A compound is an enclosed area of land that is used for a particular purpose.

glance***
[glǽns]

v. 흘깃 보다, 잠깐 보다; n. 흘깃 봄
If you glance at something or someone, you look at them very quickly and then look away again immediately.

weary**
[wíəri]

a. 피로한, 지친 (wearily ad. 지쳐서)
If you are weary, you are very tired.

drip**
[drip]

v. 방울방울[뚝뚝] 떨어지다; 가득[넘칠 듯이] 지니고 있다
When something drips, drops of liquid fall from it.

sweat^{복습}
[swét]

n. 땀; v. 땀 흘리다; 습기가 차다
Sweat is the salty colorless liquid which comes through your skin when you are hot, ill, or afraid.

grunt^{복습}
[grʌnt]

vi. (사람이) 툴툴거리다; (돼지가) 꿀꿀거리다; n. 꿀꿀[툴툴]거리는 소리
If you grunt, you make a low sound, especially because you are annoyed or not interested in something.

cot*
[kat]

n. 접이 침대, 간이[야영용] 침대; 소아용 침대
A cot is a narrow bed, usually made of canvas fitted over a frame which can be folded up.

thrill**
[θríl]

v. 감동[감격, 흥분]시키다; 오싹하다; n. 전율, 오싹함 (thrilled a. 아주 흥분한, 신이 난)
If something thrills you, or if you thrill at it, it gives you a feeling of great pleasure and excitement.

crate*
[kréit]

n. 나무 상자, (짐을 보호하는) 나무틀
A crate is a large box used for transporting or storing things.

stack*
[stæk]

v. 쌓다, 쌓아올리다; n. 더미; 많음, 다량
If you stack a number of things, you arrange them in neat piles.

face^{복습}
[féis]

v. ~을 마주보다, 향하다; 직면하다; 직시하다
If someone or something faces a particular thing, person, or direction, they are positioned opposite them or are looking in that direction.

nickname**
[níknèim]

n. 별명; v. 별명을 붙이다
A nickname is an informal name for someone or something.

tap^{복습}
[tæp]

① v. 가볍게 두드리다; n. 가볍게 두드리기 ② n. 주둥이, (수도 등의) 꼭지
If you tap something, you hit it with a quick light blow or a series of quick light blows.

rim**
[rim]

n. (둥근 물건의) 가장자리, 테두리; v. 둘러싸다, 테를 두르다
The rim of a circular object is its outside edge.

playful*
[pléifəl]

a. 장난기 많은, 명랑한; 농담의 (playfully ad. 장난스럽게)
A playful gesture or person is friendly or humorous.

spit^{복습}
[spit]

v. 뱉다, 내뿜다; (폭언 등을) 내뱉다; n. 침
If you spit liquid or food somewhere, you force a small amount of it out of your mouth.

saliva
[səláivə]

n. 침, 타액
Saliva is the watery liquid that forms in your mouth and helps you to chew and digest food.

sanitary**
[sǽnətèri]

a. 위생적인, 깨끗한
If you say that a place is not sanitary, you mean that it is not very clean.

file out

phrasal v. 줄을 지어 나가다
When a group of people file out somewhere, they exit in a line.

canteen^{복습}
[kæntíːn]

n. (휴대용) 물통; (공장·학교 등의) 구내식당
A canteen is a small plastic bottle for carrying water and other drinks. Canteens are used by soldiers.

whirl**
[hwə:rl]

v. 빙글 돌다, 선회하다
If something or someone whirls around or if you whirl them around, they move around or turn around very quickly.

collar**
[kálər]

n. (윗옷의) 칼라, 깃; (개 등의 목에 거는) 목걸이
The collar of a shirt or coat is the part which fits round the neck and is usually folded over.

terrify**
[térəfài]

vt. 무섭게[겁나게] 하다; 놀래다 (terrified a. 겁먹은, 무서워하는)
If something terrifies you, it makes you feel extremely frightened.

spigot
[spígət]

n. (수도·통 등의) 마개, 주둥이, 꼭지
A spigot is a faucet or tap.

stall**
[stɔ:l]

① n. 칸막이한 작은 방; 노점; 마구간 ② v. 시간을 지연시키다, 시간을 벌다; 핑계 대다
A stall is a small enclosed area in a room which is used for a particular purpose, for example a shower.

cannot for the life of

idiom 목숨을 걸고라도, 도저히
People say 'cannot for the life of me,' when they cannot do something, however hard they try.

figure out

phrasal v. ~을 생각해내다, 발견하다
If you figure out a solution to a problem or the reason for something, you succeed in solving it or understanding it.

1분에 몇 단어를 읽는지 리딩 속도를 측정해보세요.

$$\frac{1{,}170 \text{ words}}{\text{reading time ( ) sec}} \times 60 = (\quad) \text{ WPM}$$

Build Your Vocabulary

scratchy
[skrǽtʃi]

a. (몸에 닿으면) 가려운[따끔거리는]; 긁는 듯한 소리가 나는
Scratchy clothes or fabrics are rough and uncomfortable to wear next to your skin.

cot^{복습}
[kɑt]

n. 접이 침대, 간이[야영용] 침대; 소아용 침대
A cot is a narrow bed, usually made of canvas fitted over a frame which can be folded up.

scarcity*
[skέərsəti]

n. 부족, 결핍; 기근, 식량 부족
If there is a scarcity of something, there is not enough of it for the people who need it or want it.

knob*
[nab]

n. 손잡이; 혹, 마디; (작은) 덩이
A knob is a round handle on a door or drawer which you use in order to open or close it.

rinse*
[rins]

vt. 헹구어 내다, 씻어내다; n. 헹굼
When you rinse something, you wash it in clean water in order to remove dirt or soap from it.

suds
[sʌdz]

n. (pl.) 비누 거품
Suds are the bubbles that are produced when a substance such as soap is mixed with water.

stew*
[stjuː]

v. 약한 불로 끓(이)다; n. 스튜(요리)
When you stew meat, vegetables, or fruit, you cook them slowly in liquid in a closed dish.

mop up

phrasal v. (물기를) 빨아 들여 없애다
If you mop up liquid, you clean it up or remove it from somewhere, using something that absorbs it.

evidence***
[évidəns]

n. 증거, 흔적; vt. 증명하다
Evidence is anything that you see, experience, read, or are told that causes you to believe that something is true or has really happened.

guilt**
[gilt]

n. 유죄, 죄책감
Guilt is the fact that you have done something wrong or illegal.

courtroom
[kɔ́ːrtrùːm]

n. 법정
A courtroom is a room in which a legal court meets.

prospect**
[prá(ɔ́)spekt]

n. (어떤 일이 있을) 가망, 기대, 전망
If there is some prospect of something happening, there is a possibility that it will happen.

testify*
[téstəfài]

v. 증언하다; 증명하다, 입증하다
When someone testifies in a court of law, they give a statement of what they saw someone do or what they know of a situation, after having promised to tell the truth.

donate*
[dóuneit]

vt. (자선 사업 · 공공 기관에) 기부[기증] 하다
If you donate something to a charity or other organization, you give it to them.

homeless*
[hóumlis]

a. 노숙자의; n. (pl.) 노숙자들
Homeless people have nowhere to live.

shelter***
[ʃéltər]

n. 쉼터, 보호소; 피신처; v. 피할[쉴] 곳을 제공하다, 보호하다
A shelter is a building where homeless people can sleep and get food.

horrible**
[hɔ́:rəbəl]

a. 끔찍한, 소름 끼치게 싫은; 무서운
You can call something horrible when it causes you to feel great shock, fear, and disgust.

thief**
[θí:f]

n. 도둑, 절도범
A thief is a person who steals something from another person.

collapse**
[kəlǽps]

v. 무너지다, 붕괴하다; 쓰러지다, 맥없이 주저앉다; n. 무너짐, 붕괴
If a building or other structure collapses, it falls down very suddenly.

roll over

phrasal v. 자면서 몸을 뒤척이다, 뒹굴다
When you roll over, you turn from lying on one side of your body to the other side.

snore*
[snɔ:r]

v. 코를 골다
When someone who is asleep snores, they make a loud noise each time they breathe.

bully*
[búli]

n. 약자를 괴롭히는 사람; v. 괴롭히다, 겁주다
A bully is someone who uses their strength or power to hurt or frighten other people.

torment**
[tɔ́:rment]

vt. 괴롭히다, 고문하다; n. 고통, 고뇌
If something torments you, it causes you extreme mental suffering.

complaint**
[kəmpléint]

n. 불평, 불만, 푸념
A complaint is a statement in which you express your dissatisfaction with a particular situation.

amuse**
[əmjú:z]

vt. 즐겁게 하다, 재미나게 하다 (amusing a. 재미있는, 즐거운)
If something amuses you, it makes you want to laugh or smile.

pick on

phrasal v. (구어) 괴롭히다, 못살게 굴다; ~을 선택하다, 고르다
If you pick on someone, you treat them badly or unfairly, especially repeatedly.

arrest복습
[ərést]

vt. 체포하다, 저지하다; (주의 · 이목 · 흥미 등을) 끌다; n. 체포, 검거, 구속
If the police arrest you, they take charge of you and take you to a police station, because they believe you may have committed a crime.

retrieve*
[ritríːv]

vt. 되찾다, 회수하다
If you retrieve something, you get it back from the place where you left it.

freeway
[fríːwèi]

n. 고속도로
A freeway is a major road that has been specially built for fast travel over long distances.

overpass
[óuvərpæs]

n. (도로 · 철도 등의 위에 가설된) 다리, 고가도로, 육교
An overpass is a structure which carries one road over the top of another one.

figure out복습

phrasal v. ~을 생각해내다, 발견하다
If you figure out a solution to a problem or the reason for something, you succeed in solving it or understanding it.

recycle복습
[riːsáikl]

v. 재활용하다; 재순환하다
If you recycle things that have already been used, such as bottles or sheets of paper, you process them so that they can be used again.

seemingly*
[síːmiŋli]

ad. 보기엔, 외관상; 겉으로는, 표면적으로는
If something is seemingly the case, you mean that it appears to be the case, even though it may not really be so.

odor복습
[óudər]

n. (불쾌한) 냄새, 악취 (foot odor n. 발냄새)
An odor is a particular and distinctive smell.

coincidence*
[kouínsidəns]

n. (우연의) 일치, 부합; 동시에 일어남
A coincidence is when two or more similar or related events occur at the same time by chance and without any planning.

mere***
[míər]

a. 단지 ~에 불과한; 단순한
You use mere to emphasize how unimportant or inadequate something is, in comparison to the general situation you are describing.

miserable복습
[mízərəbəl]

a. 비참한, 초라한, 불쌍한
If you describe a place or situation as miserable, you mean that it makes you feel unhappy or depressed.

humiliate*
[hjuːmílièit]

vt. 굴욕감을 느끼게 하다, 창피를 주다
To humiliate someone means to say or do something which makes them feel ashamed or stupid.

patrol*
[pətróul]

n. 순찰, 정찰; 순찰병, 경관; v. 순찰하다
Soldiers, police, or guards who are on patrol are patrolling an area.

autograph*
[óːtəgræf]

n. 서명, 사인, 자필; vt. 서명하다, 자필로 쓰다
An autograph is the signature of someone famous which is specially written for a fan to keep.

auction*
[óːkʃən]

v. 경매로 팔다; n. 경매
If something is auctioned, it is sold in a public sale where goods are sold to the person who offers the highest price.

trial***
[tráiəl]

n. 재판, 공판; 시험, 실험
A trial is a formal meeting in a law court, at which a judge and jury listen to evidence and decide whether a person is guilty of a crime.

delay***
[diléi]

v. 미루다, 연기하다; n. 지연
If you delay doing something, you do not do it immediately or at the planned or expected time, but you leave it until later.

afford***
[əfɔ́:rd]

vt. ~할 여유가 있다; 주다, 공급하다
If you cannot afford something, you do not have enough money to pay for it.

despicable
[déspikəbəl]

a. 야비한, 비열한
If you say that a person or action is despicable, you are emphasizing that they are extremely nasty, cruel, or evil.

souvenir*
[sù:vəníər]

n. 기념품
A souvenir is something which you buy or keep to remind you of a holiday, place, or event.

discipline*
[dísiplin]

n. 규율, 훈련; vt. 훈련하다
Discipline is the practice of making people obey rules or standards of behavior, and punishing them when they do not.

improve***
[imprú:v]

v. 개선하다, 진보하다, 나아지다
If something improves or if you improve it, it gets better.

character***
[kǽriktər]

n. 인격, 성격; 특징, 특성; 문자, 서체
Your character is your personality, especially how reliable and honest you are.

jail복습
[dʒeil]

n. 교도소, 감옥
A jail is a place where criminals are kept in order to punish them, or where people waiting to be tried are kept.

vacancy*
[véikənsi]

n. 결원, 공석; 빈 방
A vacancy is a job or position which has not been filled.

34

1분에 몇 단어를 읽는지 리딩 속도를 측정해보세요.

$$\frac{3{,}781 \text{ words}}{\text{reading time (} \quad \text{) sec}} \times 60 = (\qquad) \text{ WPM}$$

Build Your Vocabulary

fleshy
[fléʃi]

a. 살집이 있는, 살찐
If you describe someone as fleshy, you mean that they are slightly fat.

jam**
[dʒǽm]

v. (세게) 밀다, 밀어 넣다; n. 혼잡, 교통 체증; (기계의) 고장
If you jam something somewhere, you push or put it there roughly.

blade**
[bleid]

n. (칼·도구 등의) 날; (프로펠러 등의) 날개; 잎
The blade of a knife, ax, or saw is the edge, which is used for cutting.

bang**
[bæŋ]

v. 탕 치다, 부딪치다, 쾅 닫(히)다; n. 쾅 하는 소리
If something bangs, it makes a sudden loud noise, once or several times.

bounce*
[bauns]

v. 튀다, 튀게 하다; 급히 움직이다, 뛰어다니다; n. 튐, 바운드
If something bounces off a surface or is bounced off it, it reaches the surface and is reflected back.

dent*
[dent]

n. 움푹 들어간 곳; vt. (단단한 표면을 세게 쳐서) 움푹 들어가게 만들다
A dent is a hollow in the surface of something which has been caused by hitting or pressing it.

vibration*
[vaibréiʃən]

n. 진동, 떨림
Vibration is the act of repeated small, quick movement.

shaft**
[ʃǽft]

n. (망치·골프채 등의 기다란) 손잡이
A shaft is a long thin piece of wood or metal that forms part of a spear, ax, golf club, or other object.

wrist^{복습}
[rist]

n. 손목
Your wrist is the part of your body between your hand and your arm which bends when you move your hand.

rattle^{복습}
[rǽtl]

v. 왈각달각 소리 나다, 덜걱덜걱 움직이다; n. 방울뱀의 꼬리; 덜거덕거리는 소리
When something rattles or when you rattle it, it makes short sharp knocking sounds because it is being shaken or it keeps hitting against something hard.

might***
[máit]

n. 힘, 완력; 세력, 권력
Might is power or strength.

sting**
[stiŋ]

vt. (stung–stung) 찌르다, 쏘다; n. 찌름, 쏨
If something stings you, a sharp part of is pushed into your skin so that you feel a sharp pain.

impression[**]
[impréʃən]

n. (표면을 세게 눌렀을 때 생기는) 자국; (사람·사물로부터 받는) 인상
An impression of an object is a mark or outline that it has left after being pressed hard onto a surface.

defective[*]
[diféktiv]

a. 결함이 있는
If something is defective, there is something wrong with it and it does not work properly.

glance[복습]
[glǽns]

v. 흘깃 보다, 잠깐 보다; n. 흘깃 봄
If you glance at something or someone, you look at them very quickly and then look away again immediately.

scoop[*]
[skúːp]

v. 뜨다, 파다; 재빨리 들어 올리다; n. 국자, 주걱
If you scoop something from a container, you remove it with something such as a spoon.

shovelful
[ʃʌ́vəlfùl]

n. 한 삽(의 분량)
shovel (명사: 삽) + ful (접미사: ~정도의 양)

dump[*]
[dʌ́mp]

vt. 쏟아 버리다, 내버리다, 아무렇게나 내려놓다; n. 쓰레기 더미
If you dump something somewhere, you put it or unload it there quickly and carelessly.

lukewarm
[lúːkwɔ́ːrm]

a. 미지근한
Something, especially a liquid, that is lukewarm is only slightly warm.

cereal[**]
[síəriəl]

n. 시리얼; 곡물, 곡류
Cereal or breakfast cereal is a food made from grain. It is mixed with milk and eaten for breakfast.

carton
[káːrtən]

n. (음식이나 음료를 담는) 곽[통]; 상자
A carton is a plastic or cardboard container in which food or drink is sold.

assign[복습]
[əsáin]

v. 맡기다, 배정하다; 배치하다
If you assign a piece of work to someone, you give them the work to do.

shed[*]
[ʃed]

n. (~을) 보관하는 곳, (작은) 헛간
A shed is a small building that is used for storing things such as garden tools.

fraction[**]
[frǽkʃən]

n. 부분, 일부
A fraction of something is a tiny amount or proportion of it.

tip[**]
[típ]

① n. (뾰족한) 끝 ② v. 뒤집어엎다, 기울이다 ③ n. 팁, 사례금
The tip of something long and narrow is the end of it.

mound[**]
[maund]

n. 더미, 무더기, 언덕
A mound of something is a large rounded pile of it.

day off

n. (근무·일을) 쉬는 날
A day off is a day when you do not go to work, even though it is usually a working day.

dig ^{복습}
[díg]

v. (구멍 등을) 파다; 뒤지다; n. 파기
If people or animals dig, they make a hole in the ground or in a pile of earth, stones, or rubbish.

character ^{복습}
[kǽriktər]

n. 인격, 성격; 특징, 특성; 문자, 서체
Your character is your personality, especially how reliable and honest you are.

helpless *
[hélplis]

a. 무력한, 속수무책의 (helplessly ad. 무력하게, 어쩔 수 없이)
If you are helpless, you do not have the strength or power to do anything useful or to control or protect yourself.

crack **
[kræk]

n. 갈라진 금; 갑작스런 날카로운 소리; v. 금이 가다, 깨다; (짧고 세게) 때리다
A crack is a very narrow gap between two things, or between two parts of a thing.

packed
[pækt]

a. 단단히 다져진; (특히 사람들이) 꽉 들어찬
Something that is packed with things contains a very large number of them.

overweight ^{복습}
[óuvərwèit]

a. 과체중의, 비만의; 중량 초과의
Someone who is overweight weighs more than is considered healthy or attractive.

pry
[prai]

① vt. (pried–pried) 비틀어 움직이다; 지레로 들어 올리다; n. 지레
② vi. 엿보다, 동정을 살피다
If you pry something open or pry it away from a surface, you force it open or away from a surface.

unearth
[Ànə́:rθ]

v. (땅속에서) 파내다, 발굴하다; 찾다, 밝혀내다
If someone unearths something that is buried, they find it by digging in the ground.

manner ***
[mǽnər]

n. (일의) 방식; (사람의) 태도, 예의
The manner in which you do something is the way that you do it.

perimeter
[pərímitər]

n. (어떤 구역의) 주위, 주변
The perimeter of an area of land is the whole of its outer edge or boundary.

awful ^{복습}
[ɔ́:fəl]

a. 지독한, 대단한; 무서운 (awfully ad. (구어) 대단히, 몹시)
If you say that something is awful, you mean that it is extremely unpleasant, shocking, or bad.

bake ***
[beik]

v. (열로) 굽다[굳히다]; (음식을) 굽다
If places or people become extremely hot because the sun is shining very strongly, you can say that they bake.

crust **
[krʌst]

n. 딱딱한 표면, 겉껍질
A crust is a hard layer of something.

blister *
[blístər]

n. 물집, 수포; v. 물집이 생기다
A blister is a painful swelling on the surface of your skin. Blisters contain a clear liquid and are usually caused by heat or by something repeatedly rubbing your skin.

ask for someone's hand

idiom 청혼하다
If you ask for someone's hand, you ask for permission to marry he or she.

puffy
[pʌ́fi]

a. 부푼, 팽창된
If you describe something as puffy, you mean it has a round, swollen appearance.

ankle*
[ǽŋkl]

n. 발목
Your ankle is the joint where your foot joins your leg.

compete*
[kəmpíːt]

vi. 겨루다, 경쟁하다
If you compete with someone for something, you try to get it for yourself and stop the other person getting it.

flowerpot
[fláuərpàt]

n. 화분
A flowerpot is a container that is used for growing plants.

plow*
[plau]

n. 쟁기; v. 갈다, 경작하다
A plow is a large farming tool with sharp blades which is pulled across the soil to turn it over, usually before seeds are planted.

delicate*
[délikit]

a. 섬세한, 고운, 예민한, 민감한
Something that is delicate is small and beautifully shaped.

spoil***
[spɔ́il]

v. (아이를) 응석받이로[버릇없게] 키우다; 망치다
If you spoil children, you give them everything they want or ask for.

shallow*
[ʃǽlou]

a. 얕은, 얄팍한, 피상적인
If you describe a person, piece of work, or idea as shallow, you disapprove of them because they do not show or involve any serious or careful thought.

forlorn*
[fərlɔ́ːrn]

a. 고독한, 쓸쓸한; 버려진, 버림받은
If someone is forlorn, they feel alone and unhappy.

sow
[sau]

① n. 암퇘지 ② v. 씨를 뿌리다, 파종하다
A sow is an adult female pig.

litter*
[lítər]

n. 한 배에서 난 새끼들; 쓰레기, 어질러진 물건; vt. 어질러 놓다, 흩어지다
A litter is a group of animals born to the same mother at the same time.

piglet
[píglit]

n. 새끼 돼지
A piglet is a young pig.

runt
[rʌnt]

n. (한 배에서 태어난 새끼들 중) 제일 작고 약한 녀석
The runt of a group of animals born to the same mother at the same time is the smallest and weakest of them.

suckle
[sʌ́kl]

vt. 젖을 먹이다; 기르다, 양육하다
When a mother suckles her baby, she feeds it by letting it suck milk from her breast.

uphill*
[ʌ́phìl]

ad. 오르막길로, 언덕 위로; a. 오르막의
If something or someone is uphill or is moving uphill, they are near the top of a hill or are going up a slope.

descendant^{복습}
[diséndənt]

n. 자손, 후예
Someone's descendants are the people in later generations who are related to them.

doom**
[dú:m]

vt. 운명 짓다, 선고하다; n. 운명, 파멸 (doomed a. 운이 다한, 불운한)
If something is doomed to happen, or if you are doomed to a particular state, something unpleasant is certain to happen, and you can do nothing to prevent it.

eternity*
[itə́:rnəti]

n. 영원, 오랜 시간
Eternity is time without an end or a state of existence outside time, especially the state which some people believe they will pass into after they have died.

curse^{복습}
[kə:rs]

n. 저주, 악담; vt. 저주하다, 욕설을 퍼붓다
If you say that there is a curse on someone, you mean that there seems to be a supernatural power causing unpleasant things to happen to them.

slope***
[slóup]

v. 경사지다, 비탈지다; n. 비탈, 경사
If a surface slopes, it is at an angle, so that one end is higher than the other.

horizon**
[həráizn]

n. 지평선, 수평선
The horizon is the line in the far distance where the sky seems to meet the land or the sea.

ray***
[réi]

n. 광선, 빛; v. 번쩍이다
Rays of light are narrow beams of light.

dizzy*
[dízi]

a. 현기증 나는, 아찔한 (dizziness n. 현기증)
If you feel dizzy, you feel as if everything is spinning round and being unable to balance.

steady***
[stédi]

v. 진정시키다, 균형을 잡다; a. 꾸준한
If you steady something or if it steadies, it stops shaking or moving about.

throw up

phrasal v. 토하다
When someone throws up, they vomit.

wasteland^{복습}
[wéistlænd]

n. 황무지, 불모지
A wasteland is an area of land on which not much can grow or which has been spoiled in some way.

trail***
[tréil]

v. ~을 뒤쫓다; (땅에 대고 뒤로) 끌다, 끌리다; n. 지나간 자국, 흔적
If you trail something or it trails, it hangs down loosely behind you as you move along.

rear*
[riər]

① n. 뒤, 배후; a. 후방의; v. 뒷다리로 서다 ② v. 기르다, 교육하다
The rear of something such as a building or vehicle is the back part of it.

pop*
[páp]

v. 급히 집어넣다; 뻥 하고 터뜨리다; 불쑥 나타나다; n. 뻥[탁] 하는 소리, 발포
If you pop something somewhere, you put it there quickly.

deft
[déft]

a. 손재주 있는, 솜씨 좋은 (deftly ad. 솜씨 좋게, 교묘히)
A deft action is skillful and often quick.

bold**
[bould]

a. 용감한, 대담한; 선명한, 굵은 (boldly ad. 대담하게)
Someone who is bold is not afraid to do things which involve risk or danger.

rip*
[rip]

v. 찢(어지)다, 벗겨내다; 돌진하다; n. 찢어진 틈, 잡아 찢음
When something rips or when you rip it, you tear it forcefully with your hands or with a tool such as a knife.

grip
[grip]

n. 움켜쥠, 꽉 붙잡음; 손잡이; v. 꽉 잡다, 움켜잡다
A grip is a firm, strong hold on something.

convince**
[kənvíns]

vt. 설득하다; 확신시키다, 납득시키다
If someone or something convinces you to do something, they persuade you to do it.

eventually**
[ivéntʃuəli]

ad. 결국, 마침내
Eventually means at the end of a situation or process or as the final result of it.

compact**
[kəmpǽk]

v. 압축하다, 꽉 채우다; a. 조밀한
To compact something means to press it so that it becomes more solid.

excavate
[ékskəvèit]

vt. (구멍 등을) 파다, 발굴하다, 출토하다
To excavate means to dig a hole in the ground, for example in order to build there.

reluctant*
[rilʌ́ktənt]

a. 마음이 내키지 않는, 마지못해 하는 (reluctantly ad. 마지못해서)
If you are reluctant to do something, you are unwilling to do it and hesitate before doing it, or do it slowly and without enthusiasm.

snout
[snáut]

n. (돼지 같은 동물의) 주둥이
The snout of an animal such as a pig is its long nose.

preposterous
[pripástərəs]

a. 말도 안 되는, 터무니없는
If you describe something as preposterous, you mean that it is extremely unreasonable and foolish.

exclaim***
[ikskléim]

v. 외치다, 소리치다
If you exclaim, you say or shout something suddenly because of surprise, fear and pleasure.

expel*
[ikspél]

vt. (공기나 물을) 배출하다; 쫓아내다, 물리치다
To expel something means to force it out from a container or from your body.

saliva ᵇᵘ
[səláivə]

n. 침, 타액
Saliva is the watery liquid that forms in your mouth and helps you to chew and digest food.

rub**
[rʌ́b]

v. 비비다, 문지르다; 스치다; n. 문지르기
If you rub a part of your body, you move your hand or fingers backwards and forwards over it while pressing firmly.

chin**
[tʃín]

n. 턱
Your chin is the part of your face that is below your mouth and above your neck.

slap[**]
[slæp]

v. 찰싹 때리다, 탁 놓다; 철썩 부딪치다; n. 찰싹 (때림)
If you slap someone, you hit them with the palm of your hand.

summon[**]
[sʌ́mən]

vt. 호출하다, 소환하다
If you summon someone, you order them to come to you.

blush[**]
[blʌ́ʃ]

v. 얼굴을 붉히다, (얼굴이) 빨개지다; n. 얼굴을 붉힘, 홍조
When you blush, your face becomes redder than usual because you are ashamed or embarrassed.

blossom[**]
[blásəm]

n. 꽃; v. 꽃이 피다, 꽃을 피우다
If someone or something blossoms, they develop good, attractive, or successful qualities.

mutter[**]
[mʌ́tər]

v. 중얼거리다, 불평하다; n. 중얼거림, 불평
If you mutter, you speak very quietly so that you cannot easily be heard, often because you are complaining about something.

sack[복습]
[sæk]

n. (쇼핑 물건을 담는 크고 튼튼한 종이) 봉지; 부대, 자루; vt. 자루에 넣다
Sacks are used to carry or store things such as vegetables or coal.

afford[복습]
[əfɔ́ːrd]

vt. ~할 여유가 있다; 주다, 공급하다
If you cannot afford something, you do not have enough money to pay for it.

dawdle
[dɔ́ːdl]

v. 꾸물거리다, 빈둥거리다
If you dawdle, you spend more time than is necessary going somewhere.

soak[**]
[souk]

v. 젖다, 스며들다; 적시다, 빨아들이다; n. 적심
If a liquid soaks something or if you soak something with a liquid, the liquid makes the thing very wet.

gesture[**]
[dʒéstʃər]

vi. (손 · 머리 · 얼굴 등으로) 가리키다, 몸짓을 하다; n. 몸짓
If you gesture, you use movements of your hands or head in order to tell someone something or draw their attention to something.

expanse[*]
[ikspǽns]

n. 넓게 퍼진 지역; 팽창, 확장
An expanse of something, usually sea, sky, or land, is a very large amount of it.

stagger[**]
[stǽgər]

v. 비틀거리다, 휘청거리다; n. 비틀거림
If you stagger, you walk very unsteadily, for example because you are ill or drunk.

wander[***]
[wɑ́ndər]

v. 돌아다니다, 방황하다; n. 유랑, 방랑
If you wander in a place, you walk around there in a casual way, often without intending to go in any particular direction.

aimless[*]
[éimlis]

a. 목적이[목표가] 없는 (aimlessly ad. 목적 없이)
A person or activity that is aimless has no clear purpose or plan.

wharf[**]
[hwɔ́ːrf]

n. 부두, 선창
A wharf is a platform by a river or the sea where ships can be tied up.

pier[**]
[piər]

n. 부두
A pier is a platform sticking out into water, usually the sea, which people walk along or use when getting onto or off boats.

foul**
[faul]

a. (성격 · 맛 등이) 더러운, 아주 안 좋은
If you describe something as foul, you mean it is dirty and smells or tastes unpleasant.

dock**
[dák]

n. 선창, 부두; **v.** (배를) 부두에 대다
A dock is an enclosed area in a harbor where ships go to be loaded, unloaded, and repaired.

deck***
[dék]

n. 갑판; (카드 패의) 한 벌
A deck on a vehicle such as a bus or ship is a lower or upper area of it.

passage***
[pǽsidʒ]

n. (배로 한 장소에서 다른 장소로 가는) 항해; 통로, 복도
A passage is a journey by ship.

aboard*
[əbɔ́:rd]

ad. 배에, 승선하여
If you are aboard a ship or plane, you are on it or in it.

harbor***
[há:rbər]

n. 항구, 항만; 피난처, 은신처
A harbor is an area of the sea at the coast which is partly enclosed by land or strong walls, so that boats can be left there safely.

envious**
[énviəs]

a. 부러워하는; 질투하는, 샘내는 (enviously **ad.** 부러운 듯)
If you are envious of someone, you want something that they have.

steep**
[sti:p]

a. (경사면 · 언덕 등이) 가파른, 비탈진; (증감이) 급격한
A steep slope rises at a very sharp angle and is difficult to go up.

clod*
[klád]

n. 흙덩어리; 흙
A clod of earth is a large lump of earth.

compound^{복습}
[kámpaund]

① **n.** (저택 · 공장의) 건물 안, 구내 ② **vt.** 합성하다, 조합하다, 만들어내다; **n.** 합성물, 화합물
A compound is an enclosed area of land that is used for a particular purpose.

weird*
[wiə:rd]

a. 이상한, 기묘한; 수상한
If you describe something or someone as weird, you mean that they are strange.

dude
[dju:d]

n. [구어] 형씨, 친구; 사내, 녀석
A dude is a man.

frizzy
[frízi]

a. (머리가) 곱슬곱슬한
Frizzy hair is very tightly curled.

stick out

phrasal v. (툭) 튀어나오다; ~을 내밀다
If something sticks out, it is further out than something else.

bob*
[bɑb]

v. 까닥까닥 흔들리다, 위아래로 움직이다
If something bobs, it moves up and down, like something does when it is floating on water.

stain**
[stéin]

v. 더러워지다, 얼룩지게 하다; **n.** 얼룩, 오점
If a liquid stains something, the thing becomes colored or marked by the liquid.

42

grave[star][star]
[greiv]

① n. 무덤, 묘 ② a. 중대한, 근엄한
A grave is a place where a dead person is buried.

lullaby[star]
[lʌ́ləbài]

n. 자장가
A lullaby is a quiet song which is intended to be sung to babies and young children to help them go to sleep.

barn[star][star]
[bɑːrn]

n. 헛간, 광
A barn is a building on a farm in which crops or animal food can be kept.

strike[star][star][star]
[straik]

v. (struck–stricken/struck) 때리다, 치다, 부딪치다; 갑자기 떠오르다;
n. 파업; 치기, 때리기
If something that is falling or moving strikes something, it hits it.

thief[복습]
[θíːf]

n. 도둑, 절도범
A thief is a person who steals something from another person.

sparkle[star][star]
[spɑ́ːrkl]

v. 반짝이다; 생기 넘치다; n. 반짝거림, 광채
If something sparkles, it is clear and bright and shines with a lot of very small points of light.

translate[star][star]
[trænsléit]

v. 번역하다; (다른 상태 · 성질로) 바꾸다, 변형하다
If something that someone has said or written is translated from one language into another, it is said or written again in the second language.

rhyme[star]
[raim]

v. (두 단어나 음절이) 운이 맞다; n. (시의) 운
If one word rhymes with another or if two words rhyme, they have a very similar sound.

woodpecker[복습]
[wúdpèkəːr]

n. [조류] 딱따구리
A woodpecker is a type of bird with a long sharp beak. Woodpeckers use their beaks to make holes in tree trunks.

bark[복습]
[bɑːrk]

① n. 나무껍질 ② v. (개가) 짖다; 고함치다; n. 짖는 소리
Bark is the tough material that covers the outside of a tree.

grimace[star]
[gríməs]

vi. 얼굴을 찡그리다; n. 얼굴을 찡그림
If you grimace, you twist your face in an ugly way because you are annoyed, disgusted, or in pain.

chunk
[tʃʌŋk]

n. 큰 덩어리, 상당한 양; v. 덩어리로 나누다
A chunk of something is a large amount or large part of it.

fling[star][star]
[fliŋ]

vt. (flung–flung) 내던지다, 던지다; (문 등을) 왈칵 열다
If you fling something somewhere, you throw it there using a lot of force.

rotate[star]
[róuteit]

v. 회전시키다, 회전하다, 돌다
When something rotates or when you rotate it, it turns with a circular movement.

chip off

phrasal v. (부서지거나 하여 작은 부분이) 떨어져 나가다[나가게 하다]
If paint or a surface chips off, it comes off in small pieces.

rim[복습]
[rim]

n. (둥근 물건의) 가장자리, 테두리; v. 둘러싸다, 테를 두르다
The rim of a circular object is its outside edge.

foothold[*]
[fúthòuld]

n. (등산 때) 발 디딜 곳; (사업 · 직업 등에서 성공의) 발판

A foothold is a place such as a small hole or area of rock where you can safely put your foot when climbing.

faint^{***}
[feint]

vi. 기절하다; **n.** 기절, 졸도; **a.** 희미한, 어렴풋한

If you faint, you lose consciousness for a short time, especially because you are hungry, or because of pain, heat, or shock.

suck^{**}
[sʌk]

v. 빨다, 빨아내다; 삼키다; **n.** 빨아들임

If something sucks a liquid, gas, or object in a particular direction, it draws it there with a powerful force.

44

chapters eight to eleven

1. Where do yellow spotted lizards live?
   A. Near water spigots
   B. Under rocks
   C. In old birds' nests
   D. In holes

2. When did Zero have a serious, almost angry look on his face?
   A. When the Lump tried to fight Stanley
   B. When X-Ray spoke about digging holes
   C. When Stanley was writing a letter to his mother
   D. When the other boys gave Stanley a nickname

3. What was Stanley's nickname?
   A. Caveman
   B. Lump
   C. Barf Bag
   D. Hole

4. What did Stanley find?
   A. A fish
   B. A fossil
   C. A gem
   D. A shiny rock

5. Who was always at the front of the line?
   A. X-Ray
   B. Magnet
   C. Squid
   D. Zigzag

6. X-Ray wanted to _____.
   A. steal Mr. Sir's sunflower seeds
   B. drink from Stanley's water canteen
   C. have anything that Stanley found
   D. trade holes with Stanley

7. What helped Stanley dig his hole?
   A. He imagined going home and beating up Derrick Dunne by himself.
   B. He imagined being taller than the other campers in Group D.
   C. He thought about his great-great-grandfather beating up Derrick Dunne.
   D. He imagined Derrick Dunne being beat up by the campers in Group D.

1분에 몇 단어를 읽는지 리딩 속도를 측정해보세요.

$$\frac{216 \text{ words}}{\text{reading time } (\quad) \text{ sec}} \times 60 = (\quad) \text{ WPM}$$

Build Your Vocabulary

curse^{복습}
[kə:rs]

n. 저주, 악담; vt. 저주하다, 욕설을 퍼붓다
If you say that there is a curse on someone, you mean that there seems to be a supernatural power causing unpleasant things to happen to them.

spotted^{복습}
[spátid]

a. 얼룩무늬의; 물방울무늬가 있는
Something that is spotted has a pattern of spots on it.

lizard^{복습}
[lízərd]

n. 도마뱀
A lizard is a reptile with short legs and a long tail.

odd**
[ɑd]

a. 이상한, 기묘한
If you describe someone or something as odd, you think that they are strange or unusual.

milky*
[mílki]

a. 우유 같은, 희뿌연; 우유로 만든
If you describe something as milky, you mean that it is pale white in color.

shade^{복습}
[ʃeid]

n. (시원한) 그늘; 색조; vt. 그늘지게 하다
Shade is an area of darkness under or next to an object such as a tree, where sunlight does not reach.

protection^{복습}
[prətékʃən]

n. 보호
To give or be protection against something unpleasant means to prevent people or things from being harmed or damaged by it.

predatory
[prédətɔ̀:ri]

a. 포식성의, 육식하는
Predatory animals live by killing other animals for food.

leap***
[lí:p]

v. 껑충 뛰다; 뛰어넘다; n. 뜀, 도약
If you leap, you jump high in the air or jump a long distance.

attack***
[ətǽk]

v. 공격하다; n. 공격, 습격; (자주 보이던 증상의 갑작스럽고 격렬한) 도짐[발발]
To attack a person or place means to try to hurt or damage them using physical violence.

prey**
[prei]

n. 먹이, 사냥감; 희생양
A creature's prey are the creatures that it hunts and eats in order to live.

insect**
[ínsekt]

n. 곤충, 벌레
An insect is a small animal that has six legs. Most insects have wings. Ants, flies, butterflies, and beetles are all insects.

cactus*
[kǽktəs]

n. [식물] 선인장
A cactus is a thick fleshy plant that grows in many hot, dry parts of the world. Cacti have no leaves and many of them are covered in prickles.

thorn**
[θɔ́ːrn]

n. 가시
Thorns are the sharp points on some plants and trees.

1분에 몇 단어를 읽는지 리딩 속도를 측정해보세요.

$$\frac{976 \text{ words}}{\text{reading time ( ) sec}} \times 60 = (\qquad) \text{ WPM}$$

Build Your Vocabulary

sore**
[sɔːr]

a. 아픈, 쓰린
If part of your body is sore, it causes you pain and discomfort.

drain**
[drein]

n. 배수관; v. 물을 빼내다, (액체가) 흘러나가다
A drain is a pipe that carries water or sewage away from a place, or an opening in a surface that leads to the pipe.

evaporate*
[ivǽpərèit]

v. 증발하다, 증발시키다; 사라지다
When a liquid evaporates, or is evaporated, it changes from a liquid state to a gas, because its temperature has increased.

crate복습
[kréit]

n. 나무 상자, (짐을 보호하는) 나무틀
A crate is a large box used for transporting or storing things.

stationery복습
[stéiʃənèri]

n. 문구류, 문방구
Stationery is paper, envelopes, and other materials or equipment used for writing.

wreck**
[rék]

n. 잔해, 다 망가지다시피 한 것; 난파; v. 망가뜨리다, 파괴하다
A wreck is something such as a ship, car, plane, or building which has been destroyed, usually in an accident.

worn-out
[wɔ́ːrn-áut]

a. 기진맥진한; 써서 낡은, 닳아 해진
Someone who is worn-out is extremely tired after hard work or a difficult or unpleasant experience.

sprawl*
[sprɔ́ːl]

v. (팔다리 등을) 쭉 펴다, 큰 대자로 눕다; 제 멋대로 뻗어 나가다
If you sprawl somewhere, you sit or lie down with your legs and arms spread out in a careless way.

bump복습
[bʌ́mp]

n. (도로의) 튀어나온 부분; 혹; v. 덜컹거리며 가다; (쾅하고) 부딪치다
A bump on a road is a raised, uneven part.

carve*
[kaːrv]

v. (글씨를) 새기다, 파다; 조각하다
If you carve writing or a design on an object, you cut it into the surface of the object.

air-conditioning복습
[ɛ́ər-kəndíʃəníŋ]

n. (건물 · 자동차의) 에어컨 (장치)
Air-conditioning is a method of providing buildings and vehicles with cool dry air.

trip***
[tríp]

v. 걸려 넘어지다; 경쾌한 걸음걸이로 걷다; n. 여행
If you trip when you are walking, you knock your foot against something and fall or nearly fall.

50

outstretch
[àutstrétʃ]

v. 펴다, 뻗다, 확장하다
When you outstretch, you are stretching or extending beyond.

lump**
[lʌmp]

n. (보통 특정한 형태가 없는) 덩어리
A lump of something is a solid piece of it.

mutter복습
[mʌ́tər]

v. 중얼거리다, 불평하다; n. 중얼거림, 불평
If you mutter, you speak very quietly so that you cannot easily be heard, often because you are complaining about something.

poke*
[pouk]

v. (손가락 등으로) 쿡 찌르다; n. 찌르기, 쑤시기
If you poke someone or something, you quickly push them with your finger or with a sharp object.

mess with

phrasal v. 방해하다, 건드리다; 손대다
If you mess with something, you cause trouble for them.

grunt복습
[grʌnt]

vi. (사람이) 툴툴거리다; (돼지가) 꿀꿀거리다; n. 꿀꿀[툴툴]거리는 소리
If you grunt, you make a low sound, especially because you are annoyed or not interested in something.

couch**
[kautʃ]

n. 소파, 긴 의자
A couch is a long, comfortable seat for two or three people.

dude복습
[dju:d]

n. (구어) 형씨, 친구; 사내, 녀석
A dude is a man.

vinyl*
[váinl]

n. 비닐
Vinyl is a strong plastic used for making things such as floor coverings and furniture.

upholstery
[ʌphóulstəri]

n. (소파 등의) 덮개; 덮개를 씌우는 일
Upholstery is the soft covering on chairs and seats that makes them more comfortable to sit on.

radiate*
[réidièit]

vi. (빛 · 열 등을) 발하다, 빛나다, 방출하다
If you radiate an emotion or quality or if it radiates from you, people can see it very clearly in your face and in your behavior.

groan**
[gróun]

v. 신음하다, 끙끙거리다; n. 신음, 끙끙거리는 소리
If you groan, you make a long, low sound because you are in pain, or because you are upset or unhappy about something.

scowl***
[skaul]

vi. 얼굴을 찌푸리다, 싫은 기색을 하다; n. 찌푸린 얼굴
When someone scowls, an angry or hostile expression appears on their face.

smash*
[smæʃ]

v. 때려 부수다, 깨뜨리다; 세게 충돌하다; n. 강타; 부서지는 소리; 분쇄
If you smash something or if it smashes, it breaks into many pieces, for example when it is hit or dropped.

sneaker복습
[sníːkər]

n. (pl.) 고무창 운동화
Sneakers are casual shoes with rubber soles.

commercial**
[kəmɔ́ːrʃəl]

n. (텔레비전 · 라디오의) 광고; a. 상업의, 무역의; 영리적인
A commercial is an advertisement that is broadcast on television or radio.

intensity*
[inténsəti]

n. 강렬함, 강함, 격렬함
Intensity is the quality of being very strong, concentrated or difficult or the degree to which something is difficult or strong.

stuff^{복습}
[stʌf]

vt. 채워 넣다, 속을 채우다; **n.** 일[것](일반적으로 말하거나 생각하는 것); 물건, 물질 (stuffing **n.** (쿠션·장난감 등의 안에 넣는) 속)
Stuffing is material that is used to fill things such as cushions or toys in order to make them firm or solid.

shrug*
[ʃrʌg]

v. (어깨를) 으쓱하다; **n.** (양 손바닥을 내보이면서 어깨를) 으쓱하기
If you shrug, you raise your shoulders to show that you are not interested in something or that you do not know or care about something.

1분에 몇 단어를 읽는지 리딩 속도를 측정해보세요.

$$\frac{900 \ words}{reading \ time \ (\quad) \ sec} \times 60 = (\quad) \ WPM$$

Build Your Vocabulary

muscle**
[mʌsl]

n. 근육
A muscle is a piece of tissue inside your body which connects two bones and which you use when you make a movement.

joint**
[dʒɔint]

n. 관절, 연결 부위; a. 공동의, 합동의
A joint is a part of your body such as your elbow or knee where two bones meet and are able to move together.

ache**
[eik]

vi. 쑤시다, 아프다; n. 아픔, 쑤심
If you ache or a part of your body aches, you feel a steady, fairly strong pain.

ankle^{복습}
[ǽŋkl]

n. 발목
Your ankle is the joint where your foot joins your leg.

shovel^{복습}
[ʃʌvəl]

n. 삽; v. ～을 삽으로 뜨다[파다], 삽으로 일하다
A shovel is a tool with a long handle that is used for lifting and moving earth, coal, or snow.

crack^{복습}
[kræk]

n. 갈라진 금; 갑작스런 날카로운 소리; v. 금이 가다, 깨다; (짧고 세게) 때리다
A crack is a very narrow gap between two things, or between two parts of a thing.

blade^{복습}
[bleid]

n. (칼 · 도구 등의) 날; (프로펠러 등의) 날개; 잎
The blade of a knife, ax, or saw is the edge, which is used for cutting.

shaft^{복습}
[ʃæft]

n. (망치 · 골프채 등의 기다란) 손잡이
A shaft is a long thin piece of wood or metal that forms part of a spear, ax, golf club, or other object.

blister^{복습}
[blístər]

v. 물집이 생기다; n. 물집, 수포
When your skin blisters or when something blisters it, blisters appear on it.

dump^{복습}
[dʌmp]

vt. 쏟아 버리다, 내버리다, 아무렇게나 내려놓다; n. 쓰레기 더미
If you dump something somewhere, you put it or unload it there quickly and carelessly.

forehead**
[fɔ́ːrhèd]

n. 이마
Your forehead is the area at the front of your head between your eyebrows and your hair.

shovelful^{복습}
[ʃʌvəlfùl]

n. 한 삽(의 분량)
shovel (명사: 삽) + ful (접미사: ～정도의 양)

awesome
[ɔ́:səm]

a. 경탄할 만한, 어마어마한, 엄청난
An awesome person or thing is very impressive and often frightening.

sore^{복습}
[sɔ:r]

a. 아픈, 쓰린
If part of your body is sore, it causes you pain and discomfort.

grunt^{복습}
[grʌnt]

vi. (사람이) 툴툴거리다; (돼지가) 꿀꿀거리다; **n.** 꿀꿀[툴툴]거리는 소리
If you grunt, you make a low sound, especially because you are annoyed or not interested in something.

canteen^{복습}
[kæntí:n]

n. (휴대용) 물통; (공장·학교 등의) 구내식당
A canteen is a small plastic bottle for carrying water and other drinks. Canteens are used by soldiers.

ray^{복습}
[réi]

n. 광선, 빛; **v.** 번쩍이다
Rays of light are narrow beams of light.

arc**
[ɑ:rk]

v. 활 모양을 그리다; **n.** 둥근[활] 모양; 호, 원호
If something arces, it moves in the shape of an curve.

horizon^{복습}
[həráizn]

n. 지평선, 수평선
The horizon is the line in the far distance where the sky seems to meet the land or the sea.

fossilize
[fɑ́səlàiz]

v. 화석화하다, 화석이 되다
If the remains of an animal or plant fossilize or are fossilized, they become hard and form fossils, instead of decaying completely.

rub^{복습}
[rʌb]

v. 문지르다, 비비다; 스치다; **n.** 문지르기
If you rub an object or a surface, you move a cloth backward and forward over it in order to clean or dry it.

outline**
[áutlàin]

n. 윤곽; 개요; **v.** 개요를 서술하다; 윤곽을 나타내다
The outline of something is its general shape, especially when it cannot be clearly seen.

peek
[pí:k]

vi. 살짝 들여다보다, 엿보다; **n.** 엿봄
If you peek at something or someone, you have a quick look at them.

barren^{복습}
[bǽrən]

a. 불모의, 메마른
A barren landscape is dry and bare, and has very few plants and no trees.

wasteland^{복습}
[wéistlænd]

n. 황무지, 불모지
A wasteland is an area of land on which not much can grow or which has been spoiled in some way.

day off^{복습}

n. (근무·일을) 쉬는 날
A day off is a day when you do not go to work, even though it is usually a working day.

fossil*
[fɑ́səl]

n. 화석
A fossil is the hard remains of a prehistoric animal or plant that are found inside a rock.

bulge*
[bʌldʒ]

n. 툭 튀어 나온 것, 불룩한 것; **v.** (~으로) 가득 차다, 툭 튀어 나오다
Bulges are lumps that stick out from a surface which is otherwise flat or smooth.

54

wipe^{**}
[waɪp]

v. 닦다, 닦아 내다; **n.** 닦기
If you wipe something, you rub its surface to remove dirt or liquid from it.

Check Your Reading Speed

1분에 몇 단어를 읽는지 리딩 속도를 측정해보세요.

$$\frac{611 \text{ words}}{\text{reading time ( ) sec}} \times 60 = (\quad) \text{ WPM}$$

Build Your Vocabulary

fossil ^{복습}
[fάsəl]

n. 화석
A fossil is the hard remains of a prehistoric animal or plant that are found inside a rock.

slam[*]
[slǽm]

v. 세게 놓다, 세게 치다; 쾅 닫다[닫히다]; n. 쾅 (하는 소리)
If you slam something down, you put it there quickly and with great force.

pry^{복습}
[prai]

① vt. (pried–pried) 지레로 들어 올리다; 비틀어 움직이다; n. 지레
② vi. 엿보다, 동정을 살피다
If you pry something open or pry it away from a surface, you force it open or away from a surface.

eyesight[*]
[άisàit]

n. 시력
Your eyesight is your ability to see.

shrug^{복습}
[ʃrʌ́g]

v. (어깨를) 으쓱하다; n. (양 손바닥을 내보이면서 어깨를) 으쓱하기
If you shrug, you raise your shoulders to show that you are not interested in something or that you do not know or care about something.

dig^{복습}
[díg]

v. (dug–dug) (구멍 등을) 파다; 뒤지다; n. 발굴
If people or animals dig, they make a hole in the ground or in a pile of earth, stones, or rubbish.

remarkable^{**}
[rimά:rkəbl]

a. 놀랄 만한, 놀라운, 주목할 만한
Someone or something that is remarkable is unusual or special in a way that makes people notice them and be surprised or impressed.

bully^{복습}
[búli]

n. 약자를 괴롭히는 사람; v. 괴롭히다, 겁주다
A bully is someone who uses their strength or power to hurt or frighten other people.

pick on^{복습}

phrasal v. (구어) 괴롭히다, 못살게 굴다; ~을 선택하다, 고르다
If you pick on someone, you treat them badly or unfairly, especially repeatedly.

senseless[*]
[sénslis]

a. 인사불성의, 의식을 잃은; 무의미한
If someone is senseless, they are unconscious.

smug
[smʌg]

a. 잘난 체하는, 점잖은 체하는
If you say that someone is smug, you are criticizing the fact they seem very pleased with how good, clever, or lucky they are.

collar^{복습}
[kálər]

n. (윗옷의) 칼라, 깃; (개 등의 목에 거는) 목걸이
The collar of a shirt or coat is the part which fits round the neck and is usually folded over.

beat up

phrasal v. 두들겨 패다, 마구 차다
If you beat up someone, you strike or kick them repeatedly.

ease***
[iːz]

v. (고통 · 고민 등을) 진정[완화]시키다; 천천히 움직이다; **n.** 편함, 안정
If something unpleasant eases or if you ease it, it is reduced in degree, speed, or intensity.

chapters twelve to fourteen

1. Why did Zero smile?
   A. Mr. Pendanski told a funny story.
   B. Stanley made a joke.
   C. Magnet told the group he liked animals.
   D. Mr. Pendanski told Zero that he was special.

2. What did Zero say he liked to do?
   A. Train animals
   B. Find fossils
   C. Write letters
   D. Dig holes

3. What did Stanley find?
   A. A shotgun shell
   B. A gold bullet
   C. A coin
   D. A gold tube

4. Why didn't X-Ray show Mr. Pendanski the discovery?
   A. His hole was nearly finished.
   B. He already had a day off.
   C. He didn't want to lie to Mr. Pendanski.
   D. Stanley would show Mr. Pendanski the item.

5. When the water truck came, _____.
   A. X-Ray stood next to Stanley
   B. Stanley stood at the front of the line
   C. Magnet stood behind Stanley
   D. Stanley stood in front of Zero

6. What happened in the morning?
   A. X-Ray thanked Stanley.
   B. X-Ray shared his breakfast with Stanley.
   C. X-Ray was rude to Stanley.
   D. Stanley couldn't find X-Ray anywhere.

7. What was X-Ray's reward?
   A. The rest of the day off, an extra meal and a double shower
   B. Double shower, an extra meal and clean clothes
   C. The rest of the day off, a double shower and clean clothes
   D. An entire day off work, a double shower and a special dessert

8. What was the other campers' reward?
   A. The rest of the day off
   B. Extra water
   C. A bigger lunch
   D. Clean clothes

Check Your Reading Speed

1분에 몇 단어를 읽는지 리딩 속도를 측정해보세요.

$$\frac{769 \text{ words}}{\text{reading time } (\quad) \text{ sec}} \times 60 = (\quad) \text{ WPM}$$

Build Your Vocabulary

drag^{복습}
[dræg]

v. 힘들게 움직이다; 끌다, 끌고 오다; n. 견인, 끌기; 빨아들이기
If you say that you drag yourself somewhere, you are emphasizing that you have to make a very great effort to go there.

compound^{복습}
[kámpaund]

① n. (저택 · 공장의) 건물 안, 구내 ② vt. 합성하다, 조합하다, 만들어내다;
n. 합성물, 화합물
A compound is an enclosed area of land that is used for a particular purpose.

nod^{복습}
[nɔd]

v. 끄덕이다, 끄덕여 표시하다; n. 끄덕임(동의 · 인사 · 신호 · 명령)
If you nod, you move your head downwards and upwards to show agreement, understanding, or approval.

spit^{복습}
[spit]

v. 뱉다, 내뿜다; (폭언 등을) 내뱉다; n. 침
If you spit liquid or food somewhere, you force a small amount of it out of your mouth.

plop
[plάp]

v. 털썩 주저앉다; 풍당[툭] 하고 떨어지다; n. 풍당 (하는 소리)
If something plops somewhere, it drops there with a soft, gentle sound.

jail^{복습}
[dʒeil]

n. 교도소, 감옥
A jail is a place where criminals are kept in order to punish them, or where people waiting to be tried are kept.

veterinarian
[vètərənέəriən]

n. 수의사
A veterinarian is a person who is qualified to treat sick or injured animals.

accomplish^{***}
[əkά(ɔ́)mpliʃ]

vt. 이루다, 성취하다, 완수하다
If you accomplish something, you succeed in doing it.

figure out^{복습}

phrasal v. ~을 생각해내다, 발견하다
If you figure out a solution to a problem or the reason for something, you succeed in solving it or understanding it.

appropriate^{**}
[əpróupriit]

a. 적절한, 알맞은; v. 사용하다, 충당하다
Something that is appropriate is suitable or acceptable for a particular situation.

mess up

phrasal v. 망쳐놓다, 어질러놓다
If you mess something up or if you mess up, you cause something to fail or be spoiled.

60

on account of	idiom ~때문에, ~으로 You use on account of to introduce the reason or explanation for something.
howl^{복습} [hául]	v. 울다, 울부짖다; n. 울부짖음 If you howl with laughter, you laugh very loudly.
worthless[*] [wɔ́:rθlis]	a. 가치 없는, 쓸모없는 Something that is worthless is of no real value or use.
glare^{**} [gléər]	v. 노려보다; 번쩍번쩍 빛나다; n. 섬광; 노려봄 If you glare at someone, you look at them with an angry expression on your face.

1분에 몇 단어를 읽는지 리딩 속도를 측정해보세요.

$$\frac{1,019 \text{ words}}{\text{reading time (} \quad \text{) sec}} \times 60 = (\quad) \text{ WPM}$$

Build Your Vocabulary

lose track of
idiom ~을 놓치다, 잊다
If you lose track of someone or something, you no longer know where they are or what is happening.

freeze**
[fríːz]
v. (froze–frozen) 얼다, 얼리다; n. (임금 · 가격 등의) 동결
If a liquid or a substance containing a liquid freezes, or if something freezes it, it becomes solid because of low temperatures.

occasional**
[əkéiʒənl]
a. 가끔의, 때때로의 (occasionally ad. 때때로, 가끔)
Occasional means happening sometimes, but not regularly or often.

tease복습
[tíːz]
v. 놀리다, 장난하다; n. 장난, 놀림
To tease someone means to laugh at them or make jokes about them in order to embarrass, annoy, or upset them.

glisten*
[glísn]
v. 반짝이다, 번들거리다
If something glistens, it shines, usually because it is wet or oily.

unsure복습
[ʌnʃuər]
a. 확신하지 못하는, 의심스러워하는
If you are unsure about something, you feel uncertain about it.

glance복습
[glǽns]
v. 흘깃 보다, 잠깐 보다; n. 흘깃 봄
If you glance at something or someone, you look at them very quickly and then look away again immediately.

squint*
[skwínt]
v. 눈을 가늘게 뜨고[찡그리고] 보다; n. 사시, 사팔뜨기
If you squint at something, you look at it with your eyes partly closed.

scoop복습
[skúːp]
v. 뜨다, 파다; 재빨리 들어 올리다; n. 국자, 주걱
If you scoop something from a container, you remove it with something such as a spoon.

curiosity**
[kjuːriά(ɔ́)siti]
n. 호기심
Curiosity is a desire to know about something.

get the better of
idiom ~을 이기다, 능가하다
If a feeling such as jealousy, curiosity, or anger gets the better of you, it becomes too strong for you to hide or control.

sift**
[sift]
v. 체로 치다[거르다]; 면밀히 조사하다, 샅샅이 살피다
If you sift a powder such as flour or sand, you put it through a sieve in order to remove large pieces or lumps.

metallic*
[mətǽlik]
a. 금속의, 금속성의
Metallic means consisting entirely or partly of metal.

precious***
[préʃəs]

a. 귀한, 소중한
If you say that something such as a resource is precious, you mean that it is valuable and should not be wasted or used badly.

rub^{복습}
[rʌb]

v. 문지르다, 비비다; 스치다; n. 문지르기
If you rub an object or a surface, you move a cloth backward and forward over it in order to clean or dry it.

engrave*
[engréiv]

vt. 조각하다, 새기다; 새겨 두다, ~에게 감명을 주다
If you engrave something with a design or words, or if you engrave a design or words on it, you cut the design or words into its surface.

outline^{복습}
[áutlàin]

n. 윤곽; 개요; v. 개요를 서술하다; 윤곽을 나타내다
The outline of something is its general shape, especially when it cannot be clearly seen.

etch
[etʃ]

v. 뚜렷이 새기다
If a line or pattern is etched into a surface, it is cut into the surface by means of acid or a sharp tool.

suspect**
[səspékt]

v. 의심하다; 짐작하다; 혐의를 두다; n. 용의자
If you suspect that something dishonest or unpleasant has been done, you believe that it has probably been done.

cabin^{복습}
[kǽbin]

n. (통나무) 오두막집; 객실, 선실
A cabin is a small wooden house, especially one in an area of forests or mountains.

oak^{복습}
[óuk]

n. 오크 나무
An oak or an oak tree is a large tree that often grows in woods and forests and has strong, hard wood.

place***
[pleis]

v. (신원·정체와 관련하여) 누구[무엇]인지를 알아보다; 놓다, 두다; n. 장소
If you say that you cannot place someone, you mean that you recognize them but cannot remember exactly who they are or where you have met them before.

fossil^{복습}
[fásəl]

n. 화석
A fossil is the hard remains of a prehistoric animal or plant that are found inside a rock.

shotgun
[ʃátgʌ̀n]

n. 산탄총, 엽총
A shotgun is a gun used for shooting birds and animals which fires a lot of small metal balls at one time.

junk*
[dʒʌŋk]

n. 폐물, 고물
Junk is old and used goods that have little value and that you do not want any more.

1분에 몇 단어를 읽는지 리딩 속도를 측정해보세요.

$$\frac{952 \text{ words}}{\text{reading time (} \quad \text{) sec}} \times 60 = (\quad) \text{ WPM}$$

Build Your Vocabulary

scratchy^{복습}
[skrǽtʃi]

a. (몸에 닿으면) 가려운[따끔거리는]; 긁는 듯한 소리가 나는
Scratchy clothes or fabrics are rough and uncomfortable to wear next to your skin.

cot^{복습}
[kɑt]

n. 접이 침대, 간이[야영용] 침대; 소아용 침대
A cot is a narrow bed, usually made of canvas fitted over a frame which can be folded up.

grumble^{복습}
[grʌ́mbl]

v. 투덜거리다, 불평하다; n. 투덜댐, 불평
If someone grumbles, they complain about something in a bad-tempered way.

snap**
[snǽp]

v. (화난 목소리로) 딱딱거리다; 딱[툭] (하고) 부러뜨리다[부러지다]
If someone snaps at you, they speak to you in a sharp, unfriendly way.

scrape**
[skréip]

v. 긁다, 긁어내다, 문지르다; 스쳐서 상처를 내다
If someone or something scrapes something else, it rubs against it, usually making a noise or causing slight damage.

stamp***
[stǽmp]

v. (발을) 구르다, 짓밟다; (도장 · 스탬프 등을) 찍다; n. 우표, 인지; 도장
If you stamp or stamp your foot, you lift your foot and put it down very hard on the ground, for example because you are angry.

blade^{복습}
[bleid]

n. (칼 · 도구 등의) 날; (프로펠러 등의) 날개; 잎
The blade of a knife, ax, or saw is the edge, which is used for cutting.

shovel^{복습}
[ʃʌ́vəl]

n. 삽; v. ~을 삽으로 뜨다[파다], 삽으로 일하다
A shovel is a tool with a long handle that is used for lifting and moving earth, coal, or snow.

pierce***
[piərs]

vt. (뾰족한 기구로) 뚫다, 찌르다
If a sharp object pierces something, or if you pierce something with a sharp object, the object goes into it and makes a hole in it.

produce^{복습}
[prədjúːs]

v. (~에서) 꺼내 보이다, 보여 주다; 생산하다; n. 생산물
If you produce an object from somewhere, you show it or bring it out so that it can be seen.

distant***
[dístənt]

a. 먼, (멀리) 떨어져 있는
Distant means very far away.

haze*
[heiz]

n. 아지랑이, 엷은 연기; v. 흐릿해지다, 안개가 끼다
If there is a haze of something such as smoke or steam, you cannot see clearly through it.

drift**
[drift]

v. (물·공기에) 떠가다, 표류[부유]하다; (자신도 모르게) ~하게 되다; n. 표류
When something drifts somewhere, it is carried there by the movement of wind or water.

canteen^{복습}
[kæntíːn]

n. (휴대용) 물통; (공장·학교 등의) 구내식당
A canteen is a small plastic bottle for carrying water and other drinks. Canteens are used by soldiers.

cab**
[kæb]

n. (버스·기차·트럭의) 운전석; 택시
The cab of a truck or train is the front part in which the driver sits.

stick out^{복습}

phrasal v. (툭) 튀어나오다; ~을 내밀다
If something is sticks out, it is further out than something else.

day off^{복습}

n. (근무·일을) 쉬는 날
A day off is a day when you do not go to work, even though it is usually a working day.

passenger^{복습}
[pǽsəndʒər]

n. 승객 (passenger side n. 조수석)
A passenger in a vehicle such as a bus, boat, or plane is a person who is travelling in it, but who is not driving it or working on it.

stud*
[stʌd]

n. 장식용 금속 단추; 못[징] (studded a. 장식용 금속 단추를 붙인)
Something that is studded is decorated with small pieces of metal for decoration.

freckle*
[frékl]

n. 주근깨, 반점
Freckles are small light brown spots on someone's skin, especially on their face.

reward**
[riwɔ́ːrd]

v. 보답하다, 보상하다; n. 보상, 보답; 현상금
If you do something and are rewarded with a particular benefit, you receive that benefit as a result of doing that thing.

wiggle^{복습}
[wígl]

v. (좌우로) 움직이다, (몸을) 뒤흔들다; n. 뒤흔듦
If you wiggle something or if it wiggles, it moves up and down or from side to side in small quick movements.

swish
[swíʃ]

v. 휙 소리 내다, 휘두르다; 튀기다; n. 휙 소리
If something swishes or if you swish it, it moves quickly through the air, making a soft sound.

authority***
[əθɔ́ːriti]

n. 권위, 권력; 권한
Authority is the right to command and control other people.

chapters fifteen & sixteen

1. What was Stanley's new job?
   A. Shovel dirt into a wheelbarrow
   B. Help Zero dig a new hole
   C. Fill up the other boys' canteens
   D. Dig a large hole with Magnet and Squid

2. Why was X-Ray rude to Stanley in the morning?
   A. X-Ray didn't want Stanley to take the tube away from him.
   B. Stanley told X-Ray that he would tell the Warden the truth.
   C. X-Ray didn't like Stanley.
   D. X-Ray believed there were cameras and microphones all over the camp.

3. Stanley _____.
   A. found something new in the wheelbarrow
   B. knew the Warden was looking for something
   C. forgot where he found the tube
   D. would tell the Warden where he found the tube

4. Why did the boys work faster?
   A. Mr. Sir left them alone.
   B. The Warden took away their water.
   C. Mr. Sir helped them dig.
   D. The Warden yelled at them.

5. Why was the landlord threatening to evict Stanley's parents?
   A. They couldn't pay the rent.
   B. There was a fire in their apartment.
   C. Their home smelled so bad.
   D. Stanley was sent to Camp Green Lake.

6. Why didn't Zero laugh at the joke in Stanley's letter?
   A. Stanley refused to share the joke.
   B. Stanley didn't explain the joke well.
   C. Zero didn't care about the joke or Stanley's letter.
   D. Zero didn't know the nursery rhyme.

1분에 몇 단어를 읽는지 리딩 속도를 측정해보세요.

$$\frac{658 \text{ words}}{\text{reading time ( ) sec}} \times 60 = (\quad) \text{ WPM}$$

Build Your Vocabulary

poke^{복습}
[pouk]

v. (손가락 등으로) 쿡 찌르다; n. 찌르기, 쑤시기
If you poke someone or something, you quickly push them with your finger or with a sharp object.

take over

phrasal v. (~로부터) (~을) 인계받다, (기업 등을) 인수하다
If you take over something from someone, you do it instead of them.

dig^{복습}
[díg]

v. (구멍 등을) 파다; 뒤지다; n. 파기
If people or animals dig, they make a hole in the ground or in a pile of earth, stones, or rubbish.

dump^{복습}
[dʌ́mp]

vt. 쏟아 버리다, 내버리다, 아무렇게나 내려놓다; n. 쓰레기 더미
If you dump something somewhere, you put it or unload it there quickly and carelessly.

get in the way

idiom 방해되다
If something gets in the way, it prevents you from doing something; prevent something from happening.

remainder*
[riméindər]

n. 나머지
The remainder of a group are the things or people that still remain after the other things or people have gone or have been dealt with.

occasional^{복습}
[əkéiʒənl]

a. 가끔의, 때때로의 (occasionally ad. 때때로, 가끔)
Occasional means happening sometimes, but not regularly or often.

still***
[stíl]

a. 정지한, 움직이지 않는; 조용한, 고요한; ad. 여전히, 아직도
If you stay still, you stay in the same position and do not move.

excavate^{복습}
[ékskəvèit]

vt. (구멍 등을) 파다, 발굴하다, 출토하다
To excavate means to dig a hole in the ground, for example in order to build there.

microphone**
[máikrəfòun]

n. 마이크(로폰)
A microphone is a device that is used to make sounds louder or to record them on a tape recorder.

paranoid
[pǽrənɔ̀id]

a. 피해망상적인; n. 편집증 환자
If you say that someone is paranoid, you mean that they are extremely suspicious and afraid of other people.

toenail
[tóunèil]

n. 발톱
Your toenails are the thin hard areas at the end of each of your toes.

68

character^{복습}
[kǽriktər]

n. 인격, 성격; 특징, 특성; 문자, 서체
Your character is your personality, especially how reliable and honest you are.

definite[*]
[défənit]

a. 분명한, 뚜렷한; 확실한, 확고한 (definitely **ad.** 분명히, 틀림없이)
You use definite to emphasize the strength of your opinion or belief.

gaze^{***}
[géiz]

vi. 응시하다, 뚫어지게 보다; **n.** 주시, 응시
If you gaze at someone or something, you look steadily at them for a long time, for example because you find them attractive or interesting, or because you are thinking about something else.

Check Your Reading Speed

1분에 몇 단어를 읽는지 리딩 속도를 측정해보세요.

$$\frac{898 \text{ words}}{\text{reading time ( ) sec}} \times 60 = (\quad) \text{ WPM}$$

Build Your Vocabulary

flesh***
[fleʃ]

n. 살; 육체; vt. (칼 등을) 살에 찌르다
Flesh is the soft part of a person's or animal's body between the bones and the skin.

couch^{복습}
[kautʃ]

n. 소파, 긴 의자
A couch is a long, comfortable seat for two or three people.

crash**
[kræʃ]

vt. 충돌하다, 추락하다; (굉음과 함께) 부딪치다; n. 쿵, 와르르 하는 소리; 충돌, 추락
If something crashes somewhere, it moves and hits something else violently, making a loud noise.

groan^{복습}
[gróun]

v. 신음하다, 끙끙거리다; n. 신음, 끙끙거리는 소리
If you groan, you make a long, low sound because you are in pain, or because you are upset or unhappy about something.

uncertain**
[ʌnsə́:rtn]

a. 자신 없는, 머뭇거리는 (uncertainly ad. 자신 없게, 머뭇거리며)
If you are uncertain about something, you do not know what you should do, what is going to happen, or what the truth is about something.

intent**
[intént]

① a. 집중된; 열심인, 여념이 없는 (intently ad. 골똘하게) ② n. 의지, 의향
If you are intent on doing something, you are eager and determined to do it.

bust
[bʌst]

v. 고장 내다, 망치다; (현장을) 덮치다; 파산하다
If you bust something, you break it or damage it so badly that it cannot be used.

dig^{복습}
[díg]

v. (dug–dug) (구멍 등을) 파다; 뒤지다; n. 파기
If people or animals dig, they make a hole in the ground or in a pile of earth, stones, or rubbish.

tend**
[tend]

① vt. 손질하다, 돌보다 ② vi. 향하다; 경향이 있다
If you tend to someone or something, you pay attention to them and deal with their problems and needs.

cart*
[ka:rt]

v. (수레나 차량으로) 운반하다, 나르다; n. 손수레, 카트
If you cart things or people somewhere, you carry them or transport them there, often with difficulty.

excess**
[eksés]

a. 제한 초과의, 여분의; n. 초과, 과잉
Excess is used to describe amounts that are greater than what is needed, allowed, or usual.

70

place복습
[pleis]

v. (신원 · 정체와 관련하여) 누구[무엇]인지를 알아보다; 놓다, 두다; n. 장소
If you say that you cannot place someone, you mean that you recognize them but cannot remember exactly who they are or where you have met them before.

lid**
[lid]

n. 뚜껑
A lid is the top of a box or other container which can be removed or raised when you want to open the container.

fancy**
[fǽnsi]

a. 화려한, 고급스러운; v. 공상(상상)하다; 좋아하다; n. 공상; 기호, 선호
If you describe something as fancy, you mean that it is very expensive or of very high quality.

sprawl복습
[sprɔ́:l]

v. (팔다리 등을) 쭉 펴다, 큰 대자로 눕다; 제 멋대로 뻗어 나가다
(sprawled a. 팔다리를 아무렇게나 벌리고 누워있는)
If you sprawl somewhere, you sit or lie down with your legs and arms spread out in a careless way.

understuffed
[ʌ́ndərstʌ́ft]

a. 속이 부족한
under (접두사: 충분하지 못함) + stuffed (형용사: 속을 채운)

sneak*
[sní:k]

v. 살금살금 돌아다니다; 슬쩍 넣다[집다]; 고자질하다; n. 밀고자
If you sneak somewhere, you go there very quietly on foot, trying to avoid being seen or heard.

presumable
[prizú:məbl]

a. 가정[추정]할 수 있는, 있음직한 (presumably ad. 아마, 짐작컨대)
If you say that something is presumably the case, you mean that you think it is very likely to be the case, although you are not certain.

afford복습
[əfɔ́:rd]

vt. ~할 여유가 있다; 주다, 공급하다
If you cannot afford something, you do not have enough money to pay for it.

breakthrough
[bréikθrù:]

n. 돌파구
A breakthrough is an important development or achievement.

sneaker복습
[sní:kər]

n. (pl.) 고무창 운동화
Sneakers are casual shoes with rubber soles.

landlord**
[lǽndlɔ́:rd]

n. 지주, 집주인
Someone's landlord is the man who allows them to live or work in a building which he owns, in return for rent.

threaten**
[θrétn]

v. 위협하다, 협박하다
If something or someone threatens a person or thing, they are likely to harm that person or thing.

evict
[ivíkt]

vt. (주택이나 땅에서) 쫓아내다, 퇴거시키다
If someone is evicted from the place where they are living, they are forced to leave it, usually because they have broken a law or contract.

odor복습
[óudər]

n. (불쾌한) 냄새, 악취
An odor is a particular and distinctive smell.

awful 복습
[ɔ́:fəl]

a. 지독한, 대단한; 무서운
If you say that someone or something is awful, you dislike that person or thing or you think that they are not very good.

startle *
[stɑ́:rtl]

v. 깜짝 놀라게 하다; 움찔하다; n. 깜짝 놀람
If something sudden and unexpected startles you, it surprises and frightens you slightly.

recycle 복습
[ri:sáikl]

v. 재활용하다; 재순환하다
If you recycle things that have already been used, such as bottles or sheets of paper, you process them so that they can be used again.

blank **
[blǽŋk]

a. 멍한, 무표정한; 빈; n. 빈칸, 여백 (blankly ad. 멍하니, 우두커니)
If you look blank, your face shows no feeling, understanding, or interest.

rhyme 복습
[raim]

n. (시의) 운; v. (두 단어나 음절이) 운이 맞다 (nursery rhyme n. 자장가, 동요)
A nursery rhyme is a poem or song for young children, especially one that is old or well known.

recite **
[risáit]

v. 암송[낭독]하다; 죽 말하다, 나열하다
When someone recites a poem or other piece of writing, they say it aloud after they have learned it.

1. What did the Warden do to Armpit?
   A. She took away his water.
   B. She smacked him on the head.
   C. She jabbed him with a pitchfork.
   D. She hit him with a shovel.

2. What happened to Stanley?
   A. He passed out because of the heat.
   B. Zigzag's shovel hit him on the heaD.
   C. Magnet poked Stanley with a pitchfork.
   D. He fell onto Zigzag's dirt.

3. What did Stanley learn about Zero?
   A. Zero didn't know how to rock climb.
   B. Zero didn't know how to read or write.
   C. Zero didn't have a family.
   D. Zero stole Stanley's box of stationary.

4. What had NOT changed about Stanley since arriving at Camp Green Lake?
   A. His hands had become tougher.
   B. He had gotten stronger.
   C. He had become less thirsty.
   D. His heart had hardened.

5. Why was Stanley awakened in the night?

    A. He heard Squid crying.

    B. He had bad allergies.

    C. He heard Squid and Magnet fighting.

    D. He was very thirsty.

6. What DIDN'T happen?

    A. Magnet stole sunflower seeds from Mr. Sir's truck.

    B. Stanley ate some sunflower seeds.

    C. Zigzag threw the sunflower seed bag to Stanley.

    D. The sunflowers spilled in Stanley's hole.

7. Stanley _____.

    A. knocked a pile of dirt back into his hole

    B. thought that X-Ray didn't close the bag properly

    C. lied to Mr. Sir

    D. felt terrible inside Mr. Sir's truck

1분에 몇 단어를 읽는지 리딩 속도를 측정해보세요.

$$\frac{471 \text{ words}}{\text{reading time ( ) sec}} \times 60 = (\quad) \text{ WPM}$$

Build Your Vocabulary

wear on	phrasal v. 지나다, 경과하다; 초조하게 만들다 If a period of time wears on, it seems to go past very slowly.
jab [dʒǽb]	v. 콱[쿡] 찌르다; 쥐어박다; n. (콱) 찌르기; 잽 If you jab one thing into another, you push it there with a quick, sudden movement and with a lot of force.
knock* [nák]	v. 치다, 부수다; (문을) 두드리다, 노크하다 If you knock something, you touch or hit it roughly, especially so that it falls or moves.
scoop [skú:p]	v. 뜨다, 파다; 재빨리 들어 올리다; n. 국자, 주걱 If you scoop something from a container, you remove it with something such as a spoon.
collapse [kəlǽps]	v. 쓰러지다, 맥없이 주저앉다; 무너지다, 붕괴하다; n. 무너짐, 붕괴 If you collapse, you suddenly faint or fall down because you are very ill or weak.
pass out	phrasal v. 의식을 잃다, 기절하다 If you pass out, you faint or collapse.
gash* [gǽʃ]	n. 깊은 상처; (지면의) 갈라진 틈; vt. 상처를 입히다 A gash is a long, deep cut in your skin or in the surface of something.
bandage* [bǽndidʒ]	n. 붕대; vt. 붕대를 감다 If you bandage a wound or part of someone's body, you tie a bandage around it.
sack [sæk]	n. (쇼핑 물건을 담는 크고 튼튼한 종이) 봉지; 부대, 자루; vt. 자루에 넣다 Sacks are used to carry or store things such as vegetables or coal.
wound* [wú:nd]	n. 상처, 부상; v. 부상을 입히다 A wound is damage to part of your body, especially a cut or a hole in your flesh, which is caused by a gun, knife, or other weapon.
nap* [næp]	n. 잠깐 잠, 낮잠 If you have a nap, you have a short sleep, usually during the day.
dizzy [dízi]	a. 현기증 나는, 아찔한 If you feel dizzy, you feel as if everything is spinning round and being unable to balance.

Check Your Reading Speed

1분에 몇 단어를 읽는지 리딩 속도를 측정해보세요.

$$\frac{555 \text{ words}}{\text{reading time ( ) sec}} \times 60 = (\quad) \text{ WPM}$$

Build Your Vocabulary

shovel복습
[ʃʌvəl]

n. 삽; v. ~을 삽으로 뜨다[파다]. 삽으로 일하다
A shovel is a tool with a long handle that is used for lifting and moving earth, coal, or snow.

swing*
[swíŋ]

v. 휘두르다. (한 점을 축으로 하여) 빙 돌다, 휙 움직이다
If you swing at a person or thing, you try to hit them with your arm or with something that you are holding.

hang around

phrasal v. (~에서) 서성거리다
If you hang around, you spend time somewhere, without doing very much.

jerk**
[dʒɔ́:rk]

① v. 휙 움직이다; n. (갑자기 날카롭게) 휙 움직임 ② n. 바보, 멍청이
If you jerk something or someone in a particular direction, or they jerk in a particular direction, they move a short distance very suddenly and quickly.

throb*
[θráb]

vi. 욱신거리다; (심장이) 고동치다, 맥이 뛰다; n. 고동, 맥박
If part of your body throbs, you feel a series of strong and usually painful beats there.

considerable**
[kənsídərəbl]

a. 상당한, 많은 (considerably ad. 꽤, 상당히)
Considerable means great in amount or degree.

swell*
[swél]

v. (swelled-swollen) 붓다; 팽창하다; (가슴이) 벅차다; (소리가) 높아지다;
n. 팽창, 증대
If something such as a part of your body swells, it becomes larger and rounder than normal.

hard-boiled

a. (달걀이) 완숙된
A hard-boiled egg has been boiled in its shell until the whole of the inside is solid.

stick out복습

phrasal v. (툭) 튀어나오다; ~을 내밀다
If something is sticks out, it is further out than something else.

remainder복습
[riméindər]

n. 나머지
The remainder of a group are the things or people that still remain after the other things or people have gone or have been dealt with.

muscle복습
[mʌsl]

n. 근육
A muscle is a piece of tissue inside your body which connects two bones and which you use when you make a movement.

callused
[kǽləst]

a. (피부가) 거칠고 못이 박혀 굳어진
A foot or hand that is callused is covered in thick skin.

spit^{복습}
[spit]

v. (spat-spat) 뱉다, 내뿜다; (폭언 등을) 내뱉다; n. 침
If you spit liquid or food somewhere, you force a small amount of it out of your mouth.

crate^{복습}
[kréit]

n. 나무 상자, (짐을 보호하는) 나무틀
A crate is a large box used for transporting or storing things.

stationery^{복습}
[stéiʃənèri]

n. 문구류, 문방구
Stationery is paper, envelopes, and other materials or equipment used for writing.

challenging
[tʃǽlindʒiŋ]

a. 도전적인, 도전 의식을 북돋우는
A challenging task or job requires great effort and determination.

obstacle^{복습}
[ábstəkl]

n. 장애(물), 방해(물)
An obstacle is an object that makes it difficult for you to go where you want to go, because it is in your way.

penetrate**
[pénitreit]

v. 간파하다; 꿰뚫다, 통과하다
If something or someone penetrates a physical object or an area, they succeed in getting into it or passing through it.

sore^{복습}
[sɔːr]

a. 아픈, 쓰린
If part of your body is sore, it causes you pain and discomfort.

count^{복습}
[káunt]

v. 중요하다; 세다, 계산하다; 포함시키다; (정식으로) 인정되다; n. 계산, 셈
If something or someone counts for something or counts, they are important or valuable.

moisture**
[mɔ́istʃər]

n. 습기, 수분
Moisture is tiny drops of water in the air, on a surface, or in the ground.

seal**
[síːl]

v. (봉투 등을) 봉인하다; 밀폐하다; n. 직인, 도장
When you seal an envelope, you close it by folding part of it over and sticking it down, so that it cannot be opened without being torn.

stamp^{복습}
[stæmp]

v. (도장 · 스탬프 등을) 찍다; (발을) 구르다, 짓밟다; n. 우표, 인지; 도장
If you stamp a mark or word on an object, you press the mark or word onto the object using a stamp or other device.

1분에 몇 단어를 읽는지 리딩 속도를 측정해보세요.

$$\frac{1{,}014 \text{ words}}{\text{reading time (} \quad \text{) sec}} \times 60 = (\quad) \text{ WPM}$$

Build Your Vocabulary

awaken***
[əwéikən]

v. (잠에서) 깨다, 깨우다
When you awaken, or when something or someone awakens you, you wake up.

frighten**
[fráitn]

v. 놀라게 하다, 섬뜩하게 하다 (frightened **a.** 겁먹은, 무서워하는)
If something or someone frightens you, they cause you to suddenly feel afraid, anxious, or nervous.

cot복습
[kɑt]

n. 접이 침대, 간이[야영용] 침대; 소아용 침대
A cot is a narrow bed, usually made of canvas fitted over a frame which can be folded up.

jerk복습
[dʒə́:rk]

① v. 홱 움직이다; n. (갑자기 날카롭게) 홱 움직임 ② n. 바보, 멍청이
If you jerk something or someone in a particular direction, or they jerk in a particular direction, they move a short distance very suddenly and quickly.

sniff**
[snif]

v. 코를 훌쩍이다; 콧방귀를 뀌다; 코를 킁킁거리다, 냄새를 맡다;
n. 냄새 맡음; 콧방귀
When you sniff, you breathe in air through your nose hard enough to make a sound, for example when you are trying not to cry, or in order to show disapproval.

allergy*
[ǽlərdʒi]

n. 알레르기, 과민증
If you have a particular allergy, you become ill or get a rash when you eat, smell, or touch something.

jaw**
[dʒɔ:]

n. 턱, 아래턱
Your jaw is the lower part of your face below your mouth.

racial*
[réiʃəl]

a. 인종[민족]간의
Racial describes things relating to people's race.

trail복습
[tréil]

v. (땅에 대고 뒤로) 끌다, 끌리다; ~을 뒤쫓다; n. 지나간 자국, 흔적
If you trail something or it trails, it hangs down loosely behind you as you move along.

canteen복습
[kæntí:n]

n. (휴대용) 물통; (공장·학교 등의) 구내식당
A canteen is a small plastic bottle for carrying water and other drinks. Canteens are used by soldiers.

exhaust**
[igzɔ́:st]

n. (자동차 등의) 배기가스; vt. 기진맥진하게 만들다; 다 써 버리다, 고갈시키다
Exhaust is the gas or steam that is produced when the engine of a vehicle is running.

fume^{**}
[fjú:m]

n. 연기, 김; v. 몹시 화내다; 연기 나다, 그을리다
Fumes are the unpleasant and often unhealthy smoke and gases that are produced by fires or by things such as chemicals, fuel, or cooking.

pop^{복습}
[páp]

v. 급히 집어넣다; 뻥 하고 터뜨리다; 불쑥 나타나다; n. 뻥[탁] 하는 소리; 발포
If you pop something somewhere, you put it there quickly.

handful[*]
[hǽndfùl]

n. 한 움큼, 손에 그득, 한 줌
A handful of something is the amount of it that you can hold in your hand.

swallow^{**}
[swálou]

v. 삼키다, 목구멍으로 넘기다; (초조해서) 마른침을 삼키다
If you swallow something, you cause it to go from your mouth down into your stomach.

wiggle^{복습}
[wígl]

v. (좌우로) 움직이다, (몸을) 뒤흔들다; n. 뒤흔듦
If you wiggle something or if it wiggles, it moves up and down or from side to side in small quick movements.

salt^{***}
[sɔ:lt]

v. 소금을 치다; n. 소금 (salted a. 소금에 절인)
When you salt food, you add salt to it.

dig^{복습}
[díg]

v. (dug–dug) (구멍 등을) 파다; 뒤지다; n. 발굴
If people or animals dig, they make a hole in the ground or in a pile of earth, stones, or rubbish.

sweep^{**}
[swí:p]

v. (빗자루로) 쓸다, 털다; n. 쓸기, 비질하기
If you sweep things off something, you push them off with a quick smooth movement of your arm.

knock^{복습}
[nák]

v. 치다, 부수다; (문을) 두드리다, 노크하다
If you knock something, you touch or hit it roughly, especially so that it falls or moves.

unthinkable
[ʌnθíŋkəbl]

a. 상상도 할 수 없는
If you say that something is unthinkable, you are emphasizing that it cannot possibly be accepted or imagined as a possibility.

unearth^{복습}
[ʌnə́:rθ]

v. (땅속에서) 파내다, 발굴하다; 찾다, 밝혀내다
If someone unearths something that is buried, they find it by digging in the ground.

day off^{복습}

n. (근무 · 일을) 쉬는 날
A day off is a day when you do not go to work, even though it is usually a working day.

mutter^{복습}
[mʌ́tər]

v. 중얼거리다, 불평하다; n. 중얼거림, 불평
If you mutter, you speak very quietly so that you cannot easily be heard, often because you are complaining about something.

ray^{복습}
[réi]

n. 광선, 빛; v. 번쩍이다
Rays of light are narrow beams of light.

bounce^{복습}
[bauns]

v. 급히 움직이다, 뛰어다니다; 튀다, 튀게 하다; n. 튐, 바운드
If someone bounces somewhere, they move there in an energetic way, because they are feeling happy.

80

appreciate[star][star]
[əpríːʃieit]

v. 고마워하다; 평가하다, 감상하다
If you appreciate something that someone has done for you or is going to do for you, you are grateful for it.

sweaty
[swéti]

a. (사람 · 몸 · 옷 등이) 땀투성이의, 땀이 나는
If parts of your body or your clothes are sweaty, they are soaked or covered with sweat.

1. What happened to Mr. Sir?
   A. The Warden hit him and he went unconscious.
   B. The Warden scratched him.
   C. He fell onto the Warden's flowered makeup bag.
   D. The Warden injected him with venom.

2. What DIDN'T happen?
   A. The Warden struck Mr. Sir across the face.
   B. Stanley lied to the Warden.
   C. Mr. Sir kicked Warden when he fell down.
   D. The Warden barely touched Stanley's wound with her nail.

3. According to Stanley's great-grandfather, how did he live so long in the desert?
   A. He found refuge on God's Thumb.
   B. He was rescued by Kissin' Kate Barlow.
   C. He found a small cabin in the desert.
   D. He spent seventeen days with rattlesnake hunters.

4. Who nearly finished digging Stanley's hole?
   A. X-Ray
   B. Magnet
   C. Armpit
   D. Zero

5. What did Zero know?

    A. Stanley ate some sunflower seeds.

    B. Stanley didn't steal the sneakers.

    C. The Warden hurt Mr. Sir with rattlesnake venom.

    D. What the gold tube really was.

6. Stanley would teach Zero _____; Zero would
   _____.

    A. to read; dig part of X-Ray's hole

    B. math; dig part of Stanley's hole

    C. English; dig a part of each camper's hole

    D. to read; dig part of Stanley's hole

7. Zero _____.

    A. was stupid

    B. didn't like answering people's questions

    C. couldn't learn the alphabet easily

    D. was selfish

8. What was the gold tube?

    A. A bullet

    B. An eye shadow container

    C. A nail polish jar

    D. A lipstick container

1분에 몇 단어를 읽는지 리딩 속도를 측정해보세요.

$$\frac{908 \text{ words}}{\text{reading time (} \quad \text{) sec}} \times 60 = (\quad) \text{ WPM}$$

Build Your Vocabulary

shade복습
[ʃeid]

n. (시원한) 그늘; 색조; vt. 그늘지게 하다
Shade is an area of darkness under or next to an object such as a tree, where sunlight does not reach.

oak복습
[óuk]

n. 오크 나무
An oak or an oak tree is a large tree that often grows in woods and forests and has strong, hard wood.

condemn**
[kəndém]

vt. 선고를 내리다; 규탄하다, 비난하다 (condemned a. 유죄 선고를 받은)
If someone is condemned to a punishment, they are given this punishment.

cabin복습
[kæbin]

n. (통나무) 오두막집; 객실, 선실
A cabin is a small wooden house, especially one in an area of forests or mountains.

knock복습
[nák]

v. (문을) 두드리다, 노크하다; 치다, 부수다
If you knock on something such as a door or window, you hit it, usually several times, to attract someone's attention.

gaze복습
[géiz]

n. 주시, 응시; vi. 응시하다, 뚫어지게 보다
You can talk about someone's gaze as a way of describing how they are looking at something, especially when they are looking steadily at it.

dread**
[dred]

n. 두려움; 두려운 것; v. 몹시 무서워하다, 두려워하다
Dread is a feeling of great anxiety and fear about something that may happen.

air-conditioned복습
[ɛ́ər-kəndíʃənd]

a. 냉난방[공기 조절] 장치를 한
If a room or vehicle is air-conditioned, the air in it is kept cool and dry by means of a special machine.

remote**
[rimóut]

n. (= remote control) 리모컨; a. 외진, 외딴; (시간상으로) 먼
A remote is a control device.

barefoot*
[bɛ́ərfùt]

a., ad. 맨발의[로]
Someone who is barefoot is not wearing anything on their feet.

freckle복습
[frékl]

n. 주근깨, 반점 (freckled a. 주근깨가 있는)
Freckles are small light brown spots on someone's skin, especially on their face.

steady ^{복습}
[stédi]

v. 진정시키다, 균형을 잡다; a. 꾸준한
If you steady something or if it steadies, it stops shaking or moving about.

sneak ^{복습}
[sníːk]

v. (snuck–snuck) 살금살금 돌아다니다; 슬쩍 넣다[집다]; 고자질하다; n. 밀고자
If you sneak somewhere, you go there very quietly on foot, trying to avoid being seen or heard.

cover up

phrasal v. (나쁜 짓 등을) 은폐하다
If you cover up something, you put something over it in order to hide or protect it.

flowered
[fláuərd]

a. 꽃으로 덮인, 꽃무늬로 장식한
Flowered paper or cloth has a pattern of flowers on it.

unclasp
[ʌnklǽsp]

v. 걸쇠를 벗기다; (쥐었던 손 등을) 놓다, 펴다
If you unclasp something, you unfasten the clasp of it.

latch [*]
[lætʃ]

n. 걸쇠, 빗장; v. 걸쇠를 걸다
A latch is a fastening on a door or gate. It consists of a metal bar which you lift in order to open the door.

jar ^{**}
[dʒáːr]

① n. 병, 단지 ② v. 삐걱거리다; n. 삐걱거리는 소리, 잡음
A jar is a glass container with a lid that is used for storing food.

nod ^{복습}
[nɔd]

v. 끄덕이다, 끄덕여 표시하다; n. 끄덕임(동의 · 인사 · 신호 · 명령)
If you nod, you move your head downwards and upwards to show agreement, understanding, or approval.

ingredient [*]
[ingríːdiənt]

n. 재료, 성분, 원료
Ingredients are the things that are used to make something, especially all the different foods you use when you are cooking a particular dish.

rattlesnake ^{복습}
[rǽtlsnèik]

n. [동물] 방울뱀
A rattlesnake is a poisonous American snake which can make a rattling noise with its tail.

venom [*]
[vénəm]

n. (독사 따위의) 독; 악의, 원한
The venom of a creature such as a snake or spider is the poison that it puts into your body when it bites or stings you.

harmless ^{**}
[háːrmlis]

a. 해롭지 않은, 무해한
If you describe someone or something as harmless, you mean that they are not important and therefore unlikely to annoy other people or cause trouble.

toxic
[táksik]

a. 유독성의
A toxic substance is poisonous.

tingle [*]
[tíŋgl]

v. 따끔따끔 아프다, 쑤시다; 설레게 하다, 흥분시키다; n. 따끔거림; 흥분, 안달
When a part of your body tingles, you have a slight stinging feeling there.

pinkie
[píŋki]

n. 새끼손가락
Your pinkie is the smallest finger on your hand.

wound^{복습}
[wúːnd]

n. 상처, 부상; v. 부상을 입히다
A wound is damage to part of your body, especially a cut or a hole in your flesh, which is caused by a gun, knife, or other weapon.

sting^{복습}
[stiŋ]

n. 찌름, 쏨; vt. 찌르다, 쏘다
If you feel a sting, you feel a sharp pain in your skin or other part of your body.

face^{복습}
[féis]

v. ~을 마주보다, 향하다; 직면하다; 직시하다
If someone or something faces a particular thing, person, or direction, they are positioned opposite them or are looking in that direction.

fireplace*
[faiərplèis]

n. (벽)난로
In a room, the fireplace is the place where a fire can be lit and the area on the wall and floor surrounding this place.

hearth**
[hɑːrə]

n. 난로 부근, 난로 (바닥)
The hearth is the floor of a fireplace, which sometimes extends into the room.

strike^{복습}
[straik]

v. (struck−stricken/struck) 때리다, 치다, 부딪치다; 갑자기 떠오르다;
n. 치기, 때리기; 파업
If you strike someone or something, you deliberately hit them.

slant**
[slǽnt]

v. 기울어지다, 비스듬해지다; n. 비스듬함
Something that slants is sloping, rather than horizontal or vertical.

clutch**
[klʌ́tʃ]

v. 부여잡다, 꽉 잡다, 붙들다; n. 붙잡음, 움켜쥠
If you clutch at something or clutch something, you hold it tightly, usually because you are afraid or anxious.

rug**
[rʌg]

n. (방바닥·마루에 까는) 깔개, 융단
A rug is a piece of thick material that you put on a floor.

moan**
[móun]

v. 신음하다, 끙끙대다; 투덜대다; n. 신음; 불평
If you moan, you make a low sound, usually because you are unhappy or in pain.

recede*
[risíːd]

vi. 약해지다, 희미해지다; (서서히) 물러나다
When something such as a quality, problem, or illness recedes, it becomes weaker, smaller, or less intense.

violent**
[váiələnt]

a. 격렬한, 맹렬한; 폭력적인, 난폭한 (violently ad. 격렬하게, 맹렬히)
If you describe something as violent, you mean that it is said, done, or felt very strongly.

shrill**
[ʃril]

a. (소리가) 날카로운; v. 날카로운[새된] 소리를 내다
A shrill sound is high-pitched and unpleasant.

twitch*
[twítʃ]

vi. (손가락·근육 따위가) 씰룩거리다; 홱 잡아당기다, 잡아채다; n. 씰룩거림, 경련
If something, especially a part of your body, twitches or if you twitch it, it makes a little jumping movement.

writhe*
[raið]

v. (고통으로) 몸부림치다, 몸을 뒤틀다
If you writhe, your body twists and turns violently backwards and forwards, usually because you are in great pain or discomfort.

86

agony
[ǽgəni]

n. 고뇌, 고통, 번민
Agony is great physical or mental pain.

frighten^{복습}
[fráitn]

v. 놀라게 하다, 섬뜩하게 하다 (frightened **a.** 겁먹은, 무서워하는)
If something or someone frightens you, they cause you to suddenly feel afraid, anxious, or nervous.

1분에 몇 단어를 읽는지 리딩 속도를 측정해보세요.

$$\frac{481 \text{ words}}{\text{reading time (} \quad \text{) sec}} \times 60 = (\quad) \text{ WPM}$$

Build Your Vocabulary

haze^{복습} [heiz]	**n.** 아지랑이, 엷은 연기; **v.** 흐릿해지다, 안개가 끼다 If there is a haze of something such as smoke or steam, you cannot see clearly through it.
desolate^{복습} [désəlit]	**a.** 황폐한, 황량한, 쓸쓸한 A desolate place is empty of people and lacking in comfort.
wasteland^{복습} [wéistlænd]	**n.** 황무지, 불모지 A wasteland is an area of land on which not much can grow or which has been spoiled in some way.
rob^{복습} [ráb]	**v.** 빼앗다, 도둑질하다 If someone is robbed, they have money or property stolen from them.
strand^{복습} [strænd]	① **v.** 오도 가도 못 하게 하다, 발을 묶다 ② **n.** (실·전선·머리카락 등의) 가닥, 끈 줄 If you are stranded, you are prevented from leaving a place, for example because of bad weather.
desert^{복습} [dézərt]	① **n.** 사막, 황무지 ② **v.** 인적이 끊기다; 버리다, 유기하다 A desert is a large area of land, usually in a hot region, where there is almost no water, rain, trees, or plants.
face^{복습} [féis]	**v.** 직면하다; ~을 마주보다, 향하다; 직시하다 If you face or are faced with something difficult or unpleasant, or if it faces you, it is going to affect you and you have to deal with it.
barren^{복습} [bǽrən]	**a.** 불모의, 메마른 A barren landscape is dry and bare, and has very few plants and no trees.
insane^{**} [inséin]	**a.** 정신 이상의, 미친 Someone who is insane has a mind that does not work in a normal way, with the result that their behavior is very strange.
refuge[*] [réfjudʒ]	**n.** 피난처, 은신처; 피난, 도피 A refuge is a place where you go for safety and protection.
twitch^{복습} [twitʃ]	**vi.** 홱 잡아당기다, 잡아채다; (손가락·근육 따위가) 씰룩거리다; **n.** 씰룩거림, 경련 If something, especially a part of your body, twitches or if you twitch it, it makes a little jumping movement.
coil[*] [kóil]	**v.** (고리 모양으로) 감다, 휘감다; **n.** (여러 겹으로 둥글게 감아 놓은) 고리 If you coil something, you wind it into a series of loops or into the shape of a ring. If it coils around something, it forms loops or a ring.

rattle ^{복습}
[rǽtl]

v. 왈각달각 소리 나다, 덜걱덜걱 움직이다; n. 방울뱀의 꼬리; 덜거덕거리는 소리
When something rattles or when you rattle it, it makes short sharp knocking sounds because it is being shaken or it keeps hitting against something hard.

pound [*]
[páund]

① v. 쿵쿵 울리다; 마구 치다, 세게 두드리다; n. 타격 ② n. 파운드 (무게의 단위) ③ n. 울타리, 우리
If your heart is pounding, it is beating with an unusually strong and fast rhythm, usually because you are afraid.

shrug ^{복습}
[ʃrʌ́g]

v. (어깨를) 으쓱하다; n. (양 손바닥을 내보이면서 어깨를) 으쓱하기
If you shrug, you raise your shoulders to show that you are not interested in something or that you do not know or care about something.

bother ^{복습}
[báðər]

v. 귀찮게 하다; 신경 쓰이게 하다, 괴롭히다; 일부러 ~하다, 애를 쓰다
If someone bothers you, they talk to you when you want to be left alone or interrupt you when you are busy.

credit ^{***}
[krédit]

n. 공, 명예, 칭찬; 학점; 신용
If you get the credit for something good, people praise you because you are responsible for it, or are thought to be responsible for it.

1분에 몇 단어를 읽는지 리딩 속도를 측정해보세요.

$$\frac{1{,}158 \text{ words}}{\text{reading time ( ) sec}} \times 60 = (\qquad) \text{ WPM}$$

Build Your Vocabulary

spit^{복습}
[spit]

v. (spat–spat) 뱉다, 내뿜다; (폭언 등을) 내뱉다; n. 침
If you spit liquid or food somewhere, you force a small amount of it out of your mouth.

laundry^{복습}
[lɔ́:ndri]

n. 세탁물; 세탁
Laundry is used to refer to clothes, sheets, and towels that are about to be washed, are being washed, or have just been washed.

**mole*
[móul]

n. [동물] 두더지
A mole is a small animal with black fur that lives underground.

point out^{복습}

phrasal v. ~을 지적하다
If you point out a fact or mistake, you tell someone about it or draw their attention to it.

worm**
[wə:rm]

n. 벌레
A worm is a small animal with a long thin body, no bones and no legs.

flap**
[flæp]

n. 덮개; 퍼덕거림; v. 퍼덕거리다, 퍼덕이다
A flap of cloth or skin, for example, is a flat piece of it that can move freely up and down or from side to side because it is held or attached by only one edge.

glance^{복습}
[glæns]

v. 흘낏 보다, 잠깐 보다; n. 흘낏 봄
If you glance at something or someone, you look at them very quickly and then look away again immediately.

crate^{복습}
[kréit]

n. 나무 상자, (짐을 보호하는) 나무틀
A crate is a large box used for transporting or storing things.

deposit**
[dipázit]

vt. (특정한 곳에) 두다, 놓다; 맡기다, 예금하다
To deposit something somewhere means to put them or leave them there.

sneaker^{복습}
[sní:kər]

n. (pl.) 고무창 운동화
Sneakers are casual shoes with rubber soles.

worn-out^{복습}
[wɔ́:rn-áut]

a. 기진맥진한; 써서 낡은, 닳아 해진
Someone who is worn-out is extremely tired after hard work or a difficult or unpleasant experience.

stationery^{복습}
[stéiʃənèri]

n. 문구류, 문방구
Stationery is paper, envelopes, and other materials or equipment used for writing.

defiance*
[difáiəns]

n. 저항, 반항; 도전
Defiance is behavior or an attitude which shows that you are not willing to obey someone.

memorize**
[méməràiz]

vt. 기억하다, 암기하다
If you memorize something, you learn it so that you can remember it exactly.

refresh**
[rifréʃ]

vt. ～의 기억을 새롭게 하다; 상쾌하게 하다, 원기를 회복하다
If someone refreshes your memory, they tell you something that you had forgotten.

recite^{복습}
[risáit]

v. 죽 말하다, 나열하다; 암송[낭독]하다
If you recite something such as a list, you say it aloud.

give away

phrasal v. 누설하다, 드러내다
If you do or say something gives you away, it shows or reveals your secret.

figure out^{복습}

phrasal v. ～을 생각해내다, 발견하다
If you figure out a solution to a problem or the reason for something, you succeed in solving it or understanding it.

print***
[prínt]

v. (글자를) 인쇄체로 쓰다; 인쇄하다; n. (인쇄된) 활자
If you print words, you write in letters that are not joined together and that look like the letters in a book or newspaper.

proper***
[prápər]

a. 고유의; 적절한, 제대로 된 (proper noun n. 고유명사)
You can add proper after a word to indicate that you are referring to the central and most important part of a place, event, or object and want to distinguish it from other things which are not regarded as being important or central to it.

lowercase
[lóuərkèis]

a. 소문자의, 소문자로 인쇄한; n. 소문자
Lowercase letters are small letters, not capital letters.

multiply**
[mʌ́ltiplai]

vt. (수를) 곱하다; 늘리다, 증가하다
When something multiplies or when you multiply it, it increases greatly in number or amount.

count^{복습}
[káunt]

v. 세다, 계산하다; 포함시키다; 중요하다; (정식으로) 인정되다; n. 계산, 셈
When you count, you say all the numbers one after another up to a particular number.

uppercase
[ʌ́pərkèis]

a. 대문자의, 대문자로 인쇄한; n. 대문자
Uppercase letters are capital letters.

divide***
[diváid]

vt. 나누다, 분할하다
If you divide a larger number by a smaller number or divide a smaller number into a larger number, you calculate how many times the smaller number can fit exactly into the larger number.

reconsider*
[rì:kənsídər]

v. 재고하다, 다시 생각하다
If you reconsider a decision or opinion, you think about it and try to decide whether it should be changed.

float***
[flóut]

v. 흘러가다, 떠돌다; 뜨다; 띄우다
Something that floats in or through the air hangs in it or moves slowly and gently through it.

writhe^{복습}
[raið]

v. (고통으로) 몸부림치다, 몸을 뒤틀다
If you writhe, your body twists and turns violently backwards and forwards, usually because you are in great pain or discomfort.

flowered
[fláuərd]

a. 꽃으로 덮인, 꽃무늬로 장식한
Flowered paper or cloth has a pattern of flowers on it.

jolt*
[dʒoult]

n. 가슴이 철렁하는 느낌; 덜컥 하고 움직임;
v. 갑자기 거칠게[덜컥거리며] 움직이다
A jolt is an unpleasant surprise or shock.

astonishment**
[əstániʃmənt]

n. 놀람, 경악
Astonishment is a feeling of great surprise.

outlaw^{복습}
[áutlɔː]

n. 범법자; vt. 불법화하다, 금지하다
An outlaw is a criminal who is hiding from the authorities.

92

1. What was Katherine Barlow's job?
   A. Chef
   B. Peach Farmer
   C. Teacher
   D. Town mayor

2. Why did most townspeople believe Katherine would marry Trout Walker?
   A. Trout was well educated and he was the most handsome young man in the county.
   B. Trout was the richest man in the county and he enjoyed making spiced peaches with Katherine.
   C. Trout had a new boat and Katherine enjoyed spending time on Green Lake.
   D. Trout was the son of the richest man in the county and his family owned most of the peach trees.

3. Mr. Sir _____.
   A. gave Stanley extra water
   B. grabbed Stanley by the neck
   C. didn't give Stanley any water
   D. told the campers what happened to his face

4. According to Sam, Mary Lou lived a long time because
_____.
   A. she'd never been sick
   B. she only ate raw onions
   C. Dr. Hawthorn took care of her
   D. she lived in the Walkers' shed

5. What deal did Sam and Katherine make?
   A. Sam would fix things around the school for jars of spiced peaches.
   B. Sam would fix Katherine's boat for reading and writing lessons.
   C. Sam would give Katherine onion medicines for jars of spiced peaches.
   D. Sam would fix things around the school for different onion medicines.

6. Why wasn't Katherine happy after the school house was finished?
   A. She didn't think Sam did a good job.
   B. She didn't want any more students attending the school.
   C. The school was too small for the new students.
   D. She ran out of things that needed to be fixed.

7. Why did Hattie Parker whisper, "God will punish you!"?
   A. She saw Katherine hug Mary Lou.
   B. She saw Sam selling sweet, hot onions.
   C. She saw Katherine and Sam kissing.
   D. She thought that Sam's onion medicines didn't work.

Check Your Reading Speed

1분에 몇 단어를 읽는지 리딩 속도를 측정해보세요.

$$\frac{629 \text{ words}}{\text{reading time ( ) sec}} \times 60 = (\quad) \text{ WPM}$$

Build Your Vocabulary

sparkle^{복습}
[spá:rkl]

v. 반짝이다; 생기 넘치다; n. 반짝거림, 광채
If something sparkles, it is clear and bright and shines with a lot of very small points of light.

shore***
[ʃɔ́:r]

n. 물가, 강기슭; vt. 상륙시키다
The shores or the shore of a sea, lake, or wide river is the land along the edge of it.

bloom**
[blu:m]

v. 꽃이 피다, 개화하다; 번영시키다; n. 꽃
When a plant or tree blooms, it produces flowers. When a flower blooms, it opens.

blossom^{복습}
[blásəm]

n. 꽃; v. 꽃이 피다, 꽃을 피우다
Blossom is the flowers that appear on a tree before the fruit.

fabulous*
[fǽbjuləs]

a. 굉장한, 멋진, 믿어지지 않는
If you describe something as fabulous, you are emphasizing that you like it a lot or think that it is very good.

spice**
[spais]

v. ~에 향신료를[양념을] 치다; n. 양념, 향신료, 양념류
Food that is spiced has had spices or other strong-tasting foods added to it.

jar^{복습}
[dʒá:r]

① n. 병, 단지 ② v. 삐걱거리다; n. 삐걱거리는 소리, 잡음
A jar is a glass container with a lid that is used for storing food.

leak*
[li:k]

v. (액체·기체가) 새게 하다, 새다; n. (액체·기체가) 새는 곳
If a container leaks, there is a hole or crack in it which lets a substance such as liquid or gas escape.

crooked**
[krúkid]

a. 비뚤어진, 구부러진; 부정직한
If you describe something as crooked, especially something that is usually straight, you mean that it is bent or twisted.

hinge*
[híndʒ]

n. (문·뚜껑 등의) 경첩
A hinge is a piece of metal, wood, or plastic that is used to join a door to its frame or to join two things together so that one of them can swing freely.

incurable
[inkjúərəbl]

a. 치유할 수 없는, 불치의
If someone has an incurable disease, they cannot be cured of it.

afflict**
[əflíkt]

v. 괴롭히다, 피해를 입히다
If you are afflicted by pain, illness, or disaster, it affects you badly and makes you suffer.

ballplayer
[bɔ́:lplèiər]

n. 직업 야구 선수
A ballplayer is a baseball player.

brag
[bræg]

v. 자랑하다, 자만하다, 허풍떨다
If you brag, you say in a very proud way that you have something or have done something.

county*
[káunti]

n. 자치주[군]
A county is a region of Britain, Ireland, or the USA which has its own local government.

disrespectful
[dìsrispéktfəl]

a. 무례한, 실례되는
If you are disrespectful, you show no respect in the way that you speak or behave to someone.

ranch*
[rǽntʃ]

n. 목장, 대규모 방목장
A ranch is a large farm used for raising animals, especially cattle, horses, or sheep.

schooling*
[skú:liŋ]

n. 학교 교육
Schooling is education that children receive at school.

stupidity*
[stju:pídəti]

n. 우둔함; 어리석음, 어리석은 짓
Stupidity is the state of being silly or unwise.

brand-new
[brǽnd-njú:]

a. 아주 새로운, 신상품의
A brand-new object is completely new.

row*
[róu]

① v. 노[배]를 젓다 ② n. 줄; 열, 줄; 좌석 줄
When you row, you sit in a boat and make it move through the water by using oars.

horrible수능
[hɔ́:rəbəl]

a. 끔찍한, 소름 끼치게 싫은; 무서운
You can call something horrible when it causes you to feel great shock, fear, and disgust.

spew
[spjú:]

v. 뿜어져 나오다, 분출하다; (먹은 것을) 토하다
When something spews out a substance or when a substance spews from something, the substance flows out quickly in large quantities.

turn down

phrasal v. 거절하다; (소리 · 온도 등을) 낮추다
If you turn someone or something down, you reject or refuse them.

1분에 몇 단어를 읽는지 리딩 속도를 측정해보세요.

$$\frac{573 \text{ words}}{\text{reading time ( ) sec}} \times 60 = (\quad) \text{ WPM}$$

Build Your Vocabulary

sight^{복습}
[sait]

n. 보기, 봄; 시력, 시야
The sight of something is the act of seeing it or an occasion on which you see it.

awaken^{복습}
[əwéikən]

v. (잠에서) 깨다, 깨우다
When you awaken, or when something or someone awakens you, you wake up.

swell^{복습}
[swél]

v. (swelled-swollen) 붓다; 팽창하다; (가슴이) 벅차다; (소리가) 높아지다;
n. 팽창, 증대
If something such as a part of your body swells, it becomes larger and rounder than normal.

jagged
[dʒǽgid]

a. 삐죽삐죽한, 들쭉날쭉한
Something that is jagged has a rough, uneven shape or edge with lots of sharp points.

good sense

n. 양식, 분별
If you have the good sense, you have the quality someone has when they are able to make sensible decisions about what to do.

carton^{복습}
[káːrtən]

n. (음식이나 음료를 담는) 곽[통]; 상자
A carton is a plastic or cardboard container in which food or drink is sold.

ladle
[léidl]

vt. (음식을 국자 등으로 듬뿍) 떠[퍼] 담다; n. 국자
If you ladle food such as soup or stew, you serve it, especially with a ladle.

stuff^{복습}
[stʌf]

n. 물질, 물건; 일[것](일반적으로 말하거나 생각하는 것); vt. 채워 넣다, 속을 채우다
You can use stuff to refer to things such as a substance, a collection of things, events, or ideas, or the contents of something in a general way without mentioning the thing itself by name.

crash^{복습}
[kræʃ]

n. 쿵, 와르르 하는 소리; 충돌, 추락; vt. (굉음과 함께) 부딪치다; 충돌하다, 추락하다
A crash is a sudden, loud noise.

choke**
[tʃouk]

v. 질식시키다, 숨이 막히다; n. 질식
When you choke or when something chokes you, you cannot breathe properly or get enough air into your lungs.

bang^{복습}
[bæŋ]

v. 부딪치다, 탕 치다, 쾅 닫(히)다; n. 쾅 하는 소리
If something bangs, it makes a sudden loud noise, once or several times.

gurgle*
[gɔ́ːrgəl]

v. (물이 좁은 공간을 빠르게 흐를 때 나는) 꼴꼴 소리 나다; (아기가) 까르륵 소리를 내다
If someone, especially a baby, is gurgling, they are making a sound in their throat similar to the gurgling of water.

gasp**
[gǽsp]

v. 숨이 턱 막히다, 헉 하고 숨을 쉬다; n. (숨이 막히는 듯) 헉 하는 소리를 냄
When you gasp, you take a short quick breath through your mouth, especially when you are surprised, shocked, or in pain.

dig^{복습}
[díg]

v. (dug–dug) (구멍 등을) 파다; 뒤지다; n. 파기
If people or animals dig, they make a hole in the ground or in a pile of earth, stones, or rubbish.

pace***
[péis]

v. (일의) 속도를 유지하다; 서성거리다; n. 속도
If you pace yourself when doing something, you do it at a steady rate.

canteen^{복습}
[kæntíːn]

n. (휴대용) 물통; (공장 · 학교 등의) 구내식당
A canteen is a small plastic bottle for carrying water and other drinks. Canteens are used by soldiers.

dare***
[déər]

v. 감히 ~하다, 무릅쓰다, 도전하다
If you dare to do something, you do something which requires a lot of courage.

grotesque*
[groutésk]

a. 기괴한; 터무니없는, 말도 안 되는
You say that something is grotesque when it is so unnatural, unpleasant, and exaggerated that it upsets or shocks you.

parched
[paːrtʃt]

a. 몹시 목마른; (날씨가 더워서) 몹시 건조한
If your mouth, throat, or lips are parched, they are unpleasantly dry.

nozzle*
[názl]

n. 노즐, 분사구
The nozzle of a hose or pipe is a narrow piece fitted to the end to control the flow of liquid or gas.

splatter
[splǽtəːr]

v. 튀다, 튀기다; n. 튀기기; 철벅철벅 소리
If a thick wet substance splatters on something or is splattered on it, it drops or is thrown over it.

absorb**
[æbsɔ́ːrb]

vt. 흡수하다, 받아들이다; 열중시키다
If something absorbs a liquid, gas, or other substance, it soaks it up or takes it in.

shrink**
[ʃriŋk]

v. (shrank–shrunk) 줄어들다, 오그라지다
If something shrinks or something else shrinks it, it becomes smaller.

1분에 몇 단어를 읽는지 리딩 속도를 측정해보세요.

$$\frac{1{,}151 \text{ words}}{\text{reading time (\quad) sec}} \times 60 = (\quad) \text{ WPM}$$

Build Your Vocabulary

donkey**
[dáŋki]

n. 당나귀
A donkey is an animal which is like a horse but which is smaller and has longer ears.

dirt road

n. (시골의) 흙길, 비포장도로
dirt (명사: 흙) + road (명사: 작은 길, 오솔길)

row복습
[róu]

① v. 노[배]를 젓다 ② n. 열, 줄; 좌석 줄
When you row, you sit in a boat and make it move through the water by using oars.

batch
[bǽtʃ]

n. 집단, 한 회분, 일괄 처리되는 묶음
A batch of things is a group of things of the same kind, dealt with at the same time.

shed복습
[ʃed]

n. (~을) 보관하는 곳, (작은) 헛간
A shed is a small building that is used for storing things such as garden tools.

charge***
[tʃɑ́ːrdʒ]

n. (상품 · 서비스에 대한) 요금; 기소, 고발; 책임, 담당;
v. 청구하다; 기소하다, 고소하다; 돌격하다
A charge is an amount of money that you have to pay for a service.

extraordinary**
[ikstrɔ́ːrdənèri]

a. 기이한, 놀라운; 비상한, 비범한 (extraordinarily ad. 비상하게, 엄청나게)
If you describe something as extraordinary, you mean that it is very unusual or surprising.

digestion**
[didʒéstʃən]

n. 소화, 소화력
Your digestion is the system in your body which digests your food.

liver**
[lívər]

n. (인체의) 간
The liver of some animals that is cooked and eaten.

lung**
[lʌŋ]

n. 폐, 허파
Your lungs are the two organs inside your chest which fill with air when you breathe in.

ointment
[ɔ́intmənt]

n. 연고
An ointment is a smooth thick substance that is put on sore skin or a wound to help it heal.

100

paste**
[peist]

n. (밀가루 등의 가루로 만든) 반죽, 풀; **v.** 풀로 붙이다
Paste is a soft, wet, sticky mixture of a substance and a liquid, which can be spread easily.

cure**
[kjuər]

v. 낫게 하다, 치유하다; **n.** 치유하는 약, 치유법
If doctors or medical treatments cure a person, they make the person well again after an illness or injury.

pimple
[pímpl]

n. 여드름, 뾰루지
Pimples are small raised spots, especially on the face.

remedy**
[rémədi]

n. 치료, 구제책; **vt.** 고치다, 치료하다
A remedy is something that is intended to cure you when you are ill or in pain.

bald^{복습}
[bɔ́:ld]

a. (머리 등이) 벗겨진, 대머리의; **vi.** 머리가 벗겨지다 (baldness **n.** 대머리, 탈모증)
Someone who is bald has little or no hair on the top of their head.

rub^{복습}
[rʌ́b]

v. 문지르다, 비비다; 스치다; **n.** 문지르기
If you rub a substance into a surface or rub something such as dirt from a surface, you spread it over the surface or remove it from the surface using your hand or something such as a cloth.

resent*
[rizént]

v. 분하게[억울하게] 여기다, 분개하다
If you resent someone or something, you feel bitter and angry about them.

folk***
[fóuk]

n. (pl.) (특정 국가 · 지역 출신 또는 특정한 생활방식을 가진) 사람들
You can refer to people as folk or folks.

concoction
[kɑnkɑ́kʃən]

n. (음료나 약물의 특이한) 혼합물
A concoction is something that has been made out of several things mixed together.

treatment**
[trí:tmənt]

n. 치료, 처치; 취급, 대우
Treatment is medical attention given to a sick or injured person or animal.

trick***
[trik]

n. 비결, 요령, 묘책; 속임수; **v.** 속이다, 속임수를 쓰다
A trick is a clever way of doing something.

distract*
[distrǽkt]

v. (마음 · 주의를) 흐트러뜨리다, 딴 데로 돌리다 (distracted **a.** 정신이 산만한)
If you are distracted, you are not concentrating on something because you are worried or are thinking about something else.

leak^{복습}
[li:k]

v. (액체 · 기체가) 새게 하다, 새다; **n.** (액체 · 기체가) 새는 곳
If a container leaks, there is a hole or crack in it which lets a substance such as liquid or gas escape.

leaky
[lí:ki]

a. (구멍 · 균열이 생겨서 물 · 가스가) 새는, 구멍이 난
Something that is leaky has holes, cracks, or other faults which allow liquids and gases to pass through.

jar^{복습}
[dʒɑ́:r]

① **n.** 병, 단지 ② **v.** 삐걱거리다; **n.** 삐걱거리는 소리, 잡음
A jar is a glass container with a lid that is used for storing food.

spice^{복습}
[spais]

v. ~에 향신료를[양념을] 치다; n. 양념, 향신료, 양념류
Food that is spiced has had spices or other strong-tasting foods added to it.

poetry**
[póuitri]

n. (집합적으로) 시, 시가
Poems, considered as a form of literature, are referred to as poetry.

poem***
[póuəm]

n. (한 편의) 시
A poem is a piece of writing in which the words are chosen for their beauty and sound and are carefully arranged, often in short lines which rhyme.

breeze**
[bri:z]

n. 산들바람, 미풍; vi. 산들산들 불다
A breeze is a gentle wind.

uphill^{복습}
[ʌ́phil]

ad. 오르막길로, 언덕 위로; a. 오르막의
If something or someone is uphill or is moving uphill, they are near the top of a hill or are going up a slope.

wobble
[wábl]

v. 흔들흔들하다, 비틀대다; 동요하다; n. 흔들림
If something or someone wobbles, they make small movements from side to side, for example because they are unsteady.

run-down
[rʌ́n-dáun]

a. 황폐한, 쇠퇴한
A run-down building or area is in very poor condition.

craft**
[kræ(ɑ:)ft]

vt. 공들여 만들다, 공예품을 만들다; n. (수)공예; 기술, 기교
If something is crafted, it is made skillfully.

admire***
[ædmáiər]

v. 감탄하며 바라보다; 존경하다, 칭찬하다
If you admire someone or something, you like and respect them very much.

general store

n. 잡화점
A general store is a rural or small town store that carries a general line of merchandise.

quiver**
[kwívər]

v. 떨다, (떨리듯) 흔들리다; n. 떨기
If something quivers, it shakes with very small movements.

punish**
[pʌ́niʃ]

v. 처벌하다, 벌주다
To punish someone means to make them suffer in some way because they have done something wrong.

1. How did Sam break the law?

    A. He kissed Katherine.

    B. He set the schoolhouse on fire.

    C. He sold the sheriff bad onions.

    D. He continued selling onions after he was told not to.

2. What happened to Sam?

    A. He was hanged.

    B. He was shot and killed.

    C. He got away in his boat.

    D. He became an outlaw.

3. What did Mr. Pendanski do for Stanley?

    A. He gave Stanley another canteen.

    B. He helped Stanley dig his hole.

    C. He let Stanley have a break from digging his hole.

    D. He let Stanley have extra water.

4. The other boys didn't like _____.

    A. Stanley speaking to Zero

    B. Stanley digging faster than them

    C. Stanley sitting around while they worked

    D. Mr. Sir giving Stanley water again

5. Why did Stanley pour his water onto the dirt?
    A. He thought that digging without water would make him stronger.
    B. He saw Mr. Pendanski put something in it.
    C. He wasn't thirsty.
    D. He thought that Mr. Sir put something in it.

6. Why did Trout and Linda go to Kate's cabin?
    A. They wanted Kate's loot.
    B. They wanted revenge.
    C. They wanted to kill Kate.
    D. They wanted to live in the cabin.

7. Trout Walker _____.
    A. married Linda for her money
    B. lost all his money because the lake dried up
    C. robbed every bank in Texas
    D. was the most feared outlaw in the county

8. How did Kate die?
    A. She was shot by Trout Walker.
    B. She was with a shovel by Linda Walker.
    C. She was bitten by a lizarD.
    D. She didn't drink enough water.

1분에 몇 단어를 읽는지 리딩 속도를 측정해보세요.

$$\frac{806 \text{ words}}{\text{reading time } (\quad) \text{ sec}} \times 60 = (\quad) \text{ WPM}$$

Build Your Vocabulary

lose track of^{복습}

idiom ~을 놓치다, 잊다
If you lose track of someone or something, you no longer know where they are or what is happening.

mob**
[mɑb]

n. (폭력을 휘두르거나 말썽을 일으킬 것 같은) 군중, 무리
A mob is a large, disorganized, and often violent crowd of people.

storm***
[stɔːrm]

vi. 돌진하다; 격노하다; n. 폭풍우
If you storm into or out of a place, you enter or leave it quickly and noisily, because you are angry.

rip^{복습}
[rip]

v. 찢(어지)다, 벗겨내다; 돌진하다; n. 찢어진 틈, 잡아 찢음
When something rips or when you rip it, you tear it forcefully with your hands or with a tool such as a knife.

bulletin board*
[búlətinbɔ́ːrd]

n. 게시판
A bulletin board is a board which is usually attached to a wall in order to display notices giving information about something.

poison**
[pɔ́izn]

v. 나쁜 영향을 주다, 해치다; 독으로 죽이다, 독살하다; n. 독, 독약
Something that poisons a good situation or relationship spoils it or destroys it.

sheriff**
[ʃérif]

n. 보안관
In the United States, a sheriff is a person who is elected to make sure that the law is obeyed in a particular county.

gasp^{복습}
[gæsp]

v. 헉 하고 숨을 쉬다, 숨이 턱 막히다; n. (숨이 막히는 듯) 헉 하는 소리를 냄
When you gasp, you take a short quick breath through your mouth, especially when you are surprised, shocked, or in pain.

drawl
[drɔːl]

n. 느린 말투; v. 느릿느릿 말하다
Drawl is a slow and not very clear way of speaking, with long vowel sounds.

urge***
[ə́ːrdʒ]

v. 몰아대다, 재촉하다; n. (강한) 충동
If you urge someone to do something, you try hard to persuade them to do it.

slap^{복습}
[slæp]

v. 찰싹 때리다, 탁 놓다; 철썩 부딪치다; n. 찰싹 (때림)
If you slap someone, you hit them with the palm of your hand.

wriggle*
[rígl]

v. (몸 · 몸의 일부를) 꿈틀거리다; n. 꿈틀거리기
If you wriggle or wriggle part of your body, you twist and turn with quick movements.

106

hang***
[hæŋ]

v. 교수형에 처하다; 걸다, 달아매다; 매달리다
If someone is hanged or if they hang, they are killed, usually as a punishment, by having a rope tied around their neck and the support taken away from under their feet.

jerk^{복습}
[dʒə́:rk]

① v. 홱 움직이다; n. (갑자기 날카롭게) 홱 움직임 ② n. 바보, 멍청이
If you jerk something or someone in a particular direction, or they jerk in a particular direction, they move a short distance very suddenly and quickly.

punish^{복습}
[pʌ́niʃ]

v. 처벌하다, 벌주다
To punish someone means to make them suffer in some way because they have done something wrong.

lakefront
[léikfrʌ̀nt]

n. 호숫가, 호수의 기슭
A lakefront is an area fronting on a lake.

hitch
[hítʃ]

① v. (밧줄 등으로) ~을 (~에) 묶다 ② v. (지나가는 차를) 얻어 타다, 편승하다
If you hitch something to something else, you hook it or fasten it there.

wade**
[weid]

v. (물 · 진흙 속을 힘겹게) 헤치며 걷다
If you wade through something that makes it difficult to walk, usually water or mud, you walk through it.

aboard^{복습}
[əbɔ́:rd]

ad. 배에, 승선하여
If you are aboard a ship or plane, you are on it or in it.

shore^{복습}
[ʃɔ́:r]

n. 물가, 강기슭; vt. 상륙시키다
The shores or the shore of a sea, lake, or wide river is the land along the edge of it.

motorized
[móutəràizd]

a. 엔진[동력]이 달린
A motorized vehicle has an engine.

roar***
[rɔ́:r]

n. 으르렁거리는 소리; 외치는 소리; 왁자지껄함;
vi. (큰 짐승 등이) 으르렁거리다, 고함치다
If something, usually a vehicle, roars somewhere, it goes there very fast, making a loud noise.

smash^{복습}
[smǽʃ]

v. 세게 충돌하다; 때려 부수다, 깨뜨리다; n. 강타; 부서지는 소리; 분쇄
If something smashes or is smashed against something solid, it moves very fast and with great force against it.

donkey^{복습}
[dʌ́ŋki]

n. 당나귀
A donkey is an animal which is like a horse but which is smaller and has longer ears.

coat***
[kout]

n. 표면을 덮는 것, 칠; 외투, 코트; v. (막 같은 것을) 덮다
A coat of paint or varnish is a thin layer of it on a surface.

outlaw^{복습}
[áutlɔ̀:]

n. 범법자; vt. 불법화하다, 금지하다
An outlaw is a criminal who is hiding from the authorities.

Check Your Reading Speed

1분에 몇 단어를 읽는지 리딩 속도를 측정해보세요.

$$\frac{895 \text{ words}}{\text{reading time (\quad) sec}} \times 60 = (\quad) \text{ WPM}$$

Build Your Vocabulary

shovel 복습
[ʃʌvəl]

n. 삽; **v.** ~을 삽으로 뜨다[파다], 삽으로 일하다
A shovel is a tool with a long handle that is used for lifting and moving earth, coal, or snow.

grunt 복습
[grʌnt]

vi. (사람이) 툴툴거리다; (돼지가) 꿀꿀거리다; **n.** 꿀꿀[툴툴]거리는 소리
If you grunt, you make a low sound, especially because you are annoyed or not interested in something.

pry 복습
[prai]

① **vt.** (pried–pried) 비틀어 움직이다; 지레로 들어 올리다; **n.** 지레
② **vi.** 엿보다, 동정을 살피다
If you pry something open or pry it away from a surface, you force it open or away from a surface.

fling 복습
[fliŋ]

vt. (flung–flung) 내던지다, 던지다; (문 등을) 왈칵 열다
If you fling something somewhere, you throw it there using a lot of force.

glance 복습
[glæns]

v. 흘깃 보다, 잠깐 보다; **n.** 흘깃 봄
If you glance at something or someone, you look at them very quickly and then look away again immediately.

sparing
[spέəriŋ]

a. 조금만 쓰는, 인색한 (sparingly **ad.** 절약하여)
Someone who is sparing with something uses it or gives it only in very small quantities.

slave*
[sleiv]

n. 노예; **v.** 노예처럼[고되게] 일하다
A slave is someone who is the property of another person and has to work for that person.

point out 복습

phrasal v. ~을 지적하다
If you point out a fact or mistake, you tell someone about it or draw their attention to it.

risk**
[risk]

v. (~을) 위태롭게 하다, ~의 위험을 무릅쓰다; **n.** 위험
If you risk your life or something else important, you behave in a way that might result in it being lost or harmed.

lousy
[láuzi]

a. 형편없는; 안 좋은, 엉망인
If you describe the number or amount of something as lousy, you mean it is smaller than you think it should be.

handful 복습
[hǽndfùl]

n. 한 움큼, 손에 그득, 한 줌
A handful of something is the amount of it that you can hold in your hand.

108

mock**
[mɑ(ɔ)k]

v. (흉내를 내며) 놀리다, 조롱하다; a. 거짓된, 가짜의
If someone mocks you, they show or pretend that they think you are foolish or inferior, for example by saying something funny about you, or by imitating your behavior.

shovelful^{복습}
[ʃʌ́vəlfùl]

n. 한 삽(의 분량)
shovel (명사: 삽) + ful (접미사: ～정도의 양)

microphone^{복습}
[máikrəfòun]

n. 마이크(로폰)
A microphone is a device that is used to make sounds louder or to record them on a tape recorder.

swelling*
[swéliŋ]

n. (살갗의) 부기, (몸의) 부어오른 곳
A swelling is a raised, curved shape on the surface of your body which appears as a result of an injury or an illness.

puffy^{복습}
[pʌ́fi]

a. 부푼, 팽창된
If you describe something as puffy, you mean it has a round, swollen appearance.

jagged^{복습}
[dʒǽgid]

a. 삐죽삐죽한, 들쭉날쭉한
Something that is jagged has a rough, uneven shape or edge with lots of sharp points.

tattoo^{복습}
[tætú:]

n. 문신
A tattoo is a design that is drawn on someone's skin using needles to make little holes and filling them with colored dye.

swish^{복습}
[swíʃ]

v. 휙 소리 내다, 휘두르다; 튀기다; n. 휙 소리
If something swishes or if you swish it, it moves quickly through the air, making a soft sound.

dump^{복습}
[dʌ́mp]

vt. 쏟아 버리다, 내버리다, 아무렇게나 내려놓다; n. 쓰레기 더미
If you dump something somewhere, you put it or unload it there quickly and carelessly.

cab^{복습}
[kǽb]

n. (버스 · 기차 · 트럭의) 운전석; 택시
The cab of a truck or train is the front part in which the driver sits.

pop^{복습}
[pɑ́p]

v. 급히 집어넣다; 뻥 하고 터뜨리다; 불쑥 나타나다; n. 뻥[탁] 하는 소리; 발포
If you pop something somewhere, you put it there quickly.

spit^{복습}
[spit]

v. 뱉다, 내뿜다; (폭언 등을) 내뱉다; n. 침
If you spit liquid or food somewhere, you force a small amount of it out of your mouth.

vile**
[vail]

a. 극도로 불쾌한, 나쁜; 비도덕적인, 절대 용납할 수 없는
If you say that someone or something is vile, you mean that they are very unpleasant.

substance**
[sʌ́bstəns]

n. 물질; 실체
A substance is a solid, powder, liquid, or gas with particular properties.

unscrew
[ʌnskrú:]

v. (병뚜껑 같은 것을 돌려서) 열다; 나사를 풀다
If you unscrew something such as a lid, or if it unscrews, you keep turning it until you can remove it.

1분에 몇 단어를 읽는지 리딩 속도를 측정해보세요.

$$\frac{840 \text{ words}}{\text{reading time (\quad) sec}} \times 60 = (\qquad) \text{ WPM}$$

Build Your Vocabulary

oak^{복습}
[óuk]

n. 오크 나무
An oak or an oak tree is a large tree that often grows in woods and forests and has strong, hard wood.

abandon**
[əbǽndən]

vt. 버리다; 단념하다, 그만두다 (abandoned **a.** 버려진)
If you abandon a place, thing, or person, you leave the place, thing, or person permanently or for a long time.

cabin^{복습}
[kǽbin]

n. (통나무) 오두막집; 객실, 선실
A cabin is a small wooden house, especially one in an area of forests or mountains.

pond***
[pɑnd]

n. (주로 인공적인) 연못
A pond is a small area of water that is smaller than a lake.

echo**
[ékou]

v. 울려 퍼지다, 메아리치다; (남의 말·의견을) 그대로 되풀이하다; **n.** 메아리
If a sound echoes, it is reflected off a surface and can be heard again after the original sound has stopped.

vast^{복습}
[væ(ɑ:)st]

a. 광대한, 거대한
Something that is vast is extremely large.

awaken^{복습}
[əwéikən]

v. (잠에서) 깨다, 깨우다
When you awaken, or when something or someone awakens you, you wake up.

blurry
[blɔ́:ri]

a. 흐릿한, 모호한
A blurry shape is one that has an unclear outline.

rifle^{복습}
[ráifl]

① **n.** 라이플총 ② **vt.** 샅샅이 뒤지다; 강탈하다
A rifle is a gun with a long barrel.

loot
[lu:t]

n. 약탈품; **v.** 훔치다, 약탈하다
Loot is stolen money or valuable objects taken by soldiers from the enemy after winning a battle.

yawn**
[jɔ:n]

vi. 하품하다; **n.** 하품
If you yawn, you open your mouth very wide and breathe in more air than usual, often when you are tired or when you are not interested in something.

redheaded
[rédhèdid]

a. 머리털이 빨간
A redheaded person, especially a woman, has red color hair.

110

rummage
[rʌ́midʒ]

v. 뒤지다; n. 뒤지기
If you rummage through something, you search for something you want by moving things around in a careless or hurried way.

drawer**
[drɔ́:ər]

n. 서랍
A drawer is part of a desk, chest, or other piece of furniture that is shaped like a box and is designed for putting things in.

knock복습
[nák]

v. 치다, 부수다; (문을) 두드리다, 노크하다
If you knock something, you touch or hit it roughly, especially so that it falls or moves.

freckle복습
[frékl]

n. 주근깨
Freckles are small light brown spots on someone's skin, especially on their face.

blotchy
[blátʃi]

a. 얼룩덜룩한, 얼룩진
Something that is blotchy has blotches on it.

scraggly
[skrǽgli]

a. 듬성듬성[들쭉날쭉] 자란
Scraggly hair or plants are thin and untidy.

jab복습
[dʒǽb]

v. 콱[쿡] 찌르다; 쥐어박다; n. (콱) 찌르기; 잽
If you jab one thing into another, you push it there with a quick, sudden movement and with a lot of force.

rob복습
[ráb]

v. 빼앗다, 도둑질하다
If someone is robbed, they have money or property stolen from them.

nod복습
[nɔd]

v. 끄덕이다, 끄덕여 표시하다; n. 끄덕임(동의 · 인사 · 신호 · 명령)
If you nod, you move your head downwards and upwards to show agreement, understanding, or approval.

livestock*
[láivstàk]

n. 가축
Animals such as cattle and sheep which are kept on a farm are referred to as livestock.

drought*
[draut]

n. 가뭄
A drought is a long period of time during which no rain falls.

fireplace복습
[faiərplèis]

n. (벽)난로
In a room, the fireplace is the place where a fire can be lit and the area on the wall and floor surrounding this place.

blast**
[blǽst]

n. 폭발, 폭파; 폭풍, 돌풍; v. 폭파하다; 후려치다
A blast is a big explosion, especially one caused by a bomb.

fire***
[faiər]

v. 발사하다; 불을 지르다; 해고하다; n. 불, 화재
If someone fires a gun or a bullet, or if they fire, a bullet is sent from a gun that they are using.

shatter**
[ʃǽtər]

v. 산산조각이 나다; 파괴하다; n. 파편, 부서진 조각
If something shatters or is shattered, it breaks into a lot of small pieces.

dig복습
[díg]

v. (구멍 등을) 파다; 뒤지다; n. 파기
If people or animals dig, they make a hole in the ground or in a pile of earth, stones, or rubbish.

wasteland^{복습}
[wéistlænd]

n. 황무지, 불모지
A wasteland is an area of land on which not much can grow or which has been spoiled in some way.

drag^{복습}
[dræg]

v. 끌다, 끌고 오다; 힘들게 움직이다; n. 견인, 끌기; 빨아들이기
If someone drags you somewhere you do not want to go, they make you go there.

pajama
[pədʒάːmə]

n. (pl.) 파자마, 잠옷; a. 파자마 같은
A pair of pajamas consists of loose trousers and a loose jacket that people wear in bed.

stud^{복습}
[stʌd]

n. 장식용 금속 단추; 못[징] (studded a. 장식용 금속 단추를 붙인)
Something that is studded is decorated with small pieces of metal for decoration.

barefoot^{복습}
[béərfùt]

a., ad. 맨발의[로] ad., a. 맨발로[의]
Someone who is barefoot or barefooted is not wearing anything on their feet.

might as well^{복습}

idiom ~하는 편이 낫다
If you say that you might as well do something, or that you may as well do it, you mean that you will do it although you do not have a strong desire to do it and may even feel slightly unwilling to do it.

blister^{복습}
[blístər]

v. 물집이 생기다; n. 물집, 수포
When your skin blisters or when something blisters it, blisters appear on it.

whack[*]
[hwæk]

v. (지팡이 등으로) 세게 치다, 탁 때리다; n. 철썩[세게] 치기, 구타
If you whack someone or something, you hit them hard.

struggle to one's feet

idiom 가까스로 일어서다
If you struggle to your feet, you try hard to stand up.

lizard^{복습}
[lízərd]

n. 도마뱀
A lizard is a reptile with short legs and a long tail.

leap^{복습}
[líːp]

v. 껑충 뛰다; 뛰어넘다; n. 뜀, 도약
If you leap, you jump high in the air or jump a long distance.

ankle^{복습}
[æŋkl]

n. 발목
Your ankle is the joint where your foot joins your leg.

lap^{복습}
[læp]

① v. 할짝할짝 핥다; (물이) 찰랑거리다 ② n. 무릎; (경주에서 트랙의) 한 바퀴
When an animal laps a drink, it uses short quick movements of its tongue to take liquid up into its mouth.

droplet
[dráplit]

n. 작은 (물)방울
A droplet is a very small drop of liquid.

leak^{복습}
[liːk]

v. (액체 · 기체가) 새게 하다, 새다; n. (액체 · 기체가) 새는 곳
If a container leaks, there is a hole or crack in it which lets a substance such as liquid or gas escape.

wound^{복습}
[wúːnd]

n. 상처, 부상; v. 부상을 입히다
A wound is damage to part of your body, especially a cut or a hole in your flesh, which is caused by a gun, knife, or other weapon.

112

screech*
[skriːtʃ]

v. 꽥[끼익] 하는 소리를 내다; n. 귀에 거슬리는 날카로운 소리
When you screech something, you shout it in a loud, unpleasant, high-pitched voice.

chapters twenty-nine & thirty

1. How had the weather changed?
   A. It was colder because there were thunderstorms in the distance.
   B. It was more humid and it rained at the camp.
   C. It was cooler but more humiD.
   D. It was hotter and more humid.

2. Stanley saw _____.
   A. a man standing on one of the mountain peaks
   B. a unusual rock formation on one of the mountain peaks
   C. a strange cloud formation during the thunderstorm
   D. lightning hit the cabin

3. Mr. Pendanski wanted _____.
   A. Mr. Sir to stop the riot
   B. Stanley and Zigzag to stop fighting
   C. Stanley to hit Zigzag
   D. Zero to punch Zigzag

4. How did Zero defend Stanley?
   A. He punched Mr. Pendanski.
   B. He chocked Zigzag.
   C. He hit Armpit.
   D. He attacked Zigzag and X-Ray.

5. What did the Warden decide after the riot?

   A. Stanley wasn't allowed to teach Zero to read.

   B. Zero wasn't allowed to dig any holes.

   C. The counselors should shoot Zero.

   D. Stanley had to dig two holes for the next month.

6. Why did the counselors point their guns at Zero?

   A. Zero punched the Warden.

   B. Zero started to run away.

   C. Zero threw a shovel at Mr. Sir.

   D. Zero hit Mr. Pendanski with a shovel.

7. What were the counselors ordered to do?

   A. Search for Zero in their trucks.

   B. Shoot at Zero.

   C. Find Zero at night.

   D. Guard the shower room and Wreck Room.

1분에 몇 단어를 읽는지 리딩 속도를 측정해보세요.

$$\frac{500 \text{ words}}{\text{reading time ( ) sec}} \times 60 = (\quad) \text{ WPM}$$

Build Your Vocabulary

unbearable*
[ʌnbéərəbəl]

a. 참을 수 없는, 견딜 수 없는 (unbearably ad. 참을 수 없을 정도로)
If you describe something as unbearable, you mean that it is so unpleasant, painful, or upsetting that you feel unable to accept it or deal with it.

humid*
[hjú:mid]

a. (대기 · 날씨가) 습한
You use humid to describe an atmosphere or climate that is very damp, and usually very hot.

drench**
[drentʃ]

vt. 흠뻑 적시다
To drench something or someone means to make them completely wet.

sweat복습
[swét]

n. 땀; v. 땀 흘리다; 습기가 차다
Sweat is the salty colorless liquid which comes through your skin when you are hot, ill, or afraid.

bead*
[bí:d]

n. (구슬 같은) 방울; 구슬
A bead of liquid or moisture is a small drop of it.

moisture복습
[mɔ́istʃər]

n. 습기, 수분
Moisture is tiny drops of water in the air, on a surface, or in the ground.

boom**
[bú:m]

n. 쿵 울리는 소리; 인기, 붐; v. 번창하다, 호황을 맞다; 쿵하고 울리다
A boom is a deep and strong sound, as of an explosion.

echo복습
[ékou]

v. 울려 퍼지다, 메아리치다; (남의 말 · 의견을) 그대로 되풀이하다; n. 메아리
If a sound echoes, it is reflected off a surface and can be heard again after the original sound has stopped.

storm복습
[stɔ:rm]

n. 폭풍우; vi. 돌진하다; 격노하다
A storm is very bad weather, with heavy rain, strong winds, and often thunder and lightning.

count복습
[káunt]

v. 세다, 계산하다; 포함시키다; 중요하다; (정식으로) 인정되다; n. 계산, 셈
When you count, you say all the numbers one after another up to a particular number.

clap**
[klæp]

n. (갑자기 크게) 쿵[탁] 하는 소리; 박수 (소리); v. 박수를 치다
A clap of thunder is a sudden and loud noise of thunder.

barren복습
[bǽrən]

a. 불모의, 메마른
A barren landscape is dry and bare, and has very few plants and no trees.

sunup
[sʌ́nʌ̀p]

n. 동틀녘
Sunup is another name for sunrise.

hazy*
[héizi]

a. 흐릿한, 안개 낀
Hazy weather conditions are those in which things are difficult to see, because of light mist, hot air, or dust.

brief***
[bri:f]

a. (시간이) 짧은, 잠시 동안의; (말·글이) 간단한 (briefly ad. 잠시; 간단히)
Something that is brief lasts for only a short time.

rattlesnake^{복습}
[rǽtlsnèik]

n. [동물] 방울뱀
A rattlesnake is a poisonous American snake which can make a rattling noise with its tail.

scorpion^{복습}
[skɔ́:rpiən]

n. [동물] 전갈
A scorpion is a small creature which looks like a large insect. Scorpions have a long curved tail, and some of them are poisonous.

spotted^{복습}
[spátid]

a. 얼룩무늬의; 물방울무늬가 있는
Something that is spotted has a pattern of spots on it.

humidity*
[hju:mídəti]

n. 습함, 습기; 습도
You say there is humidity when the air feels very heavy and damp.

frizzy^{복습}
[frízi]

a. (머리가) 곱슬곱슬한
Frizzy hair is very tightly curled.

horizon^{복습}
[həráizn]

n. 지평선, 수평선
The horizon is the line in the far distance where the sky seems to meet the land or the sea.

split second
[splít sékənd]

n. 채 1초도 걸리지 않는 시간, 일순간
A split second is an extremely short period of time.

formation**
[fɔ:rméiʃən]

n. 형성물; 형성 (과정)
A rock or cloud formation is rock or cloud of a particular shape or structure.

peak**
[pí:k]

n. 산꼭대기; (지붕·탑 등의) 뾰족한 끝; 절정, 최고점
A peak is a mountain or the top of a mountain.

fist**
[fist]

n. (쥔) 주먹
Your hand is referred to as your fist when you have bent your fingers in towards the palm in order to hit someone.

refuge^{복습}
[réfjudʒ]

n. 피난처, 은신처; 피난, 도피
A refuge is a place where you go for safety and protection.

strand^{복습}
[strænd]

① v. 오도 가도 못 하게 하다, 발을 묶다 ② n. (실·전선·머리카락 등의) 가닥, 꼰 줄
If you are stranded, you are prevented from leaving a place, for example because of bad weather.

desert^{복습}
[dézərt]

① n. 사막, 황무지 ② v. 인적이 끊기다; 버리다, 유기하다
A desert is a large area of land, usually in a hot region, where there is almost no water, rain, trees, or plants.

delirious*
[dilíəriəs]

a. 의식이 혼미한, 헛소리를 하는
Someone who is delirious is unable to think or speak in a sensible and reasonable way, usually because they are very ill and have a fever.

treat***
[tri:t]

v. 치료하다, 처치하다; 대하다; n. 특별한 선물, 대접
When a doctor or nurse treats a patient or an illness, he or she tries to make the patient well again.

dab
[dǽb]

v. (가볍게) 만지다, 토닥거리다; n. 소량, 조금
If you dab something, you touch it several times using quick, light movements.

forehead복습
[fɔ́:rhèd]

n. 이마
Your forehead is the area at the front of your head between your eyebrows and your hair.

1분에 몇 단어를 읽는지 리딩 속도를 측정해보세요.

$$\frac{2{,}312 \text{ words}}{\text{reading time ( ) sec}} \times 60 = (\quad) \text{ WPM}$$

Build Your Vocabulary

cot^{복습}
[kɑt]

n. 접이 침대, 간이[야영용] 침대; 소아용 침대
A cot is a narrow bed, usually made of canvas fitted over a frame which can be folded up.

cut in line

idiom 줄에 새치기하다
If you cut in a line, you push in front of people who have been waiting in the line.

figure out^{복습}

phrasal v. ~을 생각해내다, 발견하다
If you figure out a solution to a problem or the reason for something, you succeed in solving it or understanding it.

carton^{복습}
[kɑ́ːrtən]

n. (음식이나 음료를 담는) 곽[통]; 상자
A carton is a plastic or cardboard container in which food or drink is sold.

adjust**
[ədʒʌ́st]

v. 적응하다; 조절하다, 조정하다; (옷매무새 등을) 바로 하다
When you adjust to a new situation, you get used to it by changing your behavior or your ideas.

harsh**
[hɑːrʃ]

a. 가혹한, 냉혹한; 거친, (소리 따위가) 귀에 거슬리는
Harsh climates or conditions are very difficult for people, animals, and plants to live in.

deprive**
[dipráiv]

vt. 주지 않다; 빼앗다, 박탈하다
If you deprive someone of something that they want or need, you take it away from them, or you prevent them from having it.

awkward**
[ɔ́ːkwərd]

a. 어색한, 불편한, 곤란한
Someone who feels awkward behaves in a shy or embarrassed way.

unsure^{복습}
[ʌnʃúər]

a. 확신하지 못하는, 의심스러워하는
If you are unsure about something, you feel uncertain about it.

horizon^{복습}
[həráizn]

n. 지평선, 수평선
The horizon is the line in the far distance where the sky seems to meet the land or the sea.

jut
[dʒʌt]

v. 돌출하다, 튀어나오다; 돌출시키다, 내밀다
If something juts out, it sticks out above or beyond a surface.

impressive**
[imprésiv]

a. 인상적인, 감명 깊은
Something that is impressive impresses you, for example because it is great in size or degree, or is done with a great deal of skill.

glare 복습
[gléər]

n. 섬광; 노려봄; v. 번쩍번쩍 빛나다; 노려보다
Glare is very bright light that is difficult to look at.

rob 복습
[ráb]

v. 빼앗다, 도둑질하다
If someone is robbed, they have money or property stolen from them.

whip＊＊
[hwip]

n. 채찍; v. 채찍질하다; 휙 빼내다; (크림 등을) 휘젓다
A whip is a long thin piece of material such as leather or rope, fastened to a stiff handle. It is used for hitting people or animals.

slave 복습
[sleiv]

n. 노예; v. 노예처럼[고되게] 일하다
A slave is someone who is the property of another person and has to work for that person.

crack 복습
[kræk]

v. (짧고 세게) 때리다; 금이 가다, 깨다; n. 갈라진 금; 갑작스런 날카로운 소리
If something cracks, or if you crack it, it makes a sharp sound like the sound of a piece of wood breaking.

pal＊＊
[pǽl]

n. 친구; 동료; vi. 친구가 되다
Your pals are your friends.

insult＊＊
[insʌ́lt]

vt. 모욕하다; n. 모욕(적인 말 · 행동)
If someone insults you, they say or do something that is rude or offensive.

canteen 복습
[kæntíːn]

n. (휴대용) 물통; (공장 · 학교 등의) 구내식당
A canteen is a small plastic bottle for carrying water and other drinks. Canteens are used by soldiers.

sack 복습
[sæk]

n. (쇼핑 물건을 담는 크고 튼튼한 종이) 봉지; 부대, 자루; vt. 자루에 넣다
Sacks are used to carry or store things such as vegetables or coal.

shove＊
[ʃʌ́v]

v. 밀치다, 떠밀다, 밀어내다; n. 밀치기
If you shove something somewhere, you push it there quickly and carelessly.

lay off

idiom (명령형으로) (~을) 그만두라
People say 'lay off' to tell someone to stop doing something that irritates or annoys them.

snap 복습
[snæp]

v. (화난 목소리로) 딱딱거리다; 딱[툭] (하고) 부러뜨리다[부러지다]
If someone snaps at you, they speak to you in a sharp, unfriendly way.

fool around

idiom (하찮은 일로) 시간을 낭비하다, 빈둥거리며 세월을 보내다
If you fool around, you waste time or behave in a silly way.

astonishment 복습
[əstániʃmənt]

n. 놀람, 경악
Astonishment is a feeling of great surprise.

bully 복습
[búli]

n. 약자를 괴롭히는 사람; v. 곯리다, 겁주다
A bully is someone who uses their strength or power to hurt or frighten other people.

challenge[asterisk][asterisk]
[tʃǽlindʒ]

v. (경쟁 · 싸움 등을) 걸다, 도전하다; n. 도전
If you challenge someone, you invite them to fight or compete with you in some way.

feeble[asterisk][asterisk]
[fí:bəl]

a. 아주 약한
If you describe someone or something as feeble, you mean that they are weak.

flurry
[flə́:ri]

n. 휙하니 움직임; 소동
A flurry of something such as snow is a small amount of it that suddenly appears for a short time and moves in a quick, swirling way.

fist복습
[fist]

n. (쥔) 주먹
Your hand is referred to as your fist when you have bent your fingers in towards the palm in order to hit someone.

collar복습
[kálər]

n. (윗옷의) 칼라, 깃; (개 등의 목에 거는) 목걸이
The collar of a shirt or coat is the part which fits round the neck and is usually folded over.

rip복습
[ríp]

v. 찢(어지)다, 벗겨내다; 돌진하다; n. 찢어진 틈, 잡아 찢음
When something rips or when you rip it, you tear it forcefully with your hands or with a tool such as a knife.

yell[asterisk][asterisk]
[jél]

v. 소리치다, 고함치다; n. 고함소리, 부르짖음
If you yell, you shout loudly, usually because you are excited, angry, or in pain.

slam복습
[slǽm]

v. 세게 치다, 세게 놓다; 쾅 닫다[닫히다]; n. 쾅 (하는 소리)
If one thing slams into or against another, it crashes into it with great force.

pound복습
[páund]

① v. 마구 치다, 세게 두드리다; 쿵쿵 울리다; n. 타격 ② n. 파운드 (무게의 단위)
③ n. 울타리, 우리
If you pound something or pound on it, you hit it with great force, usually loudly and repeatedly.

gag[asterisk]
[gǽg]

① v. 말문을 막다, 재갈을 물리다; n. 재갈 ② n. 익살, 개그; v. 농담하다
If someone gags you, they tie a piece of cloth around your mouth in order to stop you from speaking or shouting.

squeeze[asterisk][asterisk]
[skwí:z]

v. (꼭) 짜다, 쥐다; (억지로) 비집고 들어가다; n. (꼭) 짜기
If you squeeze something, you press it firmly, usually with your hands.

charge복습
[tʃáːrdʒ]

v. 돌격하다; 청구하다; 기소하다, 고소하다; n. (상품 · 서비스에 대한) 요금;
기소, 고발; 책임, 담당
If you charge towards someone or something, you move quickly and aggressively towards them.

choke복습
[tʃouk]

v. 질식시키다, 숨이 막히다; n. 질식
When you choke or when something chokes you, you cannot breathe properly or get enough air into your lungs.

fire복습
[faiər]

v. 발사하다; 불을 지르다; 해고하다; n. 불, 화재
If someone fires a gun or a bullet, or if they fire, a bullet is sent from a gun that they are using.

pistol**
[pístl]

n. 권총, 피스톨
A pistol is a small gun which is held in and fired from one hand.

counselor^{복습}
[káunsələr]

n. (캠프 생활의) 지도원; 상담역, 카운슬러
A counselor is a person whose job is to give advice to people who need it, especially advice on their personal problems.

holster^{복습}
[hóulstər]

vt. 권총용 가죽 케이스에 넣다; n. 권총용 가죽 케이스
If you holster a gun, you place it in a pistol case.

riot**
[ráiət]

n. 폭동, 소동; vi. 폭동을 일으키다
When there is a riot, a crowd of people behave violently in a public place.

strangle*
[stræŋgl]

vt. 목 졸라 죽이다, 교살하다
To strangle someone means to kill them by squeezing their throat tightly so that they cannot breathe.

beat up^{복습}

phrasal v. 두들겨 패다, 마구 차다
If you beat up someone, you strike or kick them repeatedly.

boil***
[bɔ́il]

v. (화 등으로) 속이 끓다; 끓다, 끓이다
If you are boiling with anger, you are very angry.

shrug^{복습}
[ʃrʌ́g]

v. (어깨를) 으쓱하다; n. (양 손바닥을 내보이면서 어깨를) 으쓱하기
If you shrug, you raise your shoulders to show that you are not interested in something or that you do not know or care about something.

character^{복습}
[kǽriktər]

n. 인격, 성격; 특징, 특성; 문자, 서체
Your character is your personality, especially how reliable and honest you are.

might as well^{복습}

idiom ~하는 편이 낫다
If you say that you might as well do something, or that you may as well do it, you mean that you will do it although you do not have a strong desire to do it and may even feel slightly unwilling to do it.

clap^{복습}
[klæp]

v. 박수를 치다; n. 박수 (소리); (갑자기 크게) 쿵[탁] 하는 소리
When you clap, you hit your hands together to show appreciation or attract attention.

genius**
[dʒíːnjəs]

n. 천재; 특수한 재능
A genius is a highly talented, creative, or intelligent person.

concentrate**
[kánsəntrèit]

v. 집중하다, 전념하다
If you concentrate on something, you give all your attention to it.

have it in for (someone)

idiom ~에게 앙심을 품다
If you have it in for someone, you want to harm or cause trouble for them because you have had a bad experience with them.

logical**
[ládʒikəl]

a. 타당한, 사리에 맞는; 논리적인
Something that is logical seems reasonable or sensible in the circumstances.

122

mumble*
[mʌ́mbl]

v. 중얼거리다, 웅얼거리다; n. 중얼거림
If you mumble, you speak very quietly and not at all clearly with the result that the words are difficult to understand.

face^{복습}
[féis]

v. 직시하다; ~을 마주보다, 향하다; 직면하다
If you face or are faced with something difficult or unpleasant, or if it faces you, it is going to affect you and you have to deal with it.

swing^{복습}
[swíŋ]

v. (swung–swung) 휘두르다, (한 점을 축으로 하여) 빙 돌다, 휙 움직이다
If you swing at a person or thing, you try to hit them with your arm or with something that you are holding.

bat**
[bæt]

n. 방망이, 배트; 박쥐; v. (야구 · 크리켓에서 배트로) 공을 치다
A bat is a specially shaped piece of wood that is used for hitting the ball in baseball, softball, cricket, rounders, or table tennis.

blade^{복습}
[bleid]

n. (칼 · 도구 등의) 날; (프로펠러 등의) 날개; 잎
The blade of a knife, ax, or saw is the edge, which is used for cutting.

smash^{복습}
[smæʃ]

v. 세게 충돌하다; 때려 부수다, 깨뜨리다; n. 강타; 부서지는 소리; 분쇄
If something smashes or is smashed against something solid, it moves very fast and with great force against it.

crumple*
[krʌ́mpl]

v. 무너지다; 구기다, 쭈글쭈글하게 하다; 구겨지다; n. 주름
If someone crumples, they collapse, for example when they have received a shock.

unconscious**
[ʌnkɑ́nʃəs]

a. 의식[정신]을 잃은; 무의식의; 알아채지 못하는
Someone who is unconscious is in a state similar to sleep, usually as the result of a serious injury or a lack of oxygen.

bullet^{복습}
[búlit]

n. (소총 · 권총의) 총탄, 탄환
A bullet is a small piece of metal with a pointed or rounded end, which is fired out of a gun.

investigation**
[invèstəgéiʃən]

n. 조사, 연구
An investigation is an official examination of the facts about a situation, or crime.

cluster**
[klʌ́stər]

n. 무리, 집단, 떼; v. 밀집하다
A cluster of people or things is a small group of them close together.

haze^{복습}
[heiz]

n. 아지랑이, 엷은 연기; v. 흐릿해지다, 안개가 끼다
If there is a haze of something such as smoke or steam, you cannot see clearly through it.

1. Stanley's "better idea" was to _____.
   A. tell the Warden where he found the gold tube
   B. help the Warden find Zero
   C. search for Zero for three days
   D. steal the Warden's rattlesnake venom nail polish

2. Stanley hoped that _____.
   A. he could steal some extra water for Zero
   B. Zero would come back to the camp
   C. Zero would apologize to the Warden
   D. Zero had found God's thumb

3. What did the Warden order Mr. Pendanski to do?
   A. Find Zero in the desert
   B. Kill Zero
   C. Report Zero missing
   D. Destroy Zero's records

4. Why did Stanley steal the truck?
   A. He wanted to learn how to drive.
   B. Twitch told him how to steal the truck.
   C. He wanted to help Zero.
   D. He wanted to distract the counselors so Zero could steal some
      water.

5. Stanley _____.
    A. stalled the truck so it couldn't move
    B. drove the truck into a hole
    C. stole the keys from the truck's ignition
    D. drove the truck into the Warden's cabin

6. What was true when Stanley left the camp?
    A. Mr. Sir followed him in the truck.
    B. He knew where Zero was hiding.
    C. Mr. Sir shot at him with his gun.
    D. His canteen was empty.

1분에 몇 단어를 읽는지 리딩 속도를 측정해보세요.

$$\frac{845 \text{ words}}{\text{reading time (} \quad \text{) sec}} \times 60 = (\quad) \text{ WPM}$$

Build Your Vocabulary

shovel ^{복습}
[ʃʌvəl]

n. 삽; v. ~을 삽으로 뜨다[파다], 삽으로 일하다
A shovel is a tool with a long handle that is used for lifting and moving earth, coal, or snow.

eventually ^{복습}
[ivéntʃuəli]

ad. 결국, 마침내
Eventually means at the end of a situation or process or as the final result of it.

face ^{복습}
[féis]

v. 직면하다; ~을 마주보다, 향하다; 직시하다
If you have to face a person or group, you have to stand or sit in front of them and talk to them, although it may be difficult and unpleasant.

figure out ^{복습}

phrasal v. ~을 생각해내다, 발견하다
If you figure out a solution to a problem or the reason for something, you succeed in solving it or understanding it.

spigot ^{복습}
[spígət]

n. (수도 · 통 등의) 마개, 주둥이, 꼭지
A spigot is a faucet or tap.

bandage ^{복습}
[bǽndidʒ]

n. 붕대; vt. 붕대를 감다
If you bandage a wound or part of someone's body, you tie a bandage around it.

constant***
[ká(ɔ́)nstənt]

a. 끊임없는, 일정한, 불변의
You use constant to describe something that happens all the time or is always there.

watchout
[wátʃàut]

n. 경계, 주의, 조심하기
If someone keeps a watchout, they look around all the time in order to make sure there is no danger.

urge ^{복습}
[ɔ́:rdʒ]

n. (강한) 충동; v. 몰아대다, 재촉하다
If you have an urge to do or have something, you have a strong wish to do or have it.

convince ^{복습}
[kənvíns]

vt. 설득하다; 확신시키다, 납득시키다
If someone or something convinces you to do something, they persuade you to do it.

storm ^{복습}
[stɔ:rm]

n. 폭풍우; vi. 돌진하다; 격노하다
A storm is very bad weather, with heavy rain, strong winds, and often thunder and lightning.

water tower
[wɔ́:tər táuər]

n. 급수탑

A water tower is a large tank of water which is placed on a high metal structure so that water can be supplied at a steady pressure to surrounding buildings.

swell^{복습}
[swél]

v. (swelled–swollen) 붓다; 팽창하다; (가슴이) 벅차다; (소리가) 높아지다;
n. 팽창, 증대

If something such as a part of your body swells, it becomes larger and rounder than normal.

slit[*]
[slít]

n. 갈라진 틈, 틈새

A slit is a long narrow opening in something.

ward^{**}
[wɔ:rd]

n. (법원·후견인의 법률적 보호를 받는) 피보호자; (병원에서 특정 환자들을 위한) 병동

A ward or a ward of court is a child who is the responsibility of a person called a guardian, or of a court of law, because their parents are dead or because they are believed to be in need of protection.

arrest^{복습}
[ərést]

vt. 체포하다, 저지하다; (주의·이목·흥미 등을) 끌다; n. 체포, 검거, 구속

If the police arrest you, they take charge of you and take you to a police station, because they believe you may have committed a crime.

Check Your Reading Speed

1분에 몇 단어를 읽는지 리딩 속도를 측정해보세요.

$$\frac{870 \text{ words}}{\text{reading time ( ) sec}} \times 60 = (\quad) \text{ WPM}$$

Build Your Vocabulary

assign^{복습}
[əsáin]

v. 배치하다; 맡기다, 배정하다
If someone is assigned to a particular place, group, or person, they are sent there, usually in order to work at that place or for that person.

twitch^{복습}
[twítʃ]

n. 씰룩거림, 경련; vi. (손가락·근육 따위가) 씰룩거리다; 홱 잡아당기다, 잡아채다
If something, especially a part of your body, twitches or if you twitch it, it makes a little jumping movement.

fidget
[fídʒit]

v. 꼼지락거리다, 만지작거리다, 안절부절 못하다
If you fidget, you keep moving your hands or feet slightly or changing your position slightly, for example because you are nervous, bored, or excited.

crate^{복습}
[kréit]

n. 나무 상자, (짐을 보호하는) 나무틀
A crate is a large box used for transporting or storing things.

vacancy^{복습}
[véikənsi]

n. 결원, 공석; 빈 방
A vacancy is a job or position which has not been filled.

desert^{복습}
[dizə́:rt]

① v. 인적이 끊기다; 버리다, 유기하다 (deserted a. 사람이 살지 않는, 황폐한)
② n. 사막, 황무지
If people or animals desert a place, they leave it and it becomes empty.

wheel***
[hwi:l]

n. (자동차의) 핸들; 수레바퀴; v. 움직이다, 밀다; 선회하다, 방향을 바꾸다
The wheel of a car or other vehicle is the circular object that is used to steer it.

scratchy^{복습}
[skrǽtʃi]

a. (몸에 닿으면) 가려운[따끔거리는]; 긁는 듯한 소리가 나는
Scratchy clothes or fabrics are rough and uncomfortable to wear next to your skin.

cot^{복습}
[kɑt]

n. 접이 침대, 간이[야영용] 침대; 소아용 침대
A cot is a narrow bed, usually made of canvas fitted over a frame which can be folded up.

eat at

phrasal v. ~을 초조하게 만들다
If something is eating at you, it is annoying or worrying you.

crawl**
[krɔ́:l]

vi. 기어가다, 느릿느릿 가다; 우글거리다, 들끓다; n. 서행; 기어감
When you crawl, you move forward on your hands and knees.

drum**
[drʌ́m]

v. 계속 두드리다; 북을 치다; n. 북, 드럼
If you drum something on a surface, you hit it regularly, making a continuous beating sound.

shaft^{복습}
[ʃǽft]

n. (망치 · 골프채 등의 기다란) 손잡이
A shaft is a long thin piece of wood or metal that forms part of a spear, ax, golf club, or other object.

dig^{복습}
[díg]

v. (구멍 등을) 파다; 뒤지다; n. 파기
If people or animals dig, they make a hole in the ground or in a pile of earth, stones, or rubbish.

wiggle^{복습}
[wígl]

v. (좌우로) 움직이다, (몸을) 뒤흔들다; n. 뒤흔듦
If you wiggle something or if it wiggles, it moves up and down or from side to side in small quick movements.

pinkie^{복습}
[píŋki]

n. 새끼손가락
Your pinkie is the smallest finger on your hand.

pop^{복습}
[páp]

v. 급히 집어넣다; 뻥 하고 터뜨리다; 불쑥 나타나다; n. 뻥[탁] 하는 소리; 발포
If you pop something somewhere, you put it there quickly.

deft^{복습}
[déft]

a. 손재주 있는, 솜씨 좋은 (deftly ad. 솜씨 좋게, 교묘히)
A deft action is skillful and often quick.

spit^{복습}
[spit]

v. (spat–spat) 뱉다, 내뿜다; (폭언 등을) 내뱉다; n. 침
If you spit liquid or food somewhere, you force a small amount of it out of your mouth.

ignition
[igníʃən]

n. (차량의) 점화 장치; 점화
Inside a car, the ignition is the part where you turn the key so that the engine starts.

dangle[*]
[dǽŋgl]

v. (달랑달랑) 매달리다, 매달다; n. 매달린 것
If something dangles from somewhere or if you dangle it somewhere, it hangs or swings loosely.

steady^{복습}
[stédi]

v. 진정시키다, 균형을 잡다; a. 꾸준한
If you steady yourself, you control your voice or expression, so that people will think that you are calm and not nervous.

fling^{복습}
[fliŋ]

vt. (flung–flung) (문 등을) 왈칵 열다; 내던지다, 던지다
If you fling something somewhere, you throw it there using a lot of force.

pedal[*]
[pédl]

n. 페달, 발판; v. 페달을 밟다
The pedals on a bicycle are the two parts that you push with your feet in order to make the bicycle move.

rev
[rev]

v. (엔진의) 회전 속도를 올리다
When the engine of a vehicle revs, or when you rev it, the engine speed is increased as the accelerator is pressed.

roar^{복습}
[rɔːr]

vi. (큰 짐승 등이) 으르렁거리다, 고함치다; n. 으르렁거리는 소리; 외치는 소리, 왁자지껄함
If something, usually a vehicle, roars somewhere, it goes there very fast, making a loud noise.

motionless^{**}
[móuʃənlis]

a. 움직이지 않는, 부동의, 정지한
Someone or something that is motionless is not moving at all.

gear[**]
[giər]

n. 기어, 톱니바퀴; (특정한 용도의) 의복; 장비, 도구
The gears on a machine or vehicle are a device for changing the rate at which energy is changed into motion.

lurch
[ləːrtʃ]

v. 요동치다, 비틀거리다, 휘청하다
To lurch means to make a sudden movement, especially forwards, in an uncontrolled way.

jerk[복습]
[dʒə́ːrk]

① v. 홱 움직이다; n. (갑자기 날카롭게) 홱 움직임 ② n. 바보, 멍청이
If you jerk something or someone in a particular direction, or they jerk in a particular direction, they move a short distance very suddenly and quickly.

grip[복습]
[grip]

v. 꽉 잡다, 움켜잡다; n. 꽉 붙잡음, 움켜쥠; 손잡이
If you grip something, you take hold of it with your hand and continue to hold it firmly.

accelerate[*]
[æksélərèit]

v. 속도를 높이다, 가속화되다
When a moving vehicle accelerates, it goes faster and faster.

bounce[복습]
[bauns]

v. 튀다, 튀게 하다; 급히 움직이다, 뛰어다니다; n. 튐, 바운드
If something bounces off a surface or is bounced off it, it reaches the surface and is reflected back.

explode[*]
[iksplóud]

v. 터지다, 폭발하다
If an object such as a bomb explodes or if someone or something explodes it, it bursts loudly and with great force, often causing damage or injury.

lopsided
[lápsáidid]

a. 한쪽으로 기운
Something that is lopsided is uneven because one side is lower or heavier than the other.

miserable[복습]
[mízərəbəl]

a. 비참한, 초라한, 불쌍한
If you describe a place or situation as miserable, you mean that it makes you feel unhappy or depressed.

sore[복습]
[sɔːr]

a. 아픈, 쓰린
If part of your body is sore, it causes you pain and discomfort.

glance[복습]
[glæns]

v. 흘깃 보다, 잠깐 보다; n. 흘깃 봄
If you glance at something or someone, you look at them very quickly and then look away again immediately.

strap[**]
[stræp]

vt. 끈으로 묶다, 잡아매다; n. 가죽 끈, 혁대
If you strap something somewhere, you fasten it there with a narrow piece of leather or cloth.

bang[복습]
[bæŋ]

v. 부딪치다, 탕 치다, 쾅 닫(히)다; n. 쾅 하는 소리
If something bangs, it makes a sudden loud noise, once or several times.

1. Stanley _____.
   A. wanted to go to another camp
   B. knew that nobody was chasing him
   C. knew the height of the Big Thumb
   D. thought it was pointless to look for Zero

2. What DIDN'T happen?
   A. Stanley saw a family of yellow-spotted lizards.
   B. Stanley headed in what he thought was the direction of the Big Thumb.
   C. Stanley considered making a deal with the Warden.
   D. Stanley found a sack full of sunflower seeds.

3. What encouraged Stanley?
   A. The Big Thumb
   B. Believing he would find Zero
   C. Knowing that he could go back to camp
   D. Believing he could find something to put in the sack

4. What happened when Stanley yelled at the boat?
   A. His mouth became wet again.
   B. The boat moved.
   C. Someone responded.
   D. An animal crawled under the boat.

5. What did the Sploosh taste like?
   A. Apple juice
   B. Honey
   C. Pears
   D. Peaches

6. What had happened to Barf Bag?
   A. The Warden had scratched him.
   B. He had stepped on a rattlesnake on purpose.
   C. He had been bitten by a yellow-spotted lizard.
   D. He had been hit by Mr. Sir.

7. What did Zero read?
   A. The boat's name
   B. Words on the sunflower seed bag
   C. A label on a jar of Sploosh
   D. Words painted on the inside of the boat

8. Zero would rather _____.
   A. go back to camp than die in the desert
   B. stay under the boat than go to the Big Thumb
   C. die in the desert than to go back to camp
   D. dig another hole than die in the desert

Check Your Reading Speed

1분에 몇 단어를 읽는지 리딩 속도를 측정해보세요.

$$\frac{594 \text{ words}}{\text{reading time (} \quad \text{) sec}} \times 60 = (\quad) \text{ WPM}$$

Build Your Vocabulary

occasional^{복습}
[əkéiʒənl]

a. 가끔의, 때때로의 (occasionally ad. 때때로, 가끔)
Occasional means happening sometimes, but not regularly or often.

rev^{복습}
[rev]

v. (엔진의) 회전 속도를 올리다
When the engine of a vehicle revs, or when you rev it, the engine speed is increased as the accelerator is pressed.

risk^{복습}
[risk]

v. (~을) 위태롭게 하다, ~의 위험을 무릅쓰다; n. 위험
If you risk your life or something else important, you behave in a way that might result in it being lost or harmed.

refuge^{복습}
[réfjudʒ]

n. 피난처, 은신처; 피난, 도피
A refuge is a place where you go for safety and protection.

might as well^{복습}

idiom ~하는 편이 낫다
If you say that you might as well do something, or that you may as well do it, you mean that you will do it although you do not have a strong desire to do it and may even feel slightly unwilling to do it.

beg*
[beg]

vt. 빌다, 구걸하다; 부탁[간청]하다
If you beg someone to do something, you ask them very anxiously or eagerly to do it.

mercy**
[mɔ́ːrsi]

n. 자비, 연민
If someone in authority shows mercy, they choose not to harm someone they have power over, or they forgive someone they have the right to punish.

compound^{복습}
[kámpaund]

① n. (저택 · 공장의) 건물 안, 구내 ② vt. 합성하다, 조합하다, 만들어내다; n. 합성물, 화합물
A compound is an enclosed area of land that is used for a particular purpose.

cluster^{복습}
[klʌ́stər]

n. 무리, 집단, 떼; v. 밀집하다
A cluster of people or things is a small group of them close together.

systematic**
[sistəmǽtik]

a. 체계적인, 조직적인
Something that is done in a systematic way is done according to a fixed plan, in a thorough and efficient way.

fit*
[fit]

① n. 욱하는 감정; 발작 ② v. (모양 · 크기가 어떤 사람 · 사물에) 맞다; 끼우다
If you do something in a fit of anger or panic, you are very angry or afraid when you do it.

134

frustration*
[frʌ́streiʃən]

n. 불만, 좌절감
Frustration is the feeling of being annoyed and impatient because you cannot do or achieve what you want.

lottery*
[lɑ́təri]

n. 복권, 제비뽑기
A lottery is a type of gambling game in which people buy numbered tickets. Several numbers are then chosen, and the people who have those numbers on their tickets win a prize.

mound^{복습}
[maund]

n. 더미, 무더기, 언덕
A mound of something is a large rounded pile of it.

spotted^{복습}
[spɑ́tid]

a. 얼룩무늬의; 물방울무늬가 있는
Something that is spotted has a pattern of spots on it.

lizard^{복습}
[lízərd]

n. 도마뱀
A lizard is a reptile with short legs and a long tail.

leap^{복습}
[líːp]

v. (leaped/leapt–leaped/leapt) 껑충 뛰다; 뛰어넘다; n. 뜀, 도약
If you leap, you jump high in the air or jump a long distance.

collapse^{복습}
[kəlǽps]

v. 쓰러지다, 맥없이 주저앉다; 무너지다, 붕괴하다; n. 무너짐, 붕괴
If you collapse, you suddenly faint or fall down because you are very ill or weak.

encounter*
[inkáuntər]

n. 마주침; v. 만나다, 마주치다
An encounter with someone is a meeting with them, particularly one that is unexpected or significant.

cautious*
[kɔ́ːʃəs]

a. 조심스러운, 신중한
Someone who is cautious acts very carefully in order to avoid possible danger.

1분에 몇 단어를 읽는지 리딩 속도를 측정해보세요.

$$\frac{655 \text{ words}}{\text{reading time ( ) sec}} \times 60 = (\quad) \text{ WPM}$$

Build Your Vocabulary

pointless^{복습}
[póintlis]

a. 무의미한, 할 가치가 없는
If you say that something is pointless, you are criticizing it because it has no sense or purpose.

pool**
[puːl]

n. 웅덩이, 못; 수영장; (액체 · 빛이) 고여 있는 곳
A pool is a fairly small area of still water.

mirage
[mirάːʒ]

n. 신기루; 신기루 같은 것
A mirage is something which you see when it is extremely hot, for example in the desert, and which appears to be quite near but is actually a long way away or does not really exist.

shimmer*
[ʃímər]

vi. 희미하게 반짝이다, 빛나다; n. 반짝임
If something shimmers, it shines with a faint, unsteady light or has an unclear, unsteady appearance.

sack^{복습}
[sæk]

n. 부대, 자루; (쇼핑 물건을 담는 크고 튼튼한 종이) 봉지; vt. 자루에 넣다
Sacks are used to carry or store things such as vegetables or coal.

haze^{복습}
[heiz]

n. 아지랑이, 엷은 연기; v. 흐릿해지다, 안개가 끼다
If there is a haze of something such as smoke or steam, you cannot see clearly through it.

fist^{복습}
[fist]

n. (쥔) 주먹
Your hand is referred to as your fist when you have bent your fingers in towards the palm in order to hit someone.

encourage**
[enkɔ́ːridʒ]

vt. 용기를 북돋우다, 장려하다
If you encourage someone, you give them confidence, hope, or support.

thumbs-up
[θʌ́mz-ʌp]

n. 승인, 찬성, 격려 (give a thumbs-up idiom 엄지손가락을 들어 올리다)
A thumbs-up is a sign that you make by raising your thumb to show that you agree with someone, that you are happy with an idea or situation, or that everything is all right.

man-made*
[mǽn-meid]

n. 사람이 만든, 인공의
Man-made things are created or caused by people, rather than occurring naturally.

ridge**
[ridʒ]

n. 산등성이, 산마루; v. (표면을) 이랑처럼 만들다
A ridge is a long, narrow piece of raised land.

strike ^{복습}
[straik]

v. (struck–stricken/struck) 갑자기 떠오르다; 때리다, 치다, 부딪치다;
n. 치기, 때리기; 파업
If an idea or thought strikes you, it suddenly comes into your mind.

barren ^{복습}
[bǽrən]

a. 불모의, 메마른
A barren landscape is dry and bare, and has very few plants and
no trees.

wasteland ^{복습}
[wéistlænd]

n. 황무지, 불모지
A wasteland is an area of land on which not much can grow or
which has been spoiled in some way.

upside-down **
[ʌ́psàid-dáun]

a. 거꾸로, 뒤집힌 (upside down ad. (위아래가) 거꾸로, 뒤집혀)
If something is upside-down, it has been turned round so that the
part that is usually lowest is above the part that is usually highest.

drown **
[draun]

v. 익사하다, 익사시키다, (물에) 빠뜨리다
When someone drowns or is drowned, they die because they have
gone or been pushed under water and cannot breathe.

grim **
[grim]

a. 엄숙한, 단호한; 섬뜩한, 무서운 (grimly ad. 엄숙하게; 무섭게, 험악하게)
If a person or their behavior is grim, they are very serious, usually
because they are worried about something.

peel **
[pi:l]

v. 벗겨지다, 껍질을 벗기다
If a surface is peeling, the paint on it is coming away.

crawl ^{복습}
[krɔ́:l]

vi. 기어가다, 느릿느릿 가다; 우글거리다, 들끓다; n. 서행; 기어감
When you crawl, you move forward on your hands and knees.

stir ***
[stə:r]

v. 움직이다; 휘젓다, 뒤섞다; n. 움직임; 휘젓기
If you stir, you move slightly, for example because you are
uncomfortable or beginning to wake up.

Check Your Reading Speed

1분에 몇 단어를 읽는지 리딩 속도를 측정해보세요.

$$\frac{1{,}125 \text{ words}}{\text{reading time ( ) sec}} \times 60 = (\quad) \text{ WPM}$$

Build Your Vocabulary

rotten**
[rátn]

a. 썩은, 부패한; 형편없는, 끔찍한
If food, wood, or another substance is rotten, it has decayed and can no longer be used.

sunken*
[sʌ́ŋkən]

a. (눈·볼이) 움푹 들어간, 퀭한; 침몰한, 물속에 가라앉은
Sunken eyes, cheeks, or other parts of the body curve inwards and make you look thin and unwell.

droop*
[dru:p]

v. (지치거나 약해져서) 아래로 처지다, 늘어지다
If something droops, it hangs or leans downwards with no strength or firmness.

raspy
[rǽːspi]

a. 거친, 목이 쉰 듯한
If someone has a raspy voice, they make rough sounds as if they have a sore throat or have difficulty in breathing.

flop*
[flɑp]

v. 퍼덕거리다, 털썩 쓰러지다
If something flops onto something else, it falls there heavily or untidily.

get in the way^{복습}

idiom 방해되다
If something gets in the way, it prevents you from doing something; prevent something from happening.

sheepish
[ʃíːpiʃ]

a. (어리석은·잘못된 짓을 하여) 멋쩍어 하는 (sheepishly **ad.** 수줍게, 어색하게)
If you look sheepish, you look slightly embarrassed because you feel foolish or you have done something silly.

shade^{복습}
[ʃeid]

vt. 그늘지게 하다; **n.** (시원한) 그늘; 색조
If you shade your eyes, you put your hand or an object partly in front of your face in order to prevent a bright light from shining into your eyes.

forearm
[fɔ́ːràːrm]

n. 팔뚝
Your forearm is the part of your arm between your elbow and your wrist.

squeeze^{복습}
[skwíːz]

v. (억지로) 비집고 들어가다; (꼭) 짜다, 쥐다; **n.** (꼭) 짜기
If you squeeze a person or thing somewhere or if they squeeze there, they manage to get through or into a small space.

shovel^{복습}
[ʃʌ́vəl]

n. 삽; **v.** ~을 삽으로 뜨다[파다], 삽으로 일하다
A shovel is a tool with a long handle that is used for lifting and moving earth, coal, or snow.

crack^{복습}
[kræk]

n. 갈라진 금; 갑작스런 날카로운 소리; v. 금이 가다, 깨다; (짧고 세게) 때리다
A crack is a very narrow gap between two things, or between two parts of a thing.

ventilation**
[vèntəléiʃən]

n. 통풍, 환기
Ventilation is the circulation of air.

jar^{복습}
[dʒɑːr]

① n. 병, 단지 ② v. 삐걱거리다; n. 삐걱거리는 소리, 잡음
A jar is a glass container with a lid that is used for storing food.

scatter***
[skǽtər]

v. (흩)뿌리다
If you scatter things over an area, you throw or drop them so that they spread all over the area.

grunt^{복습}
[grʌnt]

vi. (사람이) 툴툴거리다; (돼지가) 꿀꿀거리다; n. 꿀꿀[툴툴]거리는 소리
If you grunt, you make a low sound, especially because you are annoyed or not interested in something.

unscrew^{복습}
[ʌnskrúː]

v. (병뚜껑 같은 것을 돌려서) 열다; 나사를 풀다
If you unscrew something such as a lid, or if it unscrews, you keep turning it until you can remove it.

lid^{복습}
[lid]

n. 뚜껑
A lid is the top of a box or other container which can be removed or raised when you want to open the container.

blade^{복습}
[bleid]

n. (칼·도구 등의) 날; (프로펠러 등의) 날개; 잎
The blade of a knife, ax, or saw is the edge, which is used for cutting.

jagged^{복습}
[dʒǽgid]

a. 삐죽삐죽한, 들쭉날쭉한
Something that is jagged has a rough, uneven shape or edge with lots of sharp points.

lick**
[lik]

v. 핥다; n. 한 번 핥기, 핥아먹기
When people or animals lick something, they move their tongue across its surface.

encourage^{복습}
[enkɔ́ːridʒ]

vt. 용기를 북돋우다, 장려하다
If you encourage someone, you give them confidence, hope, or support.

sip**
[síp]

n. 한 모금; vt. (음료를) 홀짝거리다, 조금씩 마시다
A sip is a small amount of drink that you take into your mouth.

bubbly
[bʌ́bli]

a. 거품이 이는, 거품투성이의
If something is bubbly, it has a lot of bubbles in it.

mushy
[mʌ́ʃi]

a. 죽 같은, 걸쭉한
Vegetables and fruit that are mushy are soft and have lost most of their shape.

nectar
[néktər]

n. (진한) 과일즙, (꽃의) 꿀
Nectar is a sweet liquid produced by flowers, which bees and other insects collect.

tangy
[tǽŋi]

a. (맛이) 찌릿한, (냄새가) 톡 쏘는
A tangy flavor or smell is one that is sharp, especially a flavor like that of lemon juice or a smell like that of sea air.

parched ^{복습}
[pɑːrtʃt]

a. 몹시 목마른; (날씨가 더워서) 몹시 건조한
If your mouth, throat, or lips are parched, they are unpleasantly dry.

resist **
[rizíst]

v. 저항하다, 반대하다
If you resist doing something, or resist the temptation to do it, you stop yourself from doing it although you would like to do it.

rattlesnake ^{복습}
[rǽtlsnèik]

n. [동물] 방울뱀
A rattlesnake is a poisonous American snake which can make a rattling noise with its tail.

rattle ^{복습}
[rǽtl]

n. 덜거덕거리는 소리; 방울뱀의 꼬리; **v.** 왈각달각 소리 나다, 덜걱덜걱 움직이다
A rattle is a short sharp knocking sound.

shiver **
[ʃívər]

v. (추위 · 두려움 · 흥분 등으로 가볍게) (몸을) 떨다;
n. (추위 · 두려움 · 흥분 등으로 인한) 전율
When you shiver, your body shakes slightly because you are cold or frightened.

concentrate ^{복습}
[kánsəntrèit]

v. 집중하다, 전념하다
If you concentrate on something, you give all your attention to it.

upside-down ^{복습}
[ʌ́psàid-dáun]

a. 거꾸로, 뒤집힌
If something is upside-down, it has been turned round so that the part that is usually lowest is above the part that is usually highest.

groan ^{복습}
[gróun]

v. 신음하다, 끙끙거리다; **n.** 신음, 끙끙거리는 소리
If you groan, you make a long, low sound because you are in pain, or because you are upset or unhappy about something.

helpless ^{복습}
[hélplis]

a. 무력한, 속수무책의 (helplessly ad. 무력하게, 어쩔 수 없이)
If you are helpless, you do not have the strength or power to do anything useful or to control or protect yourself.

moan ^{복습}
[móun]

v. 신음하다, 끙끙대다; 투덜대다; **n.** 신음; 불평
If you moan, you make a low sound, usually because you are unhappy or in pain.

unbend
[ʌnbend]

v. (unbent–unbent) (휘어진 것을) 펴다; (행동 · 태도가) 누그러지다, 긴장을 풀다
If you unbend something, you make or allow to become straight.

1. What was wrong with Zero?
   A. He cut his foot.
   B. He was weak from an injury.
   C. His stomach hurt.
   D. He was bitten by a rattlesnake.

2. What did Stanley and Zero do to pass the time?
   A. They talked about their families.
   B. They sang a song.
   C. They talked about Kissin' Kate Barlow.
   D. They played a word game.

3. What scared Stanley most about dying?
   A. The pain
   B. His parents not knowing what happened to him
   C. Not being able to help Zero anymore
   D. Not knowing what would happen after death

4. How did Zero help Stanley?
   A. He pulled Stanley onto the last ledge.
   B. He gave Stanley his last jar of Sploosh.
   C. He pushed Stanley forward with the shovel.
   D. He pushed Stanley up the last ledge.

5. Why did Zero's hands bleed?

    A. He cut himself on the rocks.

    B. He cut himself on a broken jar.

    C. He cut himself on the blade of the shovel.

    D. He fell and cut himself on the edge of the cliff.

6. What DIDN'T happen to Zero?

    A. He threw up.

    B. He violently swatted at the gnats.

    C. He collapsed and couldn't get up.

    D. He figured out what "l-u-n-c-h" spelleD.

7. Why did Stanley believe there was water on the mountain?

    A. He could hear the sound of rushing water.

    B. He knew it had rained in the mountains a few days before.

    C. He knew that bugs and plants need water to live.

    D. The soil on the mountain was dark and heavy.

1분에 몇 단어를 읽는지 리딩 속도를 측정해보세요.

$$\frac{1,667 \text{ words}}{\text{reading time (}\quad\text{) sec}} \times 60 = (\quad) \text{ WPM}$$

Build Your Vocabulary

thumbs-up 복습
[θʌ́mz-ʌ́p]

n. 승인, 찬성, 격려 (give a thumbs-up idiom 엄지손가락을 들어 올리다)
A thumbs-up is a sign that you make by raising your thumb to show that you agree with someone, that you are happy with an idea or situation, or that everything is all right.

canteen 복습
[kæntíːn]

n. (휴대용) 물통; (공장 · 학교 등의) 구내식당
A canteen is a small plastic bottle for carrying water and other drinks. Canteens are used by soldiers.

strap 복습
[stræp]

vt. 끈으로 묶다, 잡아매다; n. 가죽 끈, 혁대
If you strap something somewhere, you fasten it there with a narrow piece of leather or cloth.

attack 복습
[ətǽk]

n. (자주 보이던 증상의 갑작스럽고 격렬한) 도짐[발발]; 공격, 습격; v. 공격하다
An attack of an illness is a short period in which you suffer badly from it.

clutch 복습
[klʌ́tʃ]

v. 부여잡다, 꽉 잡다, 붙들다; n. 붙잡음, 움켜쥠
If you clutch at something or clutch something, you hold it tightly, usually because you are afraid or anxious.

mental **
[méntəl]

a. 정신의, 마음의
Mental means relating to the state or the health of a person's mind.

fraction 복습
[frǽkʃən]

n. 부분, 일부
A fraction of something is a tiny amount or proportion of it.

tip 복습
[típ]

① n. (뾰족한) 끝 ② v. 뒤집어엎다, 기울이다 ③ n. 팁, 사례금
The tip of something long and narrow is the end of it.

kneel **
[níːl]

vi. (knelt-knelt) 무릎 꿇다
When you kneel, you bend your legs so that your knees are touching the ground.

dig 복습
[díg]

v. (구멍 등을) 파다; 뒤지다; n. 발굴
If people or animals dig, they make a hole in the ground or in a pile of earth, stones, or rubbish.

grave 복습
[greiv]

① n. 무덤, 묘 ② a. 중대한, 근엄한
A grave is a place where a dead person is buried.

distract 복습
[distrǽkt]

v. (마음 · 주의를) 흐트러뜨리다, 딴 데로 돌리다
If something distracts you or your attention from something, it takes your attention away from it.

exhaust^{복습}
[igzɔ́:st]

vt. 기진맥진하게 만들다; 다 써 버리다, 고갈시키다; n. (자동차 등의) 배기가스
(exhausted**a.** 기진맥진한, 진이 다 빠진)
If something exhausts you, it makes you so tired, either physically or mentally, that you have no energy left.

germ[*]
[dʒə:rm]

n. 세균, 미생물
A germ is a very small organism that causes disease.

whip^{복습}
[hwip]

v. (크림 등을) 휘젓다; 채찍질하다; 휙 빼내다; n. 채찍
(whipped cream**n.** 거품을 일게 한 크림)
When you whip something liquid such as cream or an egg, you stir it very fast until it is thick or stiff.

cliff^{**}
[klif]

n. 절벽, 낭떠러지
A cliff is a high area of land with a very steep side, especially one next to the sea.

shore^{복습}
[ʃɔːr]

n. 물가, 강기슭; vt. 상륙시키다
The shores or the shore of a sea, lake, or wide river is the land along the edge of it.

situated[*]
[sítʃuèitid]

a. (특정한 장소에) 위치해[자리하고] 있는
If something is situated in a particular place or position, it is in that place or position.

slope^{복습}
[slóup]

v. 경사지다, 비탈지다; n. 비탈, 경사
If a surface slopes, it is at an angle, so that one end is higher than the other.

gradual^{**}
[grǽdʒuəl]

a. 점진적인, 서서히 일어나는; (경사가) 완만한 (gradually **ad.** 서서히)
A gradual change or process occurs in small stages over a long period of time, rather than suddenly.

frying pan[*]
[fráiiŋ pæn]

n. 프라이팬
A frying pan is a flat metal pan with a long handle, in which you fry food.

rut
[rʌt]

n. (땅에 생긴) 바퀴 자국
A rut is a deep, narrow mark made in the ground by the wheels of a vehicle.

ledge^{**}
[ledʒ]

n. (벽에서 돌출한) 선반; 바위 턱
A ledge is a narrow shelf along the bottom edge of a window.

crisscross
[krískrɔ́:s]

v. 교차하다; 십자를 그리다; n. 열십자, 십자형
If a number of things crisscross an area, they cross it, and cross over each other.

frail^{**}
[fréil]

a. 허약한, 연약한, 부서지기 쉬운
Someone who is frail is not very strong or healthy.

tremble[*]
[trémbl]

v. 떨다; 떨리다
If you tremble, you shake slightly because you are frightened or cold.

stick out^{복습}

phrasal v. (툭) 튀어나오다; ~을 내밀다
If something is sticks out, it is further out than something else.

fairly***
[féərli]

ad. 상당히, 꽤; 공정하게, 정직하게
Fairly means to quite a large degree.

foothold^{복습}
[fúthòuld]

n. (등산 때) 발 디딜 곳; (사업·직업 등에서 성공의) 발판
A foothold is a place such as a small hole or area of rock where you can safely put your foot when climbing.

boost*
[bu:st]

n. 밀어올림; 후원, 격려; vt. 밀어 올리다; 후원하다, 밀어주다
If you give a boost to someone, you push them from below.

cup***
[kʌp]

v. 두 손을 (컵 모양으로) 동그랗게 모아 쥐다; n. 컵, 잔
If you cup something in your hands, you make your hands into a curved dish-like shape and support it or hold it gently.

interweave
[intərwí:v]

v. (interwove–interwoven) (실·끈 등을) 섞어 짜다
If two or more things are interwoven or interweave, they are very closely connected or are combined with each other.

protrude*
[proutrú:d]

v. 튀어나오다, 돌출되다
If something protrudes from somewhere, it sticks out.

slab*
[slæb]

n. (두껍고 반듯한) 조각; 석판, 널빤지
A slab of something is a thick, flat piece of it.

poke^{복습}
[pouk]

v. (손가락 등으로) 쿡 찌르다; n. 찌르기, 쑤시기
If you poke someone or something, you quickly push them with your finger or with a sharp object.

shaft^{복습}
[ʃæft]

n. (망치·골프채 등의 기다란) 손잡이
A shaft is a long thin piece of wood or metal that forms part of a spear, ax, golf club, or other object.

clasp**
[klæsp]

v. (꽉) 움켜쥐다; 고정시키다, 죄다; n. 걸쇠, 버클; 악수, 포옹
If you clasp someone or something, you hold them tightly in your hands or arms.

wrist^{복습}
[rist]

n. 손목
Your wrist is the part of your body between your hand and your arm which bends when you move your hand.

brief^{복습}
[bri:f]

a. (시간이) 짧은, 잠시 동안의; (말·글이) 간단한 (briefly ad. 잠시; 간단히)
Something that is brief lasts for only a short time.

defy**
[difái]

v. (권위·법률·규칙 등에) 반항하다
If you defy someone or something that is trying to make you behave in a particular way, you refuse to obey them and behave in that way.

gravity**
[grǽviti]

n. 중력
Gravity is the force which causes things to drop to the ground.

gash^{복습}
[gæʃ]

n. 깊은 상처; (지면의) 갈라진 틈; vt. 상처를 입히다
A gash is a long, deep cut in your skin or in the surface of something.

suck^{복습}
[sʌk]

v. 빨다, 빨아내다; 삼키다; n. 빨아들임
If something sucks a liquid, gas, or object in a particular direction, it draws it there with a powerful force.

fiery^{**}
[fáiəri]

a. 불타는 듯한, 불의

You can use fiery for emphasis when you are referring to bright colors such as red or orange.

twirl[*]
[twəːrl]

v. 빙빙 돌리다, 빠르게 돌다; n. 회전

If you twirl something or if it twirls, it turns around and around with a smooth, fairly fast movement.

Check Your Reading Speed

1분에 몇 단어를 읽는지 리딩 속도를 측정해보세요.

$$\frac{513 \text{ words}}{\text{reading time ( ) sec}} \times 60 = (\quad) \text{ WPM}$$

Build Your Vocabulary

refuge복습
[réfjudʒ]

n. 피난처, 은신처; 피난, 도피
A refuge is a place where you go for safety and protection.

steep복습
[stiːp]

a. (steeper–steepest) (경사면 · 언덕 등이) 가파른, 비탈진; (증감이) 급격한
A steep slope rises at a very sharp angle and is difficult to go up.

slope복습
[slóup]

n. 비탈, 경사; v. 경사지다, 비탈지다
A slope is the side of a mountain, hill, or valley.

increase복습
[inkríːs]

v. 증가하다, 늘리다, 불리다; n. 증가, 증대
If something increases or you increase it, it becomes greater in number, level, or amount.

altitude*
[ǽltətjùːd]

n. 높이, 고도
If something is at a particular altitude, it is at that height above sea level.

increment
[ínkrəmənt]

n. (수 · 양의) 증가
An increment in something or in the value of something is an amount by which it increases.

patch**
[pætʃ]

n. (특히 주변과는 다른 조그만) 부분; 헝겊 조각; 반창고; v. 헝겊을 대고 깁다
A patch on a surface is a part of it which is different in appearance from the area around it.

weed복습
[wíːd]

n. 잡초; v. 잡초를 없애다
A weed is a wild plant that grows in gardens or fields of crops and prevents the plants that you want from growing properly.

dot**
[dɑt]

v. 여기저기 흩어져 있다, 산재하다; 점을 찍다; n. 점
When things dot a place or an area, they are scattered or spread all over it.

foothold복습
[fúthòuld]

n. (등산 때) 발 디딜 곳; (사업 · 직업 등에서 성공의) 발판
A foothold is a place such as a small hole or area of rock where you can safely put your foot when climbing.

thorn복습
[θɔ́ːrn]

n. 가시
Thorns are the sharp points on some plants and trees.

daylight**
[deiláit]

n. (낮의) 햇빛, 일광
Daylight is the natural light that there is during the day, before it gets dark.

148

swarm **
[swɔ́:rm]

n. 떼, 무리; v. 많이 모여들다, 떼를 짓다
A swarm of bees or other insects is a large group of them flying together.

gnat *
[næt]

n. 피를 빨아 먹는 작은 곤충, 각다귀
A gnat is a very small flying insect that bites people and usually lives near water.

hover 복습
[hʌ́vər]

v. 공중을 맴돌다; 계속 맴돌다; 서성이다
To hover means to stay in the same position in the air without moving forwards or backwards. Many birds and insects can hover by moving their wings very quickly.

attract **
[ətrǽkt]

v. (마음을) 끌다, 끌어당기다
If something attracts people or animals, it has features that cause them to come to it.

sweat 복습
[swét]

n. 땀; v. 땀 흘리다; 습기가 차다
Sweat is the salty colorless liquid which comes through your skin when you are hot, ill, or afraid.

swat
[swát]

v. (파리 따위를) 찰싹 치다; n. 찰싹 때림, 강타
If you swat something such as an insect, you hit it with a quick, swinging movement, using your hand or a flat object.

knock over

phrasal v. 뒤집어엎다, 때려눕히다
If you knock something over, you push or hit it and making it fall or turn on its side.

weary 복습
[wíəri]

a. 피로한, 지친
If you are weary, you are very tired.

horrible 복습
[hɔ́:rəbəl]

a. 끔찍한, 소름 끼치게 싫은; 무서운
You can call something horrible when it causes you to feel great shock, fear, and disgust.

wrench *
[rentʃ]

v. (가슴을) 쓰라리게 하다; (세게) 비틀다; n. 비틀기; 렌치 (wrenching a. 고통스러운)
If you say that leaving someone or something is a wrench, you feel very sad about it.

double over

phrasal v. (웃음·고통으로) 몸을 구부리다; 접어서 겹치다
If you double over, you suddenly bend forwards and down, usually because of pain or laughter.

frail 복습
[fréil]

a. 허약한, 연약한, 부서지기 쉬운
Someone who is frail is not very strong or healthy.

violent 복습
[váiələnt]

a. 격렬한, 맹렬한; 폭력적인, 난폭한 (violently ad. 격렬하게, 맹렬히)
If you describe something as violent, you mean that it is said, done, or felt very strongly.

throw up 복습

phrasal v. 토하다
When someone throws up, they vomit.

tangle *
[tǽŋgl]

v. 엉키다; 얽히게 하다; n. 엉킴; 혼란
If something is tangled or tangles, it becomes twisted together in an untidy way.

thorny*
[θɔ́ːrni]

a. 가시가 많은, 가시 같은
A thorny plant or tree is covered with thorns.

vine**
[váin]

n. 덩굴식물, 포도나무
A vine is a plant that grows up or over things, especially one which produces grapes.

clown*
[klaun]

n. 어릿광대, 익살꾼
A clown is a performer in a circus who wears funny clothes and bright make-up, and does silly things in order to make people laugh.

urge^{복습}
[ɔ́ːrdʒ]

v. 재촉하다, 몰아대다; **n.** (강한) 충동
If you urge someone to do something, you try hard to persuade them to do it.

chapters thirty-eight to forty

1. How did Stanley have the strength to climb?
   A. He fell in a pile of mud and realized there must be water nearby.
   B. He used the shovel as a walking stick.
   C. He smelled something in the air and it encouraged him to keep climbing.
   D. It was like the rock was a magnet pulling him towards it.

2. What did Stanley find in the mud?
   A. A hot-fudge sundae
   B. An onion
   C. A peach
   D. A potato

3. What extended all the way around Big Thumb?
   A. Muddy water about 2 inches deep
   B. Dark green, thorny weeds
   C. Greenish white flowers
   D. Brown dirt and mud

4. What did Zero confess to Stanley?
   A. He already knew how to read.
   B. He stole Clyde Livingston's shoes.
   C. He stole Stanley's shoes from the camp.
   D. He thought he was going to die.

5. Mrs. Tennyson said _____ saved her daughter Rebecca.
   A. leeches
   B. Doc Hawthorn's medicine
   C. meat from Jim the butcher
   D. onion tonic

6. Why did the townspeople laugh at Mrs. Tennyson?
   A. She thanked Sam for saving her daughter.
   B. She was wearing her bed clothes.
   C. She fed Mary Lou onions from her hand.
   D. She called Doc Hawthorn a quack.

7. Why did Stanley leave Zero alone?
   A. He went to find more onions.
   B. He wanted to pick and eat some flowers.
   C. He wanted to find the shovel.
   D. He wanted to see Camp Green Lake from the top of the mountain.

1분에 몇 단어를 읽는지 리딩 속도를 측정해보세요.

$$\frac{669 \text{ words}}{\text{reading time ( ) sec}} \times 60 = (\quad) \text{ WPM}$$

Build Your Vocabulary

forearm^{복습}
[fɔ́:rà:rm]

n. 팔뚝
Your forearm is the part of your arm between your elbow and your wrist.

upright*
[ʌ́prait]

a. 똑바른, 꼿꼿한, 수직으로 선
If you are sitting or standing upright, you are sitting or standing with your back straight, rather than bending or lying down.

stoop**
[stú:p]

v. 상체를 굽히다, 구부리다, 웅크리다
If you stoop, you bend your body forwards and downwards.

worn-out^{복습}
[wɔ́:rn-áut]

a. 기진맥진한; 써서 낡은, 닳아 해진
Someone who is worn-out is extremely tired after hard work or a difficult or unpleasant experience.

sack^{복습}
[sæk]

n. 부대, 자루; (쇼핑 물건을 담는 크고 튼튼한 종이) 봉지; vt. 자루에 넣다
Sacks are used to carry or store things such as vegetables or coal.

dangle^{복습}
[dǽŋgl]

v. (달랑달랑) 매달리다, 매달다; n. 매달린 것
If something dangles from somewhere or if you dangle it somewhere, it hangs or swings loosely.

tangle^{복습}
[tǽŋgl]

v. 엉키다; 얽히게 하다; n. 엉킴; 혼란
If something is tangled or tangles, it becomes twisted together in an untidy way.

patch^{복습}
[pætʃ]

n. (특히 주변과는 다른 조그만) 부분; 헝겊 조각; 반창고; v. 헝겊을 대고 깁다
A patch on a surface is a part of it which is different in appearance from the area around it.

vine^{복습}
[váin]

n. 덩굴식물, 포도나무
A vine is a plant that grows up or over things, especially one which produces grapes.

concentrate^{복습}
[kánsəntrèit]

v. 집중하다, 전념하다
If you concentrate on something, you give all your attention to it.

absorb^{복습}
[æbsɔ́:rb]

vt. 흡수하다, 받아들이다; 열중시키다
If something absorbs light, heat, or another form of energy, it takes it in.

foul^{복습}
[faul]

a. (성격 · 맛 등이) 더러운, 아주 안 좋은
If you describe something as foul, you mean it is dirty and smells or tastes unpleasant.

154

odor^{복습}
[óudər]

n. (불쾌한) 냄새, 악취
An odor is a particular and distinctive smell.

flatten*
[flǽtn]

vt. 평평하게 하다, 납작하게 하다
If you flatten something or if it flattens, it becomes flat or flatter.

precipice*
[présəpis]

n. 벼랑
A precipice is a very steep cliff on a mountain.

resemble**
[rizémbl]

vt. ~을 닮다, ~와 공통점이 있다
If one thing or person resembles another, they are similar to each other.

bitter***
[bítər]

a. 쓰라린; (음식 등이) 맛이 쓴
A bitter experience makes you feel very disappointed.

despair**
[dispéər]

n. 절망, 자포자기; vi. 절망하다
Despair is the feeling that everything is wrong and that nothing will improve.

occasional^{복습}
[əkéiʒənl]

a. 가끔의, 때때로의
Occasional means happening sometimes, but not regularly or often.

knock^{복습}
[nák]

v. 치다, 부수다; (문을) 두드리다, 노크하다
If you knock something, you touch or hit it roughly, especially so that it falls or moves.

tumble**
[tʌ́mbl]

v. 굴러 떨어지다, 넘어지다; n. 추락; 폭락
If someone or something tumbles somewhere, they fall there with a rolling or bouncing movement.

muddy**
[mʌ́di]

a. 진흙투성이인
Something that is muddy contains mud or is covered in mud.

gully
[gʌ́li]

n. (시냇물이나 빗물에 의해 생긴) 도랑
A gully is a long narrow valley with steep sides.

ditch**
[ditʃ]

n. (들판·도로가의) 배수로; v. (불필요한 것을) 버리다
A ditch is a long narrow channel cut into the ground at the side of a road or field.

crawl^{복습}
[krɔ́:l]

vi. 기어가다, 느릿느릿 가다; 우글거리다, 들끓다; n. 서행; 기어감
When you crawl, you move forward on your hands and knees.

gloppy
[glɑpi]

a. (gloppier–gloppiest) (기분 나쁘게) 질척거리는
Something that is gloppy is soft and soggy.

splash**
[splǽʃ]

v. 철벅 떨어지다, (물·흙탕물 등을) 끼얹다; n. 첨벙하는 소리
If you splash a liquid somewhere or if it splashes, it hits someone or something and scatters in a lot of small drops.

slap^{복습}
[slǽp]

v. 철썩 부딪치다; 찰싹 때리다, 탁 놓다; n. 찰싹 (때림)
If you slap something onto a surface, you put it there quickly, roughly, or carelessly.

soggy
[sɑ́gi]

a. 물에 잠긴, 함빡 젖은
Something that is soggy is unpleasantly wet.

pool ^{복습}
[pu:l]

n. (액체 · 빛이) 고여 있는 곳; 웅덩이, 못; 수영장
A pool of liquid or light is a small area of it on the ground or on a surface.

lick ^{복습}
[lik]

v. 핥다; n. 한 번 핥기, 핥아먹기
When people or animals lick something, they move their tongue across its surface.

scoop ^{복습}
[skú:p]

v. 뜨다, 파다; 재빨리 들어 올리다; n. 국자, 주걱
If you scoop something from a container, you remove it with something such as a spoon.

poke ^{복습}
[pouk]

v. (손가락 등으로) 쿡 찌르다; n. 찌르기, 쑤시기
If something pokes out of or through another thing, you can see part of it appearing from behind or underneath the other thing.

droplet ^{복습}
[dráplit]

n. 작은 (물)방울
A droplet is a very small drop of liquid.

drag ^{복습}
[dræg]

v. 끌다, 끌고 오다; 힘들게 움직이다; n. 견인, 끌기; 빨아들이기
If someone drags you somewhere you do not want to go, they make you go there.

wipe ^{복습}
[waip]

v. 닦다, 닦아 내다; n. 닦기
If you wipe something, you rub its surface to remove dirt or liquid from it.

peel ^{복습}
[pi:l]

v. 껍질을 벗기다, 벗겨지다
When you peel fruit or vegetables, you remove their skins.

burst ^{***}
[bɔ́:rst]

v. 터지다, 파열하다; 갑자기 ~하다; n. 폭발, 파열; 돌발
If something bursts or if you burst it, it suddenly breaks open or splits open and the air or other substance inside it comes out.

swallow ^{복습}
[swálou]

v. 삼키다, 목구멍으로 넘기다; (초조해서) 마른침을 삼키다
If you swallow something, you cause it to go from your mouth down into your stomach.

$$\frac{652 \text{ words}}{\text{reading time (} \quad \text{) sec}} \times 60 = (\quad) \text{ WPM}$$

Build Your Vocabulary

meadow**
[médou]

n. 초원, 목초지
A meadow is a field which has grass and flowers growing in it.

layer*
[léiər]

v. 층층이 놓다[쌓다]; **n.** (하나의 표면이나 여러 표면 사이를 덮고 있는) 층
If you layer something, you arrange it in layers.

streak**
[striːk]

v. (줄같이) 기다란 자국[흔적]을 내다, 줄무늬를 넣다; **n.** 줄무늬
If something streaks a surface, it makes long stripes or marks on the surface.

shade복습
[ʃeid]

n. 색조; (시원한) 그늘; **vt.** 그늘지게 하다
A shade of a particular color is one of its different forms.

tan**
[tæn]

n. 황갈색; 햇볕에 그을음; **vt.** (피부를) 햇볕에 태우다
Something that is tan is a light brown color.

coat복습
[kout]

v. (막 같은 것을) 덮다; **n.** 표면을 덮는 것, 칠; 외투, 코트
If you coat something with a substance or in a substance, you cover it with a thin layer of the substance.

roll over복습

phrasal v. 뒹굴다, 자면서 몸을 뒤척이다
When you roll over, you turn from lying on one side of your body to the other side.

sore복습
[sɔːr]

a. 아픈, 쓰린
If part of your body is sore, it causes you pain and discomfort.

swish복습
[swiʃ]

v. 휘두르다, 휙 소리 내다; 튀기다; **n.** 휙 소리
If something swishes or if you swish it, it moves quickly through the air, making a soft sound.

moan복습
[móun]

v. 신음하다, 끙끙대다; 투덜대다; **n.** 신음; 불평
If you moan, you make a low sound, usually because you are unhappy or in pain.

lap복습
[læp]

① **v.** 할짝할짝 핥다; (물이) 찰랑거리다 ② **n.** 무릎; (트랙의) 한 바퀴
When an animal laps a drink, it uses short quick movements of its tongue to take liquid up into its mouth.

jerk복습
[dʒə́ːrk]

① **v.** 홱 움직이다; **n.** (갑자기 날카롭게) 홱 움직임 ② **n.** 바보, 멍청이
If you jerk something or someone in a particular direction, or they jerk in a particular direction, they move a short distance very suddenly and quickly.

clutch ^{복습}
[klʌtʃ]

v. 부여잡다, 꽉 잡다, 붙들다; n. 붙잡음, 움켜쥠
If you clutch at something or clutch something, you hold it tightly, usually because you are afraid or anxious.

violent ^{복습}
[váiələnt]

a. 격렬한, 맹렬한; 폭력적인, 난폭한 (violently ad. 격렬하게, 맹렬히)
If you describe something as violent, you mean that it is said, done, or felt very strongly.

shovel ^{복습}
[ʃʌvəl]

n. 삽; v. ~을 삽으로 뜨다[파다], 삽으로 일하다
A shovel is a tool with a long handle that is used for lifting and moving earth, coal, or snow.

jar ^{복습}
[dʒɑːr]

① n. 병, 단지 ② v. 삐걱거리다; n. 삐걱거리는 소리, 잡음
A jar is a glass container with a lid that is used for storing food.

struggle to one's feet ^{복습}

idiom 가까스로 일어서다
If you struggle to your feet, you try hard to stand up.

precipice ^{복습}
[présəpis]

n. 벼랑
A precipice is a very steep cliff on a mountain.

cluster ^{복습}
[klʌstər]

n. 무리, 집단, 떼; v. 밀집하다
A cluster of people or things is a small group of them close together.

spit ^{복습}
[spit]

v. 뱉다, 내뿜다; (폭언 등을) 내뱉다; n. 침
If you spit liquid or food somewhere, you force a small amount of it out of your mouth.

trail ^{복습}
[tréil]

n. 지나간 자국, 흔적; v. (땅에 대고 뒤로) 끌다, 끌리다; ~을 뒤쫓다
A trail is a series of marks or other signs of movement or other activities left by someone or something.

double over ^{복습}

phrasal v. (웃음·고통으로) 몸을 구부리다; 접어서 겹치다
If you double over, you suddenly bend forwards and down, usually because of pain or laughter.

groan ^{복습}
[gróun]

n. 신음, 끙끙거리는 소리; v. 신음하다, 끙끙거리다
A groan is a deep long sound showing great pain or unhappiness.

twist ^{**}
[twíst]

v. 비틀다, 돌리다, 꼬다; n. 뒤틀림; 엉킴; 변화
If you twist something, especially a part of your body, or if it twists, it moves into an unusual, uncomfortable, or bent position, for example because of being hit or pushed, or because you are upset.

shelter ^{복습}
[ʃéltər]

n. 쉼터, 보호소; 피난처; v. 피할[쉴] 곳을 제공하다, 보호하다
A shelter is a building where homeless people can sleep and get food.

comprehend ^{**}
[kɑ(ɔ)mprihénd]

vt. 이해하다, 파악하다
If you cannot comprehend something, you cannot understand it.

delirious ^{복습}
[dilíəriəs]

a. 의식이 혼미한, 헛소리를 하는
Someone who is delirious is unable to think or speak in a sensible and reasonable way, usually because they are very ill and have a fever.

158

confession^{*}
[kənféʃən]

n. (죄의) 자백, 고백

Confession is the act of admitting that you have done something that you are ashamed of or embarrassed about.

muscle^{복습}
[mʌ́sl]

n. 근육

A muscle is a piece of tissue inside your body which connects two bones and which you use when you make a movement.

drift^{복습}
[drift]

v. (자신도 모르게) ~하게 되다; (물 · 공기에) 떠가다, 표류[부유]하다; n. 표류

If someone or something drifts into a situation, they get into that situation in a way that is not planned or controlled.

generation^{**}
[dʒènəréiʃən]

n. 세대, 대(代), 동시대의 사람들

A generation is the period of time, usually considered to be about thirty years, that it takes for children to grow up and become adults and have children of their own.

woodpecker^{복습}
[wúdpèkəːr]

n. [조류] 딱따구리

A woodpecker is a type of bird with a long sharp beak. Woodpeckers use their beaks to make holes in tree trunks.

bark^{복습}
[baːrk]

① n. 나무껍질 ② v. (개가) 짖다; 고함치다; n. 짖는 소리

Bark is the tough material that covers the outside of a tree.

Check Your Reading Speed

1분에 몇 단어를 읽는지 리딩 속도를 측정해보세요.

$$\frac{1{,}070 \text{ words}}{\text{reading time ( ) sec}} \times 60 = (\qquad) \text{ WPM}$$

Build Your Vocabulary

grateful^{복습}
[gréitfəl]

a. 고맙게 여기는, 감사하는 (gratefully ad. 감사하여)
If you are grateful for something that someone has given you or done for you, you have warm, friendly feelings towards them and wish to thank them.

gaze^{복습}
[géiz]

vi. 응시하다, 뚫어지게 보다; n. 주시, 응시
If you gaze at someone or something, you look steadily at them for a long time, for example because you find them attractive or interesting, or because you are thinking about something else.

meadow^{복습}
[médou]

n. 초원, 목초지
A meadow is a field which has grass and flowers growing in it.

intertwine
[intərtwáin]

v. 서로 얽히게 하다, 서로 엮다
If two or more things are intertwined or intertwine, they are closely connected with each other in many ways.

rub^{복습}
[rʌ́b]

v. 문지르다, 비비다; 스치다; n. 문지르기
If you rub a part of your body, you move your hand or fingers backwards and forwards over it while pressing firmly.

dig^{복습}
[díg]

v. (dug–dug) (구멍 등을) 파다; 뒤지다; n. 파기
If people or animals dig, they make a hole in the ground or in a pile of earth, stones, or rubbish.

shore^{복습}
[ʃɔ́ːr]

n. 물가, 강기슭; vt. 상륙시키다
The shores or the shore of a sea, lake, or wide river is the land along the edge of it.

robe^{★★}
[roub]

n. 가운; (특별한 의식 때 입는) 예복
A robe is a loose piece of clothing which covers all of your body and reaches the ground.

proper^{복습}
[prápər]

a. 적절한, 제대로 된; 고유의
The proper thing is the one that is correct or most suitable.

mule
[mjuːl]

n. 노새; 뒤축 없는 슬리퍼
A mule is an animal whose parents are a horse and a donkey.

fever^{★★}
[fíːvər]

n. 열, 발열; 열중, 열광
If you have a fever when you are ill, your body temperature is higher than usual.

160

credit^{복습}
[krédit]

n. 공, 명예, 칭찬; 학점; 신용
If you get the credit for something good, people praise you because you are responsible for it, or are thought to be responsible for it.

quack[*]
[kwæk]

n. 돌팔이 의사; vi. 꽥꽥 울다; 시끄럽게 지껄이다
If you call someone a quack or a quack doctor, you mean that they claim to be skilled in medicine but are not.

leech
[li:tʃ]

n. [동물] 거머리
A leech is a small animal which looks like a worm and lives in water. Leeches feed by attaching themselves to other animals and sucking their blood.

suck^{복습}
[sʌk]

v. 빨다, 빨아내다; 삼키다; n. 빨아들임
If something sucks a liquid, gas, or object in a particular direction, it draws it there with a powerful force.

tonic[*]
[tánik]

n. 강장제; 토닉(진·보드카 등에 섞어 마시는 탄산음료)
A tonic is a medicine that makes you feel stronger, healthier, and less tired.

snicker
[sníkə:r]

vi. 낄낄 웃다, 숨죽여 웃다; n. 낄낄 웃음
If you snicker, you laugh quietly in a disrespectful way, for example at something rude or embarrassing.

parade^{**}
[pəréid]

v. (과시하듯) 걸어 다니다; 전시하다; n. 행렬, 퍼레이드, 행진
If someone parades, they walk about somewhere in order to be seen and admired.

flush^{***}
[flʌʃ]

v. (얼굴 등을) 붉히다; (물이) 왈칵 흘러나오다; n. (볼 등의) 홍조
If you flush, your face goes red because you are hot or ill, or because you are feeling a strong emotion such as embarrassment or anger.

butcher^{**}
[bútʃər]

n. 정육점 주인; 도살업자; vt. 도살하다, 학살하다
A butcher is a shopkeeper who cuts up and sells meat.

contrite
[kəntráit]

a. 깊이 뉘우치는, 회한에 찬 (contritely ad. 뉘우치며)
If you are contrite, you are very sorry because you have done something wrong.

general store^{복습}

n. 잡화점
A general store is a rural or small town store that carries a general line of merchandise.

charity^{**}
[tʃǽriti]

n. 자선, 자비, 자애; 자선단체
People who live on charity live on money or goods which other people give them because they are poor.

donkey^{복습}
[dáŋki]

n. 당나귀
A donkey is an animal which is like a horse but which is smaller and has longer ears.

splash^{복습}
[splæʃ]

v. (물·흙탕물 등을) 끼얹다, 철벅 떨어지다; n. 첨벙하는 소리
If you splash a liquid somewhere or if it splashes, it hits someone or something and scatters in a lot of small drops.

stir^{복습}
[stə:r]

v. 휘젓다, 뒤섞다; 움직이다; n. 움직임; 휘젓기
If you stir a liquid or other substance, you move it around or mix it in a container using something such as a spoon.

desert^{복습}
[dizə́:rt]

① v. 버리다, 유기하다; 인적이 끊기다 ② n. 사막, 황무지
If someone deserts you, they go away and leave you, and no longer help or support you.

feeble^{복습}
[fí:bəl]

a. 아주 약한 (feebly ad. 약하게)
If you describe someone or something as feeble, you mean that they are weak.

fairly^{복습}
[féərli]

ad. 상당히, 꽤; 공정하게, 정직하게
Fairly means to quite a large degree.

trail^{복습}
[tréil]

n. 지나간 자국, 흔적; v. (땅에 대고 뒤로) 끌다, 끌리다; ~을 뒤쫓다
A trail is a series of marks or other signs of movement or other activities left by someone or something.

definite^{복습}
[défənit]

a. 분명한, 뚜렷한; 확실한, 확고한 (definitely ad. 분명히, 틀림없이)
You use definite to emphasize the strength of your opinion or belief.

indentation
[indentéiʃən]

n. (표면·가장자리를 깎거나 찍어서 생긴) 자국
An indentation is a shallow hole or cut in the surface or edge of something.

doubtful**
[dáutfəl]

a. 불확실한; 확신이 없는, 의심을 품은
If it is doubtful that something will happen, it seems unlikely to happen or you are uncertain whether it will happen.

1. Zero's mother _____.
   A. sold Girl Scout cookies
   B. tried to sell Clyde Livingston's shoes
   C. went to Cub Scout meetings in the park
   D. stole things

2. What did Zero do with Clyde Livingston's shoes?
   A. He put them back in the glass case.
   B. He threw them off an overpass.
   C. He put them on a parked car.
   D. He tried to sell them to a shoe store.

3. When was the last time Stanley felt happiness?
   A. At school
   B. Camp Green Lake
   C. He couldn't remember
   D. Last summer

4. What would Stanley need before he became a fugitive?
   A. Money
   B. His parents
   C. A car
   D. A new name

5. How did Stanley and Zero have water for their journey?
   A. They put water in the sunflower seed sack.
   B. They put water in Stanley's canteen and the sunflower seed sack.
   C. They filled some jars they found by the Big Thumb.
   D. They put water in the Sploosh jars.

6. What was the challenge between Stanley and Zero?
   A. Who could walk the fastest
   B. Who could go the longest without water
   C. Who could find the shortest way to Camp Green Lake
   D. Who could sneak into the Wreck Room without getting caught

7. What did Zero's mother do?
   A. She left Zero at Laney Park and didn't come back.
   B. She gave Zero to a homeless shelter.
   C. She took Zero to a birthday party at a park.
   D. She left Zero with his father at Laney Park.

8. Where did Stanley and Zero hide?
   A. Underneath the Mary Lou boat
   B. In adjacent holes
   C. Behind the oak trees
   D. Next to the Warden's cabin

Check Your Reading Speed

1분에 몇 단어를 읽는지 리딩 속도를 측정해보세요.

$$\frac{704 \text{ words}}{\text{reading time ( ) sec}} \times 60 = (\quad) \text{ WPM}$$

Build Your Vocabulary

improve^{복습}
[imprúːv]

v. 개선하다, 진보하다, 나아지다
If something improves or if you improve it, it gets better.

layer^{복습}
[léiər]

n. (하나의 표면이나 여러 표면 사이를 덮고 있는) 층; v. 층층이 놓다[쌓다]
A layer of a material or substance is a quantity or piece of it that covers a surface or that is between two other things.

murky
[mə́ːrki]

a. (진흙 등으로) 흐린, 탁한
Murky water or fog is so dark and dirty that you cannot see through it.

**live on
(something)**

idiom ~을 먹고 살다
If you live on something, you eat that particular type of food very frequently or all the time.

barefoot^{복습}
[béərfùt]

a., ad. 맨발의[로]
Someone who is barefoot or barefooted is not wearing anything on their feet.

contaminate[*]
[kəntǽmənèit]

v. 오염시키다, 더럽히다
If something is contaminated by dirt, chemicals, or radiation, they make it dirty or harmful.

homeless^{복습}
[hóumlis]

a. 노숙자의; n. (pl.) 노숙자들
Homeless people have nowhere to live.

shelter^{복습}
[ʃéltər]

n. 쉼터, 보호소; 피난처; v. 피할[쉴] 곳을 제공하다, 보호하다
A shelter is a building where homeless people can sleep and get food.

ward^{**}
[wɔːrd]

n. (법원·후견인의 법률적 보호를 받는) 피보호자;
(병원에서 특정 환자들을 위한) 병동
A ward or a ward of court is a child who is the responsibility of a person called a guardian, or of a court of law, because their parents are dead or because they are believed to be in need of protection.

stuff^{복습}
[stʌf]

n. 일[것](일반적으로 말하거나 생각하는 것); 물건, 물질; vt. 채워 넣다, 속을 채우다
You can use stuff to refer to things such as a substance, a collection of things, events, or ideas, or the contents of something in a general way without mentioning the thing itself by name.

shrug^{복습}
[ʃrʌg]

v. (어깨를) 으쓱하다; n. (양 손바닥을 내보이면서 어깨를) 으쓱하기
If you shrug, you raise your shoulders to show that you are not interested in something or that you do not know or care about something.

166

arrest^{복습}
[ərést]

vt. 체포하다, 저지하다; (주의 · 이목 · 흥미 등을) 끌다; **n.** 체포, 검거, 구속
If the police arrest you, they take charge of you and take you to a police station, because they believe you may have committed a crime.

sneaker^{복습}
[sníːkər]

n. (pl.) 고무창 운동화
Sneakers are casual shoes with rubber soles.

1분에 몇 단어를 읽는지 리딩 속도를 측정해보세요.

$$\frac{953 \text{ words}}{\text{reading time ( ) sec}} \times 60 = (\quad) \text{ WPM}$$

Build Your Vocabulary

eventually^{복습}
[ivéntʃuəli]

ad. 결국, 마침내
Eventually means at the end of a situation or process or as the final result of it.

live on^{복습}
(something)

idiom ~을 먹고 살다
If you live on something, you eat that particular type of food very frequently or all the time.

sundial
[sʌ́ndàiəl]

n. 해시계
A sundial is a device used for telling the time when the sun is shining. The shadow of an upright rod falls onto a flat surface that is marked with the hours, and points to the correct hour.

uphill^{복습}
[ʌ́phil]

ad. 오르막길로, 언덕 위로; a. 오르막의
If something or someone is uphill or is moving uphill, they are near the top of a hill or are going up a slope.

bitter^{복습}
[bítər]

a. (음식 등이) 맛이 쓴; 쓰라린
A bitter taste is sharp, not sweet, and often slightly unpleasant.

rot^{**}
[rát]

v. 썩다, 썩이다; n. 썩음, 부패
If there is rot in something, especially something that is made of wood, parts of it have decayed and fallen apart.

sprout[*]
[spraut]

vi. 싹이 트다, 발아하다; n. 새싹, 새순
When plants, vegetables, or seeds sprout, they produce new leaves or shoots.

stink[*]
[stiŋk]

v. (고약한) 냄새가 나다, 악취가 풍기다; n. 악취
To stink means to smell extremely unpleasant.

freeze^{복습}
[fríːz]

v. 얼다, 얼리다; n. (임금 · 가격 등의) 동결
If a liquid or a substance containing a liquid freezes, or if something freezes it, it becomes solid because of low temperatures.

miserable^{복습}
[mízərəbəl]

a. 비참한, 초라한, 불쌍한
If you describe a place or situation as miserable, you mean that it makes you feel unhappy or depressed.

bully^{복습}
[búli]

n. 약자를 괴롭히는 사람; v. 괴롭히다, 겁주다
A bully is someone who uses their strength or power to hurt or frighten other people.

pick on 복습

phrasal v. (구어) 괴롭히다, 못살게 굴다; ~을 선택하다, 고르다
If you pick on someone, you treat them badly or unfairly, especially repeatedly.

petal *
[pétl]

n. 꽃잎
The petals of a flower are the thin colored or white parts which together form the flower.

cartoon *
[kɑːrtúːn]

n. 만화 영화, 만화
A cartoon is a humorous drawing or series of drawings in a newspaper or magazine.

chin 복습
[tʃin]

n. 턱
Your chin is the part of your face that is below your mouth and above your neck.

amazing **
[əméiziŋ]

a. 놀랄 만한, 굉장한 (amazingly ad. 놀랄 만큼)
You say that something is amazing when it is very surprising and makes you feel pleasure, approval, or wonder.

flutter **
[flʌtər]

v. (빠르고 가볍게) 흔들(리)다, 펄럭이다; n. 흔들림, 떨림
If something thin or light flutters, or if you flutter it, it moves up and down or from side to side with a lot of quick, light movements.

trial 복습
[tráiəl]

n. 재판, 공판; 시험, 실험
A trial is a formal meeting in a law court, at which a judge and jury listen to evidence and decide whether a person is guilty of a crime.

delay 복습
[diléi]

v. 미루다, 연기하다; n. 지연
If you delay doing something, you do not do it immediately or at the planned or expected time, but you leave it until later.

glitter **
[glítər]

vi. 반짝반짝 빛나다, 반짝이다; n. 반짝이는 작은 장식; 반짝거림, 광채
If something glitters, light comes from or is reflected off different parts of it.

overpass 복습
[óuvərpæs]

n. (도로·철도 등의 위에 가설된) 다리, 고가도로, 육교
An overpass is a structure which carries one road over the top of another one.

strike 복습
[straik]

v. (struck—stricken/struck) 때리다, 치다, 부딪치다; 갑자기 떠오르다;
n. 치기, 때리기; 파업
If something that is falling or moving strikes something, it hits it.

coincidence 복습
[kouínsidəns]

n. (우연의) 일치, 부합; 동시에 일어남
A coincidence is when two or more similar or related events occur at the same time by chance and without any planning.

dirt road 복습

n. (시골의) 흙길, 비포장도로
dirt (명사: 흙) + road (명사: 작은 길, 오솔길)

civilization **
[sìvələzéiʃən]

n. 문명 (사회)
A civilization is a human society with its own social organization and culture.

sack^{복습}
[sæk]

n. 부대, 자루; (쇼핑 물건을 담는 크고 튼튼한 종이) 봉지; vt. 자루에 넣다
Sacks are used to carry or store things such as vegetables or coal.

canteen^{복습}
[kæntí:n]

n. (휴대용) 물통; (공장 · 학교 등의) 구내식당
A canteen is a small plastic bottle for carrying water and other drinks. Canteens are used by soldiers.

sneak^{복습}
[sní:k]

v. 살금살금 돌아다니다; 슬쩍 넣다[집다]; 고자질하다; n. 밀고자
If you sneak somewhere, you go there very quietly on foot, trying to avoid being seen or heard.

counselor^{복습}
[káunsələr]

n. (캠프 생활의) 지도원; 상담역, 카운슬러
A counselor is a person whose job is to give advice to people who need it, especially advice on their personal problems.

fugitive[*]
[fjú:dʒətiv]

n. 도망자, 탈주자; a. 도망을 다니는, 도피하는
A fugitive is someone who is running away or hiding, usually in order to avoid being caught by the police.

bother^{복습}
[báðər]

v. 일부러 ~하다, 애를 쓰다; 귀찮게 하다; 신경 쓰이게 하다, 괴롭히다
If you do not bother to do something or if you do not bother with it, you do not do it, consider it, or use it because you think it is unnecessary or because you are too lazy.

identity[*]
[aidéntəti]

n. 신원, 신분, 정체
Your identity is who you are.

pop^{복습}
[páp]

v. 불쑥 나타나다; 뻥 하고 터뜨리다; 급히 집어넣다; n. 뻥[탁] 하는 소리; 발포
If something pops, it moves or appears quickly and suddenly.

chest^{**}
[tʃest]

① n. 상자, 궤 ② n. 가슴, 흉부
A chest is a large, heavy box used for storing things.

mutter^{복습}
[mʌtər]

v. 중얼거리다, 불평하다; n. 중얼거림, 불평
If you mutter, you speak very quietly so that you cannot easily be heard, often because you are complaining about something.

170

1분에 몇 단어를 읽는지 리딩 속도를 측정해보세요.

$$\frac{2{,}183 \text{ words}}{\text{reading time ( ) sec}} \times 60 = (\quad) \text{ WPM}$$

Build Your Vocabulary

homeless^{복습}
[hóumlis]

a. 노숙자의; n. (pl.) 노숙자들
Homeless people have nowhere to live.

move out

phrasal v. (살던 집에서) 이사를 나가다
If you move out from a place, you vacate your residence or place of business.

crib*
[krib]

n. 아기 침대; 구유, 여물통
A crib is a bed for a small baby.

wrist^{복습}
[rist]

n. 손목
Your wrist is the part of your body between your hand and your arm which bends when you move your hand.

clap^{복습}
[klæp]

v. 박수를 치다; n. 박수 (소리); (갑자기 크게) 쿵[탁] 하는 소리
When you clap, you hit your hands together to show appreciation or attract attention.

clue*
[klu:]

n. 단서, 실마리
A clue is a sign or some information which helps you to find the answer to a problem.

sack^{복습}
[sæk]

n. 부대, 자루; (쇼핑 물건을 담는 크고 튼튼한 종이) 봉지; vt. 자루에 넣다
Sacks are used to carry or store things such as vegetables or coal.

daylight^{복습}
[deilàit]

n. (낮의) 햇빛, 일광
Daylight is the natural light that there is during the day, before it gets dark.

dirt road^{복습}

n. (시골의) 흙길, 비포장도로
dirt (명사: 흙) + road (명사: 작은 길, 오솔길)

sneak^{복습}
[sní:k]

v. 살금살금 돌아다니다; 슬쩍 넣다[집다]; 고자질하다; n. 밀고자
If you sneak somewhere, you go there very quietly on foot, trying to avoid being seen or heard.

squeak*
[skwi:k]

v. 끽 하는 소리를 내다; (어떤 일을) 간신히 해내다; n. 끼익[꺅] 하는 소리
If something or someone squeaks, they make a short, high-pitched sound.

evict^{복습}
[ivíkt]

vt. (주택이나 땅에서) 쫓아내다, 퇴거시키다
If someone is evicted from the place where they are living, they are forced to leave it, usually because they have broken a law or contract.

recapture*
[riːkǽptʃər]

v. (과거의 느낌 · 경험을) 되찾다; 탈환하다; 다시 체포하다
When you recapture something such as an experience, emotion, or a quality that you had in the past, you experience it again. When something recaptures an experience for you, it makes you remember it.

inexplicable*
[inéksplikəbəl]

a. 설명할 수 없는, 불가사의한
If something is inexplicable, you cannot explain why it happens or why it is true.

dunk
[dʌŋk]

v. (액체 속에) 잠그다, 적시다; 덩크 슛하다
If you dunk something in a liquid, you put it in the liquid, especially for a particular purpose and for a short time.

shovel복습
[ʃʌvəl]

n. 삽; v. ~을 삽으로 뜨다[파다], 삽으로 일하다
A shovel is a tool with a long handle that is used for lifting and moving earth, coal, or snow.

cram복습
[kræm]

v. (좁은 공간 속으로 억지로) 밀어 넣다
If you cram things into a container or place, you put them into it, although there is hardly enough room for them.

jar복습
[dʒɑ́ːr]

① n. 병, 단지 ② v. 삐걱거리다; n. 삐걱거리는 소리, 잡음
A jar is a glass container with a lid that is used for storing food.

patch복습
[pætʃ]

n. (특히 주변과는 다른 조그만) 부분; 헝겊 조각; 반창고; v. 헝겊을 대고 깁다
A patch on a surface is a part of it which is different in appearance from the area around it.

weed복습
[wíːd]

n. 잡초; v. 잡초를 없애다
A weed is a wild plant that grows in gardens or fields of crops and prevents the plants that you want from growing properly.

throw up복습
[θrou ʌp]

phrasal v. 토하다
When someone throws up, they vomit.

steep복습
[stíːp]

a. (경사면 · 언덕 등이) 가파른, 비탈진; (증감이) 급격한
A steep slope rises at a very sharp angle and is difficult to go up.

thorny복습
[θɔ́ːrni]

a. 가시가 많은, 가시 같은
A thorny plant or tree is covered with thorns.

vine복습
[váin]

n. 덩굴식물, 포도나무
A vine is a plant that grows up or over things, especially one which produces grapes.

rip복습
[ríp]

v. 찢(어지)다, 벗겨내다; 돌진하다; n. 찢어진 틈, 잡아 찢음
When something rips or when you rip it, you tear it forcefully with your hands or with a tool such as a knife.

groan복습
[gróun]

v. 신음하다, 끙끙거리다; n. 신음, 끙끙거리는 소리
If you groan, you make a long, low sound because you are in pain, or because you are upset or unhappy about something.

thorn복습
[θɔ́ːrn]

n. 가시
Thorns are the sharp points on some plants and trees.

172

retrieve^{복습}
[ritríːv]

vt. 되찾다, 회수하다
If you retrieve something, you get it back from the place where you left it.

cliff^{복습}
[klif]

n. 절벽, 낭떠러지
A cliff is a high area of land with a very steep side, especially one next to the sea.

challenge^{복습}
[tʃælindʒ]

n. 도전; v. (경쟁 · 싸움 등을) 걸다, 도전하다
A challenge is something new and difficult which requires great effort and determination.

frying pan^{복습}
[fráiiŋ pǽn]

n. 프라이팬
A frying pan is a flat metal pan with a long handle, in which you fry food.

ease^{복습}
[iːz]

v. 천천히 움직이다; (고통 · 고민 등을) 진정[완화]시키다; n. 편함, 안정
If you ease your way somewhere or ease somewhere, you move there slowly, carefully, and gently. If you ease something somewhere, you move it there slowly, carefully, and gently.

ledge^{복습}
[ledʒ]

n. 바위 턱; (벽에서 돌출한) 선반
A ledge is a piece of rock on the side of a cliff or mountain, which is in the shape of a narrow shelf.

haze^{복습}
[heiz]

n. 아지랑이, 엷은 연기; v. 흐릿해지다, 안개가 끼다
If there is a haze of something such as smoke or steam, you cannot see clearly through it.

lighten*
[láitn]

v. 가볍게 해주다, 덜어 주다; 밝아지다, 밝게 하다
If you lighten something, you make it less heavy.

camel**
[kǽməl]

n. 낙타
A camel is a large animal that lives in deserts and is used for carrying goods and people. Camels have long necks and one or two lumps on their backs called humps.

set***
[sét]

v. (해 · 달이) 지다; (물건을) 놓다; a. 고정된; n. 한 벌
When the sun sets, it goes below the horizon.

coat^{복습}
[kout]

v. (막 같은 것을) 덮다; n. 표면을 덮는 것, 칠; 외투, 코트
If you coat something with a substance or in a substance, you cover it with a thin layer of the substance.

raspy^{복습}
[rǽːspi]

a. 거친, 목이 쉰 듯한
If someone has a raspy voice, they make rough sounds as if they have a sore throat or have difficulty in breathing.

unscrew^{복습}
[ʌnskrúː]

v. (병뚜껑 같은 것을 돌려서) 열다; 나사를 풀다
If you unscrew something such as a lid, or if it unscrews, you keep turning it until you can remove it.

lid^{복습}
[lid]

n. 뚜껑
A lid is the top of a box or other container which can be removed or raised when you want to open the container.

clink
[kliŋk]

v. 쨍그랑[짤랑] 하는 소리를 내다; n. 쨍그랑, 짤랑
If objects clink or if you clink them, they touch each other and make a short, light sound.

stubborn**
[stʌ́bərn]

a. 완고한, 고집 센
Someone who is stubborn or who behaves in a stubborn way is determined to do what they want and is very unwilling to change their mind.

shady*
[ʃéidi]

a. (빛이 바로 닿지 않게) 그늘이 드리워진
You can describe a place as shady when you like the fact that it is sheltered from bright sunlight, for example by trees or buildings.

peel복습
[piːl]

v. 껍질을 벗기다, 벗겨지다
When you peel fruit or vegetables, you remove their skins.

porch***
[pɔːrtʃ]

n. (본 건물 입구에 달린 지붕이 있는) 현관, 포치
A porch is a sheltered area at the entrance to a building, which has a roof and sometimes has walls.

crawl복습
[krɔːl]

vi. 기어가다, 느릿느릿 가다; 우글거리다, 들끓다; n. 서행; 기어감
When you crawl, you move forward on your hands and knees.

swing복습
[swíŋ]

v. (한 점을 축으로 하여) 빙 돌다, 휙 움직이다, 휘두르다
If something swings or if you swing it, it moves repeatedly backwards and forwards or from side to side from a fixed point.

apiece*
[əpíːs]

ad. 각각, 하나에
If people have a particular number of things apiece, they have that number each.

lost in thought

idiom 생각에 빠진, 골똘히 생각하는
If you are lost in thought, you are not aware of what is happening around you because you are thinking about something else.

awful복습
[ɔ́ːfəl]

a. 지독한, 대단한; 무서운
If you say that someone or something is awful, you dislike that person or thing or you think that they are not very good.

diagram**
[dáiəgræm]

n. 도형, 그림, 도표
A diagram is a simple drawing which consists mainly of lines and is used, for example, to explain how a machine works.

drift복습
[drift]

v. (물·공기에) 떠가다, 표류[부유]하다; (자신도 모르게) ~하게 되다; n. 표류
When something drifts somewhere, it is carried there by the movement of wind or water.

faint복습
[feint]

a. 희미한, 어렴풋한; vi. 기절하다; n. 기절, 졸도
A faint sound, color, mark, feeling, or quality has very little strength or intensity.

blend**
[blend]

n. 혼합; v. 섞다, 섞이다, 혼합하다
A blend of things is a mixture or combination of them that is useful or pleasant.

indistinct
[indistíŋkt]

a. (형상·기억 등이) 뚜렷하지 않은, 희미한
Something that is indistinct is unclear and difficult to see, hear, or recognize.

occasional^{복습}
[əkéiʒənl]

a. 가끔의, 때때로의 (occasionally ad. 때때로, 가끔)
Occasional means happening sometimes, but not regularly or often.

distinctive*
[distíŋktiv]

a. 독특한
Something that is distinctive has a special quality or feature which makes it easily recognizable and different from other things of the same type.

bark^{복습}
[bɑːrk]

① n. 짖는 소리; v. (개가) 짖다; 고함치다 ② n. 나무껍질
A bark is a loud and aggressive shouting voice.

cluster^{복습}
[klʌ́stər]

n. 무리, 집단, 떼; v. 밀집하다
A cluster of people or things is a small group of them close together.

nod^{복습}
[nɔd]

v. 끄덕이다, 끄덕여 표시하다; n. 끄덕임(동의 · 인사 · 신호 · 명령)
If you nod, you move your head downwards and upwards to show agreement, understanding, or approval.

ray^{복습}
[réi]

n. 광선, 빛; v. 번쩍이다
Rays of light are narrow beams of light.

beat down

phrasal v. 햇볕이 쨍쨍 내리쬐다
If the sun beats down, it shines with great heat.

creep*
[kriːp]

vi. (crept–crept) 살금살금 걷다, 기다; n. 포복
If something creeps somewhere, it moves very slowly.

clank
[klæŋk]

v. 철커덕하는 소리가 나다
When large metal objects clank, they make a noise because they are hitting together or hitting against something hard.

compound^{복습}
[kámpaund]

① n. (저택 · 공장의) 건물 안, 구내 ② vt. 합성하다, 조합하다, 만들어내다; n. 합성물, 화합물
A compound is an enclosed area of land that is used for a particular purpose.

cabin^{복습}
[kǽbin]

n. (통나무) 오두막집; 객실, 선실
A cabin is a small wooden house, especially one in an area of forests or mountains.

oak^{복습}
[óuk]

n. 오크 나무
An oak or an oak tree is a large tree that often grows in woods and forests and has strong, hard wood.

dizzy^{복습}
[dízi]

a. 현기증 나는, 아찔한
If you feel dizzy, you feel as if everything is spinning round and being unable to balance.

summon^{복습}
[sʌ́mən]

vt. 호출하다, 소환하다
If you summon someone, you order them to come to you.

risk^{복습}
[risk]

v. (~을) 위태롭게 하다, ~의 위험을 무릅쓰다; n. 위험
If you risk doing something, you do it, even though you know that it might have undesirable consequences.

adjacent*
[ədʒéisnt]

a. 인접한, 가까운
If one thing is adjacent to another, the two things are next to each other.

1. What made Stanley nearly gag?
   A. The dirt from his hands
   B. The taste of cereal
   C. Water from the spigot
   D. The taste of an onion

2. What did Stanley find?
   A. A metal jewelry box
   B. A handful of diamonds
   C. A metal suitcase
   D. A cardboard box

3. Zero filled the water jugs _____.
   A. at the Warden's cabin
   B. by the Big Thumb
   C. at the showers
   D. at the Wreck Room

4. How did Stanley get the suitcase from the hole?
   A. He dug a tunnel above it.
   B. He and Zero pulled it from the side of the hole.
   C. He dug a new hole above it.
   D. He dug a tunnel below it.

5. Why did the Warden tell the counselors to wait?
   A. She wanted Mr. Sir to shoot the lizards before she went into the hole.
   B. She wanted Zero to hand her the suitcase.
   C. She wanted Mr. Sir to shoot Stanley and Zero.
   D. She wanted to wait until Stanley and Zero were killed by lizards.

6. What did the Warden say she did when she was little?
   A. She helped her parents dig holes only in the summer.
   B. She watched her parents dig holes every weekend and holiday.
   C. She listened to her parents' stories about Kissin' Kate.
   D. She watched her parents dig two holes a day.

1분에 몇 단어를 읽는지 리딩 속도를 측정해보세요.

$$\frac{1,342 \text{ words}}{\text{reading time ( ) sec}} \times 60 = (\qquad) \text{ WPM}$$

Build Your Vocabulary

creak*
[kri:k]

v. 삐걱거리(게 하)다; n. 삐걱거리는 소리
If something creaks, it makes a short, high-pitched sound when it moves.

drum복습
[drÁm]

v. 계속 두드리다; 북을 치다; n. 북, 드럼
If something drums on a surface, or if you drum something on a surface, it hits it regularly, making a continuous beating sound.

canteen복습
[kæntí:n]

n. (휴대용) 물통; (공장 · 학교 등의) 구내식당
A canteen is a small plastic bottle for carrying water and other drinks. Canteens are used by soldiers.

jar복습
[dʒá:r]

① n. 병, 단지 ② v. 삐걱거리다; n. 삐걱거리는 소리, 잡음
A jar is a glass container with a lid that is used for storing food.

stumble**
[stÁmbl]

v. 발부리가 걸리다, 비틀거리며 걷다; n. 비틀거림
If you stumble, you put your foot down awkwardly while you are walking or running and nearly fall over.

shovel복습
[ʃÁvəl]

n. 삽; v. ~을 삽으로 뜨다[파다], 삽으로 일하다
A shovel is a tool with a long handle that is used for lifting and moving earth, coal, or snow.

blade복습
[bleid]

n. (칼 · 도구 등의) 날; (프로펠러 등의) 날개; 잎
The blade of a knife, ax, or saw is the edge, which is used for cutting.

scoop복습
[skú:p]

v. 뜨다, 파다; 재빨리 들어 올리다; n. 국자, 주걱
If you scoop something from a container, you remove it with something such as a spoon.

exhale*
[ekshéil]

v. (숨 · 연기 등을) 내쉬다, 내뿜다
When you exhale, you breathe out the air that is in your lungs.

dig복습
[díg]

v. (구멍 등을) 파다; 뒤지다; n. 파기
If people or animals dig, they make a hole in the ground or in a pile of earth, stones, or rubbish.

shovelful복습
[ʃÁvəlfùl]

n. 한 삽(의 분량)
shovel (명사: 삽) + ful (접미사: ~정도의 양)

dump복습
[dÁmp]

vt. 쏟아 버리다, 내버리다, 아무렇게나 내려놓다; n. 쓰레기 더미
If you dump something somewhere, you put it or unload it there quickly and carelessly.

chest^{복습}
[tʃest]

① n. 상자, 궤 ② n. 가슴, 흉부
A chest is a large, heavy box used for storing things.

gang**
[gæŋ]

n. 패거리, 한 떼, 무리
A gang is a group of people who go around together and often deliberately cause trouble.

thief^{복습}
[θiːf]

n. (pl. thieves) 도둑, 절도범
A thief is a person who steals something from another person.

cereal^{복습}
[síəriəl]

n. 시리얼; 곡물, 곡류
Cereal or breakfast cereal is a food made from grain. It is mixed with milk and eaten for breakfast.

gag^{복습}
[gæg]

① v. 말문을 막다, 재갈을 물리다; n. 재갈 ② n. 익살, 개그; v. 농담하다
If someone gags you, they tie a piece of cloth around your mouth in order to stop you from speaking or shouting.

frost**
[frɔːst]

v. (케이크에) 설탕을 입히다; 서리로 덮다, 서리가 앉다; n. 서리
If you frost something such as a cake, you give a frostlike surface by putting sugar on it.

flake**
[fleik]

n. (얇은) 조각; v. (얇게 조각조각) 벗겨지다[떨어지다]
A flake is a small thin piece of something, especially one that has broken off a larger piece.

adjust^{복습}
[ədʒʌst]

v. 적응하다; 조절하다, 조정하다; (옷매무새 등을) 바로 하다
When you adjust to a new situation, you get used to it by changing your behaviour or your ideas.

swig
[swig]

n. 쭉쭉 들이킴; v. 마구 들이켜다
A swig is a large and hurried swallow.

take over^{복습}

phrasal v. (~로부터) (~을) 인계받다, (기업 등을) 인수하다
If you take over something from someone, you do it instead of them.

sift^{복습}
[sift]

v. 체로 치다[거르다]; 면밀히 조사하다, 샅샅이 살피다
If you sift a powder such as flour or sand, you put it through a sieve in order to remove large pieces or lumps.

pebble**
[pébəl]

n. 조약돌, 자갈
A pebble is a small, smooth, round stone which is found on beaches and at the bottom of rivers.

spigot^{복습}
[spígət]

n. (수도 · 통 등의) 마개, 주둥이, 꼭지
A spigot is a faucet or tap.

no offense

idiom (구어) (내 말 · 행동에) 기분 나빠 하지 마라
Some people say 'no offense' to make it clear that they do not want to upset someone, although what they are saying may seem rather rude.

cave in

phrasal v. (지붕 · 벽 등이) 무너지다, 함몰되다
If a roof or wall caves in, it falls down and towards the center.

shrug^{복습}
[ʃrʌg]

v. (어깨를) 으쓱하다; n. (양 손바닥을 내보이면서 어깨를) 으쓱하기
If you shrug, you raise your shoulders to show that you are not interested in something or that you do not know or care about something.

bounce^{복습}
[bauns]

v. 튀다, 튀게 하다; 급히 움직이다, 뛰어다니다; n. 튐, 바운드
If something bounces off a surface or is bounced off it, it reaches the surface and is reflected back.

chip**
[tʃíp]

v. 깨지다, 이가 빠지다; 잘게 썰다; n. 조각, 토막
If you chip something or if it chips, a small piece is broken off it.

pronounced
[prənáunst]

a. 확연한
Something that is pronounced is very noticeable.

stick out^{복습}

phrasal v. (툭) 튀어나오다; ~을 내밀다
If something is sticks out, it is further out than something else.

astonishment^{복습}
[əstániʃmənt]

n. 놀람, 경악
Astonishment is a feeling of great surprise.

lengthwise*
[léŋkθwàiz]

ad. (길이대로) 길게, 세로로
Lengthwise means in a direction or position along the length of something.

collapse^{복습}
[kəlǽps]

v. 무너지다, 붕괴하다; 쓰러지다, 맥없이 주저앉다; n. 무너짐, 붕괴
If a building or other structure collapses, it falls down very suddenly.

scrape^{복습}
[skréip]

v. 긁어내다, 긁다, 문지르다; 스쳐서 상처를 내다
If you scrape something from a surface, you remove it, especially by pulling a sharp object over the surface.

budge
[bʌdʒ]

v. 약간 움직이다, 꿈쩍하다
If something will not budge or you cannot budge it, it will not move.

jam^{복습}
[dʒǽm]

v. (세게) 밀다, 밀어 넣다; n. 혼잡, 교통 체증; (기계의) 고장
If you jam something somewhere, you push or put it there roughly.

occasional^{복습}
[əkéiʒənl]

a. 가끔의, 때때로의 (occasionally ad. 때때로, 가끔)
Occasional means happening sometimes, but not regularly or often.

stoop^{복습}
[stú:p]

v. 상체를 굽히다, 구부리다, 웅크리다
If you stoop, you bend your body forwards and downwards.

precarious*
[prikέəriəs]

a. 위태로운, 불안정한
Something that is precarious is not securely held in place and seems likely to fall or collapse at any moment.

latch^{복습}
[lætʃ]

n. 걸쇠, 빗장; v. 걸쇠를 걸다
A latch is a fastening on a door or gate. It consists of a metal bar which you lift in order to open the door.

suitcase*
[sú:tkèis]

n. 여행 가방
A suitcase is a box or bag with a handle and a hard frame in which you carry your clothes when you are traveling.

pry^{복습}
[prai]

① vt. 비틀어 움직이다; 지레로 들어 올리다; n. 지레
② vi. 엿보다, 동정을 살피다
If you pry something open or pry it away from a surface, you force it open or away from a surface.

might as well 복습

idiom ~하는 편이 낫다

If you say that you might as well do something, or that you may as well do it, you mean that you will do it although you do not have a strong desire to do it and may even feel slightly unwilling to do it.

sip 복습
[síp]

n. 한 모금; vt. (음료를) 홀짝거리다, 조금씩 마시다

A sip is a small amount of drink that you take into your mouth.

tip 복습
[típ]

① n. (뾰족한) 끝 ② v. 뒤집어엎다, 기울이다 ③ n. 팁, 사례금

The tip of something long and narrow is the end of it.

wedge *
[wedʒ]

vt. 밀어 넣다, 끼워 넣다; n. 쐐기[V] 모양(의 물건); 쐐기

If you wedge something, you force it to remain in a particular position by holding it there tightly or by fixing something next to it to prevent it from moving.

kneel 복습
[níːl]

vi. (knelt–knelt) 무릎 꿇다

When you kneel, you bend your legs so that your knees are touching the ground.

exclaim 복습
[ikskléim]

v. 외치다, 소리치다

If you exclaim, you say or shout something suddenly because of surprise, fear and pleasure.

Check Your Reading Speed

1분에 몇 단어를 읽는지 리딩 속도를 측정해보세요.

$$\frac{564 \text{ words}}{\text{reading time (}\quad\text{) sec}} \times 60 = (\quad) \text{ WPM}$$

Build Your Vocabulary

beam^{★★}
[bíːm]

n. 빛줄기; 환한 얼굴; v. 활짝 웃다; 빛나다
A beam is a line of energy, radiation, or particles sent in a particular direction.

suitcase^{복습}
[súːtkèis]

n. 여행 가방
A suitcase is a box or bag with a handle and a hard frame in which you carry your clothes when you are traveling.

lap^{복습}
[læp]

① n. 무릎; (트랙의) 한 바퀴 ② v. (물이) 찰랑거리다; 할짝할짝 핥다
If you have something on your lap, it is on top of your legs and near to your body.

barefoot^{복습}
[béərfùt]

a., ad. 맨발의[로]
Someone who is barefoot or barefooted is not wearing anything on their feet.

bare-chested

a. 윗옷을 입지 않은
bare (형용사: 벌거벗은) + chested (형용사: 가슴이 ~한)

pajama^{복습}
[pədʒáːmə]

n. (pl.) 파자마, 잠옷; a. 파자마 같은
A pair of pajamas consists of loose trousers and a loose jacket that people wear in bed.

bob^{복습}
[bab]

v. 위아래로 움직이다, 까닥까닥 흔들리다
If something bobs, it moves up and down, like something does when it is floating on water.

helpless^{복습}
[hélplis]

a. 무력한, 속수무책의
If you are helpless, you do not have the strength or power to do anything useful or to control or protect yourself.

in the nick of time

idiom 마침 제때에, 때마침
If you say that something happens in the nick of time, you are emphasizing that it happens at the last possible moment.

lizard^{복습}
[lízərd]

n. 도마뱀
A lizard is a reptile with short legs and a long tail.

statue^{★★}
[stǽtʃuː]

n. 상(像), 조각상
A statue is a large sculpture of a person or an animal, made of stone or metal.

scramble^{★★}
[skrǽmbl]

v. 기어오르다, 서로 밀치다, 앞다투어 급히 하다; 허둥지둥 해내다
If you scramble over rocks or up a hill, you move quickly over them or up it using your hands to help you.

commotion*
[kəmóuʃən]

n. 소란, 소동, 동요
A commotion is a lot of noise, confusion, and excitement.

gasp^{복습}
[gǽsp]

v. 숨이 턱 막히다, 헉 하고 숨을 쉬다; **n.** (숨이 막히는 듯) 헉 하는 소리를 냄
When you gasp, you take a short quick breath through your mouth, especially when you are surprised, shocked, or in pain.

illuminate**
[ilú:mənèit]

vt. 비추다, 밝히다
To illuminate something means to shine light on it and to make it brighter and more visible.

glance^{복습}
[glǽns]

v. 흘깃 보다, 잠깐 보다; **n.** 흘깃 봄
If you glance at something or someone, you look at them very quickly and then look away again immediately.

suppress*
[səprés]

v. (감정 · 감정 표현을) 참다, 억누르다; 진압하다
If you suppress your feelings or reactions, you do not express them, even though you might want to.

explode^{복습}
[iksplóud]

v. 터지다, 폭발하다
If an object such as a bomb explodes or if someone or something explodes it, it bursts loudly and with great force, often causing damage or injury.

sneaker^{복습}
[sní:kər]

n. (pl.) 고무창 운동화
Sneakers are casual shoes with rubber soles.

trail off

phrasal v. (목소리가) 서서히 사라지다 (trail **v.** 끌다; 뒤쫓다)
If a speaker's voice or a speaker trails off, their voice becomes quieter and they hesitate until they stop speaking completely.

claw**
[klɔ:]

n. 발톱, 집게발; **v.** (손 · 발톱 따위로) 할퀴다, 긁다
The claws of a bird or animal are the thin, hard, curved nails at the end of its feet.

chin^{복습}
[tʃin]

n. 턱
Your chin is the part of your face that is below your mouth and above your neck.

1. What was NOT included in the Warden's story about Stanley's death?
   A. Stanley ran away to look for Zero.
   B. Stanley fell in a hole.
   C. The lizards killed Stanley.
   D. Stanley ran away in the night.

2. Why had a lawyer come to Camp Green Lake the previous day?
   A. A lawyer came to investigate Zero's "death".
   B. Zero was innocent and a lawyer came to take him away.
   C. A lawyer came to speak to the different campers about Stanley and Zero.
   D. Stanley was innocent and a lawyer came to take him away.

3. How did Mr. Sir know that the lizards were hungry?
   A. A lizard bit Stanley.
   B. The lizards were licking the air.
   C. A lizard ate a tarantulA.
   D. The lizards didn't hide from the sun.

4. The Warden said that Stanley _____.
   A. tried to escape the day before
   B. couldn't leave Camp Green Lake for another sixteen months
   C. tried to kill her with a yellow-spotted lizard
   D. stole her suitcase

5. What was NOT true?
    A. The Warden told the lawyer that Stanley was suffering from hallucinations.
    B. The Warden said that the lawyer didn't have proper authorization to take Stanley the day before.
    C. The Warden said that Stanley was bitten by a yellow-spotted lizard.
    D. The Warden said that Stanley was hospitalizeD.

6. Why did Zero say the case belonged to Stanley?
    A. Stanley had found the case.
    B. It had Stanley's name on it.
    C. Stanley had stolen it from the Warden's cabin.
    D. Zero wanted to trick the Warden.

Check Your Reading Speed

1분에 몇 단어를 읽는지 리딩 속도를 측정해보세요.

$$\frac{876 \text{ words}}{\text{reading time ( ) sec}} \times 60 = (\qquad) \text{ WPM}$$

Build Your Vocabulary

cereal^{복습}
[síəriəl]

n. 시리얼; 곡물, 곡류
Cereal or breakfast cereal is a food made from grain. It is mixed with milk and eaten for breakfast.

spring*
[spríŋ]

v. 튀다, 뛰어오르다; n. 용수철, 스프링; 봄
When a person or animal springs, they jump upwards or forwards suddenly or quickly.

midair
[midéər]

n. 공중, 중천
mid (형용사: 중앙의, 중간의) + air (명사: 공기)

blast^{복습}
[blǽst]

n. 폭발, 폭파; 폭풍, 돌풍; v. 폭파하다; 후려치다
A blast is a big explosion, especially one caused by a bomb.

shatter^{복습}
[ʃǽtər]

v. 산산조각이 나다; 파괴하다; n. 파편, 부서진 조각
If something shatters or is shattered, it breaks into a lot of small pieces.

scurry*
[skə́ːri]

vi. 종종걸음으로 달리다, 급히 가다
When people or small animals scurry somewhere, they move there quickly and hurriedly, especially because they are frightened.

frantic*
[frǽntik]

a. 극도로 흥분한, 광란의 (frantically ad. 미친 듯이)
If you are frantic, you are behaving in a wild and uncontrolled way because you are frightened or worried.

flinch
[flintʃ]

v. (고통 · 공포로) 움찔하다
If you flinch, you make a small sudden movement, especially when something surprises you or hurts you.

cigarette**
[sìgərét]

n. 담배
Cigarettes are small tubes of paper containing tobacco which people smoke.

counselor^{복습}
[káunsələr]

n. (캠프 생활의) 지도원; 상담역, 카운슬러
A counselor is a person whose job is to give advice to people who need it, especially advice on their personal problems.

drag^{복습}
[drǽg]

n. 빨아들이기; 견인, 끌기; v. 끌다, 끌고 오다; 힘들게 움직이다
If you take a drag on a cigarette or pipe that you are smoking, you take in air through it.

nightmare*
[náitmeər]

n. 악몽
A nightmare is a very frightening dream.

186

grim^{복습}
[grim]

a. 섬뜩한, 무서운; 엄숙한, 단호한 (grimly **ad.** 무섭게, 험악하게; 엄숙하게)
If you say that something is grim, you think that it is very bad, ugly, or depressing.

grave^{복습}
[greiv]

① **n.** 무덤, 묘 ② **a.** 중대한, 근엄한
A grave is a place where a dead person is buried.

trail off^{복습}

phrasal v. (목소리가) 서서히 사라지다
If a speaker's voice or a speaker trails off, their voice becomes quieter and they hesitate until they stop speaking completely.

initiate*
[iníʃièit]

vt. 시작하다, 개시하다, 창시하다
If you initiate something, you start it or cause it to happen.

investigation^{복습}
[invèstəgéiʃən]

n. 조사, 연구
An investigation is an official examination of the facts about a situation, crime, etc.

release*
[rilí:s]

v. (갇히거나 구속되어 있는 상태에서) 풀어 주다, 해방하다; **n.** 석방, 풀어 줌
If a person or animal is released from somewhere where they have been looked after, they are set free or allowed to go.

delirious^{복습}
[diliəriəs]

a. 의식이 혼미한, 헛소리를 하는
Someone who is delirious is unable to think or speak in a sensible and reasonable way, usually because they are very ill and have a fever.

claw^{복습}
[klɔ:]

n. 발톱, 집게발; **v.** (손·발톱 따위로) 할퀴다, 긁다
The claws of a bird or animal are the thin, hard, curved nails at the end of its feet.

etch^{복습}
[etʃ]

v. 뚜렷이 새기다
If a line or pattern is etched into a surface, it is cut into the surface by means of acid or a sharp tool.

bundle up

phrasal v. ~를 따뜻이 둘러싸다
If you bundle someone up, you make them feel warmer by putting warm clothes on them or covering them with blankets.

hand in hand

idiom (두 사람이) 서로 손을 잡고
If two people are hand in hand, they are holding each other's nearest hand, usually while they are walking.

mitten*
[mítn]

n. 벙어리장갑
Mittens are gloves which have one section that covers your thumb and another section that covers your four fingers together.

dizzy^{복습}
[dízi]

a. 현기증 나는, 아찔한
If you feel dizzy, you feel as if everything is spinning round and being unable to balance.

fleck
[flek]

n. 작은 조각, 부스러기; 반점, 주근깨
Flecks are small marks on a surface, or objects that look like small marks.

cheery*
[tʃíəri]

a. 기분 좋은; 명랑한
If you describe a person or their behavior as cheery, you mean that they are cheerful and happy.

innocent 복습
[ínəsnt]

a. 잘못이 없는, 결백한; 순진한
Innocent people are those who are not involved in a crime or conflict, but are injured or killed as a result of it.

severe **
[səvíər]

a. 극심한, 심각한, 격렬한 (severely ad. 심하게, 혹독하게)
You use severe to indicate that something bad or undesirable is great or intense.

punish 복습
[pʌ́niʃ]

v. 처벌하다, 벌주다
To punish someone means to make them suffer in some way because they have done something wrong.

perch **
[pə:rtʃ]

v. (높은 곳에) 놓다, 앉히다; n. (새의) 횃대; 높은 자리
To perch somewhere means to be on the top or edge of something.

fist 복습
[fist]

n. (쥔) 주먹
Your hand is referred to as your fist when you have bent your fingers in towards the palm in order to hit someone.

thumbs-up 복습
[θʌ́mz-ʌ́p]

n. 승인, 찬성, 격려 (give a thumbs-up idiom 엄지손가락을 들어 올리다)
A thumbs-up is a sign that you make by raising your thumb to show that you agree with someone, that you are happy with an idea or situation, or that everything is all right.

overhear *
[òuvərhíər]

v. (overheard-overheard) (남의 대화 등을) 우연히 듣다
If you overhear someone, you hear what they are saying when they are not talking to you and they do not know that you are listening.

afford 복습
[əfɔ́:rd]

vt. ~할 여유가 있다; 주다, 공급하다
If you cannot afford something, you do not have enough money to pay for it.

sore 복습
[sɔ:r]

a. 아픈, 쓰린
If part of your body is sore, it causes you pain and discomfort.

rigid *
[rídʒid]

a. 뻣뻣한, 단단한; 엄격한, 융통성 없는
A rigid substance or object is stiff and does not bend, stretch, or twist easily.

strenuous *
[strénjuəs]

a. 힘이 많이 드는, 몹시 힘든; 불굴의, 완강한
A strenuous activity or action involves a lot of energy or effort.

1분에 몇 단어를 읽는지 리딩 속도를 측정해보세요.

$$\frac{1,291 \text{ words}}{\text{reading time ( ) sec}} \times 60 = (\quad) \text{ WPM}$$

Build Your Vocabulary

lack**
[læk]

n. 부족; v. ~이 없다. ~이 결핍되다
If there is a lack of something, there is not enough of it or it does not exist at all.

forehead복습
[fɔ́ːrhèd]

n. 이마
Your forehead is the area at the front of your head between your eyebrows and your hair.

exaggerate**
[egzǽdʒəreit]

vt. 과장하다
If you exaggerate, you indicate that something is, for example, worse or more important than it really is.

stark*
[stɑːrk]

a. 삭막한, 황량한; (불쾌하지만 피할 수 없는) 냉혹한
Something that is stark is very plain in appearance.

blotchy복습
[blátʃi]

a. 얼룩덜룩한, 얼룩진
Something that is blotchy has blotches on it.

unsure복습
[ʌnʃuər]

a. 확신하지 못하는, 의심스러워하는
If you are unsure about something, you feel uncertain about it.

crawl복습
[krɔ́ːl]

vi. 기어가다, 느릿느릿 가다; 우글거리다, 들끓다; n. 서행; 기어감
When you crawl, you move forward on your hands and knees.

momentary**
[móuməntèri]

a. 찰나의, 순식간의 (momentarily ad. 잠깐)
Something that is momentary lasts for a very short period of time.

fascinate*
[fǽsineit]

v. 매혹하다, 반하게 하다 (fascinated a. 매혹된, 마음을 빼앗긴)
If something fascinates you, it interests and delights you so much that your thoughts tend to concentrate on it.

sting복습
[stiŋ]

n. 찌름, 쏨; vt. 찌르다, 쏘다
If you feel a sting, you feel a sharp pain in your skin or other part of your body.

mere복습
[míər]

a. 단지 ~에 불과한; 단순한 (merely ad. 단지)
You use mere to emphasize how unimportant or inadequate something is, in comparison to the general situation you are describing.

leap복습
[líːp]

v. (leaped/leapt–leaped/leapt) 껑충 뛰다; 뛰어넘다; n. 뜀, 도약
If you leap, you jump high in the air or jump a long distance.

pounce*
[pauns]

vi. 갑자기 달려들다, 와락 덤벼들다
If someone pounces on you, they come up towards you suddenly and take hold of you.

stick out^{복습}

phrasal v. (툭) 튀어나오다; ~을 내밀다
If something is sticks out, it is further out than something else.

shade^{복습}
[ʃeid]

n. (시원한) 그늘; 색조; vt. 그늘지게 하다
Shade is an area of darkness under or next to an object such as a tree, where sunlight does not reach.

raspy^{복습}
[rǽːspi]

a. 거친, 목이 쉰 듯한
If someone has a raspy voice, they make rough sounds as if they have a sore throat or have difficulty in breathing.

numb[*]
[nʌ́m]

a. (추위 등으로 신체 부위가) 감각이 없는; 멍한, 망연자실한;
vt. 감각이 없게 만들다; 멍하게 만들다
If a part of your body is numb, you cannot feel anything there.

claw^{복습}
[klɔ:]

n. 발톱, 집게발; v. (손 · 발톱 따위로) 할퀴다, 긁다
The claws of a bird or animal are the thin, hard, curved nails at the end of its feet.

ankle^{복습}
[ǽŋkl]

n. 발목
Your ankle is the joint where your foot joins your leg.

ease^{복습}
[íːz]

v. 천천히 움직이다; (고통 · 고민 등을) 진정[완화]시키다; n. 편함, 안정
If you ease your way somewhere or ease somewhere, you move there slowly, carefully, and gently. If you ease something somewhere, you move it there slowly, carefully, and gently.

amazement^{**}
[əméizmənt]

n. 놀람, 경탄
Amazement is the feeling you have when something surprises you very much.

briefcase[*]
[bríːfkèis]

n. 서류 가방
A briefcase is a case used for carrying documents in.

snap^{복습}
[snǽp]

v. (화난 목소리로) 딱딱거리다; 딱[툭] (하고) 부러뜨리다[부러지다]
If someone snaps at you, they speak to you in a sharp, unfriendly way.

pajama^{복습}
[pədʒáːmə]

n. (pl.) 파자마, 잠옷; a. 파자마 같은
A pair of pajamas consists of loose trousers and a loose jacket that people wear in bed.

exclaim^{복습}
[ikskléim]

v. 외치다, 소리치다
If you exclaim, you say or shout something suddenly because of surprise, fear and pleasure.

file a charge

idiom 고소하다
If you file a formal or legal accusation, complaint, or request, you make it officially.

abuse^{**}
[əbjúːs]

n. 학대; 남용, 오용; v. 남용[오용]하다; 학대하다
Abuse of someone is cruel and violent treatment of them.

imprison^{**}
[imprízn]

vt. 투옥하다, 감금하다 (imprisionment n. 투옥, 구금)
If someone is imprisoned, they are locked up or kept somewhere, usually in prison as a punishment for a crime or for political opposition.

torture[to:rtʃər]

n. 고문, 고뇌; vt. 고문하다, 고통을 주다
If you say that something is torture or a torture, you mean that it causes you great mental or physical suffering.

sneak[sní:k]

v. (snuck–snuck) 살금살금 돌아다니다; 슬쩍 넣다[집다]; 고자질하다; n. 밀고자
If you sneak somewhere, you go there very quietly on foot, trying to avoid being seen or heard.

cabin[kǽbin]

n. (통나무) 오두막집; 객실, 선실
A cabin is a small wooden house, especially one in an area of forests or mountains.

attorney[ətə́:rni]

n. (법정에서 남을 대변하는) 변호사; (사업 · 법률적 문제의) 대리인
In the United States, an attorney or attorney at law is a lawyer.

legal[lí:gəl]

a. 법률의, 합법적인 (legally ad. 법률적으로)
An action or situation that is legal is allowed or required by law.

trace[treis]

n. 극미량, 조금; 자취, 흔적; v. 추적하다, (추적하여) 찾아내다
A trace of something is a very small amount of it.

release[rilí:s]

v. (갇히거나 구속되어 있는 상태에서) 풀어 주다, 해방하다; n. 석방, 풀어 줌
If a person or animal is released from somewhere where they have been looked after, they are set free or allowed to go.

thief[θí:f]

n. 도둑, 절도범
A thief is a person who steals something from another person.

delirious[dilíəriəs]

a. 의식이 혼미한, 헛소리를 하는
Someone who is delirious is unable to think or speak in a sensible and reasonable way, usually because they are very ill and have a fever.

proper[prápər]

a. 적절한, 제대로 된; 고유의
The proper thing is the one that is correct or most suitable.

authorization[ɔ:θərizéiʃən]

n. 권한 부여, 위임; 공인, 관허, 인증, 허가
Authorization is the power to give orders to people.

authenticate[ɔ:θéntikèit]

v. 진짜임을 증명하다
If you authenticate something, you state officially that it is genuine after examining it.

sentence[séntəns]

v. (형을) 선고하다; n. 문장; 형벌, 형; (형의) 선고
When a judge sentences someone, he or she states in court what their punishment will be.

legitimate[lidʒítəmit]

a. 합법적인, 정당한; 합리적인
Something that is legitimate is acceptable according to the law.

custody[kʌ́stədi]

n. 보호, 관리; (재판 전의) 유치, 구류
Someone who is in custody or has been taken into custody has been arrested and is being kept in prison until they can be tried in a court.

hospitalize[háspitəlàiz]

v. 입원시키다
If someone is hospitalized, they are sent or admitted to hospital.

hallucination
[həlùːsənéiʃən]

n. 환각, 환영; 환청
A hallucination is the experience of seeing something that is not really there because you are ill or have taken a drug.

delirium
[dilíriəm]

n. (병으로 인한) 망상, 헛소리
If someone is suffering from delirium, they are not able to think or speak in a sensible and reasonable way because they are very ill and have a fever.

rant
[rænt]

v. 고함치다, 큰소리로 불평하다
If you say that someone rants, you mean that they talk loudly or angrily, and exaggerate or say foolish things.

rave*
[reiv]

v. 횡설수설하다, 헛소리를 하다; 열변을 토하다
If someone raves, they talk in an excited and uncontrolled way.

ray복습
[réi]

n. 광선, 빛; **v.** 번쩍이다
Rays of light are narrow beams of light.

swing복습
[swíŋ]

v. (swung–swung) 휘두르다, (한 점을 축으로 하여) 빙 돌다, 휙 움직이다
If something swings or if you swing it, it moves repeatedly backwards and forwards or from side to side from a fixed point.

hop**
[háp]

v. 깡충 뛰다, 뛰어오르다; **n.** 깡충깡충 뜀
If you hop, you move along by jumping.

overcome**
[ouvərkÁm]

v. (overcame–overcome) 꼼짝 못하게 되다, 압도당하다; 극복하다
If you are overcome by a feeling or event, it is so strong or has such a strong effect that you cannot think clearly.

dizzy복습
[dízi]

a. 현기증 나는, 아찔한 (dizziness **n.** 현기증)
If you feel dizzy, you feel as if everything is spinning round and being unable to balance.

steady복습
[stédi]

v. 진정시키다, 균형을 잡다; **a.** 꾸준한
If you steady yourself, you control your voice or expression, so that people will think that you are calm and not nervous.

scurry복습
[skə́ːri]

vi. 종종걸음으로 달리다, 급히 가다
When people or small animals scurry somewhere, they move there quickly and hurriedly, especially because they are frightened.

stagger복습
[stǽgər]

v. 비틀거리다, 휘청거리다; **n.** 비틀거림
If you stagger, you walk very unsteadily, for example because you are ill or drunk.

jerk복습
[dʒə́ːrk]

① **v.** 홱 움직이다; **n.** (갑자기 날카롭게) 홱 움직임 ② **n.** 바보, 멍청이
If you jerk something or someone in a particular direction, or they jerk in a particular direction, they move a short distance very suddenly and quickly.

catch (someone) red-handed

idiom ~을 현행범으로 붙잡다
If someone is caught red-handed, they are caught while they are in the act of doing something wrong.

press charges

idiom 고발하다, 기소하다
If you press charges against someone, you make an official accusation against them which has to be decided in a court of law.

disbelief*
[dìsbilíːf]

n. 믿기지 않음, 불신감
Disbelief is not believing that something is true or real.

chapters forty-eight & forty-nine

1. How had the Warden changed her story?
   A. She said that Stanley didn't have any files and she couldn't release him.
   B. She said that Stanley had put the stolen items in his suitcase.
   C. She said that Stanley had tried to run her over with Mr. Sir's truck.
   D. She said that Zero had written Stanley's name on the suitcase.

2. Why didn't Stanley open the suitcase?
   A. His lawyer told him not to.
   B. There were drugs and weapons in the suitcase.
   C. He didn't have the key to the suitcase.
   D. The suitcase's lock was broken.

3. Who would take charge of the camp?
   A. The lawyer
   B. The Attorney General
   C. Mr. Pendanski
   D. Mr. Sir

4. Why could the lawyer take Zero with her?
   A. Stanley said that the Warden would kill Zero.
   B. The camp would be investigated.
   C. The Warden didn't have any of Zero's files.
   D. The Attorney General told the lawyer to take Zero with her.

5. Why didn't the lizards bite Zero and Stanley?

   A. The boys stood very still.

   B. The lizards weren't hungry.

   C. There was a rattlesnake hiding in the hole.

   D. The boys had eaten a lot of onions.

6. What did Stanley's father invent?

   A. A way to recycle old sneakers

   B. A way to eliminate foot odor

   C. A way to wash old sneakers

   D. A way to eliminate bad breath

1분에 몇 단어를 읽는지 리딩 속도를 측정해보세요.

$$\frac{1,139 \text{ words}}{\text{reading time (} \quad \text{) sec}} \times 60 = (\quad) \text{ WPM}$$

Build Your Vocabulary

law enforcement
[lɔ́: infɔ́:rsmənt]

n. 법의 집행, 시행 (집행 당국)
Law enforcement agencies or officials are responsible for catching people who break the law.

suitcase복습
[súːtkèis]

n. 여행 가방
A suitcase is a box or bag with a handle and a hard frame in which you carry your clothes when you are traveling.

comprehend복습
[kɑ(ɔ)mprihénd]

vt. 이해하다, 파악하다
If you cannot comprehend something, you cannot understand it.

daze복습
[déiz]

vt. 멍하게 하다; 현혹시키다; n. 멍한 상태; 눈이 부심 (dazed a. 멍한)
If someone is dazed, they are confused and unable to think clearly, often because of shock or a blow to the head.

hang in there

idiom 버티다, 견디다
If you tell someone to hang in there, you are encouraging them to keep trying to do something and not to give up even though it might be difficult.

carton복습
[káːrtən]

n. (음식이나 음료를 담는) 곽[통]; 상자
A carton is a plastic or cardboard container in which food or drink is sold.

exclaim복습
[ikskléim]

v. 외치다, 소리치다
If you exclaim, you say or shout something suddenly because of surprise, fear and pleasure.

cabin복습
[kǽbin]

n. (통나무) 오두막집; 객실, 선실
A cabin is a small wooden house, especially one in an area of forests or mountains.

detainee
[ditéini]

n. (정치적 이유에 의한) 억류자
A detainee is someone who is held prisoner by a government because of his or her political views or activities.

drug복습
[drʌ́g]

n. 마약; 약; v. 약을 먹이다
Drugs are substances that some people take because of their pleasant effects, but which are usually illegal.

witness***
[wítnis]

n. 목격자, 증인; v. 목격하다; 증언하다
A witness to an event such as an accident or crime is a person who saw it.

hysterical*
[histérikəl]

a. 히스테리 상태의, (히스테리) 발작적인
Someone who is hysterical is in a state of uncontrolled excitement, anger, or panic.

jurisdiction*
[dʒùərisdíkʃən]

n. 관할권, 사법권
A jurisdiction is a state or other area in which a particular court and system of laws has authority.

release복습
[rilíːs]

v. (갇히거나 구속되어 있는 상태에서) 풀어 주다, 해방하다; n. 석방, 풀어 줌
If a person or animal is released from somewhere where they have been looked after, they are set free or allowed to go.

anxious**
[ǽŋkʃəs]

a. 열망하는, 간절히 바라는; 걱정하는, 염려하는
If you are anxious to do something or anxious that something should happen, you very much want to do it or very much want it to happen.

souvenir복습
[sùːvəníər]

n. 기념품
A souvenir is something which you buy or keep to remind you of a holiday, place, or event.

thumbs-up복습
[θʌmz-ʌ́p]

n. 승인, 찬성, 격려 (give a thumbs-up **idiom** 엄지손가락을 들어 올리다)
A thumbs-up is a sign that you make by raising your thumb to show that you agree with someone, that you are happy with an idea or situation, or that everything is all right.

urgent**
[ɔ́ːrdʒənt]

a. 긴급한, 절박한 (urgency n. 긴급)
If something is urgent, it needs to be dealt with as soon as possible.

pursuant*
[pərsúːənt]

a. (규칙·법률 같은) ~에 따른
If someone does something pursuant to a law or regulation, they obey that law or regulation.

charge복습
[tʃɑ́ːrdʒ]

n. 책임, 담당; (상품·서비스에 대한) 요금; 기소, 고발;
v. 청구하다; 기소하다, 고소하다; 돌격하다
If you take charge of someone or something, you make yourself responsible for them and take control over them.

investigation복습
[invèstəɡéiʃən]

n. 조사, 연구
An investigation is an official examination of the facts about a situation, crime, etc.

blank복습
[blǽŋk]

a. 멍한, 무표정한; 빈; n. 빈칸, 여백 (blankly ad. 멍하니, 우두커니)
If you look blank, your face shows no feeling, understanding, or interest.

misplace
[mispléis]

v. 엉뚱한 곳에 두다, 잘못 두다
If you misplace something, you lose it, usually only temporarily.

outrage**
[áutrèidʒ]

v. 격분[격노]하게 만들다; n. 격분, 격노
If you are outraged by something, it makes you extremely shocked and angry.

assume**
[əsjúːm]

v. (사실일 것으로) 추정하다; (권력·책임을) 맡다
If you assume that something is true, you imagine that it is true, sometimes wrongly.

slam ^{복습}
[slæm]

v. 쾅 닫다[닫히다]; 세게 치다, 세게 놓다; **n.** 쾅 (하는 소리)
If you slam a door or window or if it slams, it shuts noisily and with great force.

curse ^{복습}
[kəːrs]

vt. 욕설을 퍼붓다, 저주하다; **n.** 저주, 악담
If you curse, you use rude or offensive language, usually because you are angry about something.

way to go

idiom 잘 했어!
You say 'way to go!' to tell someone that you are pleased about something they have done.

rattlesnake ^{복습}
[rǽtlsnèik]

n. [동물] 방울뱀
A rattlesnake is a poisonous American snake which can make a rattling noise with its tail.

glance ^{복습}
[glæns]

v. 흘깃 보다, 잠깐 보다; **n.** 흘깃 봄
If you glance at something or someone, you look at them very quickly and then look away again immediately.

dig ^{복습}
[díg]

v. (구멍 등을) 파다; 뒤지다; **n.** 파기
If people or animals dig, they make a hole in the ground or in a pile of earth, stones, or rubbish.

hesitant
[hézətənt]

a. 주저하는, 망설이는, 머뭇거리는 (hesitantly **ad.** 머뭇거리며)
If you are hesitant about doing something, you do not do it quickly or immediately.

depart*
[dipáːrt]

v. (열차 · 사람 등이) 출발하다, 떠나다; 벗어나다, 빗나가다
When something or someone departs from a place, they leave it and start a journey to another place.

authority ^{복습}
[əθɔ́ːriti]

n. 권한; 권위, 권력
Authority is the right to command and control other people.

cyberspace
[sáibərspèis]

n. 사이버 공간
In computer technology, cyberspace refers to data banks and networks, considered as a place.

confine**
[kənfáin]

vt. 제한하다, 가두다
If you confine someone to a certain place, you keep them there so that they cannot leave.

indefinite**
[indéfənit]

a. 무기한의; 분명히 규정되지 않은 (indefinitely **ad.** 무기한으로)
If you describe a situation or period as indefinite, you mean that people have not decided when it will end.

crawl ^{복습}
[krɔ́ːl]

vi. 기어가다, 느릿느릿 가다; 우글거리다, 들끓다; **n.** 서행; 기어감
When you crawl, you move forward on your hands and knees.

incarcerate
[inkáːrsərèit]

vt. 감금하다
If people are incarcerated, they are kept in a prison or other place.

1분에 몇 단어를 읽는지 리딩 속도를 측정해보세요.

$$\frac{672 \text{ words}}{\text{reading time (} \quad \text{) sec}} \times 60 = (\quad) \text{ WPM}$$

Build Your Vocabulary

spotted^{복습}
[spátid]

a. 얼룩무늬의; 물방울무늬가 있는
Something that is spotted has a pattern of spots on it.

lizard^{복습}
[lízərd]

n. 도마뱀
A lizard is a reptile with short legs and a long tail.

townsfolk
[táunzfòuk]

n. (특정한) 도시 주민
The townsfolk of a town or city are the people who live there.

desert^{복습}
[dézərt]

① n. 사막, 황무지 ② v. 인적이 끊기다; 버리다, 유기하다
A desert is a large area of land, usually in a hot region, where there is almost no water, rain, trees, or plants.

donkey^{복습}
[dáŋki]

n. 당나귀
A donkey is an animal which is like a horse but which is smaller and has longer ears.

anchor^{**}
[áŋkər]

v. (배를) 닻으로 고정시키다, 닻을 내리다; 고정시키다; n. 닻
When a boat anchors or when you anchor it, its anchor is dropped into the water in order to make it stay in one place.

shore^{복습}
[ʃɔ́ːr]

n. 물가, 강기슭; vt. 상륙시키다 (off shore **idiom** 해안에서 떨어져서)
The shores or the shore of a sea, lake, or wide river is the land along the edge of it.

stuff^{복습}
[stʌ́f]

n. 일[것](일반적으로 말하거나 생각하는 것); 물건, 물질;
vt. 채워 넣다, 속을 채우다
You can use stuff to refer to things such as a substance, a collection of things, events, or ideas, or the contents of something in a general way without mentioning the thing itself by name.

unsure^{복습}
[ʌnʃúər]

a. 확신하지 못하는, 의심스러워하는
If you are unsure about something, you feel uncertain about it.

bloodstream
[blʌ́dstrìːm]

n. 혈류; 혈액 순환
Your bloodstream is the blood that flows around your body.

workshop[*]
[wɔ́ːrkʃàp]

n. 작업장; 공동 연구회, 연수회
A workshop is a building which contains tools or machinery for making or repairing things, especially using wood or metal.

air-conditioning^{복습}
[éər-kəndiʃəníŋ]

n. (건물·자동차의) 에어컨 (장치)
Air-conditioning is a method of providing buildings and vehicles with cool dry air.

chapter forty-nine

no offense^{복습}

idiom (구어) (내 말 · 행동에) 기분 나빠 하지 마라
Some people say 'no offense' to make it clear that they do not want to upset someone, although what they are saying may seem rather rude.

patent**
[pǽtənt]

n. 특허; **v.** 특허를 받다
A patent is an official right to be the only person or company allowed to make or sell a new product for a certain period of time.

attorney^{복습}
[ətɔ́ːrni]

n. (법정에서 남을 대변하는) 변호사; (사업 · 법률적 문제의) 대리인
In the United States, an attorney or attorney at law is a lawyer.

investigate**
[invéstigeit]

v. 조사하다, 연구하다, 심사하다
If someone, especially an official, investigates an event, situation, or claim, they try to find out what happened or what is the truth.

sneaker^{복습}
[sníːkər]

n. (pl.) 고무창 운동화
Sneakers are casual shoes with rubber soles.

fish***
[fiʃ]

v. 끌어올리다, 꺼내다; 낚시질하다; **n.** 물고기, 어류
If you fish something out from somewhere, you take or pull it out, often after searching for it for some time.

redden*
[rédn]

v. 빨개지다, 붉어지다
If someone reddens or their face reddens, their face turns pink or red, often because they are embarrassed or angry.

shame**
[ʃéim]

n. 수치심, 창피; 애석한 일; **v.** 부끄럽게 하다
Shame is an uncomfortable feeling that you get when you have done something wrong or embarrassing, or when someone close to you has.

recycle^{복습}
[rìːsáikl]

v. 재활용하다; 재순환하다
If you recycle things that have already been used, such as bottles or sheets of paper, you process them so that they can be used again.

eliminate**
[ilímineit]

vt. 제거하다
To eliminate something, especially something you do not want or need, means to remove it completely.

odor^{복습}
[óudər]

n. (불쾌한) 냄새, 악취 (foot odor **n.** 발냄새)
An odor is a particular and distinctive smell.

briefcase^{복습}
[bríːfkèis]

n. 서류 가방
A briefcase is a case used for carrying documents in.

bathe**
[béið]

v. 씻다, 목욕시키다; (열 · 빛 등이) 뒤덮다, 감싸다
When you bathe, you have a bath.

200

chapter fifty

1. The curse broke when _____.
   A. Stanley's father invented a cure for foot odor
   B. Stanley found the suitcase
   C. Stanley carried Zero up the mountain
   D. Stanley and Zero were taken from Camp Green Lake

2. What happened to the Warden's land?
   A. She had to sell it.
   B. She gave it to the Attorney General.
   C. It was taken by the state of Texas to build a new camp.
   D. She built a new prison for boys.

3. What was NOT in the suitcase?
   A. Jewels
   B. Stock certificates
   C. Bars of gold
   D. Promissory notes

4. Why did the Yelnats have a party?
   A. They wanted to watch the super bowl.
   B. They wanted to see the commercial for Sploosh.
   C. They wanted to celebrate Stanley's return home.
   D. They wanted to have a party for Zero's mother.

5. Who was NOT true about Zero's mother?
    A. She sang a song that her grandmother used to sing to her.
    B. Her eyes seemed weary.
    C. She was very old and sick.
    D. Her smile seemed too big for her face.

1분에 몇 단어를 읽는지 리딩 속도를 측정해보세요.

$$\frac{1,008 \text{ words}}{\text{reading time (} \quad \text{) sec}} \times 60 = (\quad) \text{ WPM}$$

Build Your Vocabulary

curse^{복습}
[kə:rs]

n. 저주, 악담; vt. 욕설을 퍼붓다, 저주하다
If you say that there is a curse on someone, you mean that there seems to be a supernatural power causing unpleasant things to happen to them.

cure^{복습}
[kjuər]

n. 치유하는 약, 치유법; v. 낫게 하다, 치유하다
A cure for an illness is a medicine or other treatment that cures the illness.

odor^{복습}
[óudər]

n. (불쾌한) 냄새, 악취 (foot odor n. 발냄새)
An odor is a particular and distinctive smell.

generation^{복습}
[dʒènəréiʃən]

n. 세대, 대(代), 동시대의 사람들
A generation is the period of time, usually considered to be about thirty years, that it takes for children to grow up and become adults and have children of their own.

dedicate^{**}
[dédikèit]

v. (건물 · 기념물 등을) 봉헌하다; (시간 · 노력을) 바치다, 전념[헌신]하다
When a building, especially a religious building, is dedicated, there is a ceremony at which it is formally opened for use and its particular purpose is stated.

tedious^{**}
[tí:diəs]

a. 지루한, 싫증나는
If you describe something such as a job, task, or situation as tedious, you mean it is boring and rather frustrating.

character^{복습}
[kǽriktər]

n. 인격, 성격; 특징, 특성; 문자, 서체
Your character is your personality, especially how reliable and honest you are.

self-confidence
[sélf-kánfədəns]

n. 자신(감)
If you have self-confidence, you behave confidently because you feel sure of your abilities or value.

subtle^{**}
[sʌtl]

a. 미묘한, 미세한; 교묘한, 솜씨 좋은
Something that is subtle is not immediately obvious or noticeable.

suitcase^{복습}
[sú:tkèis]

n. 여행 가방
A suitcase is a box or bag with a handle and a hard frame in which you carry your clothes when you are traveling.

pry^{복습}
[prai]

① vt. (pried–pried) 비틀어 움직이다; 지레로 들어 올리다; n. 지레
② vi. 엿보다, 동정을 살피다
If you pry something open or pry it away from a surface, you force it open or away from a surface.

204

workshop^{복습}
[wə́:rkʃʌ̀p]

n. 작업장; 공동 연구회, 연수회
A workshop is a building which contains tools or machinery for making or repairing things, especially using wood or metal.

gasp^{복습}
[gǽsp]

v. 숨이 턱 막히다, 헉 하고 숨을 쉬다; n. (숨이 막히는 듯) 헉 하는 소리를 냄
When you gasp, you take a short quick breath through your mouth, especially when you are surprised, shocked, or in pain.

sparkle^{복습}
[spá:rkl]

v. 반짝이다; 생기 넘치다; n. 반짝거림, 광채
If something sparkles, it is clear and bright and shines with a lot of very small points of light.

millionaire**
[mìljənέər]

n. 백만장자, 굉장한 부자, (대)부호
A millionaire is a very rich person who has money or property worth at least a million pounds or dollars.

stack^{복습}
[stǽk]

n. 더미; 많음, 다량; v. 쌓다, 쌓아올리다
A stack of things is a pile of them.

stock^{복습}
[stάk]

n. 주식; 재고품, 저장품; 저장; 가축; (나무) 그루터기
Stocks are shares in the ownership of a company, or investments on which a fixed amount of interest will be paid.

certificate**
[sərtífikət]

n. 증서, 증명서; 자격증
A certificate is an official document stating that particular facts are true.

deed***
[di:d]

n. (주택 · 건물의 소유권을 증명하는) 증서; 행위, 행동
A deed is a document containing the terms of an agreement, especially an agreement concerning the ownership of land or a building.

trust***
[trʌ́st]

n. 신탁 재산, 신탁금; 신뢰, 신임; v. 신뢰하다, 믿다
A trust is a financial arrangement in which a group of people or an organization keeps and invests money for someone.

legal^{복습}
[lí:gəl]

a. 법률의, 합법적인
An action or situation that is legal is allowed or required by law.

laboratory**
[lǽbərətɔ̀:ri]

n. 실험실
A laboratory is a building or a room where scientific experiments, analyses, and research are carried out.

basement**
[béismənt]

n. (건물의) 지하층
The basement of a building is a floor built partly or completely below ground level.

time-out
[táim-áut]

n. 타임아웃, 중간휴식
In basketball, American football, ice hockey, and some other sports, when a team calls a time out, they call a stop to the game for a few minutes in order to rest and discuss how they are going to play.

commercial^{복습}
[kəmɔ́:rʃəl]

n. (텔레비전 · 라디오의) 광고; a. 상업의, 무역의; 영리적인
A commercial is an advertisement that is broadcast on television or radio.

amid**
[əmíd]

prep. ~으로 에워싸인; (흥분 · 공포심이 느껴지는) 가운데[중]에
If something is amid other things, it is surrounded by them.

catcher*
[kǽtʃər]

n. 포수, 캐처
In baseball, the catcher is the player who stands behind the batter.
The catcher has a special glove for catching the ball.

umpire*
[ʌ́mpaiər]

n. (테니스 · 야구 경기 등의) 심판; v. 심판을 보다
An umpire is a person whose job is to make sure that a sports match
or contest is played fairly and that the rules are not broken.

count^{복습}
[káunt]

v. (정식으로) 인정되다; 세다, 계산하다; 포함시키다; 중요하다; n. 계산, 셈
If something counts or is counted as a particular thing, it is regarded
as being that thing, especially in particular circumstances or under
particular rules.

way to go^{복습}

idiom 잘 했어!
You say 'way to go!' to tell someone that you are pleased about
something they have done.

slap^{복습}
[slǽp]

v. 찰싹 때리다, 탁 놓다; 철썩 부딪치다; n. 찰싹 (때림)
If you slap someone, you hit them with the palm of your hand.

couch^{복습}
[kautʃ]

n. 소파, 긴 의자
A couch is a long, comfortable seat for two or three people.

stink^{복습}
[stiŋk]

v. (고약한) 냄새가 나다, 악취가 풍기다; n. 악취
To stink means to smell extremely unpleasant.

fan**
[fǽn]

vt. 부채질하다; 부채꼴로 펴다; n. 부채, 선풍기
If you fan yourself or your face when you are hot, you wave a fan
or other flat object in order to make yourself feel cooler.

shush
[ʃʌʃ]

v. (손가락을 입에 대고) 쉿[조용히] 하라고 말하다; int. 쉿 (조용히 해)
If you shush someone, you tell them to be quiet by saying 'shush' or
'sh', or by indicating in some other way that you want them to be quiet.

tingle^{복습}
[tíŋgl]

n. 따끔거림; 흥분, 안달; v. 따끔따끔 아프다, 쑤시다; 설레게 하다, 흥분시키다
When a part of your body tingles, you have a slight stinging feeling
there.

treat^{복습}
[tri:t]

n. 특별한 선물, 대접; v. 대하다; 치료하다, 처치하다
If you give someone a treat, you buy or arrange something special
for them which they will enjoy.

ingredient^{복습}
[ingrí:diənt]

n. 재료, 성분, 원료
Ingredients are the things that are used to make something, especially
all the different foods you use when you are cooking a particular
dish.

neutralize*
[njú:trəlàiz]

v. (화학 물질을) 중화시키다; 무효화시키다
To neutralize something means to prevent it from having any effect
or from working properly.

fungus*
[fʌ́ŋgəs]

n. (pl. fungi) 균류, 곰팡이류
A fungus is a plant that has no flowers, leaves, or green colouring,
such as a mushroom or a toadstool. Other types of fungus such as
mould are extremely small and look like a fine powder.

clap^{복습}
[klæp]

v. 박수를 치다; n. 박수 (소리); (갑자기 크게) 쿵[탁] 하는 소리
When you clap, you hit your hands together to show appreciation or attract attention.

pat^{복습}
[pæt]

v. 톡톡 가볍게 치다, (애정을 담아) 쓰다듬다; n. 쓰다듬기
If you pat something or someone, you tap them lightly, usually with your hand held flat.

uncertain^{복습}
[ʌnsə́:rtn]

a. 자신 없는, 머뭇거리는 (uncertainly ad. 자신 없게, 머뭇거리며)
If you are uncertain about something, you do not know what you should do, what is going to happen, or what the truth is about something.

blush^{복습}
[blʌʃ]

v. 얼굴을 붉히다. (얼굴이) 빨개지다; n. 얼굴을 붉힘, 홍조
When you blush, your face becomes redder than usual because you are ashamed or embarrassed.

overstuffed
[òuvərstʌ́ft]

a. 속을 두툼하게 채운
over (접두어: 지나치게 많은) + stuffed (형용사: 속을 채운)

absent-minded
[ǽbsənt-máindid]

a. 딴 데 정신이 팔린; 건망증이 심한 (absent−mindedly ad. 멍하니)
Someone who is absent-minded forgets things or does not pay attention to what they are doing, often because they are thinking about something else.

fluff
[flʌf]

v. 부풀리다; n. 보풀, 솜털
If you fluff things such as cushions or feathers, you get a lot of air into them.

weathered
[wéðə:rd]

a. 오래된 것처럼 보이는, (바위가) 풍화된, 비바람에 씻긴
If something such as wood or rock weathers or is weathered, it changes color or shape as a result of the wind, sun, rain, or cold.

weary^{복습}
[wíəri]

a. 피로한, 지친
If you are weary, you are very tired.

hum^{**}
[hʌm]

v. 콧노래를 부르다; (벌, 기계 등이) 윙윙거리다; n. 윙윙(소리)
When you hum a tune, you sing it with your lips closed.

bold^{복습}
[bould]

a. 용감한, 대담한; 선명한, 굵은 (boldly ad. 대담하게)
Someone who is bold is not afraid to do things which involve risk or danger.

수고하셨습니다!

드디어 끝까지 다 읽으셨군요! 축하드립니다! 여러분은 이 책을 통해 총 47,079개의 단어를 읽으셨고, 900개 이상의 어휘와 표현들을 익히셨습니다. 이 책에 나온 어휘는 다른 원서를 읽을 때에도 빈번히 만날 수 있는 필수 어휘들입니다. 이 책을 읽었던 경험은 비슷한 수준의 다른 원서들을 읽을 때 큰 도움이 될 것입니다. 이제 자신의 상황에 맞게 원서를 반복해서 읽거나, 오디오북을 들어 볼 수 있습니다. 혹은 비슷한 수준의 다른 원서를 찾아 읽는 것도 좋습니다. 일단 원서를 완독한 뒤에 어떻게 계속 영어 공부를 이어갈 수 있을지, 도움말을 꼼꼼히 살펴보고 각자 상황에 맞게 적용해 보세요!

리딩(Reading)을 확실하게 다지고 싶다면? 반복해서 읽어 보세요!

리딩 실력을 탄탄하게 다지고 싶다면, 같은 원서를 2~3번 반복해서 읽을 것을 권합니다. 같은 책을 여러 번 읽으면 지루할 것 같지만, 꼭 그렇지도 않습니다. 반복해서 읽을 때 처음과 주안점을 다르게 두면, 전혀 다른 느낌으로 재미있게 읽을 수 있습니다.

처음 원서를 읽을 때는 생소한 단어들과 스토리로 인해 읽으면서 곧바로 이해하기가 매우 힘들 수 있습니다. 전체 맥락을 잡고 읽어도 약간 버거운 느낌이지요. 하지만 반복해서 읽기 시작하면 달라집니다. 일단 내용을 파악한 상황이기 때문에 문장 구조나 어휘의 활용에 더 집중하게 되고, 조금 더 깊이 있게 읽을 수 있습니다. 좋은 표현과 문장을 수집하고 메모할 만한 여유도 생기게 되지요. 어휘도 많이 익숙해졌기 때문에 리딩 속도에도 탄력이 붙습니다. 처음 읽을 때는 '내용'에서 재미를 느꼈다면, 반복해서 읽을 때에는 '영어'에서 재미를 느끼게 되는 것입니다. 따라서 리딩 실력을 더욱 확고하게 다지고자 한다면, 같은 책을 2~3회 정도 반복해서 읽을 것을 권해 드립니다.

리스닝(Listening) 실력을 늘리고 싶다면?
귀를 통해서 읽어 보세요!

많은 영어 학습자들이 '리스닝이 안 돼서 문제'라고 한탄합니다. 그리고 리스닝 실력을 늘리는 방법으로 무슨 뜻인지 몰라도 반복해서 듣는 '무작정 듣기'를 선택합니다. 하지만 뜻도 모르면서 무작정 듣는 일에는 엄청난 인내력이 필요합니다. 그래서 대부분 며칠 시도하다가 포기해 버리고 말지요.

따라서 모르는 내용을 무작정 듣는 것보다는 어느 정도 알고 있는 내용을 반복해서 듣는 것이 더 효과적인 듣기 방법입니다. 그리고 이런 방식의 듣기에 활용할 수 있는 가장 좋은 교재가 오디오북입니다.

리스닝 실력을 향상하고 싶다면, 이 책에서 제공하는 오디오북을 이용해서 듣는 연습을 해 보세요. 활용법은 간단합니다. 일단 책을 한 번 완독했다면, 오디오북을 통해 다시 들어 보는 것입니다. 휴대 기기에 넣어 시간이 날 때 틈틈이 듣는 것도 좋고, 책상에 앉아 눈으로는 텍스트를 보며 귀로 읽는 것도 좋습니다. 이미 읽었던 내용이라 이해하기가 훨씬 수월하고, 애매했던 발음들도 자연스럽게 교정할 수 있습니다. 또 성우의 목소리 연기를 듣다 보면 내용이 더욱 생동감 있게 다가와 이해도가 높아지는 효과도 거둘 수 있습니다.

반대로 듣기에 자신 있는 사람이라면, 책을 읽기 전에 처음부터 오디오북을 먼저 듣는 것도 좋은 방법입니다. 귀를 통해 책을 쭉 읽어 보고, 이후에 다시 눈으로 책을 읽으면서 잘 들리지 않았던 부분을 보충하는 것이지요.

중요한 것은 내용을 따라가면서, 내용에 푹 빠져서 반복해 들어야 한다는 것입니다. 이렇게 연습을 반복해서 눈으로 읽지 않은 책이라도 '귀를 통해' 읽을 수 있을 정도가 되면, 리스닝으로 고생하는 일은 거의 없을 것입니다.

왼쪽의 QR 코드를 스마트폰으로 인식하여 정식 오디오북을 들어 보세요! 더불어 롱테일북스 홈페이지(www.longtailbooks.co.kr)에서도 오디오북 MP3 파일을 다운로드 받을 수 있습니다.

스피킹(Speaking)이 고민이라면? 소리 내어 읽어 보세요!

스피킹 역시 많은 학습자들이 고민하는 부분입니다. 스피킹이 고민이라면, 원서를 큰 소리로 읽는 낭독 훈련(voice reading)을 해 보세요!
'소리 내어 읽는 것이 말하기에 정말로 도움이 될까?'라고 의아한 생각이 들 수도 있습니다. 하지만 인간의 두뇌 입장에서 봤을 때, 성대 구조를 활용해서 '발화'한다는 점에서는 소리 내어 읽기와 말하기에 큰 차이가 없다고 합니다. 소리 내어 읽는 것은 '타인의 생각'을 전달하고, 직접 말하는 것은 '자신의 생각'을 전달한다는 차이가 있을 뿐, 머릿속에서 문장을 처리하고 조음기관(혀와 성대 등)을 움직여 의미를 만든다는 점에서 같은 과정인 것이지요. 따라서 소리 내어 읽는 연습을 꾸준히 하는 것은 스피킹 연습에 큰 도움이 됩니다.
소리 내어 읽기를 하는 방법은 간단합니다. 일단 오디오북을 들으면서 성우의 목소리를 최대한 따라 하며 같이 읽어 보세요. 발음뿐 아니라 억양, 어조, 느낌까지 완벽히 따라 한다고 생각하면서 소리 내어 읽습니다. 따라 읽는 것이 조금 익숙해지면, 옆의 누군가에게 이 책을 읽어 준다는 생각으로 소리 내어 계속 읽어 나갑니다. 한 번 눈과 귀로 읽었던 책이기 때문에 보다 수월하게 진행할 수 있고, 자연스럽게 어휘와 표현을 복습하는 효과도 거두게 됩니다. 또 이렇게 소리 내어 읽은 것을 녹음해서 들어 보면 스스로에게도 좋은 피드백이 됩니다.
최근 말하기가 강조되면서 소리 내어 읽기가 크게 각광을 받고 있기는 하지만, 그렇다고 소리 내어 읽기가 무조건 좋은 것만은 아닙니다. 책을 소리 내어 읽다 보면, 무의식적으로 속으로 발음을 하는 습관을 가지게 되어 리딩 속도 자체는 오히려 크게 떨어지는 현상이 발생할 수 있습니다. 따라서 빠른 리딩 속도가 중요한 수험생이나 고학력 학습자들에게는 소리 내어 읽기가 적절하지 않은 방법입니다. 효과가 좋다는 말만 믿고 무턱대고 따라 하기보다는 자신의 필요에 맞게 우선순위를 정하고 원서를 활용하는 것이 좋습니다.

라이팅(Writing)까지 욕심이 난다면? 요약하는 연습을 해 보세요!

원서를 라이팅 연습에 직접적으로 활용하는 데에는 한계가 있지만, 적절히 활용하면 원서도 유용한 라이팅 자료가 될 수 있습니다.

특히 책을 읽고 그 내용을 요약하는 연습은 큰 도움이 됩니다. 요약 훈련의 방식도 간단합니다. 원서를 읽고 그날 읽은 분량만큼 혹은 책을 다 읽고 전체 내용을 기반으로, 책 내용을 한번 요약하고 나의 느낌을 영어로 적어 보는 것입니다.

이때 그 책에 나왔던 단어와 표현을 최대한 활용하여 요약하는 것이 중요합니다. 영어 표현력은 결국 얼마나 다양한 어휘로 많은 표현을 해 보았느냐가 좌우하게 됩니다. 이런 면에서 내가 읽은 책을, 그 책에 나온 문장과 어휘로 다시 표현해 보는 것은 매우 효율적인 방법입니다. 책에 나온 어휘와 표현을 단순히 읽고 무슨 말인지 아는 정도가 아니라, 실제로 직접 활용해서 쓸 수 있을 만큼 확실하게 익히게 되는 것이지요. 여기에 첨삭까지 받을 수 있는 방법이 있다면 금상첨화입니다.

이러한 '표현하기' 연습은 스피킹 훈련에도 그대로 적용될 수 있습니다. 책을 읽고 그 내용을 3분 안에 다른 사람에게 영어로 말하는 연습을 해 보세요. 순발력과 표현력을 기르는 좋은 훈련이 될 것입니다.

꾸준히 원서를 읽고 싶다면? 뉴베리 수상작을 계속 읽어 보세요!

뉴베리 상이 세계 최고 권위의 아동 문학상인 만큼, 그 수상작들은 확실히 완성도를 검증받은 작품이라고 할 수 있습니다. 특히 '쉬운 어휘로 쓰인 깊이 있는 문장'으로 이루어졌다는 점이 영어 학습자들에게 큰 호응을 얻고 있습니다. 이렇게 '검증된 원서'를 꾸준히 읽는 것은 영어 실력 향상에 큰 도움이 됩니다.

아래에 수준별로 제시된 뉴베리 수상작 목록을 보며 적절한 책들을 찾아 계속 읽어 보세요. 꼭 뉴베리 수상작이 아니더라도 마음에 드는 작가의 다른 책을 읽어 보는 것 또한 아주 좋은 방법입니다.

• 영어 초보자도 쉽게 읽을 만한 아주 쉬운 수준. 소리 내어 읽기에도 아주 적합.
Sarah, Plain and Tall*(Medal, 8,331단어), The Hundred Penny Box (Honor, 5,878단어), The Hundred Dresses*(Honor, 7,329단어), My Father's Dragon (Honor, 7,682단어), 26 Fairmount Avenue (Honor, 6,737단어)

- 중·고등학생 정도 영어 학습자라면 쉽게 읽을 수 있는 수준. 소리 내어 읽기에도 비교적 적합한 편.

Because of Winn-Dixie★(Honor, 22,123단어), What Jamie Saw (Honor, 17,203단어), Charlotte's Web (Honor, 31,938단어), Dear Mr. Henshaw (Medal, 18,145단어), Missing May (Medal, 17,509단어)

- 대학생 정도 영어 학습자라면 무난한 수준. 소리 내어 읽기에는 적합하지 않음.

Number The Stars★(Medal, 27,197단어), A Single Shard (Medal, 33,726단어), The Tale of Despereaux★(Medal, 32,375단어), Hatchet★(Medal, 42,328단어), Bridge to Terabithia (Medal, 32,888단어), A Fine White Dust (Honor, 19,022단어), Jennifer, Hecate, Macbeth, William McKinley and Me, Elizabeth (Honor, 23,266단어)

- 원서 완독 경험을 가진 학습자에게 적절한 수준. 소리 내어 읽기에는 적합하지 않음.

The Giver★(Medal, 43,617단어), From the Mixed-Up Files of Mrs. Basil E. Frankweiler (Medal, 30,906단어), The View from Saturday (Medal, 42,685단어), Holes★(Medal, 47,079단어), Criss Cross (Medal, 48,221단어), Walk Two Moons (Medal, 59,400단어), The Graveyard Book (Medal, 67,380단어)

뉴베리 수상작과 뉴베리 수상 작가의 좋은 작품을 엄선한 「뉴베리 컬렉션」에도 위 목록에 있는 도서 중 상당수가 포함될 예정입니다.

★ 「뉴베리 컬렉션」으로 이미 출간된 도서

**어떤 책들이 출간되었는지 확인하려면, 지금 인터넷 서점에서
뉴베리 컬렉션을 검색해 보세요.**

뉴베리 수상작을 동영상 강의로 만나 보세요!

영어원서 전문 동영상 강의 사이트 영서당(yseodang.com)에서는 뉴베리 컬렉션 『Holes』, 『Because of Winn-Dixie』, 『The Miraculous Journey of Edward Tulane』, 『Wayside School 시리즈』 등의 동영상 강의를 제공하고 있습니다. 뉴베리 수상작이라는 최고의 영어 교재와 EBS 출신 인기 강사가 만난 명강의! 지금 사이트를 방문해서 무료 샘플 강의를 들어 보세요!

'스피드 리딩 카페'를 통해 원서 읽기 습관을 길러 보세요!

일상에서 영어를 한마디도 쓰지 않는 비영어권 국가에서 살고 있는 우리가 영어 환경에 가장 쉽고, 편하고, 부담 없이 노출되는 방법은 바로 '영어원서 읽기'입니다. 언제 어디서든 원서를 붙잡고 읽기만 하면 곧바로 영어를 접하는 환경이 만들어지기 때문이지요. 하루에 20분씩만 꾸준히 읽는다면, 1년에 무려 120시간 동안 영어에 노출될 수 있습니다. 이러한 이유 때문에 영어 교육 전문가들이 영어원서 읽기를 추천하는 것이지요.

하지만 원서 읽기가 좋다는 것을 알아도 막상 꾸준히 읽는 것은 쉽지 않습니다. 그럴 때에는 13만 명 이상의 회원을 보유한 국내 최대 원서 읽기 동호회 〈스피드 리딩 카페〉(cafe.naver.com/readingtc)를 방문해 보세요.

원서별로 정리된 무료 PDF 단어장과 수준별 추천 원서 목록 등 유용한 자료는 물론, 뉴베리 수상작을 포함한 다양한 원서의 리뷰를 무료로 확인할 수 있습니다. 특히 함께 모여서 원서를 읽는 '북클럽'은 중간에 포기하지 않고 원서를 끝까지 읽는 습관을 기르는 데 큰 도움이 될 것입니다.

chapters one to four

1. D   But you don't want to be bitten by a yellow-spotted lizard. That's the worst thing that can happen to you. You will die a slow and painful death.

2. A   Most campers weren't given a choice. Camp Green Lake is a camp for bad boys. If you take a bad boy and make him dig a hole every day in the hot sun, it will turn him into a good boy.

3. C   Stanley was not a bad kid. He was innocent of the crime for which he was convicted. He'd just been in the wrong place at the wrong time.

4. D   At such times she neglected to mention the bad luck that befell the first Stanley Yelnats. He lost his entire fortune when he was moving from New York to California. His stagecoach was robbed by the outlaw Kissin' Kate Barlow.

5. D   "You are to dig one hole each day, including Saturdays and Sundays. Each hole must be five feet deep, and five feet across in every direction. Your shovel is your measuring stick. Breakfast is served at 4:30." Stanley must have looked surprised, because Mr. Sir went on to explain that they started early to avoid the hottest part of the day. "No one is going to baby-sit you," he added. "The longer it takes you to dig, the longer you will be out in the sun. If you dig up anything interesting, you are to report it to me or any other counselor. When you finish, the rest of the day is yours."

6. A   "Good thinking," said Mr. Sir. "Nobody runs away from here. We don't need a fence. Know why? Because we've got the only water for a hundred miles. You want to run away? You'll be buzzard food in three days."

chapters five to seven

1. B   "Mr. Sir isn't really so bad," said Mr. Pendanski. "He's just been in a bad mood ever since he quit smoking. The person you've got to worry about is the Warden. There's

really only one rule at Camp Green Lake: Don't upset the Warden."

2. C   "And that's Mom!" a boy said. Mr. Pendanski smiled at him. "If it makes you feel better to call me Mom, Theodore, go ahead and call me Mom." He turned to Stanley. "If you have questions, Theodore will help you. You got that, Theodore. I'm depending on you."

3. D   Clyde Livingston, who had once lived at the shelter when he was younger, was going to speak and sign autographs. His shoes would be auctioned, and it was expected that they would sell for over five thousand dollars. All the money would go to help the homeless.

4. B   "I was walking home and the sneakers fell from the sky," he had told the judge. "One hit me on the head." It had hurt, too. They hadn't exactly fallen from the sky. He had just walked out from under a freeway overpass when the shoe hit him on the head.

5. C   The lake was so full of holes and mounds that it reminded Stanley of pictures he'd seen of the moon. "If you find anything interesting or unusual," Mr. Pendanski had told him, "you should report it either to me or Mr. Sir when we come around with the water truck. If the Warden likes what you found, you'll get the rest of the day off."

6. C   Stanley's great-great-grandfather was named Elya Yelnats. He was born in Latvia. When he was fifteen years old he fell in love with Myra Menke. (He didn't know he was Stanley's great-great-grandfather.) Myra Menke was fourteen. She would turn fifteen in two months, at which time her father had decided she should be married. Elya went to her father to ask for her hand, but so did Igor Barkov, the pig farmer.

7. B   "I want you to carry me up the mountain. I want to drink from the stream, and I want you to sing the song to me." Elya promised he would.

8. C   After his barn was struck by lightning for the third time, he told Sarah about his broken promise to Madame Zeroni. "I'm worse than a pig thief," he said. "You should leave me and find someone who isn't cursed."

chapters eight to eleven

1. D   The yellow-spotted lizards like to live in holes, which offer shade from the sun and protection from predatory birds.

2. C   He stopped writing as he became aware that somebody was reading over his shoulder. He turned to see Zero, standing behind the couch. "I don't want her to worry about me," he explained. Zero said nothing. He just stared at the letter with a serious, almost angry look on his face.

3. A   "C'mon, Caveman, dinner," said Armpit. "You coming, Caveman?" said Squid. Stanley looked around to see that Armpit and Squid were talking to him. "Uh, sure," he said. He put the piece of stationery back in the box, then got up and followed the boys out to the tables. The Lump wasn't the Caveman. He was.

4. B   He reached down to pick up his cap, and there next to it he saw a wide flat rock. As he put his cap on his head, he continued to look down at the rock. He picked it up. He thought he could see the shape of a fish, fossilized in it.

5. A   The truck stopped and the boys lined up. They always lined up in the same order, Stanley realized, no matter who got there first. X-Ray was always at the front of the line. Then came Armpit, Squid, Zigzag, Magnet, and Zero.

6. C   "Say, listen," said X-Ray. "If you find something else, give it to me, okay?" Stanley wasn't sure what to say. X-Ray was clearly the leader of the group, and Stanley didn't want to get on his bad side. … "I mean," X-Ray went on, "why should you get a day off when you've only been here a couple of days? If anybody gets a day off, it should be me. That's only fair, right?"

7. D   Stanley played the scene over and over again in his mind, each time watching another boy from Group D beat up Derrick Dunne. It helped him dig his hole and ease his own suffering. Whatever pain he felt was being felt ten times worse by Derrick.

chapters twelve to fourteen

1. B   "Well, let me tell you something, Caveman. You are here on account of one person. If it wasn't for that person, you wouldn't be here digging holes in the hot sun. You know who that person is?" "My no-good-dirty-rotten-pig-stealing-great-great-grand-father." The other boys howled with laughter. Even Zero smiled.

2. D   "What about it, Zero?" asked Mr. Pendanski. "What do you like to do?" "I like to dig holes."

3. D   He climbed up out of his hole and sifted his fingers through the pile. He felt something hard and metallic. He pulled it out. It was a gold tube, about as long and as wide as the second finger on his right hand. The tube was open at one end and closed at the other.

4. A   "Well, I'll show it to Mom," said X-Ray. "See what he thinks. Who knows? Maybe I'll get the day off." "Your hole's almost finished," said Stanley. "Yeah, so?" Stanley raised and lowered his shoulder. "So, why don't you wait until tomorrow to show it to Mom?" he suggested. "You can pretend you found it first thing in the morning. Then

you can get the whole day off, instead of just an hour or so this afternoon."

5. D   When the water truck came, Stanley started to take his place at the end of the line, but X-Ray told him to get behind Magnet, in front of Zero. Stanley moved up one place in line.

6. C   "You got it?" he asked X-Ray the next morning at breakfast. X-Ray looked at him with half-opened eyes behind his dirty glasses. "I don't know what you're talking about," he grumbled. "You know . . ." said Stanley. "No, I don't know!" X-Ray snapped. "So just leave me alone, okay? I don't want to talk to you." Stanley didn't say another word.

7. C   "Your good work will be rewarded." She turned to Mr. Pendanski. "Drive X-Ray back to camp. Let him take a double shower, and give him some clean clothes. But first I want you to fill everyone's canteen."

8. B   "Now, these fine boys have been working hard. Don't you think it might be possible that they might have taken a drink since you last filled their canteens?"

chapters fifteen & sixteen

1. A   "...And Caveman, you'll work with Zero. We're going to dig the dirt twice. Zero will dig it out of the hole, and Caveman will carefully shovel it into a wheelbarrow."

2. D   "I wonder how she knew all our names," Stanley said as he walked back to the compound. "She watches us all the time," said Zigzag. "She's got hidden microphones and cameras all over the place. In the tents, the Wreck Room, the shower." ... He realized that was why X-Ray didn't want to talk to him about the gold tube at breakfast. X-Ray was afraid the Warden might have been listening.

3. B   One thing was certain: They weren't just digging to "build character." They were definitely looking for something.

4. A   By lunchtime the Warden was beginning to lose her patience. She made them eat quickly, so they could get back to work. "If you can't get them to work any faster," she told Mr. Sir, "then you're going to have to climb down there and dig with them." After that, everyone worked faster, especially when Mr. Sir was watching them.

5. C   Your father thinks he is real close to a breakthrough on his sneaker project. I hope so. The landlord is threatening to evict us because of the odor.

6. D   "Well, see my dad is trying to invent a way to recycle old sneakers. So the apartment kind of smells bad, because he's always cooking these old sneakers. So anyway, in the letter my mom said she felt sorry for that little old lady who lived in a shoe, you

know, because it must have smelled bad in there." Zero stared blankly at him. "You know, the nursery rhyme?" Zero said nothing. "You've heard the nursery rhyme about the little old lady who lived in a shoe?" "No."

chapters seventeen to nineteen

1. C   The Warden jabbed at Armpit with her pitchfork, knocking him backward into the big hole. The pitchfork left three holes in the front of his shirt, and three tiny spots of blood.

2. B   He dug his shovel into the side of the hole. He scooped up some dirt, and was raising it up to the surface when Zigzag's shovel caught him in the side of the head. He collapsed.

3. B   "I want to learn to read and write," said Zero. Stanley let out a short laugh. He wasn't laughing at Zero. He was just surprised. All this time he had thought Zero was reading over his shoulder. "Sorry," he said. "I don't know how to teach."

4. C   His muscles and hands weren't the only parts of his body that had toughened over the past several weeks. His heart had hardened as well. He finished his letter. He barely had enough moisture in his mouth to seal and stamp the envelope. It seemed that no matter how much water he drank, he was always thirsty.

5. A   He was awakened one night by a strange noise. At first he thought it might have been some kind of animal, and it frightened him. But as the sleep cleared from his head, he realized that the noise was coming from the cot next to him. Squid was crying.

6. B   Magnet was standing at ground level, holding a sack of seeds. He popped a handful into his mouth, chewed, and swallowed, shells and all. … "How'd you get them without Mr. Sir seeing you?" asked Armpit. "I can't help it," Magnet said. He held both hands up, wiggled his fingers, and laughed. "My fingers are like little magnets."… "Coming your way, Caveman," said Zigzag. "Airmail and special delivery …" It's unclear whether the seeds spilled before they got to Stanley or after he dropped the bag. It seemed to him that Zigzag hadn't rolled up the top before throwing it, and that was the reason he didn't catch it. But it all happened very fast. One moment the sack was flying through the air, and the next thing Stanley knew the sack was in his hole and the seeds were spilled across the dirt.

7. C   "So, tell me, Caveman," said Mr. Sir. "How did my sack of sunflower seeds get in your hole?" "I stole it from your truck."

1. B   The Warden turned to face Mr. Sir, who was sitting on the fireplace hearth. "So you think he stole your sunflower seeds?" "No, he says he stole them, but I think it was—" She stepped toward him and struck him across the face. Mr. Sir stared at her. He had three long red marks slanting across the left side of his face. Stanley didn't know if the redness was caused by her nail polish or his blood.

2. C   Stanley took a breath to steady himself. "While Mr. Sir was filling the canteens, I snuck into the truck and stole his sack of sunflower seeds." … The nail on her pinkie just barely touched the wound behind his ear. A sharp sting of pain caused him to jump back.

3. A   Somehow his great-grandfather had survived for seventeen days, before he was rescued by a couple of rattlesnake hunters. He was insane when they found him. When he was asked how he had lived so long, he said he "found refuge on God's thumb."

4. D   Then he turned to Zero, who had been quietly digging in his hole since Stanley's return. Zero's hole was smaller than all the others.

5. B   Zero stared at him. His eyes seemed to expand, and it was almost as if Zero were looking right through him. "You didn't steal the sneakers," he said.

6. D   Zero must have thought he was staring for a different reason, because he said, "I'll dig part of your hole every day. I can dig for about an hour, then you can teach me for an hour. And since I'm a faster digger anyway, our holes will get done about the same time. I won't have to wait for you."

7. B   "I'm not stupid," Zero said. "I know everybody thinks I am. I just don't like answering their questions."

8. D   He suddenly realized where he'd seen the gold tube before. He'd seen it in his mother's bathroom, and he'd seen it again in the Warden's cabin. It was half of a lipstick container.

chapters twenty-three to twenty-five

1. C   Katherine Barlow was the town's only schoolteacher. She taught in an old one-room schoolhouse.

2. D   Most everyone in the town of Green Lake expected Miss Katherine to marry Trout Walker. He was the son of the richest man in the county. His family owned most of the peach trees and all the land on the east side of the lake.

3. C   Mr. Sir opened the nozzle, and the water flowed out of the tank, but it did not go into Stanley's canteen. Instead, he held the canteen right next to the stream of water. Stanley watched the water splatter on the dirt, where it was quickly absorbed by the thirsty ground.

4. B   Sam claimed that Mary Lou was almost fifty years old, which was, and still is, extraordinarily old for a donkey. "She eats nothing but raw onions," Sam would say, holding up a white onion between his dark fingers. "It's nature's magic vegetable. If a person ate nothing but raw onions, he could live to be two hundred years old."

5. A   They made a deal. He agreed to fix the leaky roof in exchange for six jars of spiced peaches. ... By the end of the first semester, Onion Sam had turned the old run-down schoolhouse into a well-crafted, freshly painted jewel of a building that the whole town was proud of.

6. D   The only person who wasn't happy with it was Miss Katherine. She'd run out of things needing to be fixed.

7. C   He took hold of both of her hands, and kissed her. Because of the rain, there was nobody else out on the street. Even if there was, Katherine and Sam wouldn't have noticed. They were lost in their own world. At that moment, however, Hattie Parker stepped out of the general store. They didn't see her, but she saw them. She pointed her quivering finger in their direction and whispered, "God will punish you!"

chapters twenty-six to twenty-eight

1. A   "It's against the law for a Negro to kiss a white woman." "Well, then you'll have to hang me, too," said Katherine. "Because I kissed him back." "It ain't against the law for you to kiss him," the sheriff explained. "Just for him to kiss you."

2. B   The Walker boat smashed into Sam's boat. Sam was shot and killed in the water. Katherine Barlow was rescued against her wishes. When they returned to the shore, she saw Mary Lou's body lying on the ground. The donkey had been shot in the head.

3. D   Fortunately, Mr. Pendanski delivered the water more often than Mr. Sir. Mr. Pendanski was obviously aware of what Mr. Sir was doing, because he always gave Stanley a little extra. He'd fill Stanley's canteen, then let Stanley take a long drink, then top it off for him.

4. C   Although, as Stanley had expected, the other boys didn't like to see Stanley sitting around while they were working. They'd say things like "Who died and made you

king?" or "It must be nice to have your own personal slave."

5. D   Stanley was afraid to drink it. He hated to think what land of vile substance Mr. Sir might have put in it.

6. A   Trout jabbed her throat with the rifle. "Where's the loot?" "There is no loot," said Kate. "Don't give me that!" shouted Trout. "You've robbed every bank from here to Houston." "You better tell him," said Linda. "We're desperate."

7. B   "You married him for his money, didn't you?" asked Kate. Linda nodded. "But it's all gone. It dried up with the lake. The peach trees. The livestock. I kept thinking: It has to rain soon. The drought can't last forever. But it just kept getting hotter and hotter and hotter . . ."

8. C   The lizard landed on Kate's bare ankle. Its sharp black teeth bit into her leg. Its white tongue lapped up the droplets of blood that leaked out of the wound.

chapters twenty-nine & thirty

1. D   The air became unbearably humid. Stanley was drenched in sweat. Beads of moisture ran down the handle of his shovel. It was almost as if the temperature had gotten so hot that the air itself was sweating.

2. B   The horizon lit up with a huge web of lightning. In that split second Stanley thought he saw an unusual rock formation on top of one of the mountain peaks. The peak looked to him exactly like a giant fist, with the thumb sticking straight up.

3. C   "I saw what was going on," Mr. Pendanski said. He turned to Stanley. "Go ahead, Stanley," he said. "Hit him back. You're bigger."

4. B   Then, suddenly, Zigzag was off of him. Stanley managed to look up, and he saw that Zero had his arm around Zigzag's long neck. Zigzag made a gagging sound, as he desperately tried to pry Zero's arm off of him.

5. A   "Okay, from now on, I don't want anyone digging anyone else's hole," said the Warden. "And no more reading lessons."

6. D   Zero took the shovel. Then he swung it like a baseball bat. The metal blade smashed across Mr. Pendanski's face. His knees crumpled beneath him. He was unconscious before he hit the ground. The counselors all drew their guns.

7. D   The Warden ordered the counselors to take turns guarding the shower room and Wreck Room, all day and all night. They were not to let Zero drink any water. When he returned, he was to be brought directly to her.

1. A   Instead, he came up with a better idea, although he didn't have it quite all figured out yet. He thought that maybe he could make a deal with the Warden. He'd tell her where he really found the gold tube if she wouldn't scratch Zero.

2. D   His only hope was that Zero had found God's thumb on his own. It wasn't impossible.

3. D   The Warden thought a moment. "Okay, I want you to destroy all of his records."

4. C   He watched Mr. Sir fill X-Ray's canteen. The image of Zero crawling across the hot dry dirt remained in his head. But what could he do about it? Even if Zero was somehow alive after more than four days, how would Stanley ever find him? It would take days. He'd need a car. Or a pickup truck. A pickup truck with a tank of water in the back.

5. B   The truck went faster and faster across the dry lake bed. It bounced over a pile of dirt. Suddenly Stanley was slammed forward, then instantly backward as an airbag exploded in his face. He fell out of the open door and onto the ground. He had driven straight into a hole.

6. D   He ran. His canteen was strapped around his neck. It banged against his chest as he ran, and every time it hit against him, it reminded him that it was empty, empty, empty.

chapters thirty-three to thirty-five

1. B   He slowed to a walk. As far as he could tell, nobody was chasing him.

2. D   He stepped over the mounds and looked into the first hole. His heart stopped. Down at the bottom was a family of yellow-spotted lizards. Their large red eyes looked up at him. … He headed in what he thought was the direction of Big Thumb. He couldn't see it through the haze. … Then he'd have to make a deal with the Warden, tell her where he found Kate Barlow's lipstick tube, and beg for mercy. … It turned out to be an empty sack of sunflower seeds. He wondered if it was the same one Magnet had stolen from Mr. Sir, although that didn't seem likely.

3. A   Almost straight ahead of him, he could see what looked like a fist, with its thumb sticking up. … But every time he looked at it, it seemed to encourage him, giving him the thumbs-up sign.

4. C   "Hey!" Stanley shouted, hoping to scare it back inside. His mouth was very dry, and it was hard to shout very loudly. "Hey," the thing answered weakly.

5. D   It was a warm, bubbly, mushy nectar, sweet and tangy. It felt like heaven as it flowed over his dry mouth and down his parched throat. He thought it might have been some kind of fruit at some time, perhaps peaches.

6. B   "Barf Bag stepped on a rattlesnake," said Zero. Stanley remembered how he'd almost done the same. "I guess he didn't hear the rattle." "He did it on purpose," said Zero.

7. A   Zero walked around to the back of the boat and pointed to the upside-down letters. "Mm-ar-yuh. Luh-oh-oo." Stanley smiled. "Mary Lou. It's the name of the boat."

8. C   "I'm not going back," said Zero. "You've got nowhere else to go," said Stanley. Zero said nothing. "You'll die out here," said Stanley. "Then I'll die out here."

chapters thirty-six & thirty-seven

1. C   They hadn't gone very far before Zero had another attack. He clutched his stomach as he let himself fall to the ground.

2. D   "Give me some words," he said weakly. It took Stanley a few seconds to realize what he meant. Then he smiled and said, "R-u-n." Zero sounded it out to himself. "Rr-un, run. Run." "Good. F-u-n." "Fffun." The spelling seemed to help Zero. It gave him something to concentrate on besides his pain and weakness.

3. B   What scared Stanley the most about dying wasn't his actual death. He figured he could handle the pain. It wouldn't be much worse than what he felt now. In fact, maybe at the moment of his death he would be too weak to feel pain. Death would be a relief. What worried him the most was the thought of his parents not knowing what happened to him, not knowing whether he was dead or alive.

4. A   Stanley grabbed hold of the shovel as he climbed up the rock wall, using the sides of the rut to help support him. His hands moved one over the other, up the shaft of the shovel. He felt Zero's hand clasp his wrist. He let go of the shaft with one hand and grabbed the top of the ledge. He gathered his strength and for a brief second seemed to defy gravity as he took a quick step up the wall and, with Zero's help, pulled himself the rest of the way over the ledge.

5. C   Zero had deep gashes in both hands. He had held on to the metal blade of the shovel, keeping it in place, as Stanley climbed.

6. B   As the sky darkened, bugs began appearing above the weed patches. A swarm

of gnats hovered around them, attracted by their sweat. Neither Stanley nor Zero had the strength to try to swat at them. … His frail body shook violently, and he threw up, emptying his stomach of the sploosh. … Stanley didn't give him any more words, thinking that he needed to save his strength. But about ten or fifteen minutes later, Zero said, "Lunch." … He didn't get up.

7. C   As they climbed higher, the patches of weeds grew thicker, and they had to be careful not to get their feet tangled in thorny vines. Stanley suddenly realized something. There hadn't been any weeds on the lake. "Weeds and bugs," he said. "There's got to be water around somewhere. We must be getting close."

chapters thirty-eight to forty

1. D   Higher and higher he climbed. His strength came from somewhere deep inside himself and also seemed to come from the outside as well. After focusing on Big Thumb for so long, it was as if the rock had absorbed his energy and now acted like a kind of giant magnet pulling him toward it.

2. B   As he continued to widen his hole, his hand came across a smooth, round object. It was too smooth and too round to be a rock. He wiped the dirt off of it and realized it was an onion.

3. C   He struggled to his feet. He was in a field of greenish white flowers that seemed to extend all the way around Big Thumb.

4. B   "I took your shoes," Zero said. Stanley didn't know what he was talking about. … "What shoes?" "From the shelter." It took a moment for Stanley to comprehend. "Clyde Livingston's shoes?" "I'm sorry," said Zero.

5. D   "It was your onion tonic," said Mrs. Tennyson. "That's what saved her."

6. B   Other townspeople made their way to the cart. "Good morning, Gladys," said Hattie Parker. "Don't you look lovely this morning." Several people snickered. "Good morning, Hattie," Mrs. Tennyson replied. "Does your husband know you're parading about in your bed clothes?" Hattie asked.

7. C   "I think I'll go look for the shovel," Stanley said. "I'll wait here," Zero said feebly, as if he had any other choice.

1. D   "We always took what we needed," Zero said. "When I was little, I didn't even know it was stealing. I don't remember when I found out. But we just took what we needed, never more."

2. C   "... When I got outside, I ran around the corner and immediately took off the shoes. I put them on top of a parked car. I remember they smelled really bad."

3. C   It occurred to him that he couldn't remember the last time he felt happiness. It wasn't just being sent to Camp Green Lake that had made his life miserable. Before that he'd been unhappy at school, where he had no friends, and bullies like Derrick Dunne picked on him. No one liked him, and the truth was, he didn't especially like himself.

4. A   But even as he thought this, an even crazier idea kept popping into his head. He knew it was too crazy to even consider. Still, if he was going to be a fugitive for the rest of his life, it would help to have some money, perhaps a treasure chest full of money.

5. D   The next morning they headed down the mountain. They'd dunked their caps in the water hole before putting them on their heads. Zero held the shovel, and Stanley carried the sack, which was crammed with onions and the three jars of water. They left the pieces of the broken jar on the mountain.

6. B   "You thirsty?" Stanley asked. "No," said Zero. "How about you." "No," Stanley lied. He didn't want to be the first one to take a drink. Although they didn't mention it, it had become a kind of challenge between him and Zero. ... They decided to save the canteen for last, since it couldn't accidentally break.

7. A   "And then one day she didn't come back," Zero said. His voice sounded suddenly hollow. "I waited for her at Laney Park."

8. B   They climbed down into adjacent holes, and waited for the camp to fall asleep.

chapters forty-four & forty-five

1. B   Zero handed down a box of cereal. Stanley carefully poured some cereal into his mouth. He didn't want to put his dirty hands inside the box. He nearly gagged on the ultra-sweet taste.

2. C   He could just feel a corner of it. Most of it was still buried. It had the cool, smooth texture of metal. "I think I might have found the treasure chest," he said.

3. C   They finished the water that Zero had gotten from the spigot by the showers. Stanley said he'd go fill the jars again, but Zero insisted that he do it instead.

4. D   Stanley jammed the shovel into the bottom edge of his hole, and carefully began to dig a tunnel underneath the metal object. He hoped it didn't cave in.

5. D   "We wait," said the Warden. "It won't be very long." … Stanley felt tiny claws dig into the side of his face as the lizard pulled itself off his neck and up past his chin. "It won't be long now," the Warden said.

6. B   "Let her ask her questions," said the Warden. "Just so long as I have the suitcase, I don't care what happens. Do you know how long . . ." Her voice trailed off, then started up again. "When I was little I'd watch my parents dig holes, every weekend and holiday. When I got bigger, I had to dig, too. Even on Christmas."

chapters forty-six & forty-seven

1. A   "We're going to keep our story simple," said the Warden. "That woman's going to ask a lot of questions. The A.G. will most likely initiate an investigation. So this is what happened: Stanley tried to run away in the night, fell in a hole, and the lizards got him. That's it. We're not even going to give them Zero's body. As far as anybody knows, Zero doesn't exist. Like Mom said, we got plenty of graves to choose from."

2. D   "Hey, Caveman, guess what?" said Mr. Sir. "You're innocent, after all. I thought you'd like to know that. Your lawyer came to get you yesterday. Too bad you weren't here."

3. C   "Look, a tarantula," said Mr. Sir, also fascinated. "I've never seen one," said the Warden. "Except in—" Stanley suddenly felt a sharp sting on the side of his neck. The lizard hadn't bitten him, however. It was merely pushing off. It leapt off Stanley's neck and pounced on the tarantula. The last Stanley saw of it was one hairy leg sticking out of the lizard's mouth. "Not hungry, huh?" said Mr. Sir.

4. D   "All night, as you can see by the way we're dressed. They snuck into my cabin while I was asleep, and stole my suitcase. I chased after them, and they ran out here and fell into the lizards' nest. I don't know what they were thinking."

5. C   "Stanley has been hospitalized for the last few days," the Warden explained. "He's been suffering from hallucinations and delirium. Ranting and raving. He was in no condition to leave. The fact that he was trying to steal from me on the day before his release proves . . ." … "Why didn't you release him when she came to you yesterday?" the tall man asked. "She didn't have proper authorization," said the Warden.

6. B   He jerked it free. "It belongs to Stanley," he said. "Don't cause any more trouble," the Warden warned. "You stole it from my cabin, and you've been caught red-

226

handed. If I press charges, Stanley might have to return to prison. Now I'm willing, in view of all the circumstances, to—" "It's got his name on it," said Zero.

chapters forty-eight & forty-nine

1. B   "Wait!" the Warden exclaimed. "I didn't say they stole the suitcase. It's his suitcase, obviously, but he put my things from my cabin inside it."

2. A   "Stanley, as your lawyer, I advise you not to open your suitcase," said Ms. Morengo.

3. B   "Your friend is not in danger," said the Attorney General. "There's going to be an investigation into everything that's happened here. For the present, I am taking charge of the camp."

4. C   "My office is having some difficulty locating Hector Zeroni's records," the Attorney General said. "So you have no claim of authority over him?" asked Ms. Morengo. … "So what are you planning to do with him? Keep him confined indefinitely, without justification, while you go crawling through black holes in cyberspace?" … Stanley's lawyer took hold of Zero's hand. "C'mon, Hector, you're coming with us."

5. D   "We want to get some of your lizard juice," said Walter. … Sam gave each man two bottles of pure onion juice. … "Just remember," Sam told the men before they left. "It's very important you drink a bottle tonight. You got to get it into your bloodstream. The lizards don't like onion blood."

6. B   "No, he's still working on that," explained Ms. Morengo. "But he invented a product that eliminates foot odor. Here, I've got a sample in my briefcase. I wish I had more. You two could bathe in it."

chapter fifty

1. C   Stanley's mother insists that there never was a curse. She even doubts whether Stanley's great-great-grandfather really stole a pig. The reader might find it interesting, however, that Stanley's father invented his cure for foot odor the day after the great-great-grandson of Elya Yelnats carried the great-great-great-grandson of Madame Zeroni up the mountain.

2. A   The Attorney General closed Camp Green Lake. Ms. Walker, who was in desperate need of money, had to sell the land which had been in her family for

generations.

3. C   Underneath the jewels was a stack of papers that had once belonged to the first Stanley Yelnats. These consisted of stock certificates, deeds of trust, and promissory notes.

4. B   There was a small party at the Yelnats house. Except for Stanley and Hector, everyone there was an adult. All kinds of snacks and drinks were set out on the counter, including caviar, champagne, and the fixings to make ice cream sundaes. The Super Bowl was on television, but nobody was really watching. "It should be coming on at the next break," Ms. Morengo announced. A time-out was called in the football game, and a commercial came on the screen. Everyone stopped talking and watched. The commercial showed a baseball game. ... "Then a teammate told me about Sploosh," said the television Clyde. He pulled a can of Sploosh out from under the dugout bench and held it up for everyone to see. "I just spray a little on each foot every morning, and now I really do have sweet feet. Plus, I like the tingle.

5. C   A woman sitting in the chair behind Hector was absent-mindedly fluffing his hair with her fingers. She wasn't very old, but her skin had a weathered look to it, almost like leather. Her eyes seemed weary, as if she'd seen too many things in her life that she didn't want to see. And when she smiled, her mouth seemed too big for her face. Very softly, she half sang, half hummed a song that her grandmother used to sing to her when she was a little girl.